Troubling Traditions

Troubling Traditions takes up a 21st century, field-specific conversation between scholars, educators, and artists from varying generational, geographical, and identity positions that speak to the wide array of debates around dramatic canons.

Unlike Literature and other fields in the humanities, Theatre and Performance Studies has not yet fully grappled with the problems of its canon. *Troubling Traditions* stages that conversation in relation to the canon in the United States. It investigates the possibilities for multiplying canons, methodologies for challenging canon formation, and the role of adaptation and practice in rethinking the field's relation to established texts. The conversations put forward by this book on the canon interrogate the field's fundamental values, and ask how to expand the voices, forms, and bodies that constitute this discipline.

This is a vital text for anyone considering the role, construction, and impact of canons in the US and beyond.

Lindsey Mantoan is an Assistant Professor of Theatre and Communication Arts at Linfield University.

Matthew Moore is an Assistant Professor of Theatre and Performance at Muhlenberg College.

Angela Farr Schiller is an Associate Professor of Theater at Boston Conservatory at Berklee.

Troubling Traditions

Canonicity, Theatre, and Performance in the US

Edited by
Lindsey Mantoan, Matthew Moore,
and Angela Farr Schiller

LONDON AND NEW YORK

First published 2022
by Routledge
2 Park Square, Milton Park, Abingdon, Oxon OX14 4RN

and by Routledge
605 Third Avenue, New York, NY 10158

Routledge is an imprint of the Taylor & Francis Group, an informa business

© 2022 selection and editorial matter, Lindsey Mantoan, Matthew Moore, and Angela Farr Schiller; individual chapters, the contributors

The right of Lindsey Mantoan, Matthew Moore, and Angela Farr Schiller to be identified as the authors of the editorial material, and of the authors for their individual chapters, has been asserted in accordance with sections 77 and 78 of the Copyright, Designs and Patents Act 1988.

All rights reserved. No part of this book may be reprinted or reproduced or utilised in any form or by any electronic, mechanical, or other means, now known or hereafter invented, including photocopying and recording, or in any information storage or retrieval system, without permission in writing from the publishers.

Trademark notice: Product or corporate names may be trademarks or registered trademarks, and are used only for identification and explanation without intent to infringe.

British Library Cataloguing-in-Publication Data
A catalogue record for this book is available from the British Library

Library of Congress Cataloguing-in-Publication Data
Names: Mantoan, Lindsey, editor. | Moore, Matthew Robert, editor. | Schiller, Angela Farr, editor.
Title: Troubling traditions : canonicity, theatre, and performance in the US / edited by Lindsey Mantoan, Matthew Moore and Angela Farr Schiller.
Description: Abingdon, Oxon ; New York : Routledge 2022. | Includes bibliographical references and index.
Identifiers: LCCN 2021030627 (print) | LCCN 2021030628 (ebook) | ISBN 9780367468323 (hardback) | ISBN 9780367468309 (paperback) | ISBN 9781003031413 (ebook)
Subjects: LCSH: American drama--History and criticism. | Canon (Literature)--History and criticism. | Theater--United States--History.
Classification: LCC PS334 .T76 2022 (print) | LCC PS334 (ebook) | DDC 812.009--dc23
LC record available at https://lccn.loc.gov/2021030627
LC ebook record available at https://lccn.loc.gov/2021030628

ISBN: 978-0-367-46832-3 (hbk)
ISBN: 978-0-367-46830-9 (pbk)
ISBN: 978-1-003-03141-3 (ebk)

DOI: 10.4324/9781003031413

Typeset in Bembo
by MPS Limited, Dehradun

Contents

List of Figures viii
Acknowledgments x
List of Contributors xi

Introduction: Troubling Traditions 1
LINDSEY MANTOAN, MATTHEW MOORE, AND
ANGELA FARR SCHILLER

PART I
Costs of Canonicity 21

1. The Good, The Bad, and The Ugly in Theatre, Dance, and Performance Studies 23
   NADINE GEORGE-GRAVES

2. The Shakespeare Problem: A Conversation 36
   SARAH ENLOE, MADELINE SAYET, MEI ANN TEO, AND
   DAWN MONIQUE WILLIAMS

3. "Go back to India if you hate my people so much": Consequences of Troubling the "Canon" in American Academia 49
   SUKANYA CHAKRABARTI

4. Despite the Flames: A Conversation 63
   PATRICIA YBARRA, VIRGINIA GRISE, AND VICTOR I. CAZARES

5. The Black Gaze/A Different Account 79
   ERIC M. GLOVER AND ISAIAH MATTHEW WOODEN

6. Amidst the Rubble of the Ivory Tower 93
SARA BRADY

PART II
Remixing Traditions 101

7. Shaking up the Canon with Cornerstone and OSF 103
BILL RAUCH AND SONJA ARSHAM KUFTINEC

8. "Yo, Let's Steal Their Canons!": Arab and Arab American Canonical Multiplicities 121
SAMER AL-SABER AND MICHAEL MALEK NAJJAR

9. Your Heritage is Safe Here: Defining Three Indigenous Theatrical Canons 134
JAY B. MUSKETT AND JONAH WINN-LENETSKY

10. "Frenemies" of the Canon: Our Two Decades of Studying and Teaching Disability in Drama and Performance 147
ANN M. FOX AND CARRIE SANDAHL

11. The Uses of Awe 161
RINDE ECKERT AND ELLEN MCLAUGHLIN

PART III
Fluid Approaches 173

12. Toward and Away: The Dramatic Tension of a Queer & Trans Canon 175
FINN LEFEVRE

13. Dancing With/Out the Canon 188
HANNAH KOSSTRIN

14. What Do We Do with the Musical Theatre Canon? 201
STACY WOLF, WITH MASI ASARE, ROB BERMAN, RANDALL ENG, ERIC M. GLOVER, DAVID SAVRAN, GEORGIA STITT, BRANDON WEBSTER, AND SARAH WHITFIELD

15. Canons in Motion: Japanese Performance, Theatre History, and the Currents of Knowledge 217
JYANA S. BROWNE AND JESSICA NAKAMURA

16. The Kids' Table: Cross-institutional Treatment of the
    Canon and the Un-canonizable Nature of New Work   230
    CHARLIE DUBACH-REINHOLD AND MELORY MIRASHRAFI

PART IV
Departures and Re-visions   243

17. Rethinking the Canon through the Digital   245
    MIGUEL ESCOBAR VARELA AND DEREK MILLER

18. *Antigone* is Dead, Long Live *Antigone*s!: Adaptation,
    Difference, and Instability at the Heart of the Traditional
    Western Canon   257
    RACHEL M. E. WOLFE

19. Redirecting Canonicity: PhD Exams and Actor Training   273
    EERO LAINE AND PETER ZAZZALI

20. We Aren't Here to Teach What We Already Know   288
    JESSICA BRATER AND MICHELLE LIU CARRIGER

21. How Do We Do the Queer Canon?   298
    ZACHARY A. DORSEY, WITH PAUL BONIN-RODRIGUEZ,
    MICHELLE DVOSKIN, LINDSEY MANTOAN, ELEANOR OWICKI,
    JACLYN I. PRYOR, AND RAMÓN H. RIVERA-SERVERA

Index   311

Figures

4.1	Promotional Poster. *Pinching Pennies with Penny Marshall*. New York Theatre Workshop. October 2020. Photo Design Credit: Victor I. Cazares	73
4.2	Chairman Mao's four minute Physical Fitness Plan by Zeke Peña. (Included as part of Virginia Grise's *Your Healing is Killing Me.*)	76
4.3	Chairman Mao's four minute physical Fitness Plan, enacted in Tuscon, Arizona during the COVID-19 Pandemic. Photo credit: Yvonne Ballesteros	77
5.1	Fred Wilson (b. 1954). *Metalwork 1793–1880*, from *Mining the Museum*, 1992–1993 by Fred Wilson. Courtesy of the Maryland Center for History and Culture	86
5.2	Fred Wilson (b. 1954) ©. *Guarded View, 1991.* Wood, paint, steel, and fabric. Dimensions variable. Gift of the Peter Norton Family Foundation. Inv.: 97.84a-d. Whitney Museum of American Art, New York, NY, U.S.A. Digital image © Whitney Museum of American Art/Licensed by Scala/Art Resource, NY	87
7.1	The Toy Truck (1992). Angelus Plaza *Credit:* Lynn Jeffries	109
7.2	Passport for OSF's "Canon in a Decade" featuring all of Shakespeare's plays. The Tudor Guild, Oregon Shakespeare Festival	111
7.3	*Oklahoma!* (2018). Will Parker (Jordan Barbour) wonders if the intentions of Ado Andy (Jonathan Luke Stevens) are of the marital variety. Photo by Jenny Graham, Oregon Shakespeare Festival	113
7.4	Title characters Macbeth (Jeffrey King), Cinderella (Laura Griffith), and Medea (Miriam A. Laube) in *Medea/Macbeth/Cinderella* (2012). Oregon Shakespeare Festival Photo: Jenny Graham	115
7.5	1491's *Between Two Knees* (Oregon Shakespeare Festival 2019): Shyla Lefner (Irma), Ensemble. Photo by Jenny Graham	118

10.1	The actor Mat Fraser in the documentary *Code of the Freaks* (2020)	157
10.2	*Teenage Dick* by Mike Lew at Theatre Wit (2020). Directed by Brian Balcom. From left to right, performers MacGregor Arney (RICHARD) and Tamar Rozofsky (BUCK)	158
18.1	In this scene from *Antíkoni,* the title character (Fantasia Painter) appears before Kreon (Phillip E. Cash Cash) in a state of digital transfiguration. The staged reading took place in the Hearst Museum of Anthropology at UC Berkeley, which holds more than 9,000 ancestral remains, the largest collection outside of the Smithsonian. Photo credit: Irene Yi	262
18.2	Writing along the fibers. Content: Sophocles' *Antigone*. From the Papyrus Manuscript Fragments Collection, Kelvin Smith Library Special Collections, Case Western Reserve University	265
21.1	Jesús I. Valles *(Un)Documents*, 2019. Credit: Errich Petersen Photography	304

Acknowledgments

This project started off small—initially, a book co-written by the three of us—and grew into a huge edited collection with 21 chapters. Growing from the seed of an idea into a book we're deeply proud of took work not only from the three co-editors but also from collaborators far and wide. We'd like to thank Becky Chaleff for consulting on dance history, and Jim Peck, Rachel Norman, and Regina Windham for sharing their thoughts on the introduction. Matthew Goulish and Lin Hixson were early interlocutors for our ideas here. Ben Piggott and Zoë Forbes at Routledge shepherded this book through the publication process with grace and clarity. Cherríe Moraga's enthusiasm for the project bolstered our energy.

Angela would like to thank with deep gratitude: Robert Swift Jr., Pelton and Shirley Farr, Pelton Farr IV, and Micheal D. Farr for always being my biggest cheerleaders.

Lindsey is deeply grateful for her family, who created space for her to do this work: Kathryn Mantoan, Art and Barb Mantoan, and Barb and Dennis Grzenczyk. Thanks also to Linfield University for awarding her the Alan and Pat Kelley Faculty Scholar Award in 2019, which provided her with additional research time.

Matt would like to thank Becky Moore for her constant support and willingness to listen, Wesley Moore and Owen Mendes, and Muhlenberg College for awarding him the Rising Scholar Award in 2019, which provided invaluable time and research funding.

Contributors

Samer Al-Saber (he/him) is an Assistant Professor of Theatre And Performance Studies at Stanford University, where he is a faculty member of the Center for the Comparative Study of Race and Ethnicity (CCSRE) and the Abbasi Program in Islamic Studies (Global Studies). His work appeared in *Theatre Research International, Alt.Theatre, Performance Paradigm, Critical Survey, Theatre Survey, Jadaliyya, Counterpunch, This Week In Palestine*, and various edited volumes. He is the co-editor of the anthology *Stories Under Occupation and Other Plays from Palestine*. https://orcid.org/0000-0003-0528-6792

Masi Asare (she/her) is an Assistant Professor of Theatre and Performance Studies at Northwestern University. As a composer and dramatist, she holds commissions from Broadway producers and Marvel; as a scholar, she studies vocal sound and the impact of racial history for contemporary practices of musical theatre performance.

Rob Berman (he/him) is a New York-based music director and conductor. He is music director of the *Encores*! series at New York City Center and has conducted many Broadway shows. He won an Emmy Award for outstanding music direction for *The Kennedy Center Honors*, for which he served as conductor for nine years.

Paul Bonin-Rodriguez (he/him) is an Associate Professor in the Performance as Public Practice Program at The University of Texas at Austin, and also serves on faculty in LGBTQ Studies. He is currently at work on *Groundwork*, a scholarly monograph about the National Performance Network and growth of US artist networks since the 1970s. https://orcid.org/0000-0003-0030-5093

Sara Brady (she/her) is an Associate Professor at Bronx Community College of the City University of New York and Managing Editor of *TDR*. She is the author of *Performance, Politics, and the War on Terror: 'Whatever It Takes'* (Palgrave 2012), and co-editor with Lindsey Mantoan of *Performance in a Militarized Culture* (Routledge 2018). https://orcid.org/0000-0001-7071-2220

Jessica Brater (she/her) is an Assistant Professor and Coordinator of the BA and MA in Theatre Studies and graduate Certificate in Theatre of Diversity, Inclusion & Social Change at Montclair State University. Her book *Ruth Maleczech at Mabou Mines* and other publications explore the politics of representation in 20th and 21st-century avant-garde performance.

Jyana S. Browne (she/her) is an Assistant Professor of Premodern Japanese Literary and Cultural Studies at the University of Maryland. She specializes in early modern Japanese performance, particularly Chikamatsu's love suicide plays. She has published her research in *Puppetry International* and *Dai 37 kai kokusai nihon bungaku kenkyūshūkai kaigiroku*.

Michelle Liu Carriger (she/they) is an assistant professor of Theater and Performance Studies at UCLA. Her first book examines clothing controversies in nineteenth-century Britain and Japan while other publications examine kimono and "cultural appropriation," historical reality television, Japanese subcultural fashions, and the Japanese Way of Tea ("tea ceremony"). http://orcid.org/0000-0003-3573-0575

Victor I. Cazares (they/them) is a PozQueer Indigenous Mexican Artist (PQIMA for short) who has had stints at Yale, Brown, and other less prestigious centers of rehabilitation. They're the Tow Playwright-In-Residence and part of the artistic staff at New York Theatre Workshop. Plays include: *American (tele)visions* and, *Pinching Pennies with Penny Marshall* (NYTW); *When We Write with Ashes* (National Queer Theater); *Ramses contra los monstruos: Salmos para el fin del mundo*; and *We Were Eight Years in Powder*.

Sukanya Chakrabarti (she/her) is an artist-scholar and Assistant Professor, Theatre Studies at San Francisco State University. Her performance practice, scholarship, and teaching lie in the intersection of postcolonial studies, globalization studies, and urban studies, with a focus on South Asian and transcultural theatre and performance studies, experimental devised performances, and community-based performance-making. https://orcid.org/0000-0003-4737-4408

Zachary A. Dorsey (he/him) is Associate Professor in the School of Theatre and Dance at James Madison University, where he teaches classes in performance analysis, dramaturgy, and the history of dance, theatre, and musical theatre. His PhD is in Performance as Public Practice from the University of Texas at Austin. https://orcid.org/0000-0003-3095-0405

Charlie Dubach-Reinhold (they/he) is a dramaturg and public speaker who recently held the Peter F. Sloss Literary/Dramaturgy Fellowship at Berkeley Repertory Theatre. They graduated from Stanford University in 2019 with a BA in Theatre and Performance Studies, and are currently pursuing a career in transgender healthcare. http://orcid.org/0000-0001-9263-2491

Michelle Dvoskin (she/her) is Associate Professor and Theatre Program Coordinator in Western Kentucky University's Department of Theatre & Dance, where she teaches courses in areas including dramatic literature, theatre, and musical theatre theory, and the creation of new work. She has been published in *Studies in Musical Theatre*, *The Journal of American Drama and Theatre*, *The Oxford Handbook of American Drama*, and *The Oxford Handbook of the American Musical*. http://orcid.org/0000-0002-2794-4082

Rinde Eckert (he/him) is a writer, composer, singer, actor, and director whose theatre, music theatre, and dance theatre pieces have been performed throughout the United States and abroad. He has received a Guggenheim Fellowship in Music Composition, a Marc Blitzstein Award (from The American Academy of Arts and Letters), an Obie Award (*And God Created Great Whales*), a Grammy Award (*Lonely Motel*), an Alpert Award for Drama (2009), and a Doris Duke Performing Artist Award (2012). He was a finalist for the Pulitzer Prize in Drama in 2007 for his *Orpheus X*.

Randall Eng (he/him) is a composer of opera and musical theatre whose works include *Florida, Henry's Wife*, and *Before the Night Sky*. He has worked as a musical consultant on and off-Broadway, and is an Associate Arts Professor at NYU's Graduate Musical Theatre Writing Program, where he runs the Tisch Opera Lab.

Sarah Ellen Enloe (she/her) has been teaching Shakespeare and theatre for two decades. Winning both teacher of the year and an NEH fellowship, she is the rising president of the Shakespeare Theatre Association. Her current focus is on the practical application of performance techniques for classrooms and beyond. https://orcid.org/0000-0002-2943-705X

Angela Farr Schiller (she/her) is an Emmy® Award-winning Director and an Associate Professor of Theater at Boston Conservatory at Berklee. Additionally, she works as a Dramaturg-In-Residence with Atlanta-based Working Title Playwrights (WTP), the leading new play development organization in the Southeast, on new play development and teaches master classes in dramaturgy. She is co-editor of The Methuen Drama Book of Trans Plays (Bloomsbury 2021). https://www.angelaschiller.com; http://orcid.org/0000-0002-6595-6332

Ann M. Fox (she/her) is a Professor of English at Davidson College, where she specializes in literary and cultural disability studies, modern and contemporary drama, and graphic medicine. She regularly curates disability arts exhibitions and is widely published on disability and representation. http://orcid.org/0000-0002-8530-0496

Nadine George-Graves (he/him) is the Naomi Willie Pollard Professor at Northwestern University where she chairs the Performance Studies Department and has a joint appointment in the Theatre Department. She also serves as executive co-editor of *Dance Research Journal*. She is an artist and scholar whose work is situated at the intersections of African American studies, critical gender studies, performance studies, theatre history, and dance history. https://orcid.org/0000-0003-1660-1380

Eric M. Glover (he/him) is an Assistant Professor adjunct of dramaturgy and dramatic criticism at Yale where he is an expert on Black musical theatre.

Virginia Grise (she/her) writes plays set in bars without windows, barrio rooftops, and lesbian bedrooms. Her published work includes *Your Healing is Killing Me*, *blu*, and *The Panza Monologues*. In addition to plays, she has created an interdisciplinary body of work that includes dance theatre, performance installations, guerilla theatre, site-specific interventions, and community gatherings.

Hannah Kosstrin (she/her) is a dance historian and movement analyst. At Ohio State University, she is an Associate Professor of Dance and affiliate faculty with the Melton Center for Jewish Studies and Slavic Center. Kosstrin is the author of *Honest Bodies: Revolutionary Modernism in the Dances of Anna Sokolow* (Oxford University Press 2017). https://orcid.org/0000-0002-0630-8124

Sonja Arsham Kuftinec (she/her) is a Professor of Theatre at the University of Minnesota and long-time Bill Rauch fan. She has published widely on community-based and applied theatre including *Staging America: Cornerstone and Community-Based Theater* (2003). She also works as an artist and conflict transformation facilitator. Current research focuses on arts literacy and creative engagements with contested memory. https://orcid.org/0000-0002-7444-3715

Eero Laine (he/him) is the Director of Graduate Studies and an Assistant Professor in the Department of Theatre and Dance at the University at Buffalo, State University of New York. https://orcid.org/0000-0001-5762-3979

Finn Lefevre (they/them) is a dramaturg and applied theatre facilitator whose work focuses on trans and queer communities. They currently serve as a lecturer at the University of Massachusetts Department of Theater and co-VP of Freelance for the Literary Managers and Dramaturgs of the Americas. www.finnlefevre.com; http://orcid.org/0000-0002-6640-6578

Lindsey Mantoan (she/her) is an Assistant Professor of Theatre and Resident Dramaturg at Linfield University. She is the author of *War as Performance: Conflict in Iraq and Political Theatricality* (Palgrave 2018) and co-editor of *The Methuen Drama Book of Trans Plays* (Bloomsbury 2021), *Vying for the Iron Throne: Essays on Power, Gender, Death, and Performance in HBO's Game of Thrones* (McFarland 2018) and *Performance in a Militarized Culture* (Routledge 2017). She is an occasional contributor to CNN.com. https://orcid.org/0000-0003-3031-7378

Ellen McLaughlin (she/her) has worked extensively in regional, international, and New York theatre, both as an actor and as a playwright. Plays and operas include, *Tongue of a Bird, The Persians, Penelope, Ajax in Iraq, Blood Moon,* and *The Oresteia.* Producers include: The Public Theater, Classic Stage Co., New York Theater Workshop, The Guthrie, The Mark Taper Forum, Oregon Shakespeare Festival, and The Almeida Theater in London. She is the winner of the Susan Smith Blackburn Prize, the Helen Merrill Award for Playwriting, and the Lila Wallace/Reader's Digest Award, among others. She has taught at Barnard College since 1995.

Derek Miller (he/him) is John L. Loeb Associate Professor of the Humanities at Harvard University. His first book is *Copyright and the Value of Performance, 1770–1911* (Cambridge 2018). His current research uses data analysis to explore Broadway and the American theatre industry. More information at visualizingbroadway.com. https://orcid.org/0000-0002-3033-0698

Melory Mirashrafi (she/they) is a first-generation Iranian-American dramaturg, actor, and director from Hillsboro, Oregon. Melory's writing has appeared in Oregon ArtsWatch, Howlround Theatre Commons, Public Books, and the *Methuen Drama Book of Trans Plays.* https://orcid.org/0000-0002-4984-455X

Matthew Moore (he/him) is a director and Assistant Professor of Theatre and Performance at Muhlenberg College. He holds a PhD in Theatre and Performance Studies and the Interdisciplinary Humanities from Stanford University. https://orcid.org/0000-0001-9550-3003

Jay B Muskett (Dine ě) (he/him) is an Indigenous writer from Nakaibito New Mexico. He is an MFA graduate from the University of New Mexico, with a Masters in Dramatic Writing. He is currently an adjunct faculty member at the Institute of American Indian Arts in Santa Fe, New Mexico.

Michael Malek Najjar (he/him) is an Associate Professor of Theatre Arts with the University of Oregon. He authored *Middle Eastern American Theatre* (Bloomsbury) and *Arab American Drama, Film and Performance* (McFarland). He edited *Heather Raffo's Iraq Plays: The Things That Can't Be Said* and *The Selected Works of Yussef El Guindi.* https://orcid.org/0000-0003-3427-1442?lang=en

Jessica Nakamura (she/her) is an Associate Professor in the Department of Theater and Dance at the University of California, Santa Barbara, whose research focuses on contemporary Japanese theatre and performance. Her book *Transgenerational Remembrance: Performance and the Asia-Pacific War in Contemporary Japan* was published in 2020 by Northwestern University Press.

Eleanor Owicki (she/her) is an Assistant Professor in Indiana University's Department of Theatre, Drama, and Contemporary Dance. She has published articles in *Theatre Symposium* and *The New Hibernia Review* as well as chapters in several edited collections. Her current research focuses on theatre in post-conflict Northern Ireland. https://orcid.org/0000-0002-3721-4489

Jaclyn Pryor (they/them) is a Performance Studies scholar/artist specializing in devising, queer/trans theories, and the politics of time. They are an Assistant Professor of Theatre at Penn State, a Fellow at the Wolf Humanities Center at the University of Pennsylvania, and the author of *Time Slips: Queer Temporalities, Contemporary Performance, and the Hole of History*. Pryor received their PhD from the University of Texas. More at jaclynissacpryor.com. https://orcid.org/0000-0002-6005-3169

Bill Rauch (he/him) is the inaugural Artistic Director of the Perelman Performing Arts Center that is currently under construction at the World Trade Center. From 2007 to 2019 he was Artistic Director of the Oregon Shakespeare Festival, and before then he co-founded Cornerstone Theater Company, collaborating with rural and urban communities for 20 years. https://orcid.org/0000-0002-3904-6909

Ramón H. Rivera- Servera (he/him) is the Dean of the College of Fine Arts and Professor of Theatre and Dance at The University of Texas at Austin. He is author or co-editor of *Queer Latinidad: Dance Sexuality Politics, Blacktino Queer Performance, Performance in the Borderlands*, and *Queer Nightlife*.

Carrie Sandahl (she/her) is an Associate Professor at the University of Illinois at Chicago in the Department of Disability and Human Development. She directs Chicago's Bodies of Work, an organization supporting the development of disability arts and culture. Her research and creative activity focus on disability identity in live performance and film. https://orcid.org/0000-0002-3021-6932

David Savran (he/him) is a specialist in twentieth- and twenty-first-century US and German theatre, musical theatre, and social theory, whose most recent book is *Highbrow/Lowdown: Theater, Jazz, and the Making of the New Middle Class*. He is a Distinguished Professor of Theatre and Performance at the CUNY Graduate Center.

Madeline Sayet (she/her) is a citizen of the Mohegan Tribe and a Clinical Assistant Professor in Arizona State University's English Department. For her work as a theatre maker, she has been honored as a Forbes 30Under30, TED Fellow, and recipient of The White House Champion of Change Award from President Obama. www.madelinesayet.comhttps://orcid.org/0000-0002-7816-6217

Georgia Stitt (she/her) is an award-winning composer, lyricist, music producer, and pianist. Her original musicals include *Snow Child*; *Big Red Sun*; *Samantha Spade, Ace Detective*; *The Big Boom*; *The Water*; and *Mosaic*. She has released four albums: *A Quiet Revolution*; *My Lifelong Love*; *Alphabet*

City Cycle; and *This Ordinary Thursday*. Georgia is the Founder of Maestra Music. www.georgiastitt.com

Mei Ann Teo (they/she) is a queer Singaporean immigrant artist and cultural producer who makes at the intersection of artistic/civic/contemplative practice. As a director/deviser/dramaturg, they collaborate internationally in multi-form performance. They are the Associate Artistic Director of New Work at Oregon Shakespeare Festival. http://www.meiannteo.com; http://orcid.org/0000-0001-5 664-1059

Miguel Escobar Varela (he/him) is an Assistant Professor of Theatre Studies at the National University of Singapore and Academic Advisor on Digital Scholarship at the NUS Libraries. He is the author of the forthcoming book *Theater as Data: Computational Journeys into Theater Research* (University of Michigan Press 2021). He also directs the Contemporary Wayang Archive and convenes Digital Humanities Singapore. More information at miguelescobar.com.

Brandon Webster (he/him) is a NYC Composer, Dramaturg, and Storyteller committed to telling afro-futurist & afro-surrealist stories He is an alumnus of the 2013 class of BMI Musical Theater Workshop, a 2017 MCC Theater Artistic Fellow, and a MTF MAKER cohort 1 and 2021–2022 Hodder Fellowship Recipient at Princeton University.

Sarah K. Whitfield (she/her) is a Senior Lecturer in Musical Theatre at the University of Wolverhampton. Her research focuses on exploring the historiography of musical theatre and recovering the work that women and minoritized groups have done through archival research and digital humanities.

Dawn Monique Williams (she/her) is a theatre director and educator. She frequently lectures on Black theatre in the US, and Shakespeare. Her artistic practice is concerned with confronting and dismantling systems of oppression and her writing interrogates contemporary, multiracial Shakespeare performance and adaptation. Dawn holds an MFA in Directing and an MA in Dramatic Literature. http://orcid.org/0000-0002-9037-270X

Jonah Winn-Lenetsky (he/him) is an Assistant Professor of Performing Arts at the Institute of American Indian Arts. He has a PhD in Theatre. His work explores Indigenous and Eco-Activist performance and how communities can utilize theatre to address threats to the environment and to re-conceptualize ecosystems and local/global relationships.

Stacy Wolf (she/her) is a Professor of Theater and American Studies at Princeton University. She is the author of *Beyond Broadway: The Pleasure and Promise of Musical Theatre Across America*; *Changed for Good: A Feminist History of the Broadway Musical*; and *A Problem Like Maria: Gender and Sexuality in the American Musical*.

Rachel M. E. Wolfe (she/her) is a theatre historian with specialties in classics, adaptation theory, and gender. She teaches all aspects of dramatic literature and criticism at Utica College, where she is an assistant professor. Her work on adaptation and the classical tradition has appeared in numerous journals and the edited volume *Vying for the Iron Throne*. https://orcid.org/0000-0002-7474-3654

Isaiah Matthew Wooden (he/him) is a director-dramaturg, critic, and assistant professor of Theater Arts at Brandeis University. He has published widely on contemporary African American art and drama in scholarly journals, anthologies, and popular venues. http://orcid.org/0000-0003-3673-2417

Patricia Ybarra (she/her) is the author of *Performing Conquest: Five Centuries of Theatre, History and Identity in Tlaxcala, Mexico* (Michigan 2009), *Latinx Theatre in Times of Neoliberalism* (Northwestern University Press 2018), and co-editor of *Neoliberalism and Global Theatres: Performance Permutations* (Palgrave Macmillan 2012). She is currently researching projects on Reza Abdoh and theatre and debt. https://orcid.org/0000-0002-0964-2427

Peter Zazzali (he/him) is a Senior Lecturer of Acting and the Director of the BA (Hons) Acting Programme at LASALLE College of the Arts. He is the author of *Acting in the Academy: The History of Professional Actor Training in US Higher Education* (Routledge 2016) and *Actor Training in Anglophone Countries: Past, Present, and Future* (Routledge 2021). https://orcid.org/0000-0003-2288-0187

Introduction

Troubling Traditions

Lindsey Mantoan, Matthew Moore, and Angela Farr Schiller

We See You, White Eurocentric Canon

In 2020, US theatre was rocked by the release of the open letter "We See You, White American Theater," which critiqued white supremacy in the industry and demanded an immediate change in the field. Many prominent white leaders in the field exhibited emotional responses ranging from shock to disbelief, both of which revealed an immense amount of privilege as well as ignorance of the ways that power operates in contemporary US theatre. As the country witnessed the resurgence of white militia groups, the disproportionate effects of COVID-19 on Black and brown people, and the widening of the economic wealth gap, the stock market soared, and a record number of Americans filed for unemployment. In May, the world watched in horror for approximately eight minutes and 46 seconds as Minneapolis police officers murdered George Floyd, a Black man who allegedly used a counterfeit $20 bill to pay for a package of cigarettes at a corner market; this violent display of White supremacy ignited a wave of protests and calls for justice and systemic reforms from Cape Town, South Africa to Portland, Oregon and in over 150 US cities. This call to action, led in part by the Black Lives Matter movement, became a charge for racial reckoning and institutional change across US society, including the US theatre. "We See You, White American Theater" became a battle cry from Black, Latinx, Middle Eastern, Hispanic, Asian, and Indigenous artists from across the country proclaiming that "[y]ou [white American theatre] are all a part of this house of cards built on white fragility and supremacy. And this is a house that will not stand. This ends TODAY. We are about to introduce you … to yourself." Part of the work of decentering whiteness and confronting unequal power in American theatre starts with confronting canonicity.

Troubling Traditions stages a 21st-century encounter with questions of theatre, performance, and canonicity, focusing on embedded histories of power, privilege, and exclusion. Together with our contributors, we ask: what are canons, how are they formed, how do they (or could they) function, how do they influence us, how could we operate outside of them, are they inevitable, what would it mean if there were none, and what should be done

DOI: 10.4324/9781003031413-101

about the projective force of "the canon" in a changing cultural environment? Exploring the range of embodied experiences of canonicity and theorizing departures from the inherited rhetoric of great works, this book also explores whether canonization is necessarily an instrument of ideological reproduction, control, and oppression, or whether it might be reclaimed as a site for progressive social dialogue. Given the ways that canons write us (through their role in our training and experience) and compel us to perform, what alternatives exist?

Canons occupy a privileged place in the Western (read: white, Christian, male, colonial) imaginary. After all, who doesn't love a greatest hits list? But there is no formal list, no concrete, agreed-upon compendium of plays that qualify as canonical. Rather, "the canon" (to whatever extent it really exists) is the product of authoritative discourse masquerading as natural processes. For many, canonical works are those that have "stood the test of time." Perhaps, but time's test is rigged, and the purely aesthetic criteria that presume to govern canonization are mired in the realities of social inequity, textocentrism, and hegemonic control of the means of cultural production.

Despite its ephemerality, the concept of a known theatrical canon circulates; it enters discourse, classrooms, publishing meetings, and season selection debates with surprising force. "The canon," as a unified and closed system, signifies an abstract tradition, a history of aesthetic production, and a set of ideals. It promises to confer a sense of continuance, a known center, and access to cultural capital. "Canons," however, proliferate—they are lived, gathered, reshaped, cross-pollinated, and evolved over time as they inhabit bodies. Canons can be located, personal, and rooted in familiarity and affinity rather than authority. And to the extent that it is very likely that we have all in some way, as educators, artists, publishers, students, and even audiences, participated in the act of making canons, it is essential that we consider their consequences, politics, and relative value—and history.

Holy Canons

Canonization as practiced by the Catholic Church—the process of making saints—transforms lived experience into symbolic objects and instructive texts, and functions theatrically to stabilize doctrinal authority. People aspire to live according to the models of the saints, whose momentary human lives have been transposed into the immortal realm of texts (hagiography), examples to all. Feasts, festivals, and prayer engage audiences of the devout in acts of performance that establish and cultivate this aspirational relationship between the living and the dead. But Church canonization (perhaps like theatrical canonization?) is also the co-optation of the previously embodied into text; it is the scripting and authorization of acts that can be (must be?) performed again. By elevating exemplars (with some editing required) of an ideologically inflected truth, the Church creates a body-text hybrid—a saint—that can embody Christian ideals, but never die. The evacuation of a contingent body is a prerequisite to creating a figure of universal and atemporal ideological signification—we can't have living saints running around ruining the illusion of permanence and transcendence. The unfleshed figure can inhabit, hauntingly and forever, both the statuary and narrative forms that replace that body. So enshrined, they become the not-quite-human that unrealistically models what a Christian ought to be. Transposed into the symbolic, they participate in a kind of theatre without end that affirms stable moral values, functioning both as a reference point for Christian behavior, the community's past, as well as its aspirational future. To further the comparison, we might consider the moralistic drive of much 19th-century Euro-American melodrama in relation to the metaphysical pageantry of the medieval and modern Church. Both fancy a moralistic universe centered on human action—one expressed symbolically through archetypal characters that have been written to manifest ideological goals through performance.

To name such a process, the Church turned to Greek, itself an emblem of literacy and the legible discourse of an ancient culture also enshrined as origin and ideal (of culture and theatre), paganism notwithstanding. Borrowing the word *kanōn* (measuring stick), and signaling its investment in the preservation of language, the Church sought to establish its own body of literature that might be used instrumentally in a process of world-making. Aesthetic canonization, to the extent that it inherits the histories and values of its Christian/Greek referents, similarly assumes an authoritative stance in relation to practice and bodies—it elevates those that conform, making models of them and fixing them within the permanence of sacred texts. Haven't anthologies such as Norton and Wadsworth sometimes felt like they were meant to be a kind of Bible?

As its etymology suggests, the canon of saints manifests a prescriptive set of values (dare we say ideologies?) located in bodies sanctified by their appropriation to The (Christian) Word. This transcription imitates the textualization of an originary speech act that brings order to the universe: let there be light. The Word, made real in the sacred text of the Bible, conflates the presumed fact of God's physical enunciation of these words and the textual object, authored by men, that makes real that divine speech act. God speaks and men write as a way of knowing and making manifest the divine. The canon of Church texts that mediate between the divine and the human, the canonization of lived experience, and canon law all reveal a regulatory logic of the Word that promises universality, stability, and permanence based on transcription and reactivation—the texts must be lived, the words spoken, again.

This promise holds true for a dramatic canon that depends upon repeated acts of embodiment and witnessing. These repetitions constitute a process of world-making—onstage and in the real, in performance and in rehearsal—and confirm the performativity of theatre (which the Church deploys in the mass, the sacraments, pageant plays, etc). Suturing a past to the present, or an imagined world to the real, is a primary function of performance. But to what extent, and with what critical perspective, do we wish to embed the canonical past in present bodies?

To be blunt, we are talking about a history of canonical theatre that is dead, white, male, and Euro-American. "We" live in a strange moment in theatre history, at once focused on the need to address our complicity in oppressive hierarchies and simultaneously obsessed with reperformance, re-membering forms, restagings, and revivals. Perhaps indicative of a need to reclaim experiences that have been written out of the canon, we make frequent returns to the old texts, occasionally with a revisionist agenda. But even these attempts to see again, to queer, to recast, come with their own pitfalls—the legacy of power embedded in the canonized artifacts of our fraught past resists easy deconstruction, and visibility in our ocular-centric moment might trump subversion.

Obsessed with this fraught past, we speak of new work as if it were something novel, but the canon is composed of new works grown old. Valuing longevity over innovation, we fail to recognize that one thing that made those works great was their departure from the past. Canonization remarks departure as continuance, stabilizing a tradition whose center can hold. It should come as no surprise, then, that our theatre, in its obsession with the canon, has become frighteningly, habitually, perhaps even irrationally, conservative. What is it we wish to conserve? To honor? When we speak of traditions, what boundaries and conventions are we really protecting? And, what are we erasing in the process?

Answering these questions will require conversation—a modality that characterizes many of the chapters of this book. We, the editors, also have some questions for you, the reader, and for each other. The next section, in which we speak from personal positions and experience, is meant to model the kind of pluralistic, dialogic thinking we want to elevate, and to honor the differences that inform our work.

Why this Book Now?

Angela Farr Schiller: For me, the question that lies at the heart of this project is: why do we continue to elevate and participate in the practice of canon building as a foundational part of the field of theatre studies when it originates from and actively functions as an exclusionary apparatus of a white supremacist colonial state? Coming from the Western-Eurocentric religious practice of canonizing, the choreography of canon building within our field(s) has historically functioned to systematically uplift the voices of white, cis-gendered, straight men as a kind of in-house affirmative action. In the second decade of the 21st century, as educators, practitioners, and students of theatre and performance, we continue to uphold and invest in this entity called The Western Dramatic Canon as a mainstay of our field. The fruits of canonicity produce the foundation for many of the required classes within our undergraduate education systems, functioning as the backbone of season selection processes and the imagined glue that binds familiarity and distinction within our dramatic fields of study. If education, as bell hooks argues, is ultimately meant to be a "practice of freedom" for all students, what is the cost, as a field, to continually invest in a process and practice meant to hegemonically seal value into the experiences of so few? (hooks 1994: 4).

Matthew Moore: 2020 has certainly prompted more people to ask such important questions. And, in a time when the systems that regulate our social reality seem newly visible, their essential and ongoing imbrication in hegemonic truths and oppressive histories laid bare, it will, perhaps, seem fashionable to turn our critical attention to that monolithic artifact of colonial mentality in our field—the Western canon. I am grateful for the sharpened focus that our moment confers. But the issues underlying the conversations in this book are not new, and this book is, in many ways, long overdue.

Scholars of theatre and performance have pointed to the effects and politics of canonical thinking (and its perpetuating partners, canonical teaching, and canonical producing); friends have ranted and railed against the oppressive apparatus as it invades their spaces, practices, and lives, but Theatre Studies needs to explore the canon's complicity in narratives of white supremacy—a task whose urgency has become clear against the background of contemporary protests for racial justice. We lack a comprehensive mapping of *the idea of the canon* in all its historical, operative force, and performative weight, especially as it relates to race and ethnicity. We lack critical strategies for deconstructing and decentering its racialized, gendered matrix of power. Canonicity looms behind our traditions and practices, imposes its logic on them, and polices our departures, at times with the force of institutional or market authority, at others in more submerged and personal ways. As an artifact of colonial ideology and world-making, canonicity obscures its own essentially conservative, cis-gendered, white, male supremacist values, and projects its narrow, exclusive, aestheticized politics onto a future in desperate need of birth.

Here, we attempt to chart canonicity's contemporary effects and imagine ways of intervening upon its ongoing ideological reproduction. Though many who read this book will have long since internalized its criticisms, and some will see their own experiences reflected in these authors' words, we need to establish collective approaches to the ongoing problems of canonicity.

Lindsey Mantoan: To me, and I think many of the contributors in this book, the imbrication of power, privilege, and canonicity means that canons will always be, as Audre Lorde suggests, the master's tools (Lorde 1984). But others argue persuasively that access to the master's tools opens new possibilities for people previously excluded. Depending on how one defines a canon, some writers suggest that canons might be inescapable, meaning they're tools we can't put down. Are they merely lists? If so, does every syllabus create a canon? Or, perhaps they're a kind of history or genealogy—but in that case, which history, whose genealogy? I'm sort of taken with the idea that each person has their own personal canon that consists of whatever they've read, watched, experienced, and so forth—but it should be noted that what we're all exposed to is governed by oppressive systems that select what gets taught and produced.

Early in the process of editing this book, we identified three distinct approaches to "the canon" (even while all three of us resisted the singularity of any notion of "the canon"): revising it with an eye toward inclusivity (incremental change), embracing multiple canons (proliferation), or operating wholly outside canons (anarchy? chaos? beautiful expansiveness?). Some chapters lean into one or the other of these options, some operate outside of them. One of the questions I'm left with is: at what point do multiple "canons" become so diffuse that they aren't really canons at all, but something else—texts, stories, and practices in circulation for a given time until culture moves on to others? Merely a moment. A breath. Not a rigid list passed down from generation to generation. What would we call this process? Naming things imbues them with power—one reason we as editors avoided using the words "the canon" in the title of this collection. Instead, this book focuses on processes related to canonicity.

Farr Schiller to Moore: What does canonicity mean to you and how has it affected how you participate in our field?

Moore: I use the word canonicity to describe the critical, practical, cultural, and emotional investments in the idea—the tradition—of specified greatness and relevance as it has developed under the stewardship of exclusive and identitarian authoritative bodies. Ironically, canonicity feels more concrete to me than the canon itself. The canon is supposedly a corpus of texts that achieve some kind of heightened, valued, important, and universal status. But where is the authoritative list? How do we decide what belongs there? And who is "we"? Different times, places, and individuals would doubtlessly construct very different lists of plays (or not plays) based on familiarity, commercial success, artistic influence, social impact, perceived aesthetic merit, or other criteria—and they do! So, despite common references to a stable and agreed-upon list, we have to acknowledge that the referent (the canon) is ephemeral, multiple, porous, and changing. Canonicity provides a way of talking about the animating sets of ideas, affinities, values, and processes that continuously create the sense of a canon. Canonicity points to the desires that stand behind individual and collective acts of nomination to an imagined canon.

To the second part of your question, desire maps my relationship to canonicity. The journey began in my first year of graduate school when the faculty handed my cohort a list of 150 plays that would comprise our first qualifying exam, and implicitly, the (our?) canon. My desire was to prove myself worthy of their mentorship (and the degree I was pursuing), and this list provided a neat, concrete measuring stick (a *kanōn*) against which I could prove myself. My performed valuation of the canon established my belonging to an academic community in a very real and emotional way.

By the time I began teaching I had internalized the value of knowing this thing called the canon. I had found all of that reading incredibly useful and perhaps had mistaken *that* value for *the* value that I saw in studying theatre history. As I taught, I grew comfortable with repetition—of the canon and my teaching of it. I wanted to look competent and so I stuck to what I knew. I had been written by the canon.

Only after a few years did I develop desires that were focused externally. What did I want for my students? What did I believe my choices were doing in the world and what did I want to be doing? I became critical of the canon, its tight parameters, its implicit goals, and its essentially conservative outlook. I recognized some of the problems of canonicity and began trying to dismantle my service to those ideas. Now I want to be rid of canonicity altogether, to find other more relevant ways of thinking about and enacting a future less encumbered by the politics and desires that motivate a historical idea of the canon.

Farr Schiller to Mantoan: How has "the canon" or ideas of canonicity impacted your practice?

Mantoan: Early in my career, I was told I had to revise a syllabus because it wasn't canonical enough. One could argue all the texts on my syllabus *were* canonical—they were all well-known, highly produced, and frequently taught, but very few were "white" (authored by white men, centering white characters, and bolstering white supremacy). To me, the canon is a weapon that people with power wield against those without. It is a tool for maintaining the status quo of white supremacist, patriarchal, ableist culture. This experience shocked and dismayed me—I had so much less power than the people instructing me to teach other material. And yet, as a white person, I also had so much privilege to challenge their demands.

The canon is performative—it requires iteration to come into being—so we have to ask ourselves why we keep giving it our attention and what it means when people with power demand that the field never change. As artists and scholars, we have all been shaped by canonizing processes; this book explores other ways of producing knowledge, art, and culture. If canons are about the past, this book looks to future structures and modes of production. This time of global pandemic and racial upheaval requires that artists and instructors assess their values, their work, and the potential gaps between them. Put another way, it's one thing to affirm commitment to antiracist art and pedagogy, and another one to do the taxing and iterative work to dismantle oppressive systems—including ossified canons. The work requires vulnerability and self-reflection and I'm not always great at it. I make mistakes, and every mistake requires me to confront my feelings of embarrassment in order to renew my commitment to the work, a painful and ongoing process.

In some ways, moving forward without a canon can feel like jumping off a cliff without being able to see the bottom. This book provides flashlights, rope, and other essential tools to take the plunge.

Moore to Mantoan: I heard you say that the canon is performative. Can you say more about your experience of this?

Mantoan: As an MA student at UT Austin, I was a TA for undergraduate courses taught by PhD students, and the texts on their syllabi were performative in the sense that they repeated, semester after semester, across different instructors and even levels/titles of courses. Whether in courses for majors or non-majors, first years or seniors, content coalesced around Cherríe Moraga's *Hungry Woman*, José Rivera's *References to Salvador Dali Make Me Hot*, Naomi Wallace's *Slaughter City*, Anna Deavere Smith's *Twilight: Los Angeles, 1992*, and others. Given the frequency with which these texts circulated in the department, they formed what I understood to be the theatre canon—texts theatre artists, students, and scholars should be expected to know. The repetition, the iteration of these texts signalled to me their value, even though the speech act of calling them a "canon" did not occur.

Now, years later, I've collected stark experiences like the one I discuss above that signal to me that my canon was aberrant in some way—that the gravity of known texts pulled toward the white, the old, and the European, and what I understood to be common and central was in fact fringe. The environment in the Theatre and Dance Department at UT Austin was so supportive of alternative ways of being that eventually, I connected my queerness with the way that canons might be queered.

I now teach a course called "Play Reading" and every year I change up the plays on the syllabus. It's more work for me, but it's my way of signaling to students that there is no core—that everyone has a different personal knowledge base. Put another way, rather than feeling some sense of loss or shame if two people at an opening night afterparty haven't read the same plays, there can be celebration that they have new texts to share with each other.

This lack of repetition in my pedagogy—my refusal to engage in iterative processes—is my way of resisting the canon.

Moore: Can I circle back, for a moment, to the "plunge" you mentioned, Lindsey? Maybe we need to say to readers who already bristle at contemplating the trove of treasures that might be lost if we abandon the canon, that we are not after burning books. We can keep Ibsen, Shakespeare, Williams. But we need to rethink what we mean by the word "keep." Do we mean "continue to rely upon?" For what? Do we mean "continue to disproportionately center?" Why? Do we mean "sustain through a practice of repetitive embodiment?" What is being sustained?

For me, departing the familiar terrain (of my canonical education) triggers anxieties: "I'm not an expert in that!" "How will I find time to read so many things I don't already know?" "Do I have the right to teach this?" "Am I really not going to teach Sophocles?" (Who, incidentally, was not white according to any modern conception, but has been co-opted into white canonicity). But worn out (white) anxieties about ownership, expertise, and what must be excluded to allow greater inclusion all support and stabilize the status quo. As you say, Lindsey, calling yourself an ally or affirming a commitment to anti-racist art and pedagogy (especially if you are white) entails responsibilities. Some of that work is getting over ourselves.

Farr Schiller: The questions that you bring up Matt, for me, harken to a white cultural investment in perfection and an idea that all things should contain the ability to be intellectually possessed, quantified, and put into discrete packages of consumption. The fear that underlines the questions that you are raising are a formidable component of an apparatus meant to keep structural oppression in place via the anxieties that deviation from "the canon" produces, particularly for white instructors/practitioners who were not particularly challenged to read very far beyond the Western Canon during their educational experiences. Frankly, as a theatre studies student, I was raised on a steady diet of white supremacy that infused pedagogical anxieties at every turn of my educational experience.

I cannot tell you how many times I, as a Black student, was inadvertently singled out and volun-told by an obviously uncomfortable white professor to suddenly become "THE teacher" when the topic of race (aka anything pertaining to Blackness or Black adjacent) became the topic of discussion in any number of theatre classes during my undergraduate education. Let alone that anything dealing with the unpacking of whiteness was pretty much non-existent, as if focusing on non-white people *was* unpacking race.

Mantoan: Angela, I appreciate your framing of our education as a "diet," because diets are so frequently fads that come and go, and they're often unhealthy!

Moore: Yes! I also can't help but think of the old saying: "you are what you eat." Why am I being fed this diet? Do I want to become this thing I am constantly ingesting? Who planned the menu? Does this smell a little old to you?

Mantoan: Matt, that's hilarious! But also, I took a course entitled "Reading the Canon" in graduate school, and all three of us had a comprehensive exam, which Matt references above, testing us on our knowledge of a reading list of approximately 150 plays. And I have to say, I actually loved both of those experiences. I learned more about European history from those exercises than I did from my undergrad Western civilization class, and I use the knowledge almost daily. But it's only with hindsight that I am able to look back on these experiences and wish that they had been framed as a self-conscious Euro/US canon. There are other canons of course, and I want to know them all! But time is finite.

Moore: Joking aside, I am profoundly grateful for the delectable banquet I was served in graduate school, but as you say, Lindsey, it wasn't framed. Well … maybe it was. It was framed as the things I needed to know. But the reasons for the needing were never addressed, nor was the "I" that was in "need," and so, despite the graduate faculty's best intentions, we ended up training our palettes inside a highly idiosyncratic culinary tradition that passes as universal taste.

Mantoan: Angela, I'm thinking about this diet of white supremacy you were fed and wondering: What costs have the canon, as it's been fed to you, exacted from you?

Farr Schiller: The use of the terminology *exacted from* is really interesting to me. It is a reminder that the canon and the ways that it has been constructed, digested, and internalized have a cost, a toll, a payment attached to them. I have never really thought of it that way but it is true and painful to even begin to construct a tally of how deeply it has extracted from my self-worth. The cost of constantly seeing whiteness as a stand-in for the complete human experience can be deadly. Year after year, the ritual becomes a practice in learning to be okay with being relegated to the margins (if you even showed up there) and, worst-of-all, trained to not think anything about it. As a Black woman living in the United States, if this is not an example of the canon functioning as an apparatus of colonial thinking on marginalized subjects I don't know what is.

Consequently, when I went to a predominantly white university for my undergraduate degree in theatre and these were the texts that were performed in the season, read about in classes, required reading courses, utilized to write papers, I never really challenged what I was being taught. Unfortunately, I think that was the underlying point. Michael J. Babbitt in *American Theatre Magazine* writes, "Predominantly white institutions exist for one main reason: racism. However you view it—whether it's explicit, implicit, or complicit—the reason they are predominantly white is the same: racism" (Bobbitt 2020). It takes work and dedication to remain predominantly anything. Why would this be any different when it comes to educational institutions remaining largely white, long after *Brown v. Board of Education*? In order for predominantly white institutions to sustain white hegemony, the individual cogs in the wheel of education must constantly bend towards whiteness and white supremacy. When I use the term white supremacy, I mean the active—whether conscious or not—elevating of whiteness, white people, white feelings, white privilege, white aesthetics, white logic, and white culture above everything else. A historic and continued investment in canonicity is part of the labor and contribution that predominantly white theatre departments, even with the best intentions, weaponize in the forward movement to remain predominantly white. It actually makes me sad to think about how big the actual cost of this kind of educational experience has been for generations of non-white theatre students, faculty, and staff, the expense that has been *exacted on* and *extracted from* the field of theatre and performance is exorbitant.

Moore to Farr Schiller: Thank you, Angela, for speaking so personally about how the canon affected you in the context of your education. Part of me wants to believe that the pain and cost for non-white students, faculty, and staff of an education dominated by white traditions, logics, and appearances is becoming part of a real conversation about change (rather than one motivated by market forces). Inclusion is a big buzzword in the academy and many of our contributors write convincingly about revising the canon to achieve greater inclusion. What does this approach mean to you? How might it change the experiences of students, faculty, and staff?

Farr Schiller: It is of note that often the answer to a lack of inclusion in predominantly white theatre departments is swapping out a few of the low hanging fruit plays from a syllabus that does not fit the aspirational narrative of equity, diversity, and inclusion, while keeping the larger white structural hegemony in place. We swap out some white-authored plays with plays by non-white authors while never giving any sustained thought to why our disproportionately white theatre departments look nothing like the syllabi that we so desire to perform as inclusive. Your question makes me think about Lindsey's earlier nod to Audre Lorde's "master's tools," in that "[t]hey may allow us temporarily to beat him at his own game, but they will never enable us to bring about genuine change" (Lorde 1984: 112). So, to answer your question, I support all efforts that lead to genuine change as stipulated by the people who are most harmed by the master and their tools. However, the question to our field is: do we have enough collective and creative imagination, audacity, and outright will to look beyond the tools of the master's house (of which the Western dramatic canon is an iconic, dare I say classic, tool) to accomplish that? Thus far, as a whole we have not. However, this book is about the future and I always have hope for the future.

Mantoan: Matt and Angela, both of you write about the ways in which canons are aspirational, personally and professionally, which is new framing for me. Matt, you say your value as a young scholar felt wrapped up in your relation to the club of insiders that the canon constitutes. How do you understand your worth as an artist-scholar now?

Moore: Honestly, I hold some shame about my previous wholesale buying into the structures of value, knowledge, and belonging that my canonical education performed. Uncritical acceptance, or worse, an indefensible urge to please others who outranked me, led to the repetition of those structures in my own classrooms and productions. I perpetuated the harm that Angela writes about by not confronting how I was complicit in the iterative process of stabilizing hegemonic values and, frankly, whiteness. Now I measure my worth as a pedagogue, artist, and scholar by how I am able to activate critical capacities. I want to make visible, and open to critique, the implicit values of a system that conscripted me. I am working toward a kind of personal decanonization, and making that journey visible to my students and audiences is important to me—not to teach them something I have come to know, but to model vulnerability and uncertainty, to invite them to explore the landscape beyond the comfortable, to see the iniquities of canonicity as it has existed, and to imagine alternatives. I want to provoke critical conversation.

Mapping the Conversation

A collected work is already a kind of conversation; this collected work seeks to double down on the active exchange of ideas by putting dialogue, with all its hesitations, redirections, disagreements, divergent perspectives, and individual voices, literally on the page. Why? In part, because we don't believe anyone can respond to all of the myriad problems of canonicity, nor does anyone person have the range of experiences that would allow them to name all of the canonical issues that arise in classrooms, faculty meetings, university and professional production, personal development, research, and publishing. Additionally, to form thought we require other perspectives. Dialogue implies an ethical stance in relation to another, promotes listening over professing, integrates identity into debate, marks the difference, and encourages connection across differences. We dialogue to see, hear, and connect with others. Finally, dialogue is a process, not exactly a form of writing. We believe that the many dialogic manifestations contained in this volume enlarge our sense of what it means to be in conversation. Some chapters are written as literal dialogue—conversations, even plays. Some are the co-authored prose that resulted from sustained dialogue over various periods of time. Some are solo-authored pieces that grew out of dialogues or make frequent use of dialogues that shaped the author's perspective. These chapters are a beginning to a renewed conversation, full of approaches (not answers), experiences, and criticisms that will provoke further thought and, we hope, action.

This conversation has a history, of course. English Literary Studies has engaged, at length, in debates about canonicity, but the majority of those debates took place during the infamous Canon Wars of the 80s and 90s, at the same time that Performance Studies took root and our field expanded, siphoning critial focus away from canonical plays and toward the larger frame of global performance. The literary canon wars didn't address issues of embodiment, public visibility, and capitalistic imperatives in ways that are useful to rethinking the total landscape of performance practice.

Some theatre scholars did confront canonicity in the 90s. One of the most significant engagements with questions of theatrical canons came from Jill Dolan's chapter "Feminism and the Canon: The Question of Universality" in *The Feminist Spectator as Critic* ([1988] 2012). Examining the ways in which mainstream criticism upholds the canon by creating different "horizons of expectations" for plays by women, Dolan argues that "fitting a woman's play into any canon—male or female—implies that it is acquiescent to the ideology perpetuated by that canon" ([1988] 2012: 19, 40). Using the critical reception of Marsha Norman's *'Night, Mother* as an example, Dolan outlines some of the approaches to the literary canon wars that feminist critics and art-makers took, and the challenges they faced as a result.

Given the ways in which canons center white male art, it is unsurprising that the critiques and considerations of it often come from subdisciplines and specific identity positions. For example, Musical Theatre Studies include both dominant narratives that center on whiteness and maleness as well as significant texts that rewrite those histories. Stacy Wolf's *Changed for Good: A Feminist History of the Broadway Musical* (2011) challenges patriarchal views of Broadway by examining, decade by decade, female characters and feminist musical theatre conventions. In *America in the Round: Capital, Race, and Nation at Washington D.C.'s Arena Stage* (2019), Donatella Galella zooms in on the way one theatre resists and upholds oppressive systems related to economics, race, and US identity. Sarah Whitfield's 2019 edited collection *Reframing the Musical: Race, Culture and Identity* offers transnational, anti-racist historiography of musical theatre as a corrective to dominant white supremacist framing. Taken together, these books shape a powerful counter-narrative to musical theatre historiography, challenging canonical understandings and centering non-canonical pieces.

Dance likewise has its own discourse related to canonicity, including texts that reread the canon or propose new ones. Sally Banes' *Talking Dancing Women: Female Bodies On Stage* (first published in 1998) analyzes the Western dance canon through a feminist lens. In *Modern Dance / Negro Dance: Race in Motion* (2004), Susan Manning explores the relation between Negro dance in the first half of the 1900s and modern dance to outline a new way to understand dance history. Ananya Chatterjea's *Butting Out: Reading Resistive Choreographies Through Works by Jawole Willa Jo Zollar and Chandralekha* (2004) grapples with binaries shaping dance history and reads each choreographer's work through historical practices of cultural production. In *Choreographing Copyright: Race, Gender, and Intellectual Property Rights in American Dance* (2016), Anthea Kraut investigates the ways in which property, race, and gender coalesce to shape dance practices and reproduction. These texts propose reframing the canon, looking outside the canon, or rethinking the ways in which canons are formed.

Since the start of the 2000s, there has been a proliferation of curated and open-source databases dedicated to collecting plays by Black, Indigenous, Middle Eastern, Asian, Latinx, Hispanic, queer, trans, disabled, and femme authors, as well as non-Western plays. Many such lists frame their interventions in terms of creating greater visibility and access to works that traditional theatre history has marginalized. Some, like The Alternative Canon Community, which compiles a huge number of nationally and ethnically specific plays, explicitly locate their efforts outside of traditional canon-making practice. Their nonhierarchical modes of assembly, invitations to revision by users, and creation of networks of disruptive efforts (made visible by including links to similar projects, resources, and associations) subvert authoritative and gatekeeping practices that attend more traditional canonizing. Some of the most prominent organizations working against traditional canonicity include Black Theatre Network, Latinx Theatre Commons, Consortium of Asian-American Theaters and Artists, Indigenous Performing Arts Alliance (Canada), Arts Administrators of Color Network, The Kilroys, The International Center for Women Playwrights, Women of Color in the Arts, and First People's Fund. Links to all of these can be found on The Alternative Canon's public Google doc, accessible at https://sourceful.us/doc/454/alternative-canon. Dozens of articles in HowlRound Theatre Commons, a website dedicated to "amplify[ing] progressive, disruptive ideas about theatre and facilitat[ing] connection between diverse practitioners," likewise challenge canonical thinking and make accessible alternative practices and texts.

And, while canons largely concern text, training methodologies have their own canonical practices and practitioners, which scholars are likewise challenging. Bringing forth a more culturally inclusive, African-centric framework to theatre pedagogy, Sharrell D. Luckett and Tia M. Shaffer, in their groundbreaking book *Black Acting Methods,* argue that,

> the nature of pedagogy is grounded in the questions of what to teach, why to teach it, and then how to teach it. The answers to these questions reveal a complicity of intentions, a foregrounding of particular histories to perpetuate particular realities at the expense of other realities and futures. (Luckett and Tia 2016: 1)

Squarely challenging white supremacist pedagogies related to embodiment, *Black Acting Methods* elevates multi-cultural, international ways of performing and teaching performance.

Similarly focused on training, a recent issue of *Theatre, Dance, and Performance Training* (TDPT), entitled "Against the Canon," takes the primarily white and male-centric canon of embodied theatre and dance practices to task. And, in the spring of 2021, the British journal *Studies in Theatre and Performance*, will publish a curated issue: *Decentering Theatre & Performance Studies.* The CFP indicates multiple goals related to moving beyond hegemonic performance discourse (by centering work about and from "the margins"), establishing pedagogies that "provide alternatives to the underwriting of traditional canonical power," and departing modes of knowledge production that sustain "a form of cultural imperialism" in our field.

Increased attention to questions of canonicity and its harm demonstrates the vital importance of this topic to our field. Conversations have been fragmented, discontinuous, and spread across events and sources. The collective demands made by the theatre artists in the We See You letter mark a seismic shift in how and where this conversation is taking place, and perhaps how it will be received. This book participates in a move toward a more collective dialogue. Acknowledging its inevitable gaps in representation, such as scholars and practitioners working from an Africanist perspective in a US performance context or the lack of conversation around the relationship between canonicity and design, we are proud to say that the voices collected here speak from a previously unseen diversity of perspectives and positions within the field. The dialogues included in *Troubling Traditions* take place among professors of all ranks (including visiting and adjuncts); theatre, dance, and Performance Studies scholars; playwrights; literary managers; artistic directors; directors; choreographers; production, resident, and new works dramaturgs; performers; composers; arts administrators; theatre historians; and directors of major performance centers across the country. Together they offer a uniquely broad view of experiences and approaches to canonicity in our time.

Costs, Remixes, Approaches, and Departures

Chapters in this volume reframe discourse, provide new analytic lenses, suggest new language, and pivot from tired practices related to canonicity. We've divided the book into four parts: "Costs of Canonicity," "Remixing Traditions," "Fluid Approaches," and "Departures and Re-Visions." Chapters in each part form a dialogue around that topic, and converse and debate with other sections.

We've situated "Costs of Canonicity" first to frame the stakes of this conversation, which are expansive and deeply personal. Chapters in this section range from manifestos about the dangers of even engaging in a conversation about canonicity when perhaps we should abandon the word, the practice, the concept altogether, to dialogues about the complex emotional relationships individual people have to dead playwrights, to narratives about the ways in which capitalism shapes art-making. In "The Good, The Bad, and The Ugly in Theater, Dance and Performance Studies," Nadine George-Graves submits a forceful argument that any form of canonizing practice is dangerous and pedagogical practice must embrace other modes of operating. Chapter Two, "The Shakespeare Problem: A Conversation," sees Sarah Enloe, Madeline Sayet, Mei Ann Teo, and Dawn Monique Williams work through their relationship to Shakespeare's dominance and the personal and professional consequences thereof; this multifaceted, occasionally contradictory discussion reveals the complexity of questioning what we might love.

Sukanya Chakrabarti, in "'Go back to India if you hate my people so much': Consequences of Troubling the 'Canon' in American Academia," starkly demonstrates the painful consequences of being a non-white professor in an academy that centers whiteness at every turn. Continuing Chakrabarti's concerns and expanding them into the realm of playwriting, Patricia Ybarra, Virginia Grise, and Victor I. Cazares interrogate in "Despite the Flames: A Conversation" the forces that shape their aesthetics and politics, including US trade policy and its valorization of capitalism. "The Black Gaze / A Different Account," Eric M. Glover and Isaiah Matthew Wooden's investigation of the ways anti-Blackness shapes production, pedagogy, and identity, includes tools for recognizing and confronting anti-Blackness.

"Amidst the Rubble of the Ivory Tower" by Sara Brady puts her personal experiences teaching at Bronx Community College against the historic framing of Performance Studies to reveal its privileges and failings; Brady then suggests concrete alternatives. Taken together, the chapters in Part One offer rawness and vulnerability as an antidote to the injury caused by the weaponization of canons, and they mobilize personal experiences to insist on an approach to theatre and performance that operates without canons.

Part Two, "Remixing Traditions," expands the parameters of canons—the locations of their boundaries, the ways we read the texts included therein, and the cultural considerations that bear on consumption and production of these texts. This section offers alternative ways of analyzing canon formation and texts. Beginning from a place that assumes we've all been conscripted into canons, Part Two challenges the way we engage with well-known texts, expanding knowledge and critical lenses available to artists and scholars.

Bill Rauch and Sonja Arsham Kuftinec chronicle, in "Shaking up the Canon with Cornerstone and OSF," 25 years of engaging with and challenging conventional understandings of the canon by examining the practices, privileges, and innovations of Rauch's artistic work. In "'Yo, Let's Steal Their Canons!': Arab and Arab American Canonical Multiplicities," Samer Al-Saber and Michael Malek Najjar debate and frequently disagree about the possibilities and parameters of an Arab and Arab American canon and even identity, attending to the clashes of geography, historical inflection points, culture, and translation. Jay B. Muskett and Jonah Winn-Lenetsky's "Your Heritage is Safe Here: Defining Three Indigenous Theatrical Canons" argues that, given the brutal erasure of Indigenous cultures and traditions, and the problematic ways white playwrights have represented indigenous characters in US theatre, a Native canon by Indigenous playwrights is essential and must sit beside—not under—the traditional Western canon.

Disability scholars Ann M. Fox and Carrie Sandahl provide alternative lenses for understanding texts by canonical playwrights, asking what those plays can do for disability, in "'Frenemies' of the Canon: Our Two Decades of Studying and Teaching Disability in Drama and Performance." Ellen McLaughlin and Rinde Eckert examine their artistic practices and heritages as playwrights, performers, and librettists through their interactions with ancient and operatic canons in "The Uses of Awe." Collectively the chapters in Part Two consider the central questions of this book through production, theory, and history.

Part Three of the book, "Fluid Approaches," examines specific subdisciplines of Theatre and Performance Studies, including queer and trans performance, dance, musical theatre, Asian performance modes, and new play development. Each subfield comes with its own challenging interrelations among embodiment, text, power, and genealogy. The authors in this section challenge assumptions about material realities, notions of quality and value, and critical authority.

The first chapter in Part Three, "Toward and Away: The Dramatic Tension of a Queer & Trans Canon" by Finn Lefevre, explores the potentiality, desire, and dissent wrapped up in queer and trans canons, which are as multiple in definition as queerness itself. Hannah Kosstrin's "Dancing With/Out the Canon" examines how embodied knowledge is part of and affected by canonical practices, paying close attention to the implications for dance studies. Stacy Wolf's polyvocal chapter brings together eight scholars and practitioners, Masi Asare, Rob Berman, Randall Eng, Eric M. Glover, David Savran, Georgia Stitt, Brandon Webster, and Sarah Whitfield, to respond via microessays to the question "what do we do with the musical theatre canon?"

In "Canons in Motion: Japanese Performance, Theatre History, and the Currents of Knowledge," Jyana S. Browne and Jessica Nakamura identify multiple canons associated with Japanese history, Japanese performance forms, and theatre history courses, and weave these currents of knowledge together. "The Kids' Table: Cross-institutional Treatment of the Canon and the Uncanonizable Nature of New Work," by literary and dramaturgy apprentices Charlie Dubach-Reinhold and Melory Mirashrafi, reads higher education from the perspective of recent undergraduates, and regional theatre from the perspective of new play development, examining the dissonance between the way theatre is taught and produced. Together, the authors in this section emphasize the importance of ongoing revisions to our ossified intellectual and artistic engagement with our fields.

The book concludes with Part Four, "Departures and Re-visions," a section that takes up questions of alternative processes besides canonicity. "Rethinking the Canon through the Digital," Miguel Escobar Varela and Derek Miller's chapter, demonstrates the ways in which the digital opens new understandings of theatre history, leaning into abundance as a methodology for resisting the scarcity of canonicity. "*Antigone* is Dead, Long Live *Antigones*!: Adaptation, Difference, and Instability at the Heart of the Traditional Western Canon" by Rachel M. E. Wolfe challenges the assumptions of adaptation theory, arguing that adaptations are like genetic descendants, retaining less and less DNA of the original over generations.

In "Redirecting Canonicity: PhD Exams and Actor Training," Eero Laine and Peter Zazzali provide close readings of requirements for graduate students and the ways in which they reproduce tired approaches rather than innovative methodologies. Jessica Brater and Michelle Liu Carriger provide, in "We Aren't Here to Teach What We Already Know," a concrete approach to the mechanics of canonicity, arguing for the value of a repository containing teaching materials accessible to all who contribute. The final chapter, organized and contributed to by Zachary Dorsey, offers microessays written by Paul Bonin-Rodriguez, Michelle Dvoskin, Lindsey Mantoan, Eleanor Owicki, Jaclyn I. Pryor, and Ramón H. Rivera-Servera addressing the titular question "How do We Do the Queer Canon?" Together, these authors embrace queerness as a *process* rather than a set of texts or way of being. Collectively, these chapters shift the focus from lists and valorized texts to methodologies for expanding engagement with the practices—historical and contemporary—of our vast field.

We Believe In You, Future of US Theatre

Toward a Future

"We See You White American Theater" concludes with the assertion: "We stand on this ground as BIPOC theatremakers, multi-generational, at varied stages in our career, but fiercely in love with the Theatre." This statement references August Wilson's iconic 1996 speech "The Ground on Which I Stand," delivered at Theatre Communications Group's national conference, held at Princeton University. Wilson's speech takes to task the structures of US theatre, highlighting that of the 66 LORT theatres in the US at the time, only one could be considered Black. Wilson faults liberal practices such as "colorblind casting" for re-entrenching exclusion and upholding white supremacy. This speech spurred significant discussion across the theatre industry and inspired a 1997 debate about race and US theatre between Wilson and American Repertory Theatre's Artistic Director Robert Brustein, moderated by Anna Deavere Smith. On the 20th anniversary of Wilson's speech, Princeton hosted a symposium entitled "The Ground on Which We Stand," which included a reading of Wilson's speech followed by responses examining the status of US theatre in the two decades since. The genealogy of critique of US theatre—from W.E.B. DuBois's "Criteria of Negro Art" to Wilson's "Ground on Which I Stand," and through "We See You," reveals that even as we move deeper into the 21st century, white supremacy continues to function as the invisible (or not so invisible) guiding structure of our field(s). This critique demands we acknowledge that whiteness, as a systemic apparatus, will never unseat itself; we have to venture outside the box for that.

Despite a long history of interventions into the workings of American performance, the field of Theatre Studies has not made substantive changes in response to the criticisms that compose this genealogy of dissent. The canon suggests a future written in terms of the past, operating according to the logic of the durable text, and conscripting bodies into ongoing narratives of reality and social values. If we wish to reorient our values, we need to rethink our relationship to text and futures, move away from singularity toward multiplicity, and decentralize authority.

In "The Ground on Which I Stand," Wilson concludes,

> I believe in the American theatre. I believe in its power to inform about the human condition, I believe in its power to heal, 'to hold the mirror as'twere up to nature,' to the truths we uncover, to the truths we wrestle from uncertain and sometimes unyielding realities. All of art is a search for ways of being, of living life more fully. (Wilson 1996)

It's profoundly moving and important that a man who roundly critiques an industry to which he has committed his life's work—an act that comes from a place of pain and exclusion—can also express such optimism about it. The panoply of contributors to this book bolster this belief in the field, and their arguments originate from a place of love and care. Those involved in US theatre at every level must commit to doing the work. We believe in you; we believe in the future of US theatre.

Works Cited

Bobbitt, Michael J. 2020. "Let's Be Real: These Programs Won't End Racism at Your Theatre." *American Theatre*, 22 December. Accessed 28 December 2020. https://

www.americantheatre.org/2020/12/22/lets-be-real-these-programs-wont-end-racism-at-your-theatre/?fbclid=IwAR1To8VUiBPRBppKz3eEPUcezGL8PJuFnayJg35TNt8IboQrHocx7ihj68A

Dolan, Jill. [1988] 2012. *The Feminist Spectator as Critic*, 2nd edition. Ann Arbor: University of Michigan Press.

hooks, bell. 1994. *Teaching to Transgress: Education as the Practice of Freedom*. New York and London: Routledge.

Lorde, Audre. 1984. *Sister Outsider*. Freedom, CA: Crossing Press.

Luckett, Sharrell, and Tia M. Shaffer. 2016. *Black Acting Methods: Critical Approaches*. New York and London: Routledge.

Wilson, August. [1996] 2016. "The Ground on Which I Stand." *American Theatre*, 20 June. Accessed 30 December 2020. https://www.americantheatre.org/2016/06/20/the-ground-on-which-i-stand/

Part I
Costs of Canonicity

1 The Good, The Bad, and The Ugly in Theatre, Dance, and Performance Studies

Nadine George-Graves

Disciplining

There is a story (perhaps apocryphal) from my undergraduate days that comes to mind as I consider the future of the Canon (with a capital "C") and acts of canonization through the professoriate. Apparently, Harold Bloom ("literally" the author of *The Western Canon*) was on his way to give a lecture and stopped off at Atticus, a local coffee shop (named after the now not-so-great white male savior of an arguably canonical novel). Upon leaving, he paused, lost in thought with his hat in his hand when a passerby put a quarter in it. He stopped the would-be good Samaritan and said, "Excuse me, madam, you've made a terrible mistake. I am the preeminent literary critic!" Of course, the exclamation point is mine and I can only surmise at his tone. Beyond the metaphor that one person's preeminent literary critic is another person's bum, I invite us to consider more deeply not only the question of who gets to decide what is "good" enough to enter the canon but also (and more importantly) why we think we need a canon in the first place. Why was his reproachful retort rooted in his job and position of power? Clearly, he was not the preeminent fashion critic, but he also seemed to be saying I don't need your quarter, lady, because I tell people what to read.

In this chapter, I consider the practices, challenges, and ethics of the canon in theatre, dance, and performance. I also ask us to take a step further out and interrogate "canonical thinking" writ large and its consequences. The editors of this collection of essays asked us to think about the ways in which the next generation of scholars and artists are introduced to texts and the idea of the canon. I'll admit that my first response was: asked and answered, move on. The death knell has rung for the canon by the paradigm shift in arts and humanities education away from "the good books" model to one of critical discourse. But, perhaps, the canon is dead, long live the canon. And perhaps the work of dismantling canonical thinking rooted in late-20th century academic culture war challenges is incomplete. To think through my position, I engaged in a number of conversations with others (scholars, artists, students, my kids, myself—a brutal interlocutor, and friends) around our work as professors tasked with providing knowledge about performance to undergraduates. Initial conversations with my

DOI: 10.4324/9781003031413-1

OSU colleague Professor Hannah Kosstrin around the themes of this project for Dance Studies provided important foundations for my reasoning. These dialogues have led me to argue in this essay that while English and Literature manifest canonicity in disciplinary and disciplining ways, and while it is important to examine important works in Theatre, Dance, and Performance Studies, what is more important is to entertain the idea of abandoning the canon, attempts at improving the canon (like expanding or pluralizing into "canons"), and the whole business of canonical thinking from our jobs altogether.

The most well-rehearsed criticism of the canon is that the power to define the parameters for inclusion and to "allow" works into the canon rests in the hands of too few—historically old, white men in elite English departments. This is certainly true but, I argue, the power underlying acts of canonization is dangerous in *any* hands and should not be the pedagogical work of university professors. The conferring of canonical status is a kind of speech-act—a saying that does. It is a beatification like the Christian dubbing of knighthood and the Catholic canonization of saints. As such, the ideology underlying the canon is not benign and is always part and parcel of our deceptively smaller educational practices. This is also not just a matter of semantics, with "canon" being interchangeable with "list," "personal opinion," or some other less controlling exercise. Canonicity is rooted in beliefs about the Western concept of the primacy of a shared origin, the universal acceptance of the values therein, the ritualistic rehearsal (through preaching or teaching) of these ideologies, and the maintenance of consistent unalterable messaging. Canonizing sanctifies, often with extreme hubris and prejudice, and it is a mistake to dismiss or underestimate these underlying foundational tenets from the past even as we look to the future. As such, we need to attend to this ideology as distinct from acts of curating materials to examine in class, making lists of works that belong to a category, or recognizing works as part of (or even emblematic of) a particular tradition. List-making can be useful, canonizing can be dangerous. Canons make works and people sacrosanct and untouchable. I argue that if one goes about organizing a body of materials to examine under the mindset of, or with the mandate towards, creating a canon, one necessarily subscribes to the hegemonic, imperial occidental systemic power structures that are inextricably linked to the original concept of The Western Canon, even if one works towards improving the ideology of canonical thinking. The argument that more voices from more diverse perspectives are needed is valid, though under-realized in nearly all endeavors. Yes, all lists should be rich, diverse, and inclusive. Yes, a diverse pool of judges, with varied points of view, and a wide range of definitions of "good" promises to yield a broader range of winners for any accolade. But this issue is more complex than attempts to "fix" an imperfectly "fixed" system. Canons of the good are *necessarily* exclusionary and will *never* attend to all definitions of the good. Yes, syllabi, reading lists, references, etc. should be well-defined, diverse, equitable, and inclusive. But they should not be canonical.

The Western Canon is considered to be the body of high culture that is the most valued thereby attaining the status of classic (read "best" and sometimes read "universal"). In *The Western Canon*, Bloom defends the canon of western literature by discussing the 26 central canonical writers according to *his* definition of literary merit. He condescendingly defines academic modes of inquiry that complicate his criteria by attending to things like race, class, gender, politics, or social awareness as "Schools of Resentment" (Bloom 1995: 4). Relatedly, attempts to expand the canon for broader representation and attempts to question those works included in the canon on grounds of social morality should be rejected out of hand, according to him and others. As if caring about the world renders one incapable of recognizing good art. This logic is also a declaration that things like racism, classism, sexism, and anything that might be politically or civically problematic have no place in the criteria for assessing canonical merit. Therefore, the critique of the canon for its lack of diversity in representation is simultaneously valid and invalid. The canon lacks diversity because it was made that way—literally. Allowing Toni Morrison in doesn't really solve the problem. (For the record, I think Morrison was a brilliant author. I'm glad she was recognized and so was she. But this is not the point.) The tactic of upholding canonical thinking by recognizing a few non-traditional examples can become a complicated trap.

As long as the canon exists, yes, it should be diverse but it is important to recognize the potential costs of these moves. Diversifying canons through representation like the race, gender, or ability of the creator usually maintains definitions of "good" that still tend to reject primary aesthetics from other populations. When examining these moves towards diversity and inclusion, we must interrogate the underlying disciplining in at least three ways. 1. Moves towards diversity and inclusion do not necessarily address assumptions about the aesthetic criteria of the canon. For example, Lorraine Hansberry's *A Raisin in The Sun* is a canonical play in part because it mainly adheres to Western definitions of a "well-made" realist play. 2. Token diversity and inclusion in the canon can also be used as an argument to suppress calls for equity and justice as Robert Brustein accused August Wilson of having a "failure of gratitude" in his call for more opportunities for Black artists in American theatre. (Wilson, Brustein 1996) 3. This conferring of canonical status can lead to more attention to the original tenets of the canon like white male privilege. Again, *A Raisin in The Sun*, couldn't just be a canonical Black play. It took some time, but Bruce Norris managed to firmly insert whiteness into one of the few Black plays to "make it" into the canon. I've written about this elsewhere (George-Graves 2018), but for my purpose here, I'll add to that argument that *Clybourne Park* was so highly praised *precisely* for its work disciplining a Black example of the theatrical canon. *A Raisin in The Sun* is fiction (though based on Hansberry's real experiences) but our investment in this family is real. With the success of Norris' demonstration that white men have access to everything, the play adjusted our pathos for a Black family. *A Raisin in the Sun* is the play that always moves some white undergraduate students to approach me after lecture wanting to talk about how much they "identified" with the characters. White people really want in. With Norris' intervention, white students can have their way "in" by identifying with the white characters.

Sitting on the subway with my daughter one day, we noticed a woman carrying a bag with her school's logo. Maya asked why she didn't know her from school and they figured out that the woman taught at the high school. (Maya was in middle school at the time.) Maya asked her what she was teaching at the moment and the white woman beamed about teaching the "sequel" to *A Raisin in the Sun* and how wonderful the story was. She went on and on about the white characters (notably not the few Black ones) and I bit my lip. I talked to Maya when we got home. The fact that this high school teacher thinks *Clybourne Park* is a sequel, the fact that it is sometimes taught *without* teaching *A Raisin in The Sun*, and the fact that other plays written by Black playwrights in response to the Black canonical text will never receive the same amount of attention is only part of the reason to trouble the argument around the ameliorative actions of diversifying the canon. If I can't persuade us out of canons and folks are still convinced that diversifying the canon is the way to go, know that there will always be a catch because hegemony finds a way. Diversify lists. Abolish canons.

Performing arts academic disciplines attempt to replicate the logocentric thinking of English and Literature departments by willing the primacy of Western classical music recorded in scores, text-based theatre traced to the ancient Greeks and Romans, and the royal roots of ballet for concert dance. Even the most embodied performing art, dance, maintains written systems of notation, albeit less recognized than scores and scripts but equally rooted in Western ideology. A number of important scholars and artists have contested these assumptions and contribute to the troubling of canonical enterprises. Diana Taylor (2003) challenges the dominance of the text/archive (dramatic literature and written history) in theatre by showing that the repertoire (embodied performance and history-keeping through scenarios, instead of plays) is ignored by performance scholars who only value text-based definitions of theatre and performance to the detriment of knowledge. It is not a coincidence that the repertoire is mainly humanist artistry in the Global South vs. Western play texts. The canon does not recognize the repertoire. Saidiya Hartman (1997) models a scene-based historiography that allows us to analyze the power dynamics at the root of privileged narrative history writing. bell hooks repeatedly challenges us to first decolonize our minds. Abandoning canonical thinking and championing other pedagogical foundations for our work is part of that project. Phenomenologists, affect theorists and even cognitive theorists investigate the importance of embodied knowledge—the stuff of theatre and dance. These are profound yet under-researched areas in which theatre and dance can offer valuable insight from a non-text-based perspective. Regrettably, neither discipline has fully embraced the ways in which scholarship that is not text-based (and is less interested in disciplining audiences' aesthetic preferences) are important epistemological matrices.

Because both theatre and dance have inferiority complexes in the academy, the replication of traditional models, including championing the canon, holds sway. Parts of Performance Studies attempt to undo these systems but the subfield has even less influence in the academy. All of these deeply embodied fields fall short of the promise of the body's challenge to the mind in the production and dissemination of knowledge in higher education. We still hold on to the idea that dramatic literature is theatre's best bet for ascending in intellectual status and respect.

Dance, a discipline that was later to the academy, coming of age at the same time as Bloom's "Schools of Resentment," has been led primarily by white women, many of whom define themselves as feminists. As such, it had the greatest potential to trouble the institution in terms of rejecting old models, including the idea of the canon. Instead, the lure of academic prestige resulted in the advocacy of dance as equal in aesthetic import to literature, fine art, music, and even theatre by building the field on analogous examples of the good. The championing of white ballet, modern, and postmodern dance traditions as part of the larger western canon became the path to success in the academy. Despite the discipline coming of age during a time of critical discourse, canonizing dance works and artists according to labels of good, bad, and ugly persist. Conversations in dance departments are still rooted in definitions of what is aesthetically "good" dance defined by narrow (though widening) standards. Predictably, this leads to a general resistance to adopt more diverse, equitable, and inclusive histories and technique classes and willful incomprehension of the necessity to cut previous examples in order to make room for other discussions. In order for students to learn about a wider range of artists, traditions, techniques, and definitions of good art, they might not learn about a white person currently on the syllabus. This is the nuanced sticking point that no number of lists of "other" examples can fix, not until canonical thinking is addressed. Although it seems obvious, it bears stating that thinking that white artistic traditions are *the best* (or even *better*) is part of white *supremacy*. Pretending white traditions aren't about identity politics is racist. We can't maintain white supremacy and practice actual diversity, equity and inclusion no matter how many examples are substituted. The canon will never look like the world. There will never be more of "us" than "them" (despite global demographics) in the canon.

"Decolonizing" is the current articulation of progressive attempts to reckon with the fallout of settler-colonialism and its imperial strategies of dominance and oppression. Our fields and our work as educators are certainly part of this grander project. As someone who has dedicated 25 years of my professional life to this work—I believe in the importance of the arts for social change. The undoing (with extreme "resentment") of the canon, canonization, and canonicity as colonial projects is crucial for this work. Without this, any act of list-making risks re-inscribing colonial value judgments about worth, hierarchy, and status. If we are serious about decolonizing the academy, we must recognize the support structures that uphold colonial disciplining and undo them. This takes radical decolonizing of minds and faith that *students will learn* even if we don't all teach the same things. This requires relinquishing control which is a dangerous prospect for fields the larger academy already considers out of control, with our unruly bodily practices and somatic wisdom. I am arguing that perhaps the reason the performing arts have yet to fully "make it" in the academy in terms of respect and resources is because, like the "schools of resentment," we were never intended to make it. Doomed to fail in many ways (including canon-making), we should stop playing the game and focus on what we do best, including methodologies, pedagogies, and systems of disseminating knowledge that other disciplines lack.

Is revisiting the canon now a progressive way to return to the right to name the "good" with a dubious promise that the new canon will be "better" because of our undoubtedly enlightened efforts? As we say in theatre, everything is a choice, and, in terms of the canon, all choices are exclusions. I have no faith in the creation of a non-power-based canon. Any canon is an echo of The Western Canon.

The Important and The Persuasive

So, then what do we *do* as college instructors?

It is possible, I argue, for us to imagine a path forward in the academy in which telling people what is good, bad, or ugly is not a part of a professor's job description. Audre Lorde warns that the master's house cannot be taken down with the master's tools. (Lorde 1984: 110) Although I don't wholly subscribe to this mantra, I posit that the canon is one of the most pernicious tools in the master's chest. Hubris, desire, and control are part and parcel of gaining access to the master's tools and canonization is particularly dangerous. After Foucault, I submit that more than serving truth, the canon serves power. Having the power of a tastemaker or, as I tell my students, "the 'they' who say," is a power to be taken very seriously even when the mechanisms behind master narratives (or the masters' narratives) are exposed. Relinquishing control of this power is anathema to some of us. But, I submit, releasing our controlling, disciplinary impulses around canonical thinking is not as radical as it might seem. Contrarily, I argue that it requires a *greater* level of intellectual rigor.

I am not under the delusion that college and university faculty do not wield power and do not serve as gatekeepers in many ways. We can still have standards for the conferring of degrees. We can still engage in profound conversations. We can still get at humanist meaning with examples. We can still be opinionated and try to convince others to see things as we see them. We can still talk about examples we like. We do not need to set PhD seminars at an every-person level of broad cultural literacy (Hirsch 1988). We can do all of these parts of our job and more without the canon. Rather than creating a carnivalesque free-for-all with ideas running amok, unhandcuffing ourselves from the canon raises the bar for our profession. Without the canon, replete with pre-packaged fodder for 101 courses, we won't be able to just rely on what someone like Bloom says is good. The internet and the corporate university have destroyed the notion of the syllabus as intellectual property. Although sometimes communities of scholars engage in equitable exchanges of ideas to support each other creating syllabi, more often months of hard work that has gone into reading, watching, deliberating, and choosing examples for a course ends up cherry-picked by others without recognition or compensation—as if professors are canon-spitting syllabi machines. Teaching the canon is easy. Teaching a more diverse canon is less easy. Thinking deeply about more complicated ways to teach performance, even at a foundational level, takes expertise. Creating courses around things other than the canon opens up possibilities for truly diverse, equitable, and inclusive conversations. We don't *have* to start with ballet or modern. We can start with Bharatanatyam, never "manage" to get to modern, and still produce deeply knowledgeable students in dance studies.

At this point, I feel like I should say (only half sarcastically) that some of my very favorite artists are dead white men. I was a Philosophy and Theater major at Yale, an institution that is older than the country. I've taught at elite liberal arts colleges and large state universities. I've been well-schooled in traditional notions of what constitutes knowledge and the role of higher education and actually subscribe to a number of them. I've taught and cited the ideas of many people who would have hated me. To be clear, I absolutely and impenitently "resent" centuries of systematic, global terror, violence, hate, and oppression perpetrated on the majority of the world's population by the elite few who tend to be of the same race, class, and gender as the people historically empowered to create canons. I do not believe that divorcing one's experiences of the world is a hindrance to aesthetic enjoyment and the adjudication of artistic excellence. This seems a rule conveniently created by people with privileged experiences who would likely not benefit from others paying attention to reality when engaging artistry or scrutinizing the canon. On the contrary, I think the richer one's perspective the more astute one is likely to be at judging the beautiful. Also, I believe I'm capable of recognizing masterful and sublime examples of my subjective aesthetic taste by artists of any race, gender, and class. There is no such thing as objectively good works of art that everyone would agree to place in the canon. Relatedly, I believe that virtuosity is possible from a diverse range of artists—a statement I suspect would be controversial if more people were honest about the role of the canon. And although I think I have excellent taste and would welcome the opportunity to be the sole arbiter of what everyone thinks is good, I find the prospect of such an enterprise preposterous. And to those who argue that criticism of the canon is based primarily in political interests, I counter that defending the canon is based primarily in the political interests of people who are just as culturally relativist as everyone else.

My argument against the canon has nothing to do with any individual artist or work of art. Rather, I'm advocating for the separating of aesthetic taste in acts of list-making from intellectual conversations about art that is/was influential or played an important role in history regardless of whether or not the work is "good" by anyone's standards. As a theorist, historian, and instructor my approach towards all material is through the intellectual lens of what the work or person "does" in the world. Creative work _____ is meaningful or important because _____. The same holds for any scholarly argument. _____'s idea about _____ is meaningful or important because _____. Those blanks should be filled with examples that represent a diverse, equitable, and inclusive array of perspectives from current and historical moments. This is our responsibility to our students. But I believe there is no single example that *must always* be included in those blanks—not even Alvin Ailey. This is a crucial difference between canonical thinking and thinking like an intellectual. I submit that professors should be focused on intellectual discourse over canonizing projects. This is also not about over-intellectualizing the joy out of art, but rather about recognizing the joy in deeply understood art. In other words, it is okay to stop "liking" something once a teacher explains that it is totally sexist or homophobic or the creator was an agent of evil. It's also okay to engage with the work differently with greater knowledge.

This also gets to a nuance about our professional roles in the academy. Whose role is it to tell people what is good, bad, or ugly? How will they know? I do not dispute the job of the critic to give her opinion about the quality of any work or artist as defined by her aesthetic judgment or criteria. This is particularly useful when considering spending hard-earned money on tickets or precious time at an event. I don't mind seeing bad art (because bad art can be important art) but I recognize not everyone wants to do this. The work of the critic and the work of the scholar are often elided, and both get called "professor" in the academy. Critics have PhDs and teach classes. Scholars write performance reviews. And there are scholars of criticism. According to Wikipedia, Harold Bloom was a "critic" and he said as much to the woman on the street. He was also a professor. I value the work of critics and have my go-to sources for insight about whether or not I might "like" something. Generally, the critic judges based on a concept of good/bad or beautiful/ugly. Those criteria change over time—one generation's devil's music is another generation's soothing NPR Sunday programming. As a scholar, historian, and intellectual, I'm more concerned with the *changes* and the *reasons why* people at a particular point in time might have found a work or style good or an idea compelling. The good, beautiful, worthy, compelling, persuasive, etc., and even the correct are fluid, slippery concepts and attempts at fixing or perfecting them (like through canons) are exercises in futility. Rather, studying how these concepts move over time and the real and imagined implications of their impact are the heart of the noble humanist pursuit of knowledge that is our work as college and university instructors. This is not to say that taste doesn't factor into what we teach and that critics aren't concerned with what is important. There are certainly classes in criticism—such as both epistemology and art appreciation. But we must parse the implications of our academic labor (especially in terms of negotiations of power). Beyond a semantic difference between a critic and a scholar, this also gets at the nuances between teaching students *what* to think vs teaching them *how* to think. Rather than chasing definitions of the canonical good, we can focus on ways of analyzing and understanding what is *important* and/or *persuasive* about *any* example. If we are good at our jobs, we will necessarily curate conversations that are diverse, equitable, and inclusive. Without the canon, there is no excuse to maintain white Western notions of primacy.

I propose that educators focus on creating environments of increasingly sophisticated levels of conversation around critical thinking about what is and has been "important" or "persuasive" in our fields over what is good. Teaching the important and persuasive opens up possible subject matters in a more responsible way without negating any particular example of someone's canonical good. I teach many works that I do not think are good, but I believe to be important. Some of my students are frustrated when I refuse to say at the outset whether or not I "like" something. Some are belligerent when I have not included a particular artist or work that they "know" should be there because of the perceived canonical status and their 18 years of life experience. Some are dumbfounded when I am dissatisfied with their "personal belief" that something is good as the end of a conversation. The fostering of educational spaces for critical inquiry that respect differing opinions (as long as they are not rooted in agendas of oppression or hate) should be our goal. Thinking about what is important allows us to shape discourse around ideas over taste and make value judgments within richer contexts.

As professors, of course, we need to make choices for our classes, pick readings/viewings, and curate experiences for our students. Part of the appeal of the canon is the fear that without a canon we will wander aimlessly in a sea of possibilities with no common references or assumed body of knowledge thereby preventing any predictable level of conversation and certainly impeding our ability to push the field forward. Welcome to my world. I can *never* assume that my students have *any* familiarity with *any* examples from African American performance history—at *any* level. If you don't see a problem with this but see a problem if someone asks who Shakespeare is, then that is part of the problem. This concern about common knowledge is not unfounded but the assumption that the canon is the agreed-upon base of knowledge is invented. We hope to have conversations with a degree of common knowledge relative to the level of study. PhD programs are a liminal space by the end of which students become professors or the "they" who say. It is a time to reckon with the responsibility and authority of that transition. We are certainly imbued with a degree of power and status as we shape the thoughts and approaches of our students. Adopting principles for curricular design (syllabi, course offerings, reading/viewing lists, etc.) that are diverse, equitable, and inclusive is clearly a more ethical and responsible way to provide our students the education they deserve. I have had too many graduate students in my classes (including African American grad students) furious that they were not taught more African American theatre or dance history earlier. And then their eyes open to what else they were deprived of learning earlier resulting in suspicion (and resentment) of the field in general. This must be corrected, no doubt, but not by reinscribing the logics that rejected a more diverse earlier educational experience. Also, we can't ignore the fact that people want guides to aesthetic experiences, and those of us who have dedicated our lives to studying creative works know a thing or two. I think we can certainly tell our students what we like and don't like and why. But we should not try to force our aesthetics on them through canonical gestures. (The fact that I am articulating a mandate here is not lost on me. I hope this reads as the conclusion of a persuasive argument rather than the power-hungry, controlling impetus I'm trying to dismantle. I'm far too colonized to think I'll actually be persuasive but too Clay/Caliban-educated not to try to use my words.)

I offer a few more dialogues that I hope help prove my point. My family has an audible.com subscription that I recently visited to download a guilty-pleasure sci-fi novel for my new COVID-era constitutionals around the parking lot and bougie sci-fi book club gatherings with my brownstone Brooklyn college friends. (This is a guilty pleasure for me because it is not work-related, not because of the genre or mode of delivery.) The Audible home page had this statement:

> Audible believes Black lives matter, and we stand with those fighting for racial justice. Below you will find collections of works from Black creators, performers, scholars, activists, and some allies who are forwarding the conversation that is so crucial right now—and always.

It also displayed these curated links: the collections "Raising Up Black Voices," "The Best Trans & Nonbinary Listens by Queer Authors," and the article "The Hidden Histories of Black Americans." With this essay in mind, I clicked on the "Classic Literature" section of the company's project of raising up Black voices recognizing the synonymous nature of classic and canonical. I might take time to quibble with what is on their list but, to practice what I preach, I submit that the opening salvo is more important for discussion than the contents of the list.

> One less-considered place that Black voices have had a hard time entering is "the canon." Worse, there have been times when Black words were miscast, and performed by narrators who didn't connect with the spirit of the authors. These classics, brilliantly rendered by Black performers, deserve a place in the canon, and dare we say every school syllabus. By Staff

I invite a meditation on a few points here. One is the gesture of placing "the canon" in quotation marks perhaps troubling the effort from the outset. Second is the passive voice of the second sentence acknowledging without laying blame or naming names for what I gather is the practice of casting of non-Black voice actors as Black characters who did bad jobs at narration by euphemistically not "connecting" with the spirit of the authors. Third, staff is not only featuring some classics (without attending to assumptions about what those are), but also highlighting that they made intentional casting choices to match the race of the performers with the race of the characters. Fourth, staff boldly declares that what they have deemed worthy should be in every school system—every! And on top of all of this, this manifesto is for the *audio* version of these stories. What would Harold Bloom think? Does listening to the good books diminish their canonical status since we can probably get through more of the boring ones faster? I couldn't pin down the members of "staff" by navigating the website. Is this a democratic move to wrest control of the canon from the Blooms of the academy or even *all* of us in the academy. Or is it an indication that the new canon is devoid of the old power? But then why the familiar righteousness? Maybe we academics can take solace in the fact that members of "staff" probably went to college.

Final Thoughts: Undead White Men

So, why won't the canon stay dead? It's not because it is inherently superior. It is because our minds have been so colonized that we can't let go of our need to fix the beautiful and the sublime, control knowledge, and make ideas behave in an orderly fashion in order to feed the academic machine of leveling up. People have deep psychological connections to works introduced to them at an early age as the best, perhaps by a parent or a wonderful teacher tying the experience to feelings of love, and just can't bear challenges to that connection. I find fascinating the collective willing of *Go Set a Watchman* out of existence, or dismissed as not good or not canonical because we cannot bear the fact that Atticus is not the great white male savior and Calpunia didn't love Scout. Why are we surprised? What do we need from these canonical types? We cannot accept the found novel and the first novel—the novel Lee wanted to write. What about all those people who named their sons Atticus? The canon works to make us who we are and how we see others—for some in a gentle, loving, hegemonically pleasing disciplining. For others as a subtle exercise in self-loathing and internalized racism until shocked woke from the matrix.

Recently, my sci-fi book club read some stories by H.P. Lovecraft and some spinoffs by writers of color in the same vein in conjunction with HBO's new series Lovecraft Country. The book club is made up of college friends and friends once removed—so mainly Yalies, sprinkled with some Berkeley, Brown, and Amherst type alums here and there. I am the only Black person in the club but not the only person of color. There are two Asian men (one doesn't come much anymore), a few Jews, WASPS, and sundry other Christians. We are all relatively able-bodied as far as I can tell, though we are reaching "of a certain age" status and starting to have "procedures." Some are single, some in gay and straight marriages, some getting divorced. We are former Theater, History, and English majors, so we are well-steeped in canonical thinking. We are mostly men but not as white male as it would have been were it not for early efforts in diversifying the club—read my white male sci-fi fanboy husband convinced me to join in 2015. Because I was overworked, I was going to skip this meeting because I hadn't read the books, didn't know anything about Lovecraft, and still feel like a guilty undergrad about not being fully prepared, even though it is a very casual gathering. Two friends convinced me to at least read The Ballad of Black Tom and come to socialize. Since it was on Zoom and I had pandemic cabin fever, I read as much of the novella as I could and joined in to hear the conversation and see folks but stated early I wasn't going to comment because I hadn't read much. I'm glad I listened to the conversation and I did end up chiming in at the end with a question rooted in my charge for this essay. I briefly explained my arguments around the decolonizing project of dismantling the canon and canonical thinking and laid out the intersection with the discussion as I saw it. To summarize, the conversation started with one woman asking why we read Lovecraft to begin with because she found the texts unbearable to read and racist. There was a fruitful and interesting discussion about the texts, but one comment stood out to me. Someone mildly defended Lovecraft's racism by saying the racism was part of the charm of the books. I have to admit that moment caught me off guard, to say the least. Although I had not read the stories, I really couldn't imagine any circumstance in which I would think racism adds to charm. I had enough cultural literacy about Lovecraft and the surrounding nerd boy fandom that I posited that defense of Lovecraft as charmingly racist and moves to rescue his works by creating diverse spinoffs that uphold his canonical status are rooted in deeply held beliefs about the good. When a friend of novelist Nnedi Okorafor pointed out that the World Fantasy Award she received in the form of a bust of Lovecraft was in honor of a man who had written the poem *On The Creation of Niggers*, she had understandable "resentment" about the fact that no one seemed to think this was important for her to know earlier. She also questioned the upholding of a proud racist in this way. Were it not for his canonical stature and the fact that racist is not a deal-breaker, changing the honor (different bust in someone else's honor) so that it doesn't pose this valid objection would be easy.

The flaws of the canon and principles for canonical thinking are not just the unfortunate but benign results of misguided early adopters soon to be rectified with time and more enlightened canonizers. They are endemic. Because of this, the stakes are high for our work as academics around our attitude towards the canon. There is a direct line between our beliefs about good culture and the sanctioning of hate. If a person's culture doesn't matter, it is easy to conclude that neither does his/her life. Our work to make sure people are educated good citizens boils down to not just what we have them examine, but more importantly how we teach them to understand. The seeming noncritical place of the performing arts in society and the academy often renders the importance of these considerations undervalued. Rejecting the canon and acts of canonization does not mean rejecting content or arguing ourselves out of existence. Shifting this focus away from a canon towards different pedagogical approaches of engagement better affords our students the ability to discuss a variety of works—good, bad, or ugly—from more intellectually rigorous expectations. Professors maintaining the canon as our goal are destined for identity crises if the power of such endeavors can rest with both the "preeminent literary critic" and "staff."

Works Cited

Bloom, Harold. 1995. *The Western Canon: The Books and School of the Ages*. New York: Riverhead Books.

George-Graves, Nadine. 2018. "An Environment of Cascading Consequences." In *Theatre, Performance and Theories of Change*, edited by Tamara Underiner and Stephani Etheridge Woodson, 99–109. New York: Palgrave-MacMillan.

Hansberry, Lorraine. 1959. *A Raisin in the Sun: A Drama in Three Acts*. New York: Random House.

Hartman, Saidiya V. 1997. *Scenes of Subjection: Terror, Slavery, and Self-Making in Nineteenth-Century America*. Oxford: Oxford University Press.

Hirsch, E. D., Joseph F. Kett, and James Trefil. 1988. *Cultural Literacy: What Every American Needs to Know*. New York: Vintage Books.

Lee, Harper. 2006. *To Kill a Mockingbird*. New York: Harper Perennial Modern Classics.

Lorde, Audre. 1984. *Sister Outsider*. Freedom, CA: Crossing Press.

Norris, Bruce. 2012. *Clybourne Park*. New York: Dramatists Play Service.

Taylor, Diana. 2003. *The Archive and the Repertoire: Performing Cultural Memory in the Americas*. Durham: Duke University Press.

To Kill a Mockingbird, adapted by Aaron Sorkin. Dir. Bartlett Sher. Shubert Theatre, New York, November 2018–March 2020.

Wilson, August, and Robert Brustein. October 1996. "Subsidized Separatism: Responses to 'The Ground on Which I Stand.'" *American Theatre*.

2 The Shakespeare Problem: A Conversation

Sarah Enloe, Madeline Sayet, Mei Ann Teo, and Dawn Monique Williams

How do you Identify in the World, and What is your Relationship to the Work of William Shakespeare?

Madeline Sayet: I'm Madeline Sayet (she/her), the Executive Director of the Yale Indigenous Performing Arts Program, a freelance director, writer, and performer. I'm also a citizen of the Mohegan Tribe, and hold Masters Degrees in Shakespeare, Arts Politics and Post-Colonial Theory. My relationship to Shakespeare has shifted dramatically. I have grappled with my initial love for the plays and the ways in which I have had to come to terms with their weaponization.

I was raised on traditional Mohegan stories and Shakespeare. My mom took me to see outdoor Shakespeare performances every summer from age six on. I began performing in these plays as a teenager, believing that Shakespeare was capable of giving me the voice I did not feel I had on my own. Recently, I abandoned the pursuit of a PhD on the relationship between Shakespeare and the indigenous peoples of America because I couldn't undo the colonial infrastructure within Shakespeare academia and the Shakespeare system.

To process my relationship with Shakespeare and colonialism, I created a solo performance piece, called *Where We Belong*. It documented my journey across the ocean to study Shakespeare, a journey echoing that of my ancestors in the 1700s on diplomatic missions to England, in service of our people. *Where We Belong* chronicles my struggle with the role of Shakespeare and my wish that my Mohegan culture and language were equally valued. It was performed at Shakespeare's Globe, making it the first work by a Native American playwright to be performed in that space, and Mei Ann directed.

Mei Ann Teo: I'm Mei Ann Teo (they/she). I'm a director/dramaturg/deviser who works at the intersection of artistic, civic, and contemplative practice and am the Associate Artistic Director of New Work at Oregon Shakespeare Festival. I grew up and was educated in Singapore and the

United States, both colonized places. I am here to engage with these questions as a culture producer and educator in the field who has studied and directed Shakespeare. As a witness to my society, I deeply believe that what we see onstage can powerfully change our belief systems, just as it can cement them.

I found myself last summer directing Maddy's "Where We Belong" at Shakespeare's Globe in the Sam Wanamaker theatre. As a director, a doula of an artistic voice, I wouldn't have chosen any one of Shakespeare's plays above Maddy's to direct in that space, because of the complexities I feel about the continual perpetuation of Great Man Theory. Maddy's voice and story are exactly the kind of disruption of that narrative we need.

Dawn Monique Williams: I'm Dawn Monique Williams (she/her). I'm a freelance director, and as the Associate Artistic Director of Aurora Theatre Company in Berkeley, CA, I produce cultural events. My relationship with Shakespeare is an evolving one. As a young teenager, I hated Shakespeare. In junior high and high school, when I was forced to read it, I hated it. I thought it was a foreign language I couldn't understand. I was one of those people who thought, "I don't get this, I must be dumb." At the same time asking, "he's a dead white guy, so what does he have to do with me?" The language didn't make sense, teachers were showing us old movie versions, and it was boring. It wasn't until I was a budding actor in conservatory training that I really fell in love with Shakespeare. The words, the language, the expansiveness of emotion—it's so great to be in that. But not great to presume that only one author can offer us that.

Sarah Enloe: I'm Sarah Enloe (she/her). I'm the director of education at the American Shakespeare Center, a small theatre in a small town in Virginia. I started my relationship with Shakespeare at a young age, but didn't act in Shakespeare until after college. I now hold two Masters' Degrees in Shakespeare and Performance (emphases: Teaching and Dramaturgy). I'm still investigating what it means for us to be producing Shakespeare and how Shakespeare can raise these very difficult questions for us as artists to wrestle with—all well and good in the rehearsal room, but how do we prepare our audiences? And why? Why are we still doing it?

How do you see Shakespeare's Work Operating Systemically up until this Point within Society?

Enloe: Shakespeare's plays give us a cultural icon to latch onto. Currently, we judge everything against Shakespeare. His work is also a measure of intellect. Some think, "If I 'get' Shakespeare, then I'm smart," but I think that Shakespeare's not that difficult to "get," I think we have been conditioned to use Shakespeare as a ruler against which we measure intellect and culture.

Sayet: Lately, I've been wondering: why is it so important that we "get" him at all? My young exposure to Shakespeare put me at ease with his poetry. As I grew up, I benefited from the fact that I was "better" at it than other people. But what is that measurement, and why does it matter in our society? The notion that Shakespeare "made me smart," gave me access to opportunities. *I couldn't choose to learn my Mohegan language growing up, instead.* American policies actively erased indigenous languages. Our culture was not deemed valuable. How is "value" attributed? Why are we lifting up this skill set in this way? Only in my senior year of college did I learn there were Native playwrights. That is no accident. America has intentionally created policies that promote the deification of Shakespeare, while indigenous arts have been opposed throughout most of American History.

Shakespeare was a cultural touchpoint of common ground with people outside my tribal nation, which helped me connect. But, honestly, that's because Shakespeare, nowadays, has become a form of fanfiction. So many know the work and converse about it, even without agreeing on what the play is about. It's strange that a commercial playwright, who was just trying to make money, has now become an emblem of high culture, supremacy. He wasn't the most educated playwright of his time, but he's become weaponized in such a way that being able to speak his language is a badge of success. The positionality of Shakespeare means that because of my knowledge of Shakespeare I will be listened to about things that have nothing to do with Shakespeare.

Williams: It's been "Shakespeare the Supreme." Shakespeare has dominated theatre. Certainly in the US, but globally as well. In order to investigate that you have to talk about cultural imperialism, colonialism. That famous factoid that we've all heard, that as westward expansion happened in the US, the two most coveted books were Shakespeare and the Bible, is true. And there are, of course, business reasons to produce Shakespeare. The plays are held in the public trust and royalty-free, no estate to get permission from, there's title recognition, and you can build educational programs around him (Shakespeare is the only named playwright in the United States Common Core, which 41 states have adopted). We've built whole systems around upholding this one author.

I built my career around directing Shakespeare plays. I'm also a Shakespeare scholar, but it has been close to two years since I've directed a Shakespeare play because I find myself questioning the elasticity of the plays that I've been so excited and passionate about. These plays were written to reflect the cultural norms of a particular time and place and perhaps by centralizing those plays as the primary thing in American Theatre, we are perpetuating a lot of harm. My approach had been to subvert some of that. Thinking, "I can cast people of color, cast women, and non-binary actors in more roles"–how I said elasticity–but so many people push back on that.

I've developed a lot of emotion around the gatekeeping we do with Shakespeare; how many white male artistic directors I have to pitch to and explain production approaches that are actually outside of their cultural experience, and therefore invalidated. Rarely have I been allowed to be the authority on Shakespeare in the room. In the last few years, I've been trying to focus more on Black playwrights, living playwrights. I have an unreconciled sadness about Shakespeare. The story I've been telling lately is that we're on a trial separation. I hope it doesn't end in divorce, but I need to know who I am without him.

Enloe: What makes Shakespeare culturally dominant? Schools teach his work, which means teachers of today (and tomorrow, likely) will teach it. Theatres produce Shakespeare (because theatres have a built in audience, the schools). We train actors to perform his plays. Therefore: he is culturally dominant. He dominates because he has, is, and will be taught, and this cycle is both founded in our educational system (and all of the accompanying supports such as textbook production and training) and, likewise, in our arts consumption. The Shakespeare industrial complex pays thousands of people per year, to teach, act, produce, print the plays. And so what do we do with that? And how do we either use that, or make a choice that is central to not using it?

I work with a masters program that is very anti-bardolatry; the (Mary Baldwin's Shakespeare and Performance) program's director, Paul Menzer, requires that we consider other playwrights and investigate if Shakespeare is worthy of the worship.

Not to point fingers but some in the academy have given us the impression that we "need to be carefully taught," taught almost to the extinction of liking Shakespeare because it is only something to achieve. The editions of Shakespeare with footnotes or definitions for each line, but students don't require all of the "help" editors and the academy are offering if teachers invite them to think about it in terms of playing, of performance. Then, we, the people, can go and break down the text ourselves without intervention from the academy. Basically, the three inches of explanation at the bottom of every page communicates to students that they don't have what it takes to "get" it. Those notes are not necessary, but, as readers, we begin to believe that they are.

Teo: The Great Man Theory posits that some people are born with the necessary and supreme attributes for making historical impact and then frames their accomplishments as single-handed, erasing the work of teams, networks, and communities who built movements. Even in saying "Shakespeare," and not "Shakespeare's Collective," we erase that they were an ensemble of actors who created together. I'm interested in those systems of distribution and valuation that perpetuate Shakespeare getting credit for the "invention of the human" (Bloom 1998). It's so typical of Western imperialism to name towards singular ownership. It's that system which distributes Shakespeare and solidifies and perpetuates how we see ourselves as human beings.

I remember around 10 years ago going to the Singapore Theatre Festival, the first of its kind to stage the work of local playwrights. Everything I saw had this strange connection; all of a sudden, someone would be quoting Shakespeare. It felt like each writer needed to throw it in as a touchstone in order for them to be a dramatist. I remember feeling so much pain about that—I wanted to hear about Singapore. What I heard was the colonized mind and what we are cultured to want to be.

Global cultural touchstones, however, are deeply powerful ways of connecting us. For instance, I remember at 3AM finding myself at a BBQ restaurant in Korea with friends who had just come from rehearsal. They were working on *The Seagull*, which I had also just directed. I don't speak Korean, and they didn't speak much English, but we were able to communicate and exchange ideas about human nature by invoking "Masha" and other characters. We spoke Chekhov. Now, I'd been railing against Chekhov the same way I'm railing against Shakespeare—but at that moment, I understood the power of connecting over a common source.

But who gets to choose that source? It's about tracking the systems that brought us to this point where Shakespeare is still the most produced playwright and recognizing all of the lost production opportunities for new work that might have new visions for us. I ask: What if we completely stopped funding for everything Shakespeare and put it toward new work that continued to ask us what it is to be human? How are we human? Can you just imagine what that would be like? Even if we did that for just one year? How would that actually change our frame, our philosophy, our understanding, the way we value something?

What do you think the Role of Shakespeare should be Within Theatre Training and the Field in General?

Enloe: I recently heard a former ASC actor, René Thornton, Jr, talking about what Shakespeare's language gives an actor. He said something along the lines of: "Shakespeare provides all of the needed information, whereas with a modern playwright, I (René) get 6 words to figure out the whole character, in Shakespeare, it is all already there." If only to reflect on the difference we find in contemporary writing, studying the construction of characters in Shakespeare offers an artist space to draw comparison.

I feel like hatred is a pretty legit frame for a lot of people's experience with Shakespeare. Introducing Shakespeare to students but not taking responsibility for how he is received is a problem. We should teach Shakespeare early but with the objective of giving students ownership. I am tired of teachers telling us that Macbeth is wrestling with fate because I'd rather the students decide what Macbeth is wrestling with. I advocate for giving the students tools to break the text down and put it back together like an actor or director does. That's what's great about, for instance, scansion, students who find an irregular line can then talk about their discovery and debate its meaning.

I think students want to have clarity about what a character is saying and also the ability to make a specific choice. Students need to be able to feel confident in ownership of the text, having the courage to work with it. Gaining confidence in their ability to wrestle with complex things and express them in a courageous way.

Williams: I've been a theatre kid my whole life, but even as a theatre kid in high school I had no interest in Shakespeare. Then I spent the early phase of my career trying to prove that as a Black woman I could do it, that I had the skills and that I understood it, and that I could decode the texts and understand the historical moments around them. By the time I was in grad school Shakespeare was my vocational passion. I took a Shakespeare seminar with the English PhD students, and begged the faculty in my directing program to assign me a Shakespeare play for my thesis production. I told my advisors, "if you don't let me do it here and get it on my resume, then no one out there will ever hire me to direct Shakespeare professionally." It was a big deal for me, I crafted my education around it, maintaining Shakespeare as my birthright. I've ranted about this for years. Then on the other side I am confronted with the Audre Lorde quote: "the master's tools will never dismantle the master's house" (Lorde [1984] 2018). You cannot use the tool of oppression to undo oppression. And that's where I get heartsick, because if we are talking about middle school and high school children, who have no choice, Shakespeare has done horrendous damage, denying many of them opportunities for their own cultural expression; I'm still having to justify why I might want some Cardi B. in a production. And yet, I have seen Shakespeare aligned with global liberation movements. So, master's tools or elastic? Can these texts be subverted?

Shakespeare's cultural primacy can be diminished in scale. He is no greater than any number of artists we might study. In terms of volume, Lope de Vega wrote an epic number of plays. I think of August Wilson, what August Wilson symbolizes especially for Black theatre-makers. We can recognize his genius, his brilliance, and also create space for Dominique Morriseau, Suzan-Lori Parks, Tarell Alvin McCraney, Marcus Gardley, y'know? It doesn't take away from Wilson's shine to say that there's a whole new generation of playwrights who have been nourished by him and are now doing their own thing. Yes, we have Shakespeare! Many of those plays are great. The words are great. Let's continue to have Shakespeare, let's also illuminate some other artists and writers who might have been fed or nourished by Shakespeare or left undiscovered because we stuck to this one thing for so long that we didn't even do the work of looking at what other plays have been written in the last

400 years. For it to remain relevant off the page, for it to be something that I think kids should be forced to see, they must be able to discover themselves in the work.

Teo: There is a story in the foreword of Elie Wiesel's *The Trial of God*. (Not to say that Shakespeare is God ... but we certainly treat him as such.) When he was in the death camps of Auschwitz, Wiesal witnessed a group of Jewish scholars hold a trial of God. After several days and nights, they came to a unanimous verdict that the Lord God Almighty, Creator of Heaven and Earth, was guilty of crimes against creation and humankind. And then the sun was on the horizon. One of them said, "It's time for evening prayers," and then they prayed.

We can hold systems accountable and love the poetry. I can still hold in my heart, "We are such stuff as dreams are made on and our little life is rounded with a sleep." There are no words that describe the ephemerality of life more beautifully. But just as beautiful and potent? Rumi. Thich Nhat Hanh. The Dhammapada, the Bible, the Bhagavad Gita, and so on and so on.

We should teach everything in context. Sarah talks about the skill set that we need in order to take text apart and put it back together. Yet if we centralize Shakespeare in that skill-building, we are still getting indoctrinated into a particular mindset of singularity. If we're looking at skill and content and the perspective that Dawn invoked—that kind of education helps us assess our position in the world. The most profound moments of education for me have been rooted in the pain of knowing my place and the expansiveness of knowing my place. The trajectory of education that encourages us to become larger than our own frame, to be more inclusive global citizens. This means that each society, each culture, each neighborhood, each family *gets* to—is not imposed upon, but gets to—form how we think about and interrogate Shakespeare's work and its position in theatre tradition/education. Currently, we ache to be told what to do, in a system where education functions as factory, our learning becomes stifled into industry. We need to build an academia that is engaged not only in supplying the industry, but also envisioning the field.

Sayet: The works must be placed amongst instead of above. The hierarchy is dangerous. It's not a matter of simply relocating another playwright to his place. There are worse things than Shakespeare in theatre education. When I began my undergraduate training with the Atlantic Theatre Company at Tisch School of the Arts, I lost Shakespeare, with its poetry and magical realism, and found myself at the altar of David Mamet, the new god I was supposed to worship. It was painful for me to be in a space where theatre was sparse, patriarchal, and cold. The things that inspired me in theatre were gone. How different a person might I have become, had I been able to engage with Native theatre first? If I was encouraged to love myself and my voice and my ancestors, instead of being taught that someone else's were more powerful and important?

Now, when I think on what was considered a "good" or "bad" habit, in acting training, my stomach turns. A lot of that training is harmful because actors are often being trained into colonial standards of speech and behavior, instead of how their unique voices might function as the place from which transformation can occur. Compared to many of the playwrights I was confronted by in college, Shakespeare at least leaves some room for interpretation, expression, and scale. At that time, Shakespeare was the escape, because we were in such a deeply colonized framework. His poetry is what had connected me to other people, and, as Dawn said, the expansiveness of that. Until recently, I had met all my romantic partners by speaking Shakespeare to them. And how terrifying is that? That my voice was deemed so inadequate that even my relationships were only ever formed through his words. What if I lived in a world where I could have fallen in love speaking Mohegan instead?

Teo: I love that, you're decolonizing your love life.

How would you Train Theatre Makers? What do you see as Most Important to that Training?

Enloe: I've been talking to some Shakespeare Association of America folks (#ShakeRace), Shakespeare literature professors, and some are horrified by the way some Shakespeare theatres approach Shakespeare in the time of identity and expression, that theatres are not on top of the tough questions. I honestly want to find a way to talk to theatres about doing Shakespeare with more consideration for how audiences will read it. How can theatres deploy this icon to serve social justice? As a negative example, I saw a production of *Romeo and Juliet* in Ohio last summer. Every single cast member was white, except for the nurse who was this beautiful and talented black woman; she was cast as the nurse. I love that role, but that was the worst casting I have ever seen in my life. The only person of color playing a servant, a wet-nurse. Moreover, this production set the play in the antebellum south. Sitting there, surrounded by Shakespeare academics, feeling how blind that choice was. We have to think about our casting, our design, the story those tell when paired with Shakespeare the icon.

Personally, because of who the audience for plays is at ASC, theatre education is not where my focus has been. We see more English/Language Arts students in our work. My BFA didn't require a Shakespeare course, so I never took one.

The structures Shakespeare wrote in—rhetoric, meter, and the stage he wrote for—all work together to tell us about what can be done with his characters. We should teach students how to interpret it. They should own it. We need to give students the tools to break text down and put it back together—then when they confront other theatre practitioners and theatre playwrights they will have those tools and they can use them in those arenas as well.

Williams: When we are talking about theatre training and actor training specifically, Shakespeare can be elective. I didn't always feel that way. I was one of those people that perpetuated the notion that if you're classically trained you can do so much more. But now I've seen how "classically trained" pedagogy has been weaponized against people. Everyone does not need the same training, it is not one size fits all. It should be possible to get a four year theatre degree and opt into or out of Shakespeare. You can throw "Styles," period acting, acting Shakespeare, in a course catalogue and you'll have people who want to take them. The idea that that's the only path or the standard, the only way to be an actor or a theatre maker is just starting to feel really ridiculous to me. Which is such a radical departure from what I would have said to you two years ago. Maybe two months ago. I just don't see it as being as important anymore. Especially because it doesn't leave space for some other things, and I think space for other things is long overdue.

Theatrical discipline aside, it's less about studying theatre, and more about being a student of life. It's about engaging with other humans. I take so much pride in being a director, but how can I be a cultural worker if I am not in tune with my culture and if I am not engaging with other people around their culture, if I am not smelling things, tasting things, hearing things, watching bad tv and reading the finest literature, I just think there has to be a holistic approach to it. Theatre is a way of unlocking the world, especially for those for whom the key isn't a history text or a great novel or a symphony; the goal is really about unlocking the world, which comes back to the broadest based global approach to learning we can manage. If I were to develop a specific actor training curriculum I would always come back to the breath. Any text can do that. I wanted Shakespeare so bad, but any playwright that resonates for a person, we can use that material to help them articulate, to engage the core, to project, to be an active listener, to tap into emotional response. Any text that resonates for an individual can be used to make that individual a better actor if we're in a space that's about unlocking creativity. I stress clarity of thought. I love image work and want actors to be painting pictures with language at all times. That tends to branch into how we're using meter, how we're using punctuation, our cadences now are different and it means something different for somebody if they can say "girlllll" as opposed to whatever it coulda shoulda woulda sounded like 450 years ago. Those are my approaches. That's with Shakespeare and everything else I touch too.

Sayet: I was thinking about what Dawn said, and it made me remember how, as an undergrad, I became frustrated by acting in a void, training without context in the world. Once I took classes in other fields again, I was grateful for new information to process, as theatre had become meaningless. I've resisted teaching acting because, I couldn't fathom telling someone else how to be. As a director, I facilitated their performances within the world but that's within context. How can I teach someone how to exist fully without a deeper understanding of who they are? As a student I was not offered a model that didn't make me feel like becoming an actor required giving up a part of myself that made me who I was. I teach interdisciplinary subject matter because it allows art to be examined in relationship to other things. Shouldn't acting be that too? Wouldn't that make actors feel more empowered to make choices and be creative in response to that information? Why can't I teach acting the way I teach adaptation? The goal should be to create a space in which participants feel empowered in their own voice and own choices. To train them to find their mission, first and foremost.

Working on *Where We Belong*, I realized rules I had been taught were getting in the way of my ability to perform. I had been trained to never look in the mirror. Yet I reached a point where, to figure out who these many people were in my body, it seemed incredibly useful to just look in the mirror. There were so many rules that were so specific about how I use my voice, how I should stand, how I should not use my arms. It was easier not to act, than to do so in a colonized straightjacket. Now I question why I accepted these rules as fact. Why was I receiving rules instead of a toolkit for exploration. I was removing everything that fundamentally made me me, in order to follow these rules. I was scared to teach acting, for fear of taking other peoples' sense of self. Now, when I teach, I lean into the expansiveness and context of each student to express themselves. That's what a decolonized teaching model must be: one with space for the full range of expression and identity.

Teo: Paulo Freire, in *Pedagogy of the Oppressed* (1970), breaks down education as a banking model, where we deposit knowledge into students without critically engaging with our role and biases in the mutual relationship of learning. I believe in knowledge, complexity, and courage as the key pillars of education. Without understanding the complexity of ourselves and our context, we will never understand the complexity of any other culture.

When I taught Contemporary Chinese Drama at Hampshire College, I started by having the students tell their own stories to help them understand their own biases. Once we establish the multiplicity and diversity of form, even while they are located in the same milieu, we begin to understand the complexities and in real-time see the effect of bias. When we read contemporary Chinese drama, we have built the precedent that there is not only one lens. Understanding the limitations of our frame while exploring the complexity of it is a vital learning wholly missing from many education models.

When we talk about Shakespeare in context we must ask, what is power in this world? How are we looking at power right now and how is that being examined in this world today? In order to actively dismantle dominance that has been harmful, we need Courage. What a beautiful thing to be able to continually ask for Courage, to step outside of ourselves and go deeper. Wrestle with Both/And instead of Either/Or.

If it is to be Taught, How Would you Teach Shakespeare?

Enloe: I am a big advocate for connections and context. I would want to look at the Greek theatre, the storytelling traditions of native populations and study what they share with Shakespeare and what is lost. Teaching theatre, theatre history, playwriting, dramaturgy, all of it as a journey, and also thinking about what are the influences on Shakespeare that forced his plays into the shape that they are in and why? So we aren't just looking at the plays as brilliant pieces of literature but as part of a time and part of a complex. I don't think we are teaching him authentically and in context. I don't think we've trained our teachers or given our teachers tools to use to teach Shakespeare, to teach drama, in a way that actually is meaningful. I think we should be looking at how it was done, how it can be done, how to do less of it, and how to introduce other playwrights. We need to surround him with the world before and the world after.

Teachers must realize that, in Shakespeare, there isn't *a* right answer, there are a thousand right answers to be explored. That's what's great about considering meter, a student can say: "I think this is an irregular line." Then students can talk about what they have found and debate its meaning. Too, Shakespeare studied hundreds of figures of rhetoric as a schoolboy and he deployed them when he was writing his plays. The hundreds of figures of rhetoric that he deployed create different voices for every single character that he wrote. If you play a king in one play or in another play they're different because they use different rhetorical figures. So the way that he shapes character is through the word order, word choice, and deployment of those figures in order to create a moment and an embodiment of a particular voice. So the words' arrangement is the ladder upon which a character is built, and it provides insights into how a character can be played. For the actor who asks: "Why did the playwright give me these words in this order? What is that?" And then making a choice and embodying it and living it.

Sayet: When I teach indigenizing Shakespeare workshops, I start with the stretchiness of the text and interpretation. I begin by offering a text without telling them who is saying it and what has happened in the play. So that the first context they encounter it in, is their own. I ask them what images in their own life, community, experience, or imagination it is conjuring for them. Because it's poetry, and it can mean any number of things. But it is certain that it doesn't mean now what it meant 400 years ago. If it is to matter, it is the uniqueness of every human being on planet Earth that is keeping it alive. Some people are afraid of Shakespeare because they have been told they were wrong about what it did or didn't mean. It has become weighed down by the baggage of its performance history, instead of the possibility of its performance future. Because of the history of colonization attached to Shakespeare, I offer Native students the power of their own interpretive gaze first. The plays have been forced on us. So why shouldn't we make meaning of them through our own eyes and center our own experiences within the work, even our own languages and how they might be incorporated. We must acknowledge and confront the racist, sexist, and colonial elements within the text, and decide what to do with them. When we do bring in the play's history, what aspect of the history are we in conversation with? Instead of reinforcing the hierarchies, let's break down the ways in which immigration, race, gender operated at his time and interrogate that for our moment.

Teo: If I were to teach Shakespeare, the first step is to really understand what I have been taught about Shakespeare. To synthesize and face all the harms perpetuated as the foundation for truly reckoning with my current moment in history. Working to examine my own biases so I don't pass them on, so that I am able to engage with texts knowing all that I know and can frame it in a way that offers those learning the freedom of their imagination and the wealth of their consciousness.

In training with the SITI company, I learned "the text is just the bones" and we must fill it with our bodies and all of who we are. We're not trying to achieve Titania, it's not about that. It's Titania emerging from us, and the text is the bones on which we hang our whole selves in order to become. It's the expansion of our own ideas of ourselves, and in so doing, we can understand the complexity and expand the possibilities of our collective society.

Williams: Something I'm understanding now in this moment, as I'm in so many conversations about taking space and making space, is that Shakespeare will have more meaning, more value, if we stop treating him as the supreme. We should let him live among all the other authors of equal, sometimes greater significance. In hip hop, you're the baddest when you're capable of beating the baddest. So if Shakespeare is a baddie he can hold his own. Shakespeare will not be tarnished.

Works Cited

Bloom, Harold. 1998. *The Invention of the Human*. New York: Riverhead Books.
Freire, Paulo. 1972. *Pedagogy of the Oppressed*. New York: Herder and Herder.

Lorde, Audre. 2018. *The Master's Tools Will Never Dismantle the Master's House*. Penguin Classics.
Where We Belong. 2019. *Written and Performed by Madeline Sayet*. London: Shakespeare's Globe, 17 June.

3 "Go back to India if you hate my people so much": Consequences of Troubling the "Canon" in American Academia

Sukanya Chakrabarti

I am a 5 ft 2″, 120 lb theatre artist-scholar from India. In the Fall of 2010, with a Master's in English literature and a dream to pursue higher education in Theatre and Performance Studies, I arrived in America to earn my PhD. I spent the first few years in America adjusting to new cultural and academic norms. My papers came back with comments to "write in active voice," a suggestion I repeat now as an instructor. I spent a long time thinking about "voice." What is this "voice?" Being raised and indoctrinated in an urban Indian education system, handed down by the British, I learnt that formal essays are written in passive voice. In switching from passive to active voice, I discovered that the performance lies in taking responsibility for the "voice"—I learnt to write with more authority, clarity, and directionality.

What constitutes the academic voice? Do I adopt a certain voice to perform academia? Apart from the written voice, what about my physical, audible voice? The voice that carries through words that resonate in a classroom and (hopefully) reaches my students?

Scene 1

In my first year as a South Asian professor in American academia, I am employed as a Visiting Assistant Professor in a Research 1 institution in the American South, to teach survey theatre history courses to undergraduate students. I have been mandated to use the *Wadsworth Anthology of Drama, Sixth Edition* (Worthen 2010). There are seven sections in this almost 1900-page volume—Theater of Classical Europe: Athens and Rome; The Theater of Classical Japan; The Theater of Medieval and Renaissance England; Early Modern Europe; Modern Europe; The United States; and World Stages. The only two sections housing non-Western texts, Theater of Classical Japan and World Stages, together have 14 plays (the former including only two), while the rest of the sections with European and American plays have 51 plays together (three plays by Shakespeare alone in the third section). Such unequal and irregular organization in an anthology of plays and critical texts does three things:

DOI: 10.4324/9781003031413-3

First, the anthology doubly marginalizes the non-Western content, by not only thematically, but also visually, Othering it. When an expansive volume of theatre history includes 65 plays, out of which only 14 can be considered non-Western, or extra-canonical, the anthology establishes a certain kind of "polar imagination" (Schwarz 1992: 155), while also performing an illusion of inclusion. Daniel R. Schwarz explains and opposes the tendency of American academia to imagine a polarity between a hegemonic cultural pattern (including primarily white Western culture) and anything falling outside the realm (often categorized as "cultural" studies). This imagined oppositional relationality is what Schwarz terms "polar imagination."

Second, the functionality of this anthology, adopted as a textbook for undergraduate education in an R1 institution in America, lays a problematic claim to authority and credibility, as the production of knowledge systems is interconnected with the reproduction of culture—"[e]ducation systems legitimate the canon by producing 'aware consumers' as well as 'sacralizing commentaries'"(Holderness 2014: 77).

Third, such polarization of knowledge systems, minimizing the importance of non-Western theatre while prioritizing and sacralizing Western white theatre, establishes BIPOC scholars and their scholarships as marginal to the central "canonical" knowledge. As an Indian first-generation immigrant scholar, teaching the established "canon" marginalizes my presence and my positionality even in my classroom, not only theoretically and conceptually, but physically as well. How many plays that we read from the anthology have characters looking like me, life experiences relatable to a person of color? How many characters that we analyze in our classrooms can someone like me embody on stage? With such lack of representation, or exoticized and skewed representation, of BIPOC stories and characters in academia, in our classrooms, on stage, and in the media, we further perpetuate that sense of shame and insufficiency, along with a need to accept and conform to white culture's beliefs about racial minorities in the form of internalized racism, which is "theorized to reinforce inequalities at cultural and institutionalized levels in that affected individuals unknowingly behave in accordance with dominant narratives (e.g., inferiority of racial minorities) that reinforce their own oppression" (Choi et al. 2017: 53). On the other hand, my invisibility and absence from American mainstream stages, canons, classrooms, curriculum, and media representations, ironically, render me hypervisible while simultaneously diminishing my credibility.

In my exploration of these scenes in American academia, I have realized that one cannot think of the canon in isolation. If we are to engage with the canon, we ought to engage with histories of colonialism and establishment of dominant cultures through a rigorous engagement with critical revisionist historiography. De-canonization is directly associated with decolonization. The Latin, Anglo-French, and Middle English roots of the word "canon" being associated uncomfortably with the Christian church ("a regulation or dogma decreed by a church council;" "an authoritative list of books accepted as Holy Scripture") (*Merriam-Webster*, s.v. "canon"), the term carries the load of the oppressive histories of sacral hegemonic forces responsible for large-scale "epistemic violence" (Spivak 1994: 76).

Frank Kermode assigns to canonicity the quality and condition of "perpetual modernity" (Kermode 1985: 62), arguing that the classics gain their place in the canon because of their ability to interact and engage with the "modern" at all times. George Hunter further contends that in the context of theatre, an art form dependent on immediacy and the present, the actors carry the relevance of the text through their interpretive mediation, and therefore converse between the past text and the present performance, diffusing the sacral quality of the text. Engaging with Kermode's claim of canon being opinion that becomes knowledge, he explains,

> Historians of style can only operate by continually reinventing the past their sense of style creates for them. But if we are to *use* the past thus created, and communicate it to a public, we must allow sufficient distance between that past and our own present so that perspective, dialogue, "conversation" become possible. It is here, it seems to me, that "knowledge" is relevant, for only knowledge can provide the stable framework of agreed norms that permits cultural conversation to take place [...] [K]nowledge can perhaps extend the lifetime of opinion by providing a basis for widely shared talk—and what we can go on talking about we have an interest in still believing. (Hunter 1991: 86)

Even though Hunter destabilizes the fixity of the canonical text by introducing the concept of relevance, there is still a presumption of an objective and neutral "knowledge," and a conversation among a seemingly homogenous "we" with shared interests. When knowledge systems alone become the instruments of control and hegemony, how can underrepresented (or even erased) knowledge systems stand a chance of prolonging an opinion? The only way forward is to recognize the uneven terrain of knowledge production and the inequity in the recognition of knowledge systems that prolong opinions, which are further limited by those dominant structures of power. In essence, unless we exit this vicious cycle of knowledge and power production associated with the very idea of a canon, it is remarkably challenging for generative conversations around inclusion to be possible.

Kermode further elaborates that "the work of preservation and defense is carried on by many voices co-operating, however unwillingly [and if I may I add, *coercively*], to one end, and not by a central authority resisting its challenges" (Kermode 1985: 79). The work of preservation, defense, or even destabilization (as envisioned by Hunter) of a canon, therefore, necessarily is embedded in the history of erasures and exclusions of voices. Here, "voices" are not only literal and physical but also metaphorical and figurative. As a woman-of-color scholar in American academia, in order to continue the work of preserving the canon, already established in a white, heteronormative, male, Christian, colonial power structure with "voices [that are heard] cooperating" and dissenting voices muted, I have to not only adopt a voice of authority recognized by the canon but also suppress my own voice that is discordant with traditionally accepted canonicity. But no matter how much I rehearse the performance of authority and knowledge, the optics of a short brown woman disrupts the correlations and expected associations between knowledge, power, race, and gender.

Scene 2

Before I walk into my classroom, I spend a few minutes checking my clothes, my shoes, my hair, and I practice a short walk—do I look tall enough, authoritative enough, knowledgeable enough, academic enough? Do I smile too much? Should I change the pitch of my voice and appear more somber? I even practice a couple of voice warmup exercises to speak in a lower register. A part of the preparation for the academic job market, and eventually, working in academia, involved buying blazers—a friend suggested that a blazer makes everyone look "professorial." I rehearse my "professorial" self while walking through the corridors leading to my classroom. After each class, committee meeting, or college meet-up, I review my performance.

In their chapter, "They See Us, but They Don't Really See Us," Jessica Lavariega Monforti and Melissa R. Michelson review this simultaneity of invisibility and hypervisibility of women-of-color (WOC) in academia. They observe (adding their voices to other scholars' reports such as Constantine et al. 2008) that,

> [f]aculty of underrepresented backgrounds are also more likely to have to be especially careful about their tone of voice, facial expressions, body language, and dress in the classroom because these choices can have direct consequences for perceived levels of competence. (Monforti and Michelson 2020: 62)

From being mocked for my "accent" while teaching, to students and colleagues mispronouncing my name and asking me where I am from, to unsolicited advice on teaching, grading, and designing my syllabus from students and colleagues expecting justification for my pedagogical choices, and eventually to outright aggressive and racist rhetoric in teaching evaluations, I have become accustomed to my knowledge, authority, and legitimacy being questioned.

Yolanda Flores Neimann observes,

> Existing academic structures facilitate different realities and rules of the game for members of historically underrepresented groups as compared to those of their white, heterosexual colleagues. These disparate realities create shaky ground for women of color and provide evidence that no matter how hard they work, how many degrees they possess, what titles they earn, or what levels and/or positions they acquire, they are still vulnerable to malevolent experiences as faculty members. The more -isms associated with their identities, the more personally directed is the antagonism and the more oppressive is the unchallenged, status-quo environment. (Neimann 2012: 448)

While a part of my navigation of such "presumed incompetence" has been to perform the image of the white male professor, another part has resisted it simultaneously, treading a fine line between conformism and resistance. My forms of resistance have been similar to the "intellectual judo move" that my former PhD cohort member Dr. Myrton Running Wolf explains:

> I think of the "intellectual judo move" [as effective], which is to use the power of the archive against it. To topple it on its head, to subvert it. I don't think it's an either-or—we teach to the canon, or we teach against the canon. How do we take the canon, reinvestigate it, so that we enable and empower our students to flip that on its head to move forward in another way, to where we can give them the skills to master the canon, so that you can disrupt the canon. (2020)

While I perform the "white male professor," wearing my blazer and adjusting my voice, I reinforce my non-whiteness and advocacy for dismantling the existing power structures by including WOC playwrights in the syllabus and adding images of Artists and Academics of Color on my PowerPoint presentations, therefore destabilizing the image and monotone of whiteness.

I fracture my own performances—one day, I wear my neatly ironed blazer, the next day, I appear in my salwar kameez. I *obey* by indicating the Wadsworth anthology as "required text" on my syllabus, while simultaneously designing assignments that require students to find plays from the same time period, but outside of the anthology. In addition to teaching Shakespeare's *The Tempest*, I teach *A Tempest* by Aimé Césaire. I ask my students to investigate not only *what* is in the syllabus, but *why* it is in it, and how we now look at those texts that are not included. I encourage them to look at not only historical documentation and archival work, but the gaps, fissures, and limitations of the archive. What happens to plays that never get printed? to oral culture? What are the problematics of studying history with a linear perspective, assuming that print culture is an evolved form of oral culture, English an evolved form of language, and that someone without an American accent deserves to be mocked? In a way, I am in a double bind—while I teach my students to question, if not disrupt, existing power structures, my authority as "the bearer of knowledge" is questioned and disrupted continuously because of my own subjectivity.

This questioning is shaped and determined by race, gender, color, and nationality. In Neimann's words,

> The challenges these authors [and academics of color] have faced are grounded largely in the quadruple threat of racism, sexism, homophobia, and class-based subordination. This combination of "isms" can be lethal to their careers, bodies, and spirits in the culture of the predominantly white, male, heterosexual, and upper-middle-/upper-class academy. (Neimann 2012: 446)

I argue that the canon is a residue of the assumed dominance of "the culture of the predominantly white, male, heterosexual, and upper-middle-/upper-class academy." In order for us to rethink the canon, it is not enough to view the canon only as a collection of texts and ideas, but also as a reinforcement of cultural superiority. We need to reexamine the culture of preservation and defense of the traditions and practices that support the canon.

Scene 3

Building on Pierre Bourdieu's ideas on "familiarization" (Bourdieu 1996: 159–160), Holderness elaborates on how a "gradual process of 'conscious or unconscious inculcation' leads people into accepting an established hierarchy of authors as 'self-evident'" (Holderness 2014: 77). Therefore, naturally, the question of familiarization leads to questions of habit and indoctrination. One needs to unlearn *habits* in order to dismantle the canon.

As a first step, how about we break the habit of using the term "canon" itself? The word, as I have established already, has uncomfortable associations with Christianity and Empire. To dismantle the hegemony of the canon, we need different terms, or perhaps, no terms at all. I am, in no way, suggesting a complete negation of the works of literature that we have considered canonical for so long, but proposing that we change our frames of thinking about them. Instead of thinking of certain texts as falling within the canon, how can we think of materials that *matter* instead, in the present, but also in the past, contextualized in history? I suggest we look at the historical and socio-political significance of the works in question, and arrange materials in survey classes according to topics rather than historical movements relating only to Europe and America. Even that process, I recognize, entails selection and, therefore, a kind of exclusion.

Instead of thinking of the canon and canonicity in their representativeness, we may focus on the loopholes of representation, the holes of history, and what Robert Dale Parker identifies as representing "unrepresentativeness itself" (Parker 1993: 105). He goes on to explain:

> The point is not to prescribe some particular set of principles for selecting texts but exactly the opposite: it is to argue against the adequacy, the representative sufficiency, of any principle of selecting texts, and thus to argue only for making each system—for we will still have our systems, and a great many of them—not only represent what it systemizes but also advertise the limits of its own systematicity. (Parker 1993: 106)

As educators, it is not enough to only impart knowledge—it is crucial for us to provoke critical thinking and encourage a pursuit of meta-knowledge. What can we understand from not only the texts represented in the syllabus but those excluded, especially in survey courses? What are the consequences of unsettling what Bourdieu recognizes as "the market of symbolic goods" (Bourdieu 1984)?

Scene 4

An advocate of polyvocality as an essential tool for cultural examination, I initiated a conversation around canonicity with some of my colleagues. In order to understand the canon from the perspective of a theatre practitioner with broad experience in Filipino, Canadian, and American education systems and industry, I spoke with Prof. Chari Arespacochaga, who is currently working in American academia as an Assistant Professor of Performance.

Sukanya Chakrabarti: In your experience as a theatre scholar, practitioner, academic, teacher, what would you define as the "canon?" If you were to design a syllabus that would disrupt that idea of the canon, what would it include?

Chari Arespacochaga: Such a hard question! Because it presumes right away that we need a canon. To me, it is problematic just because it makes the canon a fixed point. Of course, we need to read about the Greeks, know our Shakespeare, but we need to be mindful of what we are neglecting or ignoring, or maybe we are not actively ignoring, just not knowing about. How do we keep the canon expanding so it keeps up with the new ways theatre can be done? And how do we include knowledge and storytelling and performance traditions that have nothing to do with a beginning, middle, and end? I think those are the things we all should be thinking about. Because we've not really fully addressed that, and we're also still obligated to churn out students who are ready to audition because they have a Classical monologue, [or] a comic monologue—it's also rebalancing because we need to prepare the students for the industry. They still need to know a Golden Age music theatre song to walk into an audition room, right?

Chakrabarti: I recognize how big that is in terms of envisioning change not only in academia, but also envisioning a change in the theatre industry, in the publishing industry ...

Arespacochaga: And ... where will that change start ...? Because it is already problematic that certain things are upheld as a canon. And then who defines that canon? And where did that even come from?

Chakrabarti: It also becomes problematic for us to rethink the canon, when we, "we" as in right now I'm talking about you and I ... who are coming from a history of colonial context ...

Arespacochaga: But we were educated on the canon! The go-to first titles in my head are Shakespeare, and all of the Western canon.

Chakrabarti: If we were to design a new Introduction to Theater and Performance Studies course for incoming Freshmen, what happens if we don't include what we recognize as the canon? What if we don't include *Oedipus* or Shakespeare?

Arespacochaga: I think that's a great idea! What is the purpose of introducing a student to theatre now? So if you are introducing students to theatre as it is now, maybe that should be the guiding thought. Or, if the purpose of introducing new students to theatre is to imagine the ways theatre might be, then you necessarily have to depart from the canon. But it's also hard, because you have to balance not just how they can imagine how theatre can be, but also for them to discover what they can be doing in that landscape that they're imagining, right? It's also difficult because our definitions of a good skill set are also based on our education. But I think that's a great idea to ... mindfully depart from the canon. Maybe we don't need to be reading *Oedipus* in this class, or in every class that we go to.

> One of the key points that came out of my conversation with Prof. Arespacochaga was also the starting point for my conversation with my graduate school cohort, Dr. Joy Brooke Fairfield and Dr. Myrton Running Wolf, both of whom are academics in our broader field of theatre, performance, and cultural and media studies—the idea of intellectual lineage, and how an adherence to the lineage that we are fed as students becomes part of the preservation of the canon and existing power structures.

Joy Brooke Fairfield: I think it's important to be upfront with students, and ourselves, about what our intellectual and artistic lineages are. Because we are completely shaped by those lineages. We are often fed just one, or two, or three, or four cultural histories, and there are infinite. Some of them are more canonized than others. Some of them have a greater attrition of power, and [some others have more] access to wealth and resources, legal systems built up around [...] them. Canons are important so far as people who are teaching must acknowledge what they have been fed, as they are teaching, feeding the next generation. To not do that is dishonest. Diversifying who is in charge of teaching and what lineages are being introduced pedagogically will help shift the canon.

Chakrabarti: That's exactly what my biggest challenge has been. I did a Bachelor's and a Master's in English literature, which is taught in a postcolonial context, but of course it is very Euro-American. Having said that, I'm also bred by my cultural specificity, and that informs what I gain from the world and what I want to impart to the world. And I think that has been my biggest challenge coming to the West. Because, in our PhD list of required readings—the list of 120 plays or something—nothing was non-Western, nothing from the Global South.[1] But what do I say to somebody who says "but you are in America. You are physically located in American academia, you ought to be obviously thinking about canon from that perspective."

Fairfield: Why are we speaking in English? You should be studying the literature of the place you are in, you should be studying the literature of indigenous California. Central Valley. So then there's no reason why you should have to have read all of those British plays, Euro-white American plays.

Chakrabarti: And also, canon assumes the knowledge of printed text. What happens to oral cultures? How are we to think of canon if we want to include something that is oral and non-textual?

Myrton Running Wolf: I looked up one definition: "The body of rules, principles, or standards, accepted as axiomatic and universally binding in a field of study or art" (*Dictionary.com*, s.v. "canon"). Who is making the rules? Who defines the principles? Who sets the standards? ... And the dominant culture takes on the idea that the canon is common sense. That the idea of canon is not only intuitive but also righteous. They have the sense [...] this is the right way of being, and if you don't know that, you are somehow outside of what is considered right, or you are primitive. So, when you [question that], they were like, "Because we say so." "You are coming here to our country, our territory, these are the standards we go by, these are the rules and principles we operate by." The reason why I speak English is because of the boarding school assimilation period, right? That "we are here to retrain you in the Western way of being." There was a proverb which was "Kill the Indian, and save the man." Again, that idea of righteousness. Save the person, the individual, teaching him how to exist in these Euro-American ways of being. It truly is like "Well, once you're elevated in your thinking, you're going to see that the Western canon is the most powerful, most righteous, and highest gold standard that there is, and you should know that coming in. Because otherwise, if you don't, then get out of here." Which is really an aggressive move. It's not benign ... it is an indictment of the individual and the culture you are coming from.

Chakrabarti: The one response that I repeatedly get is that "Well, there is only so much you can teach in a semester. And something has to give." And "something has to give" will always be those plays that are not considered important enough to be part of the canon. I think it is a vicious cycle that until we recognize something as part of the canon, we won't even allow it to exist.

Running Wolf: We also have to think in terms of historiography. We have to think about the way that history has been shaped and formed ... If you asked me, "what are the live performance traditions for the Blackfeet?" I wouldn't be able to tell you. Not because it's not there. Because it has been erased and marginalized and has been eradicated from our ways of thinking and being. But that doesn't mean it didn't exist, that they don't have as much of a claim on truth as anything else ...

Fairfield: Reading the "important plays" and deciding on the "important plays" is for me a disciplinary residue of the fact that Theatre Studies came out of English literature, this colonial academic system which we all know has a bunch of historical violence baked into it. Part of breaking the canon is about the form too. It cannot be that the most important plays are the ones that have been written the longest time ago, as you said, and performed the most number of times. Because if it's just the historical popularity contest, we all know who is in charge of the popularity machine since the dawn of European colonialism. It just makes me think of our whole field ... Getting away from texts and textual superiority has to be part of the project.

Running Wolf: Do you think that changing the canon changes society and changes the field? If we change the canon, if we update the canon to feature half non-Western stuff, would that change the field itself? The practice? Would that change our colleagues? Or would they be like "Eh, it's a good experiment."

Chakrabarti: I think it goes back to the idea of habit—academic habit, industry habit, habit as practitioners, and it also goes back to the idea of what we choose to prioritize and the intellectual lineage. Because if we redefine the canon for our students, they are at least aware that there is a whole world of theatre outside of the American theatre industry. It brings some equity in knowledge systems. If that becomes a habit in academia, that becomes a habit as intellectual lineage, to a large extent.

I invite my students to ask the question, why is this play in the syllabus? Why is it in the anthology? To question the predominance of print culture or raise questions of inclusion, of history, or historicity. But, in doing that, I also face resistance, as I already mentioned to you.

Running Wolf: Can you repeat that [student feedback]? Because that was mind-blowing that you got that.

Chakrabarti: Yes, let me read it out to you:

> Plays were boring and seemed like communist propaganda. I know for a fact that during the last 200 years not everyone was pushing this faggot shit in literature. Only play that should remain in the syllabus is Death of a Salesman, not because it is any good or because the message is worth wasting any brain power on (man sad in NY, man kills self, everyone cry for this "very human story"), rather because it is a play that I had heard of before so it has some relevance to history whereas plays like Hungry Woman, M. Butterfly, and the boohoo apartheid plays were just about feeling bad for people who are faggots or would still be eating people if Europeans didn't oppress them into knowing that is morally wrong.

> Class sucked, boohoo people got colonized and aren't grateful to the merciful white man who brought them plumbing, industry, literacy, etc. Shove this entire antiwhite agenda up your fucking ass you durka durka retard. Go back to India if you hate my people so much.

In these comments alone, we see how presumptions of a racial hierarchy are integrated with an entitlement to decide what works *should* be included in the syllabus. Their opinion is clearly formulated by the presumptions of white supremacy, and the narratives of coloniality, indicated by the "white savior" approach. The student also merits their own knowledge of a play reason enough to demand its inclusion in the syllabus. And what we include in the syllabus, or have included habitually in it for the past 200 years, determines whose stories get told.

We need to remember that theatre is not merely entertainment, that theatre history is not merely a school subject, but a shaper of education, society, and culture, that our students are not merely young adults in the academic bubble forever, but the future itself. They will decide how our culture will be shaped and history will be archived.

I am deeply impacted by repeated discrimination, persecution, stereotyping, and race-based violence—the presumed dominance of whiteness just as much as the presumed ignorance, guilt, insufficiency, criminality of the other. When we imagine destabilizing the canon, we reshuffle the way power has operated systemically in academia, industry, and culture. It is not merely a revision of academic curricula, but a rearrangement of power structures in our culture and society. It is essential not only that we question the canon, but also that we point toward the relationship that canonicity shares with colonialism and cultural hegemony. When Amy Cooper, a white woman, threatens Christian Cooper, a black man, saying she will call 911 to "tell them there's an African American man threatening my life" (Harriot 2020), it serves as a "performative utterance" (Austin 1975). She recognizes not only the consequences of those utterances, but also their potency reinforced by historical repetition to become a performance of race inequity, injustice, and violence in the social landscape of America.

By no means do I intend to compare the enormity of scale in police brutality and systemic racism to a student evaluation. Nonetheless, the impulses of presuming superiority/inferiority are shared in these instances. And these presumptions are historical *habits*, repeated and rehearsed, which manifest themselves in either minute acts of racism in the classroom, academia, industry, and curricular practices, covertly; or repeated occurrences of brutality and oppression, overtly. When students refuse to recognize knowledge in a brown body; when walking into a classroom feels like walking into a room full of eyes judging you not only for your knowledge (or presumed lack of it), but for the way you look, how you speak and what you wear; when the textbooks your brown body teaches reflect and reinstate value-placement by erasing or marginalizing you and your stories; when you spend all your energy and time preparing for class lectures, and yet it's not enough;[2] and when you, then, further internalize that lack of faith in your knowledge and question your own legitimacy; we see knowledge, power, gender, and race interact and intersect.

This is where I propose our approach toward what we choose to deem "of value" be reexamined, and *habits* be re-imagined and re-formed, not just by faculty of color, but by our white, cis-gendered, heteronormative, male colleagues as well. I propose that we interrogate all existing canons for survey-based theatre courses, identify the lacunae, and work toward equal distribution and representation of diverse plays. I suggest, instead of text-focused theatrical discussions, we make space for re-membering body-based, experiential, and ancestral knowledge systems. I also suggest that theatre departments review, revise, and redesign their curriculum and season-planning keeping social justice, equity, diversity, and inclusion in focus; hire more professors of color with diverse education and experiences, not as tokenism, not just to repeat and reiterate the canon by teaching it, but necessarily to interrupt and depart from it.

Perhaps, then, we will learn to trouble the existing narratives of entitlement and righteousness, of presumed hierarchy of knowledge based on the color of our skin. Perhaps, then, to envision and practice an expanded approach to theatre, I will not have to "go back to India," after all.

Notes

1 For the sake of accuracy, I would like to correct myself here. There were 141 plays in the list, out of which two were non-Western—Athol Fugard, Kani, and N'tshona, *The Island*; and Tang Xianzu, *The Peony Pavillion*.
2 In my conversation with Dr. Running Wolf, he mentioned a similar experience: "walking into the classroom seems like walking into my dissertation defense every time; I have 20 pages of notes, and we get to only 2 pages, but even that amount of work is not enough."

Works Cited

Austin, J. L. 1975. *How to Do Things with Words*, edited by J. O. Urmson and Marina Sbisá. Cambridge, MA: Harvard University Press.

Bourdieu, Pierre. 1984. *The Field of Cultural Production: Essays on Art and Literature*. New York: Columbia University Press.

Bourdieu, Pierre. 1996. *The Rules of Art: Genesis and Structure of the Literary Field*. Stanford: Stanford University Press.

Choi, Andrew Young, Tania Israel, and Hotaka Maeda. 2017. "Development and Evaluation of the Internalized Racism in Asian Americans Scale (IRAAS)." *Journal of Counseling Psychology* 64, 1: 52–64.

Constantine, M. G., L. Smith, R. M. Redington, and D. Owens. 2008. "Racial Microaggressions against Black Counseling and Counseling Psychology Faculty: A Central Challenge in the Multicultural Counseling Movement." *Journal of Counseling & Development* 86, 3: 348–355.

Dictionary.com November 2020. s.v. "canon," accessed 5 https://www.dictionary.com/browse/canon#:~:text=the%20body%20of%20rules%2C%20principles,the%20canons%20of%20good%20behavior.

Harriot, Michael. 2020. "Amy Cooper is the Kind of White Woman Black Families Warn their Children about." *The Washington Post*, 29 May. Accessed 31 May 2020. https://www.washingtonpost.com/outlook/2020/05/29/amy-cooper-white-woman/

Holderness, Graham. 2014. "'An Arabian in My Room': Shakespeare and the Canon." *Critical Survey* 26, 2: 73–89.

Hunter, George. 1991. "The History of Styles as a Style of History." In *Addressing Frank Kermode: Essays in Criticism and Interpretation*, edited by Margaret Tudeau-Clayton and Martin Warner. Urbana and Chicago: University of Illinois Press.

Kermode, Frank. 1985. *Forms of Attention*. Chicago: University of Chicago Press.

Lee, Young Jean. 2009. *Songs of the Dragons Flying to Heaven*. In *Songs of the Dragons Flying to Heaven and Other Plays*. New York, NY: Theatre Communications Group.

Merriam-Webster, s.v. "canon," accessed 31 May 2020, https://www.merriam-webster.com/dictionary/canon

Monforti, Jessica Lavariega and Melissa R. Michelson. 2020. "They See Us, but They Don't Really See Us." In *Presumed Incompetent II: Race, Class, Power, and Resistance of Women in Academia*, edited by Yolanda Flores Neimann, Gabriella Gutiérrez y Muhs, and Carmen G. Gonzalez. Colorado: University Press of Colorado; Utah: Utah State University Press.

Myrton Running Wolf (Assistant Professor of Race and Media, Reynolds School of Journalism, University of Nevada, Reno), and Joy Brooke Fairfield (Assistant Professor of Theatre, Rhodes College) in conversation with the author, 21 May 2020.

Neimann, Yolanda Flores. 2012. "Lessons from the Experiences of Women of Color Working in Academia." In *Presumed Incompetent: The Intersections of Race and Class for Women in Academia*, edited by Gutiérrez y Muhs, Gabriella, Yolanda Flores Niemann, Carmen G. Gonzalez, and Angela P. Harris. Colorado: University Press of Colorado; Utah: Utah State University Press.

Parker, Robert Dale. 1993. "Material Choices: American Fictions, the Classroom, and the Post-Canon." *American Literary History* 5, 1: 89–110.

Schwarz, Daniel R. 1992. "Review-Essay: Canonicity, Culture, and Pluralism-A Humanistic Perspective on Professing English." *Texas Studies in Literature and Language* 34, 1: 149–175.

Spivak, Gayatri Chakravarty. 1994. "Can the Subaltern Speak?" In *Colonial Discourse and Postcolonial Theory*, edited by Patrick Williams and Laura Chrisman, 66–111. New York: Columbia University Press.

Worthen, W. B., ed. 2010. *The Wadsworth Anthology of Drama*, 6th Edition. Boston, MA: Cengage Learning.

4 Despite the Flames: A Conversation

Patricia Ybarra, Virginia Grise, and Victor I. Cazares

These are not the titular flames, but these flames and their smoke echoed through our conversations:

> I'm breathing in smoke … I'm breathing in trees that are older than me, older than you, older than this state, older than this corrupt nation. I'm breathing in the witnesses to our destruction, the only recorded history my people had. … And mixed inside this smoke I'm breathing now as I write this, is also inorganic material, more evidence of our destruction: plastics, rubber, corrosive metals, and actual toxins. Poison. My lungs now hold that record. My lungs will not become a tree.—message from Victor during the 2020 Oregon Wildfires as delivered in *Pinching Pennies with Penny Marshall.*

Methodology, or Why We Could Not Help but Make Such a Mess of a Straightforward Question About the US Theatrical Canon

When one of the editors first approached me, Patricia Ybarra, about a possible contribution to this volume, we were not yet in the throes of COVID-19 as a nation. Rather, the disaster we thought we'd be writing in was ecological: the series of wildfires in Southern California and the human lives deemed expendable. The title of this contribution is taken from a 28 October 2019 headline from an *LA Times* article "Getty Fire: Housekeepers and gardeners go to work despite the flames." "Despite the flames" haunted us as an accurate and harrowing phrase to describe the conditions of Latinx domestic workers in the US, who, alongside prison laborers *forced* to go put out the flames, went to work at their own peril. The story reveals that a number of largely wealthy employers simply "forgot" to tell their employees not to show up for work in the midst of an evacuation notice. This coercion is normalized.

In hindsight, the 2019 headline and the entire incident was prophetic. It foretold the plight of the now rhetorically lauded, but still violently mistreated, class of "essential workers" who would be asked to go to work despite the flames, or despite the virus, or asked not to work so as not to infect their employers and instead go hungry.

DOI: 10.4324/9781003031413-4

We were struck by the stark difference in how people in the theatre, the workers, were notified about the coming disaster of a complete and total shutdown of all our stages. Everyone knew that we could not show up to work and that we were not essential. And it isn't only COVID-19 that has impacted the theatre world, which would have remained in suspended animation had it not been for the Movement for Black Lives that arose from the murders of Breonna Taylor, George Floyd, and Ahmaud Arbery. It is in the shadow of this movement that We See You White American Theatre emerged—without demands and without saying their names. (They would, weeks later, emerge with a list of demands for a neoliberal technocratic—and yes, capitalist—form of theatre-making.)

As non-essential workers or workers who could work from home, we have been home safe. Because we are the children of essential workers, we recognize the lack of regard essential workers face and know that when they are made into "heroes" in the times of COVID-19 it is to hide their disposability.

To begin our collaboration, Victor I. Cazares, Virginia Grise, and I shared writing. The word essay in English is a bit of an overstatement for what we shared. But remembering that in Spanish the word for essay is also the word often used for rehearsal (ensayo)—perhaps "ensayo" is a term we can use.

After we shared these ensayos with each other, we sat down for two interviews. Here are the questions I offered Cazares and Grise:

1. Each of you speaks in the ensayos about a feeling of exclusion—exclusion that is not necessarily because you are Latinx, but because your aesthetics do not fit certain expectations. Can you each say more about how and why you think your aesthetics and politics are challenging to mainstream commercial theatre?
2. Can you all react to something Quiara Alegría Hudes said recently about aesthetics in her 2018 essay in *American Theatre*: "I struggle increasingly with the atheist white male aesthetics I inherit" (2018).
3. Each of you have found yourself in a new artistic home recently and I wonder if you could talk about that experience in relation to your past experiences?
4. Do you feel like you are part of a Latinx canon of dramatic work, or why not? How and why do you resonate with the challenges of We See You, White American Theatre as a mode to interrogate the very kind of season, canon, and supporting infrastructure that this volume interrogates? How and when can the critique of racism also be a critique of capitalism?
5. Why do you hate capitalism?

The answers coalesced into a group-written oral history that follows the best instincts of our storytelling traditions, in which past, present, and future collide. The question we answer over the course of this essay is: why do we continually step aside from the canonical American theatre—and what consequences and benefits does that have? But it takes a while for us to get to that point—we beg the readers' patience on this point.

Where We are from and Why it Matters (or, Why We All Ended Up Talking About Land, Place, and Space to Talk About Theatre)

Patricia Ybarra: Recently, after a complex moment in my personal history, I decided that looking to where I was from was the best way to understand where I am now. What I learned was that both sides of my family—my norteño Mexican side and my white Anglo settler side—have largely been confined to this continent for over 250 years. There have been literal moves west and north (I grew up in Whittier, California). But, there have also been moves sideways, as well as up and down in the larger sense of class mobility. I see phenomena people think are new—people who do not change classes or earnings from generation to generation, people who go to college but do not become white collar professionals. I see intelligent people whose lives are greatly altered by trauma and substance abuse. I see people who do not overcome but are not entirely overcome.

Victor I. Cazares: I grew up in El Paso, Texas, in the shadow of Wal-Mart's American Capitalism and NAFTA and the Second Amendment and a school curriculum that taught us New England's four seasons even though we lived in the desert. I grew up thinking there was something wrong with our trees because they never turned orange or red, just brown. Our skies darkened with dust storms, not rain. And I don't know what seasonal weather pattern they represented, but Border Patrol agents would come to our schools to show us how they caught bad guys: with trained German Shepherds and a cute robot named Rudy. The bad guys were our parents, our neighborhood, our colonia, in the outskirts of El Paso, where nobody with a choice lived. Where the undocumented and the marginal could disappear into the sand. In the desert, all we do is pray for rain.

Virginia Grise: And I grew up in San Antonio, Texas—one of the city's major industries is tourism so I grew up watching our culture being packaged and sold as a commodity. It is a highly militarized city. With four active military bases, San Antonio is officially known as Military City USA (trademarked and everything). The army has maintained an active presence in the city since the annexation of Texas and before that (lest we forget) there was the Alamo, one of five Spanish colonial missions still standing (colonization and militarization go hand in hand). And even though San Antonio is a city with a Mexican/Mexican American majority population, the people with power, that make decisions about the city, continue to be white men, business owners, and developers who own the banks, the newspapers, the media, and I would argue the city's politicians, too. Every year we celebrate Fiesta in San Antonio, a 10-day city-wide festival in commemoration of the Battle of San Jacinto, an important turning point in the Mexican-American War that ended in 1848 when Mexico ceded over 50% of its lands to the United States including parts of Arizona, California, New Mexico, Utah, Colorado, Nevada, and Texas. Many of the people I know from San Antonio can trace their family history to before the fall of the Alamo but that is not my family's story. I am the daughter of a Chinese Mexican immigrant and a working class white father. We have no other family in Texas.

Cazares: The problem is that Mexicans + Mexican Americans are always already dead: our stories, our nation, our lives. I forget that we are 11.3% of the US population. We rarely, if ever, see ourselves on the stage, on the screen, or on a book display at Powell's. I do see us cleaning tables, packing chicken in meat plants, and some more cleaning of various types, and at all levels of the respectability spectrum. I see us in cages, in prisons, in the fields, and on the floors of speckled linoleum, blood pooling underneath in a Wal-Mart in El Paso on August 3, 2019. One of the many, many times that the loaded gun that descended a staircase back in June 2015 has gone off. Chekhov's narrative theory, like America's founding fathers, did not imagine automatic weapons. What I mean by this, is that Chekhov got it wrong: placing a loaded gun on stage in act one doesn't mean it has to go off in act three; it means that it has to multiply exponentially, doubling every two years and at half the cost. The Donald Trump that descended the staircase in June 2015 has multiplied into 70 million votes in 2020. The single shot musket of the second amendment in the 18th century, now in act three of this country, is loaded and can shoot millions of bullets per second.

On Why Home is a Four-Letter Word:

Grise: I recently moved back to Texas after being gone for over a decade, but for the most part, I stayed traveling, on the road with my work. In 2019, the longest stretch of time I was home was two weeks consecutively the entire year. The pandemic forced me to go home really and it wasn't until then that I realized that I had spent the past two years of my life running away from home, sometimes out of necessity, as I try to piecemeal a living as a working artist in this country. So much of my life as an artist has felt uncertain, transient, unstable. I had not been home in a very long time and I have not felt home anywhere for at least the past decade. I once had a friend—anytime I would talk about not feeling at home he would suggest that I read Althusser. Home is a four-letter word he'd say. I've read Althusser. I still have this longing for home. Maybe because I come from a long line of runaways and refugees that tried to make home in places that did not want them, maybe because growing up, the home I lived in never felt safe.

Cazares: One of the ways I ground myself is by addressing my past self—in this case, when I was a child in elementary school: "Being from the border doesn't mean you're from two countries, two places; it means you belong to neither. In the future when you learn the word unheimlich in a performance studies class, you'll finally find a home. And its professor will tell you to go back to Mexico (when you complain about the passport agency that's holding up your Brazil visa). The word means un-home-like. An uncanny sense that this is not home even though it is. It's a projection. It's a cetacean that finds itself on land, again."

Why Race Matters, Why Class Matters, but Mostly Why Race and Class Matter

Grise: We often talk about race without talking about class in this country. We still only talk about race in a black and white binary. The Latinx community doesn't talk enough about race in general. And I think, now more than ever, we have a hard time seeing how struggles are interconnected.

Cazares: In the US in Latinx communities, we've often referred to our differences and prejudices based on skin color as colorism. But the latest data from Mexico calls it what it is: racism. Gathering extensive demographic data, a study from the 2016/2017 Latin American Public Opinion Project at Vanderbilt University, discussed in a 2017 article in *The Conversation*, determined that race is the biggest determining factor of a "Mexican citizen's economic and educational attainment." In order to get this racial data, however, the pollsters themselves had to categorize respondents since race is not reflected on census data. Likewise, in the US we have insufficient data on our Latinx communities: grouping Indigenous, Black, Asian, and White Latinx without parsing through their racial data paints an inaccurate picture of community needs.

Ybarra: When I look at my family history, what I see is a long history of essential workers. On my Anglo mother's side farmers become grocers and travelling grocery salesmen. On my father's side, many of his male relatives were miners. My grandfather, Tito Olivas Ybarra followed the copper across the border into Arizona in the 1920s, eventually settling in Phoenix as an urban laborer. He was a clothes washer, a printer, and eventually, an ad salesperson. His male children all joined or were drafted into the armed forces—Mexican and US born alike. The Mexican nationals in the family, when they return from war, apply for naturalization. These are people destroyed and saved by the US settler state in equal measure.

Grise: My father was an airplane mechanic. When he got home every night he would have to wash the grease off his hands with Lava soap. Grease like that doesn't come off in one washing. I have this memory of the time my father wanted me to apply to the private university on the hill in San Antonio. He asked me to meet him at the university. He left work early to get there, so when we walked into the admissions offices at the school he was still wearing his Dickies work clothes and his hands still had grease on them. I remember the way the secretary looked at him, up and down, and I decided at that moment I didn't want to go to a school that treated my father poorly. When I received the Whiting Award, I wore a pair of Dickies to my reading.

We don't like to talk about class in this country.

On Why We Hate Capitalism (and Why We Hate NAFTA Specifically)

Ybarra: I have often wondered about two things: why am I so greatly disheartened and uninterested in entrepreneurship as a mode of subject making? And, why am I so given to staying in semi-brutal labor situations? I wrote a book to figure this out, but was still left guessing. I guess the answer is in my blood. Six generations of being within the machine of extractive capitalism is a hard habit to break.

Grise: It's hard to think outside of capitalist logic when you live in the belly of the beast. I think we can easily name all the ways that capitalism hates us, especially now when the ways it's actually killing us are so clear. I hate capitalism because it hates us. I hate capitalism because it is killing the people I love. The logic of capitalism isn't logical. The free market is not free. I hate capitalism because it is extractive, because it does not care about our health, our well-being as a people, our happiness. Imagining something new, building it, creating it, when you live in the belly of the beast, comes with sacrifice and consequences.

Ybarra: My father worked in a non-unionized factory. My father was working on a machine when I was a small child. Something went wrong and the machine malfunctioned and basically came down on his arm and shattered his entire elbow. There was no compensation for the injury. That is capitalism. Soon after, the decline of the aerospace industry happens in the late 80s and early 90s (on the way to NAFTA), and sets up antagonisms between documented and undocumented workers. My father despite his horrible labor experiences takes the side of the documented and begins to blame undocumented workers for his oppression rather than the factory itself. He is suspicious of the union. That is capitalism. It is immoral.

Cazares: Capitalism has made food taste the same: engineered for mass appeal and their market suitability (i.e., this variety of banana won't bruise, its flavor doesn't matter just as long as it looks like a perfect banana). Corn, apples, they've lost their flavor. Capitalism wants to make things the same or efficient. What I'm saying is I hate efficiency. My grandpa would say that the fruit from the US does not taste the same. I thought he was just being ridiculous. Honestly, I thought: you just hate the US because they abused you and deported you and didn't pay you when you worked and they sprayed you with DDT, like, you're just saying all these things because you hate the US. But no, it's actually true. There have been studies that show that flavor has changed.

Food is blander than it used to be and they're creating a mono culture. So that's a superficial reason, but I think it's endemic. Capitalism homogenizes.
Grise: It feels to me like that answer relates to this question of theatre, too—this idea of everything tasting the same. I want to see your work because only you can make it. How do we encourage artists to be free, messy, uniquely themselves?
Cazares: A thing I derive joy from is that my grandpa was part of a collective of organizers, was part of a land reform movement in Mexico. During the 70s, they took land from one of the famous landowners. There were like 33 or 34 of them in the collective, and they finally got land rights. Now only my grandfather and his brother have retained their land and they will not sell. But they also no longer have collective power, especially not in Chihuahua, Mexico. They've been approached to sell, and at some point, they're going to be forced to sell. *Capitalism separates people.* This thing that they fought for together eventually was dissolved by capitalism.
Grise: What capitalism tries to destroy is our lived realities and daily practices of collective ownership and care, our knowledge base, what we know to be true and the ways we know how to create together and grow together as a people. I don't want to lose that, our collective knowledge, the ways that we feed each other, take care of each other. And I don't look for that in organizations and institutions but in each other, in small ways and, like theatre, maybe it's not forever but moments, spaces that we create, however temporary, for those types of relationships.
Ybarra: When we started this conversation, I did not know what a flashpoint the 1994 passage of the North American Free Trade Agreement, which greatly disenfranchised Mexican farmers *and* some US workers, would be.
Grise: I think it's because we started by talking about how we grew up. I graduated high school in 1994.

1994 marks the implementation of NAFTA, which was actually signed in San Antonio by the presidents of Canada, the US, and Mexico two years prior. One of the first protests I can remember attending was an anti-NAFTA protest. My entire family went. 1994 is also the year that the Zapatistas, an armed indigenous rebel army in Chiapas, declared war on the Mexican government. In their First Declaration of the Lacandon Jungle, the Zapatistas denounced the Mexican government, the implementation of NAFTA, and neoliberalism.

I was greatly inspired by the Zapatistas, both politically and artistically. The Zapatista movement gave me a language to begin to understand and articulate how neoliberalism was affecting all of us, on both sides of the border, how it was affecting us globally. If you think about it artistically, through encuentros, assemblies, and communiques (that were political but also funny and poetic and just good stories), the Zapatistas had a critique of global capital but they were also staging another reality, other possibilities for how we could live outside of capitalist logic. I was sent to the Intercontinental Encuentro Against

Neoliberalism and for Humanity as a delegate of Accion Zapatista, a pro Zapatista collective in the US. So much of the way that I make art was informed by those early days of organizing. I make art like an organizer. I am committed to collective study and work that is rigorous and I am most excited by theatre when it disrupts and disorientates, when it becomes an embodiment of autonomy and freedom and offers us possibilities for new futures.

Aesthetics, or Reading Things We Were not Supposed to Know About

Cazares: When I was in a workshop in grad school, I brought in Pasolini's *The Gospel of St. Matthew* as an example of my aesthetic. Which, in this case, was repurposing a classic Renaissance technique of telling Bible stories but in contemporary clothing and making it local. The professor wasn't familiar with this adaptation by Pasolini and then asked me how I knew about him and it. I'm sure he mentioned it innocently, but there is always this dynamic of a straight white man asking me how I know something, and the underlying: how did someone like you, from the border, know about this? And so the discussion becomes about how someone taught me Pasolini while I was at Yale and not about how Pasolini's work also centered on the margins like my own work. Pasolini looked outside of Rome and was trying to rescue dialects outside of Rome and bringing them to the center. I thought oh, that's what I wanted to do. I was 18 or 19 when I first encountered him valorizing the people that are not mainstream or people that are not in the center. He was controversial just for that. It was a radical act to bring people from the outside in. And here I guess I'm having the discussion about Pasolini that I would have liked to have had that day instead of explaining how I knew about Pasolini.
Grise: My father never graduated high school but he made sure I always had a book with me. He said it would keep me from being bored but it also kept me from feeling lonely. Growing up in a working-class family, in a predominately brown, working-class city, where today 1 out 4 people are functionally illiterate, the library was a place I visited with my father often and reading was my escape, my earliest memory of dreaming. My working class white father also introduced me to foreign films, filmmakers like Almodovar and Tsai Ming-liang. He read somewhere that people that went to college watched foreign films so it became something we did together on a weekly basis.
Cazares: In terms of cinema in Mexico, there was a channel, Canal Cinco, and they broadcast different international movies, like Hong Kong cinema. During the early 90s, we grew up watching those movies.
Ybarra: My mother, who did not finish high school, gave me Richard Wright's *Black Boy* to read when I was 10 or 11. In the 70s it was a mass

market paperback. This is how one grows up working class and develops radical politics and aesthetic taste. And the misguided question becomes: how would you as a working class person have access to this work? The assumption is that we only have access to less formally inventive work and are expected to reproduce canonical aesthetics and ideologies. But what we forget is that culture is not always inaccessible to working class people—libraries, antennas, and mass market publishing can allow autodidactic curiosity to flourish outside of the academy as well as inside of it.

Cazares: Also, our own lives engage structures associated with avant-garde aesthetics. I grew up in a shantytown—that's the basic translation of a colonia, which means we didn't have city water or sewage. When we drove towards El Paso, it was sort of like traveling through time, like getting to modernity and to current amenities or technologies. So I grew up sort of in a past as well. And knowing that, I realized that there's something artificial about time, that you can manipulate it in order to make it make sense to yourself. I think that must have shaped the way I see time. The way I use time is one of the things that I think marks me as aesthetically out there. We're not doing anything that *Un Chien Andalou* did not do in terms of playing with time, but, this playing with time is what makes me different. It's how I grew up. I grew up in different time zones. I had different areas where I had privilege and it was like a temporal privilege in a way.

The Canon, or Why When We Try to Talk About Aesthetics We Talk About Politics and Vice-Versa

Grise: When I think about Quiara Hudes's comment about struggling with the atheist white male aesthetics she inherits, I realize that just ain't my struggle or my inheritance. I was raised as an artist by queer, Black women in Austin, Texas. And that community of artists wasn't separate from activist communities of color. It wasn't until I went to graduate school that I discovered white straight men make theatre.

Cazares: I want to respond to several things. When I saw that I wasn't moving anywhere in terms of, like, my work, I did decide that I wasn't going to compromise myself. And, yes, I developed a meth addiction. But maybe it pickled me and preserved my aesthetic. It allowed me to stay, if not completely sane as a person, then at least it maintained my integrity as an artist.

It excluded me from mainstream theatre's way of thinking, the way of developing and valorizing the people that are professionals. It's not even a decision. I just can't be like that because of who I am. I'm a drug addict. I am HIV positive. I couldn't work in that typical way. So my play *Ramses Contra Los Monstruos* (2013) is about this person in Juárez who dissolves bodies for the cartels and one day, his bodies stopped dissolving and it's also a queer love story and an AIDS play. There was a lot of autobiography in it. No, I wasn't in a relationship with someone that dissolved bodies for the cartels, but I had a fling with someone that was close to this world. And while I didn't feel like I could tell people how close the central elements of the story were to me, I also felt that the play could stand on its own merits without my autobiography. But I also don't know who would have helped me to say: Oh, this is my story. This is biographical. I know this world intimately.**Grise:** Growing up, I always felt like I needed translation. As an artist, I'm trying to find the spaces where I do not need to translate myself. I think about that when I think about the list of demands to White American Theatre. Maybe I should start a list of every time I was told by someone that they didn't know how to sell or market my plays or how I should write for a more mainstream audience or how they wish I wrote uplifting characters or how I didn't know how to write characters cuz I was more interested in style, or why don't I just tell one story from one character's point of view, or how nobody changes in my plays, or how we don't need another Latino gang play, or how I don't understand structure, or how someone actually drew out that damn story arc diagram for me on a bar napkin once as if I had never heard of Aristotle, or how I was told people of color don't make experimental theatre and that women of color playwrights (specifically Latinas) are difficult, or that nonlinear storytelling is "out" now, or the time someone told my classmate not to associate with me cuz somehow my politics would ruin their career.

Every single person that told me those things signed the letter to White American Theatre and some are now at the helm of major regional theatres.

We See You White American Theatre, or How to Self-Deport from the Regional Theatre

Cazares: I think one of the biggest roadblocks to justice is bland theatre. And this movement does nothing but perpetuate bland theatre. The blandness of it all just hit me. Like, I've been at New York Theatre Workshop working with the WSYWAT document and working on the response at the same time I'm writing my zoom play *Pinching Pennies with Penny Marshall* (2020) in which people of color are playing white legacy roles. There's like a sort of censorship that I'm fighting against because of the document, which frames our human rights as a PR problem instead of an actual mission statement. So it's been interesting. I've just realized how much I have to fight against this document, not just politically and because this document was made by people that have excluded me and people like me, but also because it does have an aesthetic parameter. I'm only finding this out in the writing of this new play because of the censorship that it has tried to transmit to me about what is admissible in a "BIPOC" world as we are asked to take our racial identity as a fact and not something to interrogate or make sense of. For me the document is speaking to a world that I'm actually not a part of, for the most part. I had problems with the regional theatre as a model in the first place.

Despite the Flames: A Conversation 73

Figure 4.1 Promotional Poster. *Pinching Pennies with Penny Marshall*. New York Theatre Workshop. October 2020. Photo Design Credit: Victor I. Cazares.

Grise: And not just because of the regional theatre's whiteness, but because of its blandness—think about what Victor was saying earlier about how capitalism homogenizes everything. When we are asked to challenge the canon, it assumes there's a center, the challenge is to make the center more inclusive and again the assumption is that we all want to be a part of that center. I don't know if I want to be in those pictures.

Yes, the American Theatre, like the United States of America, has a race problem—that is obvious. It also has a gender problem, a class problem, so many problems. But if you think about it, the current conversation we are having about representation still centers the White American Theatre. That is not the center of my theatre-making cuz, like I said before, what they are serving tastes bland. I spend money on good wine, good liquor, and good food. I want the food at the table I'm sitting at to be good. And while I don't have a problem taking their money, I have never aspired to be a part of White American Theatre. I have never been interested in a conversation about inclusion and diversity in White American Theatre. So much money is being thrown at these institutions to fix problems they created, entire industries are being designed to fix their problems. I certainly don't think it's my job to clean up their mess.

For over 15 years, I have committed to making theatre as an artist with and for communities of color. All of my work has been made predominantly, though not exclusively, with women, queers, black and brown folks. I promise you the food at the table I am sitting at tastes damn good, though I wouldn't mind a little more money for some brown liquor. **Ybarra:** I think the most interesting thing about the document is its call to change the labor schedule of the professional theatre.

Grise: I also feel getting rid of the concept of the main stage and second stage, so that everybody gets paid the same amount of money, is an important demand. I have worked with theatres that don't actually have a physical theatre space that are still using the language of the main stage and second stage. But you don't even have a stage! And yet they hold tightly to the regional theatre as the only model for theatre making. When I work with smaller theatres that try to do this I always tell them if you do not have the resources of a regional theatre, why are you trying to produce theatre like a regional theatre? What is the thing that only you can do? Plant the corn that can only grow in your soil. In recent years, I have really taken control of my own process of developing work, finding monies, and creating partnerships (often outside of theatre) to support longer processes for development because I also have a problem with the model of 4-6 week rehearsals. The last two shows I created had a 3-4 year process of development and I really like working that way.

Cazares: I have trouble reading the document without reading the list of names and in the list of names seeing people who have literally been gatekeepers that made me feel unwelcome in the American theatre. This is a story of one of these names:

I was having a one-on-one sit down with Howard Shalwitz, the former artistic director of the Woolly Mammoth Theatre Company.

I remember walking into the lobby of the Woolly Mammoth Theatre Company while Howard Shalwitz was still the artistic director. I felt nervous and out of place. When you're darkly Indigenous and Mexican in multi-million dollar spaces, you can't shrink yourself lest you become invisible at best, removable at worst. I looked for the front desk, "You belong here. I belong here," I whispered to myself. Then, aloud, to the receptionist: "Hi. I'm here to see Howard."

The receptionist/intern looked at me, he knew me from somewhere and thought I might be delusional. "But does Howard know that?" he asked, as if someone like me could show up to a White American Theatre and ask to speak to the boss without an appointment, without being documented in a ledger. I'd made the appointment over the phone with Miriam so I didn't have an email (or a smartphone) to show him some sort of confirmation.

"Yes. He does." But did he? What if I am delusional and I only imagined that the Artistic Director of this great White American Theatre would meet with me, a nobody from a shanty town in the desert?

I remember the receptionist/intern/gatekeeper looking at me, not believing me, pausing as if to give me time to tell the truth before I was publicly humiliated. "I belong here," I told myself. He picked up the phone, called Howard's assistant and said, "There's a Victor here to see Howard?"

"Yes. Send him up." He looked at me, shocked and disappointed, and let me through, like many border guards have done before when I came to their little checkpoint.

That was ten years ago. And I still walk up to receptionists, making sure I have an email on my iPhone, ready to show that I do in fact have an appointment.

Grise: I left New York when I staged a play in a women's prison in Arizona. Doing that work there brought me home. Full circle. Home wasn't a place. It was a group of people—the incarcerated, the displaced, brown, black, indigenous, queer, artists, and dreamers. I suited up in my Dickies again when I went to work. Like my father, I want to make something with my hands.

Where We Find Our Homes Now, or Some Kind of Happy Ending

Cazares: I found my home in the great tradition of Mexicans that overstayed their visa. I think that's basically what I did at New York Theatre Workshop. As a Tow Fellow, I was invited to all the artistic meetings and like everyone gets to have an opinion. It's very lateral. Everybody contributes to the fellows, and all levels of the staff.

Grise: I have a playwriting fellowship at Cara Mia Theatre through the Mellon Foundation. The fellowship supports a playwright who is on staff at a theatre for three years. It was important to me that I apply with a theatre where I felt like I had complete and total artistic freedom and autonomy. And in the great tradition of Mexicans bringing their family with them, I am very excited about how supportive they have been of my longstanding collaborative relationships and supporting that work, particularly with directors Kendra Ware and Elena Araoz, actor Florinda Bryant, designer Tanya Orellna and my mentors Sharon Bridgforth and Omi Osun. Of course, the pandemic has shifted a lot of our original plans but I also feel it has challenged the theatre to really reevaluate its relationship to the community and to social justice movements. And so for me, I feel like I'm in a theatre where I can have challenging political and artistic conversations.

Ybarra: I found my place at Brown University. On the good days it feels like utopia. On the more challenging days, I just call one of you and you help me remember why I do this (Figure 4.2).

Figure 4.2 Chairman Mao's four minute Physical Fitness Plan by Zeke Peña. (Included as part of Virginia Grise's *Your Healing is Killing Me*.)

A Coda, from Virginia Grise's *Your Healing is Killing Me* (2017)

Capitalism is toxic. No amount of body butter or eczema creams will act as a salve for its toxicity. As a system, it cannot be fixed. The only way to defend ourselves is to destroy it. The only way to destroy it is to create something better. In the process, we must be willing to assess, to prepare, to study, to fight, but we must also be willing to live to listen to ourselves and each other, to change, to transform, to care for ourselves and each other.

> It's a process.
> A daily practice.
> Embodied.
>
> Do you like your job?
> Yes, I have to admit.

I am an artist. As an artist I believe my greatest creative project is to imagine, to imagine something, something better where our dreams matter, where as a people we are free (2017: 83).

Figure 4.3 Chairman Mao's four minute physical Fitness Plan, enacted in Tuscon, Arizona during the COVID-19 Pandemic. Photo credit: Yvonne Ballesteros.

Works Cited

Cazares, Victor I. October 2020. *Pinching Pennies with Penny Marshall. Episode 2*, Directed by Borna Barzin New York Theatre Workshop online.

Grise, Virginia. 2017. *Your Healing is Killing Me*. Pittsburgh: Plays Inverse Press.

Hudes, Quiara Alegria. 2018. "The High Tide of Heartbreak by Quiara Alegría Hudes," *American Theatre*, October 2018. Accessed 1 November 2020. https://www.americantheatre.org/2018/09/27/high-tide-of-heartbreak/.

Jasso, Carlos. 2017. "Study Reveals Racial Inequality in Mexico Disproving Race Blind Rhetoric." *The Conversation*, 13 December. Accessed 20 November 2020. https://theconversation.com/study-reveals-racial-inequality-in-mexico-disproving-its-race-blind-rhetoric-87661.

Mejia, Brittny. 2019. "Getty Fire: Housekeepers and Gardeners Go to Work Despite the Flames." *LA Times*, 28 October. Accessed 1 November 2020. https://www.latimes.com/california/story/2019-10-28/getty-fire-housekeepers-arrive-to-work.

We See You White American Theatre. Accessed 14 October 2020. https://www.weseeyouwat.com/statement.

5 The Black Gaze/A Different Account

Eric M. Glover and Isaiah Matthew Wooden

This chapter proceeds from our shared investment in interrogating prevailing pedagogical, artistic, and institutional norms and illuminating the ways they serve to reinforce antiblackness. We write from our positions as African American scholar-artists who have worked extensively in both academic and professional theatre settings and, correspondingly, who consider ourselves dedicated supporters of and advocates for the art form. Our experiences over the years have revealed just how so many people working in the theatre view and treat antiblack racism dismissively. This dismissiveness is not without effects or consequences. Indeed, one of the most persistent and pernicious ways that we have experienced its impact in our classrooms, rehearsal spaces, and conversations with students and colleagues is through an outright disregard for the rich contributions of Black theatre artists. It is striking how quick some are to reject these contributions—and, to be sure, the people who make and enjoy them—as inferior or insignificant. Equally striking is how often they do so while confidently admitting to knowing very little about the breadth and depth of Black theatre history and dramatic literature. That these kinds of incidents have repeated so frequently in our professional and everyday lives has made it necessary that we develop tools and strategies to confront and call out manifestations of antiblackness whenever and wherever they emerge. We reflect on some of these tools and strategies in what follows, sharpening particular focus on the ways they have empowered us to trouble and thwart efforts aimed at perpetuating a very narrow understanding of what constitutes theatre history and, correspondingly, the dramatic canon. We have opted for a consciously discursive approach. By writing and sharing dialogic exchanges that combine personal recollections with critical insights and provocations, our aim, in part, is to reckon with scholar Sara Ahmed's contention that "to account for racism is to offer a different account of the world" (Ahmed 2013: 3). We also aim to illustrate some of the fresh possibilities that a refusal of antiblackness and white supremacy can open up for upending the stronghold that the Eurocentric canon continues to maintain in theatre practice and pedagogy.

DOI: 10.4324/9781003031413-5

I The Black Gaze

Isaiah Matthew Wooden: We have spent many hours over the years talking about and thinking through what it means to teach courses on Black dramatic literature and theatre history in spaces that do not always see the value in these topics. Perhaps you might begin by reflecting on some of the insights that teaching in these areas have yielded for you?

Eric M. Glover: I have found that teaching Black theatre, the always already radical retelling of Blackness on the stage, often precipitates "offensive mechanisms" from instructors and students who disguise hostility toward and opposition to the subject area as concern about the sanctity of a curriculum (Pierce 1970). That instructors are so often cathected to racist and white supremacist ideas about Black people and theatre history—for example, that the musicals of the Chitlin Circuit are inherently inferior to the plays of the avant-garde—also indicates that students remain used to Black theatre history being at the margin. These limits of performance pedagogy and professional development, taken together, are a powerful concurrence of factors that creates and maintains this hierarchy of fields because of the uncritical acceptance, by artists and scholars, of the canon of white American and European drama and performance as the zenith of the theatre.

Wooden: What are some of the personal and pedagogical consequences of this?

Glover: My life as an artist and a scholar has been adversely affected by offensive mechanisms directed at me through the canon. In 1970, Chester Pierce, a Black doctor, coined *offensive mechanisms* to describe the ways in which, through speech acts designed to harm us spiritually, whites create and maintain racial hierarchy over Blacks. He writes, "Offensive mechanisms, the small, continuous bombardments of micro-aggression by whites to Blacks is the essential ingredient in race relations and race interactions" (Pierce 1970: 282). Book collections like *Presumed Incompetent* and journal articles like Koritha Mitchell's "Identifying White Mediocrity and Know-Your-Place Aggression" further encapsulate my experiences in everyday life and live performance (Gutiérrez y Muhs et al. 2012; Mitchell 2018). I have been subjected to deeply disrespectful comments like: "Are you sure you teach by yourself?" "Do you even have books on musicals?" "Do you know the plays of Molière?" "Does this look ethnic enough to you?" "How do you know all of this?" "I'm not interested in reading about that." "Nigger." "There's no power in representation." What's more, I reported microaggressions to a trusted adviser, only for her, also Black, to invite my bully later to my PhD dissertation defense. Even though the fine arts masquerade as what you call "a putative bastion of progressive thinking," on and off stage artists and scholars lead the way in perpetuating antiblackness in my experience (Wooden 2019: 184). I remained somewhat in denial about the extent to which the canon remained a contested space until I started to work in the ivory tower.

Wooden: Might you say more about how you've seen these issues manifest in your professional practice, in particular?

Glover: Working as a production dramaturge for Lorraine Hansberry's *A Raisin in the Sun* (Yale Repertory Theatre, University Theatre, New Haven, 2020), the first production of the play in over twenty-five years in the city, also invited offensive mechanisms my way unintentionally. For example, at an event at the Repertory Theatre's artistic director's home to meet and greet other instructors and students, a faculty colleague and I talked about entering into the field of theatre and performance studies through a conservatory and a graduate school, respectively. Regrettably, I confided in them that in a required course on PhD dissertation proposals in the graduate school at Princeton University, the instructor asked me if the history of Black theatre started with Hansberry's play. I thought it was a stupid question, especially since the person asking me knew that Langston Hughes's and Zora Neale Hurston's musicals were my objects of study. "It's a terrible play," my faculty colleague interjected, before adding, "I don't know why we're even doing it ... it's not even one of the better Black plays." This faculty colleague went on to say, "I'm surprised to hear you say that," when I noted that Hansberry's drama was one of my favorite plays of all time. What I found particularly pernicious was that this person knew that I was teaching a course on Black women playwrights that fall, in which Hansberry's last plays figured prominently. They also knew that I was set to work as one of two dramaturges on the production of *A Raisin in the Sun* at the Rep that spring.

The exchange reminded me of ad hominem personal attacks I overheard from a distinguished alumnus who came to deliver an invited lecture at my school. According to this person, Lloyd G. Richards, the first Black dean of Yale School of Drama (1979–1991), who plied his trade on Broadway, Off-Broadway, regional theatre, and the West End of London prior to his appointment at the School, had neither the necessary experience nor qualifications to hold that position. It must be Richards's race 'cause it ain't his résumé. I have known who Richards was since I was a child. And the gag is, I did not know who this "distinguished alumnus" was until they were introduced to me. And I still do not know who they are. I learned quickly that, though I value the history of Black theatre at the School, the field was not necessarily valued by all of my peers. Presented with an opportunity to build on Black theatre history that was made possible by Richards's appointment, I renewed a vow then to teach MFA student dramaturges criticism, history, and theory at the School, but Blacker. For example, I created the course, "Black Theatre History in the Making at Yale School of Drama," to teach my students early dramatic works by early MFA student playwrights. Also imparted in the course is the history of Black theatre at the School, from when John M. Ross entered in 1931 as the first Black student in the then-department to when the late Richards exited in 1991 as the first Black dean of the now-school. As a result, such offensive mechanisms have reanimated my work as an artist and a scholar in offering MFA student dramaturges Black theatre history courses.

Wooden: Are there myths about Black people and theatre history that you think we need to dispense with?

Glover: Yeah, absolutely. For one, I am sick and tired of going to the theatre and seeing plays by and about Black people who know nothing about their history. I experienced erasure for the first time when my college roommate and I went to see Tanya Barfield's *Blue Door: A Play with Original Songs* in 2006 at Playwrights Horizons. I was enjoying the show until an extended moment of direct address in which the central character, a middle-aged instructor, is confronted by a spirit. Were it not for the fact that I was in the middle of the orchestra and in a seat for which I had paid top dollar, I would have walked out of the Peter Jay Sharp Theatre if I could have because of the centering of white constituent audiences at the expense of the centering of Black constituent audiences in the scene: "You got a buncha white people sitting up in your head being your audience. You livin' under a White Gaze. And, to be clear, if you think Black folks gonna wanna haul their asses into this theatre—I'm talkin' 'bout this theatre—watch you deny life, where they suppose [sic] to sit down and not talk back then, brother, you are sorely mistaken. And it's time to take a look at that" (Barfield 2007: 17). While other theatregoers were eating the scene up, there I was, smack dab in the middle of the orchestra, incensed. Do you know what it's like to be alienated at the theatre? To enter excited at the prospect of a new play, only to realize fifteen minutes into it that the playwright had not even anticipated you dramaturgically? I do not begrudge those Black playwrights writing for white audiences, but I wish they would let a brother know ahead of time so that he can stay home. That experience with erasure led me to develop a close reading practice that pays attention to the plays that cast me out and invite me in.

There was a meet and greet after the performance with Reg E. Cathey, who played the instructor, and André Holland, who played the spirit, at which Barfield made a beeline for Corey and me. I realized that I was not Barfield's target audience when she asked me how I had heard about the show and, intrinsically, it did not seem to register to her that Black people frequently go to the theatre:

TB: *(Veiled curiosity.)* How did you hear about us?
Glover: On the Internet.
TB: *(Suspicion.)* But how did you hear about us?
Glover: On the Internet.
TB: *(Scorn.)* But how did you hear about us?
Glover: *(Disapproval and side-eye.)* On the Internet.

The processes of dramatic composition and theatrical representation alone do not account for Black people's erasure in the audience. Musical theatre writers and playwrights learn racial stereotypes and internalize them in their musicals and plays because of the persistence of myths about Black people and theatre history that will not die. What is ironic is they are cathected to the very same racist and white supremacist ideas about Black people and theatre history they resist. That Black people do not frequently go to the theatre. That Black people cannot afford to, even. And yet, Tyler Perry's musicals charge as much as, if not more than, Scott Rudin's—and sell out consistently. If I read another story in the *New York Times* where a Black playwright perpetuates the narrative that Black people do not frequently go to the theatre, I'm going to scream. Black people do frequently go to the theatre. Some of us don't like musicals and plays about white people's problems or musicals and plays that neglect the Black gaze.

I encounter just as much hostility and opposition to Black theatre history from Blacks as I do other non-Black people of color and whites. Instructors in a liberal arts college setting are bound by the limits of academic freedom, but instructors in a conservatory setting are bound by the limits of performance pedagogy and professional development: "For years, Black professors have experienced exclusion from, and marginalization within, their disciplines because of their race and because of their willingness to debunk myths and pseudo-science about race" write Stephen C. Finley, Biko Mandela Gray, and Lori Latrice Martin in response to what they recognize as matters of racial battle fatigue in higher education (Finley et al. 2019: 3). In addition, Blacks for whom knowing everything *but* Black theatre history is a point of pride desperately seek to conscript others into their antiblackness. A Black BFA student actor once told me that performing in the plays of August Wilson would be far less rewarding artistically than performing in the plays of Arthur Miller. They, by their own admission, knew the former in name only and only knew the latter because of the uncritical acceptance of the canon. Now that I teach in a conservatory where MFA student artists go on to promising careers, I tell students not to forget about Black people when they begin to develop their works. It's important to me as a dramatic critic.

Wooden: To return to your comment about developing a close reading practice that attends to whether a theatrical text casts you out or invites you in, can you say more about what that might look like? Are there particular criteria that you use to make your assessments?

Glover: I still believe that putting on historical plays by and about Blacks who like and love other Blacks—and not in the abstract—remains a truly necessary act. As George C. Wolfe argues, there is much at stake in representing the Black theatrical past: "Given the dynamics of this country, you may find yourself at a point where your story is no longer valuable, acute, or attractive, and if it hasn't been recorded, if you haven't recorded it or if you haven't put into motion people to record it, then it won't be there" (Rowell 1993: 612). I taught myself everything I know about Black theatre history in college and graduate school (though that need not be the case for everybody). If students were to learn about Black theatre history from slavery and freedom to the contemporary period, then students would see that historical Black artists perfected the art of writing for different audiences simultaneously. I would it were so that the Black artists working in the present did just that, not the same old, same old, yet again.

I have developed what I like to call "The Glover Test" ironically. Whereas the cartoonist Alison Bechdel wants new films to pass The Bechdel Test with flying colors, I want new musicals and plays by and about Black people to fail The Glover Test. To evaluate a play over and against this test is to take note of its characters, events, and given circumstances. If representational Black death were all it took to bring down a white supremacist regime around us, then *Ragtime*, in which Sarah and Coalhouse Walker, Jr. are murdered, would have eradicated police brutality already. The more I go to the theatre to see musicals and plays on Broadway and elsewhere, the more I see musical theatre writers and playwrights falling into the same old traps dramaturgically:

The Glover Test

1   acts of violence should take place on stage to teach basic emotional life lessons—about antiblack racism and white supremacy—that do not take
2   a Black performer should break the fourth wall to directly address their audience and misrecognize them as white constituent audiences despite the demographic data
3   a Black performer should disparage Black constituent audiences for engaging in call-and-response, a serious breach of good breeding and obedience that exhibits poor etiquette
4   a play by and about Black people should include white performers in speaking parts/roles claiming and occupying as much space and time as possible

The fact that these tropes, designed with the white gaze in mind dramaturgically, recur as often as they do speaks to the unlearning that we need to do as a community if the American theatre is to become more inclusive. What I like about early Black dramatic works—such as Eulalie Spence's *The Fool's Errand* (1927), the first play by a Black woman to be produced on Broadway, through W. E. B. Du Bois and the Negro Little Theatre Movement—is that they anticipate and take the Black gaze seriously. To teach early Black dramatic works, then, is to show my MFA students other ways of telling a story about Black people theatrically.

To return to an earlier point, you put on *A Raisin in the Sun* because of the affective and cognitive powers of representational visibility over those that see the production. Hansberry, in a classic play relevant as ever to today's world, chooses to handle her Black constituent audience with care, so much so that she sees us and we see her too. In the foreword to James V. Hatch and Errol G. Hill's *A History of African-American Theatre*, Richards, writing about the affective and cognitive powers of representational visibility, argues that in his experience:

> I certainly never read a chapter in a theatre history book on the Black theatre in America. Nor did it appear on any of the required or suggested reading lists that I encountered. Purposefully or carelessly we were being educated toward the fact that we did not count. It is a wonder that I survived my education to spend my life in the theatre. (Hatch and Hill 2003: xii)

Richards complements and complicates widely accepted theatre history by showing instructors and students the right way to take our Black constituent audience's gaze seriously. Hansberry's *Les Blancs, The Drinking Gourd, The Sign in Sidney Brustein's Window*, and *What Use Are Flowers?* represent the breadth and depth of her storytelling, which is always already worthy of in-class discussion. The larger point is one that bears repeating: *A Raisin in the Sun* was and remains one of the best, if not the best, stage works in the canon of great literature.

II A Different Account

Glover: The politics surrounding canon formation—and, indeed, the idea of the "canon" itself—have been of great concern to many African American artists, scholars, and teachers. For those of us who study and teach Black drama and theatre in particular, contending with the various ways that antiblackness manifests in these conversations becomes central to our work. Thinking about your own pedagogy, what resources and strategies have you turned to for inspiration to thwart and trouble efforts aimed at perpetuating and reifying a very narrow understanding of what constitutes the dramatic canon?

Wooden: Let me first say that art has consistently taught me how to feel more deeply, think more sharply, teach more generously, and live more boldly. It is for these reasons that I regularly turn to the work of other artists for insights on honing my pedagogy. I want to reflect briefly here on the practices of two artists who have not only been instrumental in exposing and unsettling for me the white supremacist logics that often animate the process and practice of canon formation but have also encouraged me to reflect on ways to preempt the perpetuation of antiblackness in my teaching and creative work. The first person I want to turn attention to and acknowledge for the inspiration he has provided me on these fronts is multidisciplinary visual artist Fred Wilson.

I have been an admirer of Wilson's work since first encountering his sculptural installation *Grey Area (Black Version)* (1993) on one of my many excursions to the Tate Modern in London. Tracing its origins to the 1993 Whitney Biennial—which remains notorious for the frenzy it generated amongst the art establishment's self-appointed, mostly white, critical gatekeepers—the piece's five individually-mounted, monochromatically-painted plaster replicas of the Egyptian queen Nefertiti's iconic bust exemplify Wilson's broader commitments to activating debate about the assumptions and beliefs that continue to structure how we determine and perceive what is significant, valuable, and/or meaningful. While Wilson has demonstrated these commitments throughout his career, he has perhaps done so most spectacularly in what art historian Huey Copeland calls his "site-specific museum interventions" (Copeland 2013). Among the most critically discussed and celebrated of these "interventions" is the exhibition that the artist presented at the Maryland Historical Society (in conjunction with The Contemporary Museum), entitled *Mining the Museum* (Figure 5.1).

Figure 5.1 Fred Wilson (b. 1954). *Metalwork 1793–1880*, from *Mining the Museum*, 1992–1993 by Fred Wilson. Courtesy of the Maryland Center for History and Culture.

Opening on 4 April 1992—24 years after a racist assassin murdered Martin Luther King, Jr. in Memphis and just a few short weeks before the acquittal of the four police officers captured on video brutally beating Rodney King would spark widespread outrage and unrest throughout Los Angeles—the project marked a watershed moment in Wilson's practice and in the broader conversation about the politics and culture of museum display. Remarkably, by scouring the vast collection of artifacts and objects that the Historical Society kept hidden away in storage—fugitive slave posters, iron shackles, an authentic jailhouse whipping post, and a Ku Klux Klan hood, among others—and strategically placing them on view alongside some of the pieces favored and displayed by the museum, Wilson served "to illuminate the ways in which museums constitute their publics from a white hegemonic perspective" (Copeland 2013: 20). He also provided important lessons about the suppressions and denials that make possible the triumphalist narratives museums often convey—lessons that, for me, also inspired new ways of thinking about theatrical canon formation and the attendant investments in spinning triumphalist narratives about the trajectory of dramatic literature and theatre history.

Glover: Wilson's sculpture, *Guarded View* (1991), from two years earlier, is one of my favorite artworks because he highlights the ways in which museums see and treat us not as museumgoers but as guards meant to be seen and not heard. When the sculpture circulated as part of a traveling exhibition in the

Figure 5.2 Fred Wilson (b. 1954) ©. *Guarded View*, 1991. Wood, paint, steel, and fabric. Dimensions variable. Gift of the Peter Norton Family Foundation. Inv.: 97.84a-d. Whitney Museum of American Art, New York, NY, U.S.A. Digital image © Whitney Museum of American Art/Licensed by Scala/Art Resource, NY.

1990s across the country, Wilson followed, dressed up as a guard, only to be ignored by museumgoers admiring his work. I have also found Wilson helpful for creating and maintaining visual literacy as a theatre artist in the classroom and in rehearsal and performance (Figure 5.2).

Wooden: Yes! And, Wilson would notably bring many of these lessons into even greater focus in *Speak of Me as I Am*, the 2003 installation he created to represent the United States at the 50th Venice Biennale. Drawing its title and inspiration from the Italian city's close association with one of Shakespeare's most iconic characters, Othello, the Moor, Wilson assembled works that brought attention to the ways that "the African, the Black, the Negro, the Moor remains an unacknowledged yet constant lingering presence in Venice, inhabiting both its past, as seen in Venetian visual culture, and its contemporary life," as art historian Salah M. Hassan puts it (Hassan 2004: 16). He, for example, enlisted a Senegalese street vendor to sell one-of-a-kind merchandise outside of the exhibition's venue (an act that would notably attract the attention of the police) and framed its main entrance with two large-scale banners featuring photographs of the Black figures

Melchior Barthel sculpted for the monument to Doge Giovanni Pesaro housed in the tourist hotspot, the Frari. In so doing, he reminded attendees of the ways that the Black presence is quite often *hidden in plain sight*—in both the past and present. He also further underscored the capacity of Blackness to challenge the conventions and assumptions forestalling our access to the lines of inquiry, interpretation, and meaning that a thoughtful engagement with it inevitably opens up. In so doing, he further opened up vital questions for me about ways I might fully embrace the idea of Blackness as intervention in my pedagogical and creative work.

Glover: That's such an interesting interpretation and meaningful revelation. I'm curious to learn more about the second artist who has inspired you.

Wooden: Toni Morrison is the second artist I want to turn to here briefly. Morrison has no doubt provided similar reminders as Wilson in and through her influential body of work. Indeed, a literary giant amongst literary giants, Morrison's ability to render the lives and souls of Black folk with incredible grace, depth, and beauty is certainly singular in American letters. Every single page of her virtuosic novels reveals and reflects the deep and profound care and dedication with which she crafts worlds and gives language to characters that reaffirm the brilliance and perseverance of Black people. While there are a million examples from her fiction that I could surely pull from to illuminate the ways her creative output reveals how an engagement with Blackness often inspires and necessitates the development of new styles, grammars, and categories—and, concomitantly, new ways of knowing, thinking, and creating—I want to draw attention to the challenges she boldly poses to the status quo in her critical writing.

As scholars Angela Davis and Farah Jasmine Griffin observe in an essay they published soon after their cherished friend's passing in 2019, Morrison's literary achievements often garner the most praise from admirers of her work, and rightly so. Nevertheless, "her political vision—using language to combat the devastating effects of white supremacy, sexism and all dehumanizing ideologies—remains a profound and underexplored aspect of her identity and impact" (Davis and Farah 2019). For me, Morrison's political vision achieves particular clarity and resonance in the studies on literature she carried out throughout her career. *Playing in the Dark: Whiteness and the Literary Imagination*, which she originally published in 1992, a year before she was awarded the Nobel Prize in Literature, has proven especially generative and instructive (Morrison 1992).

Morrison supplies many rich observations in the book about the central, though often unremarked-upon impact of race in the makings of the American literary canon. Significantly, she reveals the folly of a view shared among many white literary historians and critics: notably, what they regard as "canonical American literature" is somehow fundamentally "free of, uninformed, and unshaped by the 400-year-old presence of, first Africans and then African-Americans in the United States" (Morrison 1992: 4–5). Such a view, Morrison points out, runs counter to all of the evidence affirming the crucial role that Blackness and Black people have played in shaping the nation's founding myths and documents and, correspondingly, its history, culture, and identity. The Black presence (or what Morrison refers to as the "Africanist presence") has equally been critical to developing any sense or idea of "American literature" as a coherent category. Much as Wilson does with his "site specific museum interventions," Morrison illustrates just how prevalent and pervasive this presence is and, correspondingly, makes the case that *not noticing* it requires active effort. Of course, it is *not noticing*—and, indeed, actively suppressing—the Black presence that enables the conflations of "whiteness" and "quality" that remain so central to and present in many of the conversations on canonicity.

Glover: Your thoughts on Morrison's and Wilson's works remind me that the study of Black theatre is incomplete without the study of literature and culture. I cannot truly know Langston Hughes the musical theatre writer and playwright or Zora Neale Hurston the actress and the choreographer, for example, if I do not know Hughes the poet and Hurston the folklorist too.

Wooden: Oh absolutely. I have certainly discerned a lot from Wilson and Morrison's wide-ranging creative practices too. While I draw attention to some of their work here, in part, to show appreciation for the ways they have brought me tremendous pleasure over the years, my primary aim is to acknowledge and think through how they have made *not noticing* an impossibility for me. There are no doubt countless ways that both artists' work have encouraged and empowered me to pursue the kinds of interventions that might aid in refashioning and reframing what I have been inculcated over the years to believe and accept as the standard, status quo, or norm. I have particularly benefited from the reminders and calls they have provided to understand and treat antiblackness as a project, one that only endures because too many of us often refuse to recognize and confront the ways we are complicit in advancing and sustaining its aims, especially in our teaching.

Glover: I'm curious: Has Wilson's work in the museum helped you reconsider, in any way, how you teach your students a play like George C. Wolfe's *The Colored Museum* (1986)? What about Robert O'Hara's *Bootycandy* (2014)? Or Jordan E. Cooper's *Ain't No Mo'* (2019)?

Wooden: That's a really great question. And, absolutely. Wolfe's dramaturgical practice has been as impactful on my pedagogy as Wilson's artistic and museological practices. I have long argued, in fact, that Wolfe's *The Colored Museum* is one of the most important and influential experimental theatre texts of the twentieth century. I find it both notable and telling, correspondingly, that the play rarely receives mention in most projects that claim to trace the history of experimental theatre and drama. Wolfe not only inaugurates a personal commitment to defying conventions and challenging tastes and expectations with the play, but he also provides rich evidence in his dramaturgy of the ways this commitment might be mobilized by others to open up fresh possibilities for theatrical and aesthetic innovation. The play's importance, to my mind, is perhaps best measured by and reflected in the various dramas it has inspired over the years, which include O'Hara's *Bootycandy* and Cooper's *Ain't No Mo'*. What I find compelling about both plays are the ways that they draw on and extend the formal and dramaturgical risk-taking Wolfe displays throughout his text to venture their own bold, rich commentary on Black history, life, and experience.

Glover: I want to pivot back to your point about confronting antiblackness when and where it emerges. In my experience, white allies have no identity outside of thinking that they are superior to Black people whom they see as their inferiors. When they meet a Black person who is gifted, who does not apologize for who they are, and who has confidence that they do not have, they feel unmoored and turn violent. Have you had similar experiences in your career?

Wooden: Certainly. And, to be sure, I myself have not always been as forceful about calling out antiblackness as I strive to be. Indeed, I can recall offering very little pushback when, early on in my teaching career, a well-meaning colleague suggested that I should revamp a syllabus that I designed for an introductory dramatic literature course because, in their view, the inclusion of several plays by people of color made the readings seem more appropriate for a special topic, "cultural studies" course. Perhaps even more egregious was the time that I said nothing when, while serving on a search committee for a new faculty hire, a colleague openly expressed concern that a candidate was likely a one trick pony who was "only good at the *Black* thing"—this, despite the candidate's experience and materials indicating a range of knowledge and depth of expertise that far exceeded that colleague's own. It is noteworthy that, in both instances, the colleagues expressing these problematic ideas were also people who considered themselves advocates for making the classroom and broader university community more diverse, equitable, and inclusive. When presented with opportunities to challenge the white supremacist status quo, they chose instead to become agents working on its behalf. Through my silence, I no doubt had too.

In looking back, what I have come to take away from episodes like these (which, to be sure, I experienced as deeply harmful and painful in the moment) are the ways they compelled me to become more thoughtful and self-reflexive about how I might take up the charge of folks like Wilson and Morrison—Wolfe too—who, through their work, continue to call us to cultivate and engage strategies and practices that not only expose the ideological and material workings of antiblackness and white supremacy but also serve to dismantle them.

Glover: How does this connect back to the original question about the canon?

Wooden: To the question of the "canon" and ways we might further upend investments in it, I just want to advocate that we continue to answer Wilson and Morrison's calls to *notice* and *intervene*. Among the most meaningful ways that I do this is by situating Blackness at the center of all the work that I do as a theatre artist, scholar, and teacher. This means fully embracing the ways that an engagement with Blackness and Black presence can further upend investments in the teleological narratives that too many of us spin in our classrooms, rehearsal spaces, and scholarly writing about the trajectory of dramatic literature and theatre history. It is a narrative that gets reinforced when, say, we only include one or two works by Black theatre-makers on our syllabi and frame those works as representative of the diverse array of theatrical texts that constitute the aesthetically capacious category of Black drama. I don't think it is an accident that the exploration of these works is often relegated to the final weeks of the course. It bolsters the idea that Blackness is, at best, marginal and, at worst, irrelevant to the history and development of the dramatic canon and, more broadly, the theatrical art form. Part of what returning to the work of figures like Wilson and Morrison helps to illuminate, I think, is just how misguided continuing to adopt such an approach is. Surely, it is as misguided as declaring that racism in America is over (as so many, including the linguist and provocateur John McWhorter, did in the aftermath of the election of Barack Obama in 2008 [McWhorter 2008]). Like Wilson and Morrison—and scholar Sara Ahmed too—my commitment is to spotlighting the "different accounts of the world" that centering Blackness in my work can engender (Ahmed 2013). At this point, I am much more interested in bolstering these "different accounts" and appreciating all they have to offer us, than I am in trying to recuperate the canon to make it more capacious and inclusive.

Works Cited

Ahmed, Sara. 2013. *On Being Included: Racism and Diversity in Institutional Life*. Durham: Duke University Press.

Barfield, Tanya. 2007. *Blue Door: A Play with Original Songs*. New York: Dramatists Play Service, Inc.

Copeland, Huey. 2013. *Bound to Appear: Art, Slavery, and the Site of Blackness in Contemporary Art*. Chicago: University of Chicago Press.

Davis, Angela and Farah Jasmine Griffin. 2019. "Toni Morrison, Revolutionary Political Thinker." *New York Times*, 7 August. Accessed 10 May 2020. https://www.nytimes.com/2019/08/07/opinion/angela-davis-toni-morrison.html

Finley, Stephen C., Biko Mandela Gray, and Lori Latrice Martin. 2019. "Endangered and Vulnerable: The Black Professoriate, Bullying, and the Limits of Academic Freedom." *Journal of Academic Freedom* 10: 1–17.

Gutiérrez y Muhs, Gabriella, Yolanda Flores Niemann, Carmen G. González, and Angela P. Harris. 2012. *Presumed Incompetent: The Intersections of Race and Class for Women in Academia*. Boulder: Utah State University Press.

Hansberry, Lorraine. 1959. *A Raisin in the Sun: A Drama in Three Acts*. New York: Random House.

Hassan, Salah M. 2004. "Fred Wilson's Black Venezia: Fictitious Histories and the Notion of Truth." *Nka: Journal of Contemporary African Art* 19: 12–19.

McWhorter, John. 2008. "Racism in America Is Over." *Forbes.com*, 30 December. Accessed 10 May 2020. https://www.forbes.com/2008/12/30/end-of-racism-oped-cx_jm_1230mcwhorter.html#394b935949f8

Mitchell, Koritha. 2018. "Identifying White Mediocrity Know-Your-Place-Aggression: A Form of Self-Care." *African American Review* 15, 4: 253–262.

Morrison, Toni. 1992. *Playing in the Dark: Whiteness in the Literary Imagination*. New York: Verso Books.

Pierce, Chester. 1970. "Offensive Mechanisms." In *The Black Seventies: Leading Black*

Authors Look at the Present and Reach into the Future, edited by Floyd B. Barbour, 265–282. Boston: Porter Sargent.

Richards, Lloyd G. 2003. "Foreword." In *A History of African-American Theater*, by James V. Hatch and Errol G. Hill, xii–xiii. New York: Cambridge University Press.

Rowell, Charles H. 1993. "'I Just Want to Keep Telling Stories': An Interview with George C. Wolfe." *Callaloo* 16, 3: 602–623.

Wooden, Isaiah Matthew. 2019. "The Complex Racial Politics of *Smart People*." *Modern Drama* 62, 2: 171–190.

6 Amidst the Rubble of the Ivory Tower

Sara Brady

When Richard Schechner first published "Performance Studies: The Broad Spectrum Approach" in 1988, his provocative statement challenged theatre departments to wake up to the larger context of Performance Studies (PS). That call evoked a body of work, a set of examples, a "spectrum of performances" that exceeded conventional/traditional definitions of theatre. The project reflected a larger move toward an understanding of expressive behavior that went beyond the privileged position of "theatre" and challenged the conservative trends of theatre departments that had to seek legitimacy from larger university systems for so many years. "What needs to be added" to performing arts curricula, Schechner writes,

> is how performance is used in politics, medicine, religion, popular entertainments, and ordinary face-to-face interactions. The complex and various relationships among the players in the performance quadrilog—authors, performers, directors, and spectators—ought to be investigated using the methodological tools increasingly available from performance theorists, social scientists, and semioticians. (1988: 5)

Theatre, in other words, lives within the larger world of performance together with so many more examples of physical, cultural, and social expression.

Years later, in *Performance Studies: An Introduction*, Schechner summarizes the broad spectrum as "Compris[ing] everything from stage acting and ballet dancing to arguing a case in court to displaying different emotions by smiling, weeping, frowning, or glaring in anger" (2020: 76). Divergent performance forms overlap:

> Performing onstage, performing in public ceremonies, and performing in everyday life are a continuum occurring in widely divergent circumstances, from solo shows before the mirror to large-scale public events and rituals, from shamanic healing to identity-shifting trances, from theatre and dance to the great and small roles of everyday life [...] This broad spectrum of performing is a continuum, each category leading to, and blending into, the next [...]. There are no clear boundaries separating

DOI: 10.4324/9781003031413-6

everyday life from family and social roles or social roles from job roles, church ritual from trance, acting onstage from acting offstage, and so on. (2020: 77)

To take on the broad spectrum means to include performances that leave the conventional (legitimate) proscenium and go … out into the streets. If the canon is "a sanctioned or accepted group or body of related works,"[1] the broad spectrum was intended to be *anticanonical*, more repertoire than archive (Taylor 2003). The brilliance of the broad spectrum was the call to think outside of the box—to "see" other performances that are equally valid subjects of study. The broad spectrum challenges us to consider examples less "sanctioned," to consider performances that not only take place outside proscenium theatres but that may be created by people who don't have, use, or care about proscenium theatres. In other words, theatre studies assumed the privilege of the college student who had access to the proscenium, which the broad spectrum asked us to look beyond.

Now here's the problem: the broad spectrum asked us to look beyond but failed to deal with that same assumed privilege of the college student. What I argue is that that project never took on the privilege of higher education—it always assumed the student who would study all of these other performances would still be the privileged university student. A discussion of the canon—in terms of the introductory theatre or PS class—needs to not only embrace the broad spectrum; it must admit to a fundamental truth: theatre studies only makes sense to the privileged who have been to the theatre. Schechner asked us to leave the proscenium, but never to leave the ivory tower. The broad-spectrum approach, therefore, leaves behind a true reworking of the canon by never acknowledging the shifting realities of higher education. The contemporary US college student is more often than ever before not white (between 1976 and 2017 "the percentage of [w]hite students fell from 84% to 56%"), not male (56% female in 2017), and not in the ivory tower (more than one-third of undergraduate students in the US are now enrolled in two-year schools) (see NCES 2020). As the economic foundation of elite colleges crumbles, community colleges remain an affordable degree option and most definitely the future of undergraduate education (see Cohn 2019 and Mintz 2019). College itself has left the ivory tower. And it's time for the broad spectrum to acknowledge that reality.

The canon isn't just problematic because of all those white men but also because it's full of texts that inhabit and embody privilege. Diana Taylor takes on this problem in "Acts of Transfer," where she points out that performance "is not, like theatre, weighed down by centuries of colonial evangelical or normalizing activity" (2003: 15). Performance, on the other hand, "carries the possibility of challenge, even self-challenge, within it" (15). Wouldn't the radical move then be to challenge the privilege inherent in learning theatre and PS? But those conversations happen every day in the academy, don't they? I argue that there is something missing from those arguments. PS claims to be an area of academic scholarship that is conscious of its conscience. Taylor writes:

> By taking performance seriously as a system of learning, storing, and transmitting knowledge, performance studies allows us to expand what we understand by "knowledge." This move, for starters, might prepare us to challenge the preponderance of writing in Western epistemologies. (2003: 16)

PS values cultural diversity and expressive behavior. PS validates the marginalized and the powerless. If we really look beyond conventional theatre with the broad spectrum, why don't we acknowledge the privilege that goes with so much higher education? What about the broad spectrum of education? If we leave the proscenium to consider unconventional examples of performance then we also need to rethink what higher education is, but more importantly, what higher education can do.

Let me explain. The context that I teach in is an open-enrollment public community college: Bronx Community College of the City University of New York. BCC is located in one of the poorest Congressional districts in the US (see Segers 2020). 98% of the student population is of color. 72% receive financial aid. 40% of the students live in households with incomes less than $15,000/year, and, not surprisingly, 37% are food-insecure (see BCC 2021). My Introduction to Theatre class at Bronx Community College can't be taught in any traditional manner. My students come from an extremely diverse and often poor population. To assume that conventional theatre is a point of reference assumes too much. At BCC the broad spectrum is not only about considering unconventional examples of theatre; it's about opening the stage to a larger and more inclusive set of student perspectives. What I've discovered in my own teaching at a public, two-year, open-enrollment institution is that we begin with a broad spectrum not only of performance but also of education.

I've taught there since 2011. It's not where I thought I would build a career after completing a PhD in PS at NYU. But the truth is, my NYU training is precisely the reason I found a real sense of duty at BCC that I never felt teaching so-called traditional college students. I was drawn to the job in particular after giving a sample teaching lesson where I first met students who are as confounding as they are amazing. I soon learned, after a semester with them, that they are some of the strongest people I have ever met. Many are not born in the US; more than a few are undocumented; a good handful are veterans; some are homeless. Most, however, have been underserved by the disaster that is the NYC school system. 64% of BCC students need remediation.[2]

When I started at BCC, Introduction to Theatre was a course taken only by the Liberal Arts Performing Arts "option" students—that is, students getting an associate degree in liberal arts with a concentration in performing arts. I remember how shocked I was to learn that "performing arts" was a privileged subject at BCC: until CUNY's academic restructuring (CUNY Pathways) in 2013, students in the most dire financial circumstances, receiving the most aid, were not allowed to choose the Liberal Arts Performing Arts degree (see Nightingale et al. 2002: 51). When I first taught the course, I thought the students were joking when a few told me they had never seen a play. One student, who was from Palestine, insisted he didn't know what theatre was. I put on my PS hat and challenged him: "sure you do: you've seen a football game, right?" and he finally smiled; he had something to talk about that interested him. I went with it, but he still shot me down, explaining that the soccer he watched was only on TV and never live. Another student in that same section was from Togo. She sat with a neutral face and explained to me that she shouldn't take the class because she didn't know anything about theatre. She too had never seen a play. Trying to convince her that she knew enough about performance to join the discussion was far more difficult than any PS course ever prepared me for. The foundation of the discussion was not there. What seemed so obvious to my own privileged mindset—the move from the proscenium to the street, from the West End to the West Indian parade—fell flat. There was a translation problem that wasn't really linguistic. For Taylor, "the problem of untranslatability [...] is actually a positive one, a necessary stumbling block that reminds us that 'we'—whether in our various disciplines, or languages, or geographic locations throughout the Americas—do not simply or unproblematically understand each other" (2003: 15). I found her proposal "that we proceed from that premise—that we do not understand each other—and recognize that each effort in that direction needs to work against notions of easy access, decipherability, and translatability" (15) made sense, but I was discovering that really living the kind of challenge that a PS paradigm allows is not only complex but rare. Taylor begins with such hope for performance:

> Civic obedience, resistance, citizenship, gender, ethnicity, and sexual identity, for example, are rehearsed and performed daily in the public sphere. To understand these as performance suggests that performance also functions as an epistemology. Embodied practice, along with and bound up with other cultural practices, offers a way of knowing. (2003: 3)

Amazing, right? This is everything—this is where we need to be—acknowledging and analyzing the knowledge in embodied practice! I still could not articulate what was missing, because what was missing was the translatability of the privilege of higher education. I couldn't use the same terms, the same series of steps, to bring my students with me. I had to go farther from the proscenium than I ever imagined.

In the early days, I would brag that my marginalized, diverse population of students knew so much about performance, from carnival to sports to religious and secular rituals. And then I realized how short-sighted that was in an essentialist, ethnocentric, even racist way. I would assume things: The Caribbean students will know carnival, which I thought I knew something about (why? Because I've attended a Caribbean carnival once?). I would get in front of the students with talk of all the theatre and performances *I* knew about. I would encourage students to seek out free ticket offers without realizing things like: not every student of color is comfortable in every NYC theatre space. I once had a student who did nothing with the extra ticket she had for a popular Broadway show. I was shocked! Why didn't you just stand outside and find someone? The student laughed and told me she would never do that. Too risky.

I've been trying to negotiate this tension now for years in an open, honest, and humble way. Because there *was* unique knowledge that my students came to class with. I've had students who undertook the Hajj; I had two students who lived much of their lives in a refugee camp in Albania. They were used to that knowledge being undervalued. The BCC student population has significant numbers of students born outside the mainland US (the CUNY community college average is 37.9%)[3] It took a lot of effort, but I finally started to devise lessons that took on representation and cultural expression as a way into theatre and performance. I started to listen a lot more, and the truly diverse group of students spoke first-hand about cultural traditions far from the mainstream of hegemonic white privilege. I was embarrassed, ashamed, but also delighted. Because the broad spectrum came full circle for me: not only was it important to consider performance outside of theatre; it was the only way forward. And to not teach from a broad spectrum perspective was literally an insult to my students.

I used to think my intro class was so innovative; that it was a true theatre–PS hybrid; that I brought down the Western canon because I was cool. Now my class continues to adapt; what began as a lesson on Carnival has become a regular class-sharing presentation project; I've read performance reviews of middle school choirs in the South Bronx and Togolese weddings. I've encouraged my students to go to free and cheap performances all over New York City, and so many have come back to tell me they saw things they never thought they would, from protest performances to a pole-dancing *Rent*. Some things have remained: the lesson on commedia dell'arte is always a favorite because students love discovering that a centuries-old tradition is still alive and well in television sitcoms; our discussions of wrestling, dance, and cricket get better every semester. And, as I've relaxed a bit and listened more, I've realized that sometimes the quietest students are ones who have seen more Broadway than I, thanks to some impressive NYC school programs. I've also had some of the most interesting requests for paper extensions, from court dates to homelessness, from going into labor to being called up to escort former Secretary of State Colin Powell. Nothing surprises me anymore.

In my latest rendition of the class, I had to create a custom syllabus for an independent study for one student, an extremely bright young woman who earned straight A + s for all of her classes at BCC shortly after immigrating from Yemen. She avoided the "Creative Expression" CUNY requirement until it was about to stop her from graduating. She "couldn't" study art, theatre, music, or anything creative for that matter. It was against her religion. After several conversations and much consulting with her family, she finally agreed to my independent study version of Introduction to Theatre, where she took on her own robust research project on theatre and performance in Yemen, where, she initially told me, there was no theatre.

I first met this student—we'll call her Nadia—in an introductory communication class several semesters ago. On the first day, I approached the classroom with my regular physical and mental preparation for the start of another semester. I suddenly hesitated before opening the door--through the door's glass window, there was Nadia, sitting in the front row, literally covered in black. Thoughts flew through my head: cultural relativism; this is OK; who makes her *wear that?* How will I be able to communicate with her? How will she give a speech in class (it's required!)? As I crossed the room to the computer podium, I caught her eyes, and, even though I couldn't see her whole face, I could tell she was smiling. I was disarmed. Nadia introduced herself early on in the class discussion. She had only been in the US for two years; she was extremely nervous about her English, she told me. I could tell immediately that her skills were not that different from many students for whom English was not their first language. I found out later that she only attended school through eighth grade and had taught herself English and taken the GED to get into community college. She was only 17. Nadia not only put me at ease; she quickly began to teach me.

After that first communication course—in which she delivered a well-researched and well-rehearsed speech in front of the class—Nadia often visited my office hours and updated me on her accomplishments. She wanted to pursue a healthcare career so that she could return to Yemen and serve the people and place she knew. I looked at her impressive progress on her transcript and reminded her that she still had not fulfilled the "Creative Expression" requirement. In her serious but always optimistic way, she replied with some reason why she "didn't need" one of those classes. It wasn't until her graduation audit that the problem became real. I had a conference call with Nadia and her mother to explain what Introduction to Theatre entailed; we went almost lesson by lesson through the semester and several times Nadia muted herself as she discussed with her mother whether the content would be appropriate. Finally, we came to an agreement for Nadia to complete an independent study theatre class. I adapted my regular course to Nadia's abilities and needs, and, although I've already created a course that supposedly avoids Western bias, I thought my customization for Nadia was, well, something else.

Again Nadia taught me how wrong I was. I gave her a variety of readings (a boring textbook was definitely not enough); she tore through journal articles, playtexts, and translations. Since I tried to provide context from Arabic theatre studies, I often assigned scholarship from that area. But Nadia would, to be blunt, rip it apart. She would bring in historical context and research that upended the static given of introductory theatre and PS. I kept thinking about how theatre and performance are supposed to show, to reveal, to express, and how Nadia's own sense of self as her own performer in everyday life was both spectacular (in that it's not mainstream US American to wear a niqab and it's much more obvious than many other religious customs) and at the same time invisible—private, unseen (in that she is still visually opaque to me).

When I had her look at a reading on women in Arab theatre, she critiqued the critics, pointing out the context they don't understand about the Arab world and about women in that world. She repeatedly inserted the historical realities of the complex Middle East—imperialism, corruption, war, resource depletion. She had little time for an outsider view, a Western interpretation. What remained, for her, and for me reading her responses to what she read, was a reminder that the truth about Western bias is that it's so pervasive that "we" really cannot get past it. She brought my attention to the absurdity, for example, of Yemeni actors performing Shakespeare soliloquies amidst the rubble of Sana'a. In this short film project called "Shakespeare in Yemen," the actors, whose lives were upended by the war in Yemen, came together and probably took a significant risk to perform Shakespeare in Arabic and discuss the "meaning" of doing so. Unlike the actors, Nadia saw little connection between the texts and the stories of these actors' lives in war-torn Yemen. As I watched the video again after reading her critique, I felt like a blindfold had been removed. I could suddenly access what she meant: there was something completely ridiculous in their project. They didn't need to do it. There was something absurd in the translation and recitation of Shakespeare among the debris of a bombed-out city. Why did these actors need this badly to show that Shakespeare is relevant? What if they really didn't have to? What if we really did look without an agenda at theatre and performance around the world?

Nadia's story is distinctive and enlightening and challenging and uplifting. But her story is just one of so many others that have convinced me that it's time for those who teach theatre and PS to recognize that the privilege inherent in what we teach is so deeply embedded that the humility required to engage with the broadest spectrum is going to take an enormous amount of work. The first step is the most difficult one: we need to admit there is a problem, which is difficult for academics to do. We need to admit that the ivory tower isn't all it's cracked up to be; that we need to tear it down once and for all. Let's admit that there's so much we haven't read because it's not translated; that there are so many performances that we have never seen. Let's go back in the classroom grateful, open-hearted, and ready to work. Let's get comfortable amidst the rubble of the ivory tower.

Notes

1 *Merriam-Webster online*, s.v. "canon," accessed 12 December 2020, https://www.merriam-webster.com/dictionary/canon.
2 It is worth noting that CUNY has essentially ended remedial classes. See https://www.highereddive.com/news/how-colleges-are-reshaping-remedial-education/557120/.
3 See https://www.cuny.edu/wp-content/uploads/sites/4/page-assets/about/administration/offices/oira/institutional/data/current-student-data-book-by-subject/ug_student_profile_f19.pdf

Works Cited

Bronx Community College (BCC). 2021. "Facts and Figures." Accessed 23 January. http://www.bcc.cuny.edu/about-bcc/facts-figures/.

Cohn, Scott. 2019. "The Other College Debt Crisis: Schools are Going Broke." *CNBC*, 3 December. Accessed 23 January 2021. https://www.cnbc.com/2019/12/03/the-other-college-debt-crisis-schools-are-going-broke.html.

Mintz, Steven. 2019. "Community Colleges and the Future of Higher Education." *Inside Higher Ed*, 9 March. Accessed 23 January 2021. https://www.insidehighered.com/blogs/higher-ed-gamma/community-colleges-and-future-higher-education.

National Center for Education Statistics (NCES). 2020. Fast Facts: Enrollment. Accessed 27 December 2020. https://nces.ed.gov/fastfacts/display.asp?id=98.

Nightingale, Demetra Smith, Nancy Pindus, Fredrica D. Kramer, John Trutko, Kelly Mikelson, and Michael Egner. 2002. "Work and Welfare Reform in New York City During the Giuliani Administration: A Study of Program Implementation." Washington, DC: The Urban Institute Labor and Social Policy Center.

Schechner, Richard. 1988 "The Broad Spectrum Approach." *The Drama Review* 32, 3 (Autumn): 4–6.

Schechner, Richard. 2020. *Performance Studies: An Introduction*, 4th ed. London: Routledge.

Segers, Grace. 2020. "It's the Poorest and Bluest Congressional District in America. An Anti-gay, Pro-Trump Democrat is Leading." *CBSNews.com*, 22 June. Accessed 30 January 2021. https://www.cbsnews.com/news/ruben-diaz-sr-conservative--democrat-could-win-primary-in-bronx-new-york-district/.

Taylor, Diana. 2003. *The Archive and the Repertoire: Performing Cultural Memory in the Americas*. Durham, NC: Duke University Press.

Part II
Remixing Traditions

7 Shaking up the Canon with Cornerstone and OSF

Bill Rauch and Sonja Arsham Kuftinec

When I (Bill) applied for the position of Artistic Director at the Oregon Shakespeare Festival (OSF), I talked about how its work brought together multiple strands of my life: the American classics (Williams, Odets, Miller) that I watched as a child at the Westport Country Playhouse, the European classics that I studied in college (Brecht, Chekhov, Lorca), and the new community-based plays—like *The Pretty Much True Story of Dinwiddie County* (1987)—that I had helped develop with Cornerstone theatre Company.

When I (Sonja) first started attending Cornerstone and later OSF productions, I noted how they repeated, transformed, and blew open the theatrical canon as I knew it from my suburban New England high school, rural college, and community musical theatre experience. I witnessed Faust as a family of seven in a Watts community center, Brecht adapted to a post-LA uprising context, Macbeth in a three-ring circus with Cinderella and Medea.

Canons have power, especially in theatre, where we often revisit dramatic stories. The plays in these canons viscerally tie us to history, like the mirrored lineage of Banquo's progeny in *Macbeth* (c. 1606).[1] At the same time, mirrors refract as they reflect; and Hamlet's advice to the Players dwells on the theatre's capacity to hold the mirror not to ourselves, but to human *nature* and to time itself (III: 2). To do so suggests an invitation to shift the lens, play with images, even alter poetics and poetry. To lean further into this metaphor, the emotional connection we feel to the familiar can also obscure who and what may be left out of our canonical lineages, beyond the frames of our mirrors.

In this chapter, we explore and model challenges to canonicity through the lens of two companies led by Bill Rauch: Cornerstone theatre Company (1986–2006) and OSF (2007–2019). We do so in conversation with each other and with the notion of "canons," a conversation we have been having together as artist-producer and scholar-audience for the past quarter-century. Through this dialogue, we deepen our communion with one another as well as with the thousands of years of theatre history that form multiple canons. We consider specific projects that represent three avenues of shaking up the canon: (1) re-examining classical texts that are commonly accepted as canonical (*Hamlet*; *Oklahoma!*); (2) expanding our understanding of the classical canon within and outside of the boundaries of Europe and the United States; and (3)

DOI: 10.4324/9781003031413-7

creating new works (from often marginalized voices) that redefine the notion of canon and push back against institutions like OSF that sustain canonicity.

To engage these conundrums around theatrical canonicity, we dive into "canon" as a term. Like Shakespeare's clowns, we tune in to the aural playfulness of language—the way that "canon" suggests not only rules and variations but also explosions.

According to John Guillory, "canon" descends etymologically from the ancient Greek *kanon* or "reed," used as an instrument of measurement. That notion of a "kanon" as measure later developed into the sense of "rule" or "law" and, in the 4th century CE, came to refer to a list of Biblical texts or authors. In this usage, the term carries meaning as a "principle of selection connoting worth or value" (1990: 233). That principle, Guillory argues, is both sustained and shifted via institutions such as university English departments or, we would add, US regional theatres. While carrying a sense of "rule" and value, canon can also connote variation. In musical terms, the canon, or round, can be playful: inverted, augmented, and dynamized, tripping through elaborated variations around a familiar melody line. Finally, cannons as projectiles (through tubes or "reeds") can blow holes through foundations, clearing the way for new formations. We take up these canonical variations as a way to think through Cornerstone and OSF's theatrical responses to canonicity.

We begin by considering two distinctly valued genres—Shakespeare and the American musical—with a note about expanding canons to include a Sanskrit classic. We focus on arguably the most canonical works in each category. In both *Hamlet* (c. 1600) and *Oklahoma!* (1943) canonicity relies on a blend of repetition and innovation. *Hamlet* takes up a familiar "revenge" plot and steeps it in meditations on consciousness through heightened verse. With *Oklahoma!* Rodgers and Hammerstein craft what has become marked as the emergence of the integrated musical, though still relying on the "rules" of heterosexual relationship arcs forged within a white settler-colonial framework. We examine two distinct productions of *Hamlet* directed by Rauch that differently poke at its rules and revelations, reference canonical expansion via *Mṛcchakatika* (*The Little Clay Cart* c. 5th century CE), and then consider OSF's gender-bending queer take on *Oklahoma!* in order to tease out the notion of canon as both measure and variation. In each case we ask: what does it mean to shake up the rules of theatre?

A. Navigating Canonical Rules with *Hamlet* and *Oklahoma!*

Hamlet is perhaps the most canonical drama in the Western oeuvre—a play considered of great "worth and value" (in Guillory's formulation) in part because of its numerous reproductions. Yet, while seemingly settled, there is no one stable editorial text. And companies rarely, if ever, stage the production "word for word." They cut, rearrange, tweak, and make casting, design, and staging choices to engage distinct thematics. *Hamlet* is thus both reiterated and altered each time it is produced. It is in many ways a "ghost story," haunted not only by the title character's royal father, but also by its genealogy as a revenge tragedy, and its abiding questions of what we inherit and owe to our ancestors (including the source texts that Shakespeare drew upon). Like Ophelia's open grave, housing bones of the previously interred, the play evokes a palimpsest of critical readings and theatrical renderings. Despite (or perhaps because of) its iterability, *Hamlet* carries weighty assumptions. Within the institutional space of OSF, *Hamlet* has been lauded, foundational to the theatre's sense of identity and cultural currency with audience members, many of whom check off Shakespeare plays on a Canon in A Decade passport. Yet outside of such spaces, *Hamlet* is haunted by a quite different set of assumptions, associating Shakespeare with detached drama obscurely enunciated by men in tights.[2] It was this latter connotation that prompted the nascent Cornerstone theatre Company to break some rules with a 1986 production of *The Marmarth Hamlet* in rural North Dakota.

Bill—what would you say are some reasons you chose Hamlet in North Dakota and what were some of the canonical rules Cornerstone valued and breached in this production?

We pulled up on the dirt Main Street of the Badlands town of Marmarth, North Dakota (population 190) having already decided that we were producing *Hamlet*. We chose *Hamlet* because we thought there might be an interesting connection between the text set in Denmark and the largely Scandinavian roots of the [*Sonja: current*][3] inhabitants of this butte-marked part of the world; the regional dialect of [*settler*] North Dakotans has a distinctly Scandinavian lilt. Perhaps we were simply seeking an intellectual justification for the fact that, as so many young theatre artists before and after us, we wanted to tackle one of the greatest of the "great" plays of The Canon. In the end, however, the regional dialect used by the local cast members lent a great sense of local authenticity to the production. It was one of the most important ways that Cornerstone joyfully broke what felt to us like an industry-standard rule of "mid-Atlantic speech," of what we rejected as a charade of pretending to be in some nether world in the Atlantic ocean, "mid-"way between England and the US. We instead embraced the specific reality of time and place in how rural late-20th century [*settler*] North Dakotans sounded as they made almost 400-year old verse into their own language. [*Bill: Thank you so much for your necessary emendations—yes, yes, yes.*]

So, you broke the rules around accent. But what about the canonical text itself? Why invite this small town to return to a 400-year old tale rather than creating a new story?

Although we would eventually develop an iterative community-rooted process for determining content (in part inspired by Roadside theatre's story circles), and would often create original work with communities, in Cornerstone's earliest years our ensemble selected the source texts. In addition to wanting to wrestle with the "great works" ourselves, we hoped to connect often geographically isolated and low-income communities with the richness of our common theatrical legacies and to illuminate those stories by doing so. At the outset, however, our community auditioners challenged us on the inaccessibility of the archaic language. We helpfully pointed out footnotes, but the retort was immediate: "the audience won't be reading those." We tap-danced about clarity of acting choices and clever props to illustrate meaning, but our community collaborators' response would re-set Cornerstone's course. "If you kids really want to reflect our community, why don't you just change the words?" This was blasphemy to our Ivy League-educated selves, breaking the cardinal rule of the canon. Even with vivid characterizations and plots, most practitioners and scholars would argue that the energy of "Shakespeare" radiates from *the language itself*. In many ways, Shakespeare *is* the language.

So ... to keep the play, you chose to break its canonical rules around language. How did you determine what to keep and what to alter? How did the community respond?

Our belief in our mission and our respect for our collaborators won the day and in one quick week, we rewrote *Hamlet*. We substituted inaccessible words, often with contemporary slang, but we kept the verse structure and even the "thee's" and "thou's" intact. We then gathered our community cast to read aloud our version. The next morning, a rancher/cast member knocked on the door of our railroad bunkhouse to quit. "I can't be in this play Saturday night and stand in front of the kids as a Sunday school teacher the next morning." His issues were not just what would later be called our "smart-ass college humor"; it was also about Shakespeare's language and its relation to church rules. "When Hamlet calls 'O God God,' is he praying or is he blaspheming?" If we couldn't answer the question, the rancher wouldn't be in the play. An emergency meeting of the town Historical Society was called, and we found ourselves around a table with a group of elderly ranchers and their wives. We had marked up a script; blue post-it notes for our words that might trigger dissent, pink for Shakespeare's. We ended up sitting back and listening to the community have a debate with itself about the spoken and unspoken "rules" of their society and of art-making. Men might use some of these words, but not in front of the women. Women might use some of these words, but not in front of the men. Even conceding that some of this language might be accurate, doesn't art have a moral purpose to show a sanitized version of life? Or is its larger purpose to show the complexity of life as it is? It was then that our community partners turned back to us: we needed to get beyond our collegiate swear words and instead choose language that reflected their local rural culture. For instance, we had substituted "downright prick" for "arrant knave"; our community partners suggested "horse's rear." Our next draft was more collaborative, and the rancher/Sunday school teacher didn't quit. Although it wouldn't be for a few more months during our residency in West Texas that we would hit on the obvious next aesthetic step to actually set the adaptation in the community itself, the Cornerstone adaptation of a classic was born on the buttes of North Dakota.

That's a well-told tale! Although, you might say that you actually sustained the canon through linguistic shifts and community co-creation. Could you argue that Cornerstone's "disruptive" adaptations in fact reiterated the centrality of the Western canon? What does it really mean for Cornerstone to break the rules of theatre?

We were indeed reiterating the centrality of the canon, but I would argue that we were also deeply challenging the canon by changing its very DNA, the language itself. We would go on to disrupt the Western canon in other community-based adaptations of "heavy hitters": Molière in Midwestern farmlands, Aeschylus on a Paiute reservation, Brecht in a Pacific Northwest timber town, Chekhov in coal-mining country, and Ibsen in abandoned sardine canneries on coastal Maine. We'd return to Shakespeare a few more times. In our bi-racial *Romeo and Juliet* (1989) in a segregated Mississippi town, "what's in a name?" became the somewhat awkward but charged "what's in a skin?" Casting often drove our adaptation choices. The abundance of prospective female cast members in Port Gibson led to a complete matriarchy with Lord Capulet becoming Juliet's grandmother "Mamaw Capulet" as well as a female Tybalt. For *The Winter's Tale: An Interstate Adventure* (1991)—which brought together participants from Cornerstone's first five years of community residencies—we informally polled non-scholars and learned that the vast majority of US Americans [*inaccurately*] believed that "thee" and "thou" were formal, while the more contemporary "you" was informal. We decided to boldly swap the second-person pronouns throughout our adaptation, changing every "thee" to "you" and singular "you" to "thou." We broke the rules, constructively building on a common misunderstanding; such was the fierceness of our commitment to accessibility. And yet … the idea of upholding white supremacy by upholding the "canon" is a topic we'll get to deeper in our dialogue. We must. I promise myself and you and our readers.

In my view, Cornerstone learned to navigate a set of relationships with communities and canons. Within those negotiations, community and its networks of relationships became animated through performance.[4] But I'm still thinking about when a "fierce commitment to accessibility" ends up sustaining the canon, especially in a settler "American" framework that can elide the complexity of colonization.[5] [In support of what you're saying, and frankly in part inspired by your questions over the years, Sonja, we evolved our mission language from "American" to "the

United States"—although of course, even the construct of the United States is problematic and complex.]

Though Cornerstone worked with several Native communities, the company initially centered [European and American] classics. I know Cornerstone later shifted this practice—crafting original tales with community, expanding the stories told to non-Western drama like The Little Clay Cart. *The company was relatively young and nimble, with the capacity to shift modes of textual adaptation and storytelling, changing the rules of engagement with communities. How did that navigation around sustaining and breaking the "rules" of canonical texts and their reception change when you moved to OSF—a much more established, canonically centered, and larger institution? What does it mean to break and sustain the rules of theatre in that space?*

Variations on a Sanskrit Classic

Before dwelling with that major institutional shift, I want to sustain the theme of variations within Cornerstone. We moved to Los Angeles in part to build bridges *between* as well as *within* communities—arriving just before the city's 1992 insurrection in response to the acquittal of officers charged with brutally beating an unarmed Black man. As one strategy in our larger effort to reinvent ourselves into a multi-racial company, we sought to broaden our definition of classics beyond those of Europe and the United States. The first text we adapted in Southern California was *The Little Clay Cart,* a 1,500-year-old Sanskrit city comedy attributed to King Sudraka. The central love story unfolds between an impoverished Brahmin and a courtesan, but the packed plot also involves a corrupt leader, a fugitive political revolutionary, and a gambler on the lam who becomes a Buddhist monk. Little did we know how resonant aspects of the plot would be, as auditions began the Monday after the L.A. uprising (Figure 7.1).

Another connection emerged unexpectedly in regards to language. Produced at the Angelus Plaza, the nation's largest housing project for low-income senior citizens, many of our cast members were monolingual speakers of languages other than English and so our adaptation included characters who spoke in Spanish, Mandarin, Korean, and Tagalog as well as English. (Only retrospectively did we learn that the original play had been performed in multiple dialects that were essentially different languages.) Much of our creative energy in producing what we called *The Toy Truck* (1992) went into communicating the story with clarity across boundaries of language. Banners in all four languages (other than English) offered a brief synopsis of each scene. As various audience "plants" took turns complaining about their language being insufficiently represented, our Chorus Leader would not only explain a key plot point in the appropriate language but also eventually recruited the complainants into a dancing chorus, using devices such as giant arrows to introduce new characters in as many as four languages.

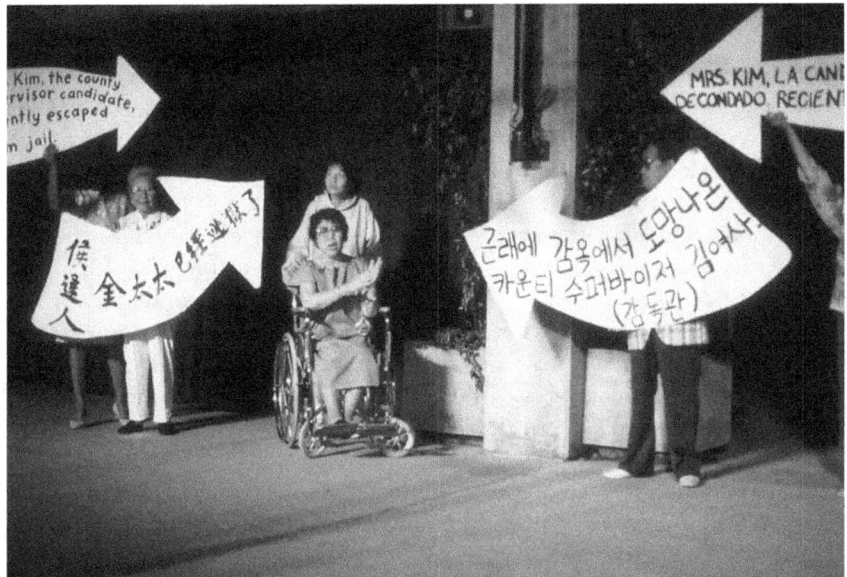

Figure 7.1 The Toy Truck (1992). Angelus Plaza *Credit:* Lynn Jeffries.

Sixteen years later, I found myself back in rehearsal for a production of *The Clay Cart* (2008), this time as the first production in my inaugural season as the artistic director of OSF. After 20 years with Cornerstone, my curiosity about working on a different scale and with different aesthetic concerns had led me to make a transition. As a new artistic director, I wanted to expand how the country's largest-scale classical theatre defined "classics," and so we made the bold decision to run *The Clay Cart* all season long in a slot that had been traditionally devoted to US and European comedies (Kaufman and Hart, Coward, Wilde, etc.) To produce a 1,500-year-old Sanskrit text at all was transgressive, but to run it 120 times broke all the rules of what an American classical theatre should program.[6] In a well-intentioned move that I would later regret, we cast the production "like Shakespeare" with a full representation of our multi-racial acting company, including actors who were white, Black, Latinx, Asian American, and mixed race. It was not until years later when OSF hosted the bi-annual conference of the Consortium of Asian American theatres that I publicly acknowledged that we had engaged in the problematic practice of propagating yellowface casting. It took time and mentorship by brilliant colleagues of color for me to fully understand that, within the white supremacist culture of the United States, casting white actors to play characters in a South Asian classic was absolutely *not* aesthetically or morally equivalent to casting actors of color to play characters in a European classic.

We've talked at length about what I think of as OSF's "color conscientious" casting and its distinction from "color blind" casting.

Yes, my predecessors at OSF had established a long-term commitment to racially diverse casting in Shakespeare. During my tenure, we expanded casting to include disabled actors and speakers of languages other than English. For example, a deaf actor performed *The Music Man's* (2009) song "Shipoopi" in American Sign Language and the text of *La Comedia of Errors* (2019) was 50% Spanish. Unlike in previous OSF eras, casting of classics might also *highlight* race and gender (when that felt appropriate to the storytelling), or explore gender as performative (as Shakespeare does so brilliantly in plays like *Twelfth Night*). However, while audiences tended to accept many of these innovations in Shakespeare, some struggled more actively and vocally with casting disruptions in classics of the American canon. In my first season as artistic director, a multi-racial *Our Town* (2008) on our flagship outdoor stage was greeted with surprising resistance. "You wouldn't cast white actors in August Wilson," was a common argument I heard, one that dramatically reveals a lack of understanding of the unequal racial playing field in American theatre and culture at large (Figure 7.2).

You bet. As embedded in its very name, OSF *exists* to uphold the Canon, in particular the work of William Shakespeare. Over the 12 years of my tenure, as a producer or director, I oversaw productions of almost every play attributed to Shakespeare. Although OSF would go on to commission contemporary "translations" of the entire canon through the *Play on!* program, most of our rule-breaking with Shakespeare in this more established institutional space involved interpretive choices through production. In directing *Hamlet* in 2010 I sought to expand artistic possibilities through multiple rule-breaking innovations: through staging (Hamlet alone on stage with his father's casket for the entire pre-show or Hamlet instructing the Players from the booth behind the audience); through textual rearrangement (soliloquies were embedded into scenes while the rest of the cast froze); through casting (Rosencrantz and Guildenstern as a lesbian couple); and through the introduction of a hip hop aesthetic (Hamlet's favorite Players from his university town were a hip hop troupe). In what seemed to augur well for my tenure, *Hamlet* played to 99% of capacity for its 120-plus performances. Not even the die-hard audience pilgrims whose families had come to Ashland for generations seemed to blink at a hip hop Player King and Queen.

It's so interesting to consider which innovations are deemed "acceptable" and what changes audiences and institutions resist. It seems that struggles to accept shifts in casting or season curation can illuminate unspoken rules around who or what gets centered. Within that framework, how did the introduction of musical theatre to OSF play out?

Shaking up the Canon 111

Figure 7.2 Passport for OSF's "Canon in a Decade" featuring all of Shakespeare's plays. The Tudor Guild, Oregon Shakespeare Festival. *Even with conscientious casting, aren't there limitations to expanding (or exploding) the canon of classics within a theatre that quite literally centers Shakespeare?*.

112 *Bill Rauch and Sonja Arsham Kuftinec*

Rule-breaking is always about context: we broke a big rule in turning to Golden Age musicals at OSF—for introducing what some might think of as "middle-brow" fare into the "high" cultural space of a Shakespeare Festival. But as a closeted queer kid growing up in suburban 1970s America, musicals offered a safe haven. Even though I know that classic musicals can reiterate problematic tropes around gender and race, their storytelling often feels to me generous and even utopic. The heightened and rigorous style, the direct audience address, and the breaking into song seem complementary to Shakespeare (who so often uses music in his plays). So, after some initial institutional resistance, and then successfully introducing musicals like *The Music Man* (2009), *Guys and Dolls* (2015), and *The Wiz* (2016) to our OSF audiences, I wanted to tackle a more radical intervention. Actually, this was a decades-long obsession. The story of a queer *Oklahoma!* as canonical variation begins for me in high school.

High school is so often the space of inauguration into the Golden Age canon and its paradoxes around queer inclusivity, heteronormative representation, and the conundrum of what Stacy Wolf refers to as "racial drag". (2019: 3)

Yes, I was a horrendously miscast Ali Hakim in my senior year of high school, which is when Rodgers and Hammerstein's classic musical first entered my psyche. As "canon" musicals began to be interpreted with racially diverse casts, it struck me that interpretive taboos remained around gender and sexual orientation. Could relationships that were conceived as heterosexual be reinvented as queer? What if Laurey and Curly were both women, Will and Ado Andy were two men, and a transgender Aunt Eller was the moral pillar of an LGBTQ-inclusive rural community that encompassed chorus members who would explore their non-binary and gender-fluid identities?[7] In fact, it was *because* the musical rigidly foregrounded gender that this approach to *Oklahoma!* felt possible, even necessary. Could we, with casting choices and some simple pronoun changes, contemporize and broaden the inclusive reach of this canonical musical? When I dared to articulate my vision to a few colleagues, I was warned that it would never happen, not with the R&H estate and especially not with their most iconic work. So, I privately nursed my dream for 25 years. Adapting the work of a writer who has been dead for four centuries is a very different proposition from wanting to radically interpret the copyright-protected work of living or more recently deceased authors. This kind of intervention requires a distinctly different institutional navigation (Figure 7.3).

After a careful and long courtship *[what a word, Bill!]* that built on our prior relationship around *Medea/Macbeth/Cinderella* (discussed below), the historically cautious Rodgers and Hammerstein estate granted permission for this bold reinvention—a respectful period production with minor textual changes. Despite significant fears from some corners, the 2018 production was a box office "hit" as well as an artistic success. In fact, *[in contrast to your closeted high*

Shaking up the Canon 113

Figure 7.3 *Oklahoma!* (2018). Will Parker (Jordan Barbour) wonders if the intentions of Ado Andy (Jonathan Luke Stevens) are of the marital variety. Photo by Jenny Graham, Oregon Shakespeare Festival.

school experience] school groups waved rainbow flags from the audience in response to every same-sex kiss. Over the course of its joyful run, we realized that we had recreated the conditions of what made the musical so groundbreaking in 1943. [*White*] Americans at the height of World War II needed and embraced Rodgers and Hammerstein's optimistic view of a *[particularly imagined]* inclusive American community. Seventy-five years later, at an especially dark and fraught time in terms of our partisan politics, our revolutionary rendition gave audiences a chance to feel optimism about a new kind of inclusive American society. I would posit that, by disrupting the tropes of the gender binary, we had honored and revitalized the *spirit* of the musical's original authorial intent.

(*A beat*)

Before I (Sonja) ever saw a production of *Oklahoma!* I grew up listening to the cast album in my family's rural New Hampshire summer cabin. Songs of cowmen and surreys, of shotgun weddings and emergent states, are imprinted in me as deeply as the grooves of that vinyl record. My Croatian-born father's father sang opera professionally in Europe. So, like the early 20th-century Jewish immigrants who crafted the American musical, its songbook affected our family's acculturation to American ideas. Musicals offer a mode of myth-making built on integration and democratic community as well as erasure and exclusion.[8]

I say all this to you, Bill, because it's part of a conversation we've been holding since we met. I celebrate the ways you expanded the community of *Oklahoma!* including the title song reprise choreographed with a Native spiral dance. At the same time, I challenge the limits of inclusion that remain. Your production certainly gestured not only to queer inclusion but also to the erasure of Indian Territory (through allotment and theft) preceding the state. And I love how you encouraged choral ensemble members to name themselves and craft ethnic and gendered back-stories. As you have noted, these choices spoke to the diversity actually present in the early 20th-century Oklahoma Territory. At the same time, the production drew attention to enclosures and constraints. Yet, even your inclusive conception required Jud's communal banishment and death, sealed with the civic ritual of a hastily staged trial exonerating Curly. In this queer utopian imaginary, certain characters still can't be integrated. And perhaps intentionally, the hasty trial felt uncomfortably close to how the US negotiated treaties as mock legal ways to claim territory and transform land into property.[9] *[All valid observations, Sonja, but it is also important to note that our production's community intervened to save Curly, a Black queer woman, from the likely racist and homophobic traditional "justice" that awaited her.]*

(*Another beat.*)

We've considered together what it means to break the canonical rules of theatre by revisiting *Hamlet* in North Dakota, *Oklahoma!* in Oregon, and *The Clay Cart* in Los Angeles. We have wondered about whether these interventions and expansions end up re-centering classical drama. In varying the canon, we've also considered what kind of rule-breaking audiences demand, resist, and, sometimes surprisingly, celebrate. We've begun to think through the role of institutions in sustaining and shifting canons. Bill, maybe we need to get at this question of theatrical rule-breaking and canonical variation from another perspective. Let's together relate the story of *Medea/Macbeth/Cinderella*—a piece crafted from three title-character plays representing what your mentor Peter Sellars referred to as the three great populist movements of *[Western]* theatre: Greek Tragedy, Elizabethan Drama, and the Golden Age American musical. What does this meta-theatrical experiment—that interweaves canonical works by Euripides, Shakespeare, and Rodgers & Hammerstein, and has been

Figure 7.4 Title characters Macbeth (Jeffrey King), Cinderella (Laura Griffith), and Medea (Miriam A. Laube) in *Medea/Macbeth/Cinderella* (2012). Oregon Shakespeare Festival Photo: Jenny Graham.

produced *[so far]* across four decades at Harvard, Cornerstone/The Actor's Gang, Yale Rep, and at OSF—tell us about canonicity? (Figure 7.4).

B. Variations on Canonical Hauntings: *Medea/Macbeth/Cinderella*: A polyvocal fugue in three columns

A ghost light flickers on a stage. Or in a college dorm basement. Or a repurposed industrial space. We hear the whispers of three title characters eternally performing, launching their intertwined struggles of power.

Bill: A casual comment from Peter Sellars lit a match. What alchemy might come from mashing together three pillars of 2,000 years of Western theatre history? I had ambitions.

> **Sonja:** I kept returning: LA, Yale, rehearsals in Ashland. Wrestling with the keys to this production; this meta-story.

Bill: The astonishing ensemble work of the Wooster Group shook me. A company experimenting with form to retake the rhythms of tales previously told. Could I leave a mark my final college semester by working with an *ensemble* on one epic, chaotic undertaking?

"In my own little corner, in my own little chair, I can be whatever I want to be…"

Sonja: How would they do it this time? Teach the rules of each genre and the Inter-dependence of theatrical rhythms?

The dagger Macbeth "sees" is clasped at first in Medea's revenge-plotting hand, then in Cinderella's, who pares an apple while imagining her envious stepsisters turning "a queer sort of sour apple green."

Sonja: How would they relate the Meta-Story of Universal Suffering and of the ensemble telling these stories? Ambition meets hubris as title characters move up or down a three-level stage! Would there be disassemblage? Elaborate costumes mapping the distinctiveness of each world—women in half-masks, men in doublets, a technicolor medieval fairy tale—gradually shed. The ensemble in stage blacks fluidly transforming from Birnam woods, to Greek choral mourning, to a line of squealing women eager to try on a glass slipper.

"When shall we three meet again?"

Bill: Who owns the stories? Who are the gatekeepers? I needed the key.

Sonja: Yale Dramaturg Mark Bly says the "fourth story"—the Meta Story told through the interweavings of three title character tales—is about Time.

Bill: For the first time, I overestimated the aesthetic adventurousness of the OSF audience. We'll need to try again.

"Why must a man always be seeking something?"

Sonja: How will you tell the story this time, Bill?

Bill: The tales return again and again, within and outside this production, overlapping, ever-repeating, always with variations—like the contrapuntal compositional technique of a "canon." *M/M/C* is a tale of obsession, for the characters and for many of us who have worked on it. Ripping out pages and laying them side by side on my dorm room floor, having my young mind blown that the Macbeths' banquet falls at the same point in the story as Cinderella's ball. Tracy Young joining as co-adapter and co-director when she was with The Actors' Gang in L.A., becoming as haunted by the challenges as me James Bundy boldly inaugurating his distinguished tenure at Yale with *M/M/C*! "It's about how men keep fucking up the world." I couldn't wait to share it at my home theatre in Ashland, so confident that OSF's passionate theatre-loving audience would embrace this event unequivocally. I've still not fully recovered from their mixed response. As I conjure these memories, the Perelman Center—which I now artistically lead—forwards an email advocating for a future production of *M/M/C* ... "The experiment is in radically juxtaposing what's accessible times three." Almost 40 years after the original college venture, I am as moved as I've ever been by the uncanny synchronicity that *M/M/C* reveals and what it says about the shared rhythms of storytelling across cultures and millennia. And yet, the project centers Eurocentricity in a way that's made me increasingly uncomfortable with its potential irrelevance, perhaps even its danger. On the other hand, Cinderella has many ancient "cousins", including from Asia. All of these stories are told and retold and retold.

This is the power of the canon. Which keeps mutating to stay alive. To stay alive within us and for us ... For "us?"

C. Can(n)ons

BOOM! When is a can(n)on a weapon to uphold white supremacy—guarding culture from on high? The playbill expands but some patterns remain. Performance slots are not equal: which titles can run all season long or "sell" all those outdoor seats? Only in the twelfth of twelve seasons do two new plays by contemporary writers of color run all season long.

BOOM! When Lear speaks of a woman's genitalia as "the sulfurous pit," when a "brow of Egypt" is the opposite of what is to be admired in beauty, when we are supposed to sigh with relief that the boy who fell in love with another boy is actually a girl after all (although still a boy actor, at least back in the day) ... how often has the can(n)on been used to blow holes in the self-confidence of young people of color, of young queer kids? Is it an exaggeration to raise the idea of *carnage* caused by the weapon of the can(n)on? Is it the fault of the texts themselves that they have been weaponized, or our educational and producing institutions that uphold the notion of can(n)ons? Who is responsible for turning plays into cultural weapons? Has the time come to tear down these monuments? Maybe we need to acknowledge and/or create new can(n)ons to blow holes in the existing ones. Decenter the [white] [artistic] director. The singular playwright. The rules of institutional representation.

BOOM! The season selection process at OSF—called *Boarshead* as a reference to the joyful, chaotic confluence of humanity found in Falstaff's favorite tavern—expands beyond department heads to include carpenters, stitchers, ushers. Younger voices with less organizational power end up having some of the strongest input.

BOOM! In OSF's 75th anniversary season, Audience Development Manager Freda Casillas confronts the two executive leaders: they are painfully out of synch on their values when it comes to building new audiences. After months of soul-baring meetings, an Audience Development Manifesto is created that will guide the organization's next decade of work.

BOOM! American Revolutions: The United States History Cycle. Commissioning 37 plays reflecting on transformations in what has come to be called America. In 2010, the "Revolutions" launch with Culture Clash, a Chicano ensemble. *American Night: The Ballad of Juan José* conjures a dreamscape of hundreds of years of events on this soil playing out the night before a citizenship test. It's a public conversation about the "we" that constitutes US history.

Curated by Cornerstone co-founder Alison Carey, American Revolutions augments—no, explodes—no, *reinvents* the canon with new stories of Presidential politics (Robert Schenkkan's LBJ Plays 2012; 2014) and Other Americas: in Black Panthers and Young Lords (Universes' *Party People* 2012), in abandoned working-class pockets (Lynn Nottage's *Sweat* 2015), and in lesbian desire playing out across Yiddish and Broadway stages (Paula Vogel's *Indecent* 2015).

But "Other Americas" and "moments of change in US history." That's a complicated story to tell from a Native perspective … (Figure 7.5)

BOOM! It's 2019 and the 1491s bust onto the stage. We are *Between Two Knees* with this Inter-tribal comedy troupe. Literally exploding Native stereotypes. The

Figure 7.5 1491's *Between Two Knees* (Oregon Shakespeare Festival 2019): Shyla Lefner (Irma), Ensemble. Photo by Jenny Graham.

set, a collage of mascots—the Cleveland Indian and Land 'o Lakes Princess—targets at a shooting arcade. Narrator-guide Larry greets the presumptive white OSF audience. "That's what it feels to be confronted with the source of your social power... but it's ok! I promise when you leave you will still own everything." By the end, it's the Lakota Ghost Dance realized. A disco ball drops and the cast cheerily gets the audience to wave along as they sing: "So Long, White People ..."

BOOM! One year earlier, across the street from the Bowmer theatre where the queer rendition of Rodgers and Hammerstein plays. Cherokee/lawyer/playwright Mary Kathryn Nagle subverts the *Oklahoma!* frontier narrative. *Manahatta* (2018) unsettles temporal and spatial rules, moving fluidly between 17th- and 21st-century Manhattan and Oklahoma. Witness the violence of securitization and linguistic assimilation. This is no cause-and-effect march of progressive history. This is Continuous Native Presence.

BOOM! After years of foot-dragging, OSF finally adds a full-time Director of Equity. For all the progress in achieving equity in the acting company (over 70% actors of color), for all the progress in expanding the playbill, the company still hasn't produced a work by a differently-abled author or a Middle Eastern author or a self-described conservative playwright. Of course, these goals raise questions about who holds power and commands representational space. What are the inherent limitations of a large-budget classical institution with a (still) overwhelmingly white audience? In a season selection conversation, Black company members cite the lack of safety and accompanying exhaustion in having to perform certain Black narratives in front of a progressive white audience. They suggest that Black theatres might better serve these stories.

BOOM! 2019. Nataki Garrett is the first woman and the first Black leader in the American theatre to run an institution of OSF's current scale.

BOOM! 2020. "Dear White American theatre" letter is signed by multiple self-defined BIPOC (Black, Indigenous, and People of Color) theatre artists. weseeyouwat.com/statement *[Bill: I took every single sentence of that letter personally. As I should have. That is the point.]* The subsequent demands for change, a fierce blueprint for equity. weseeyouwat.com/demands *"This is a house that will not stand ..."*
Canons.
Canons. ♪♩
Can(n)ons.

What's next?

Notes

1 Macbeth refers to the "glass" held by a Kingly apparition conjured by the Witches in IV:1 (117–129). One could imagine that Shakespeare and his "King's Company" patron, King James—who claimed to be descended from Banquo—would be seated in a way that the glass reflected his own "Kingly" image back to him. This reflective moment additionally alludes to the power of theater to extend beyond the representational plane, illuminating the structures of power in which theater is so often embedded.
2 In fact, Mayor Patty Perry, who invited Cornerstone to co-create *The Marmarth Hamlet* in 1986, did so with the caveat that there would be "no tights."
3 When we intervene in each other's prose, we mark this with editorial bracketing.
4 I (Sonja) elaborate this argument in *Staging America: Cornerstone and Community-Based Theater* (2003). I draw on anthropologist Victor Turner's work. In *The Ritual Process* Turner proposes that narratives, rituals, and performances can structure and create meaning for a society. Experience becomes meaningful and complete when "expressed" or "pressed out" through the performance event (1969: 13–14).
5 The emergence of US community theater as enunciated by such early twentieth century practitioners as Louise Burleigh, Constance MacKay, and Percy MacKaye marks it as a civic practice rooted in parables of progress and Patriotic assimilation. For more see *Staging America* (Kuftinec 2003: 28–30).
6 During my (Bill's) time at OSF, we also expanded the stories told on our stages to include plays rooted in Brazilian, Chinese, Japanese, Korean, Mexican, Nigerian/Yoruba, and Vietnamese cultures.
7 In almost every rural community that Cornerstone worked in we encountered (often closeted) queer folks.
8 For more on the American musical as national folk practice enabled by the emergence of the LP record in the 1940s and by community productions in sites ranging from Jewish summer camps to Colorado dinner theaters to high schools nationwide, see Stacy Wolf's excellent ethnographic study *Beyond Broadway: The Pleasure and Promise of Musical Theatre Across America* (2019).
9 In July 2020, as we drafted our article, the US Supreme Court ruled that the Eastern half of Oklahoma remains Muscogee (Creek) territory.

Works Cited

Guillory, John. 1990. "Canon." In *Critical Terms for Literary Study* edited by Frank Lentriccia and Thomas McLaughlin, 233–249. Chicago: University of Chicago Press.
Kuftinec, Sonja. 2003. *Staging America: Cornerstone and Community-Based Theater.* Carbondale, IL: Southern Illinois University Press.
Turner, Victor. 1969. *The Ritual Process: Structure and Anti-Structure.* Chicago: Aldine.
2020 weseeyouwat.com/statement. Accessed 20 July 2020.
Wolf, Stacy. 2019. *Beyond Broadway: The Pleasure and Promise of Musical Theatre Across America.* Oxford: Oxford University Press.

8 "Yo, Let's Steal Their Canons!": Arab and Arab American Canonical Multiplicities

Samer Al-Saber and Michael Malek Najjar

Introduction

We began our discussion on issues surrounding this idea of the canon by drawing on the introduction of Najjar's book *Arab American Drama, Film, and Performance* (2015), where he suggested that an Arab American identity emerged following the Naksa (Six-Day War) and in the aftermath of the occupation of what is known today as the 1967 Occupied Palestinian Territories. Najjar claimed that 1967 was a critical moment in defining an Arab American canon in the United States, and explicitly referenced Edward Said's early beginnings as a scholar who was truly connected with his Arab-Palestinian roots. Najjar's definition of an Arab American consciousness relies on Said's essay "The Arab Portrayed," which he wrote after the Naksa. Previously Najjar believed that Said began his cultural critique with *Orientalism*, which was published in 1978. Once he read that early essay, he realized that Said was thinking about media misrepresentation of Arabs and Muslims almost a decade earlier. This, along with the formation of the Arab American University Graduates (AAUG) in 1967, led Najjar to conclude that Arab American identity was forged in the aftermath of the war Arab novelist Halim Barakat called "Days of Dust" (Barakat 1983).

This starting point puzzled Al-Saber, who often claimed that he did not believe an Arab American identity defined him or his work. While 1967 was important in Al-Saber's understanding of Arab identity, it was not crucial for a definition. For Al-Saber, political subjecthood and representation are not markers of identity as much as linguistic and cultural practices that are firmly reliant on lineage and performed cultural heritage. As scholars who share Arab Theatre as our field, we both had to contend with long-standing differences in discourses of Arab identity at home and in the diaspora. In this dialogic debate, we represent an internal conversation among scholars of Middle Eastern and Arab culture. How would Arab canons exist at home and/or abroad? Who has the right to claim a canon? Why would such canons be formed? What comes first, the Arab or the American in diasporic formations? As we argued, agreed, and disagreed on these ideas, we continued to firmly believe that they function

DOI: 10.4324/9781003031413-8

within an area of study called Middle Eastern Theatre at times, and Arab Theatre at others, whether this theatre is produced at its country of origin or in the diaspora.

The reader will notice that a central argument does not govern this chapter. Rather, we bring forward a negotiation of the idea of canon within our fields of expertise through a nuanced conversation. We debate the canon in terms of key structural criteria: identity, geography and periodization, authorship, critical intervention, and function.

Identity

Samer Al-Saber: How did you conceive of this Arab American identity as distinct from your later work in relation to Middle Eastern American Theatre? In both cases, you must have had to contend with a particular notion of the canon. I am referring to the broadest definition of the canon as the codified expression of the most notable works in a field of knowledge.

Michael Malek Najjar: It was when Jamil Khoury and I collaborated on Silk Road Rising's inaugural production of *Precious Stones* (2003) that I came to realize that I needed to focus my time and energy on plays that portray Arabs and Arab Americans. Gradually, through the work of companies like Silk Road Rising, Golden Thread Productions, New Arab American Theatre Works, and Noor Theatre, an Arab American theatre canon has arisen. I decided that I had to get Arab American plays published if they were ever to gain legitimacy in the eyes of American theatre practitioners and scholars. A post-9/11 Arab American theatre identity has arisen, but it had been there since the early 1900s with writers like Kahlil Gibran, Mikhail Naimy, and Ameen Rihani, who were also playwrights. Although their plays were primarily read, not produced, they were writing plays and contributing to the Arab cultural awakening (*al Nahda*). Samer, did you see an Arab identity emerging in a similar manner in the Middle East?

Al-Saber: Contemporary Arab identity in the Middle East and in the Americas are converging as the world gets smaller. Yet, we are continuing to contend with our history. For example, in the 1950s, the peoples of the Middle East were trying to deal with this idea of what is Arab and whether there is an Arab nation under Gamal Abdel Nasser. Does Arabness in the "Arab World" suggest a hegemonic culture or can it co-exist with other minoritarian identities? When we collect an Arab American theatre canon here in the US, do we honor or choose to erase the histories that came with us from our countries of origin?

Najjar: When I originally wrote my book I thought that I had to begin broadly, so I began with "Arab American" instead of a micro-focus on, say, Maronite playwrights from 1900s that hailed specifically from the Lebanese mountain villages. We can get really microscopic or we can pull back and say "Arab American," but of course not everyone who comes from these Arabic-speaking countries considers themselves Arab. Therefore, what do we label those who do not wish to be called Arab? What do you believe constitutes an "Arab" canon?

Al-Saber: Arabness constitutes a multiplicity of canons. After all, half a billion Arabic speakers are a critical mass that has the capacity to create significant literary and performative repertoires. What is Arab culture within the Arab world? Isn't it just culture? And yet, politically and historically, there were attempts to unify this idea of Arabness in the 50s and 60s in particular. Nasser had a vision for Arab culture that essentially erased religious and ethnic pasts in favor of a secular socialist future. Arabs listened to Um Kulthum as the quintessential Arab singer. Other singers did not openly divulge their ethnic or religious heritage. Farid Al-Atrash sang in an Egyptian accent but was Lebanese and Druze. Leila Murad was Jewish. That Nasserite experiment actually failed, despite its inherent embrace of pluralist values under secularism. Egypt exported its own brand of culture in the form of the novel, the autobiography, film, and poetry as well. Who didn't want to be like Naguib Mahfouz in the 1970s? Taha Hussein became the consummate intellectual and Tawfiq Al-Hakim theorized a quintessential Arab theatre in the 1960s. How do we contend with this idea of a pan-Arab canon in the heart of the Empire? Are we trying to reconstitute ourselves in one canon despite the pluralism of the geographies to which we belong?

Geography and Periodization

Najjar: I would like to ask you, from a historical perspective, does the idea of canon in the Middle East and the Arab World mean the same thing to the Arab World as it means here?

Al-Saber: A canon is a mechanism of exclusion and inclusion. The Arab word for canon is an Arabization of the English word. It's a construction that attempts to be definitive, but in that process, it is definitively exclusionary. In my article "Arabic Facts in Palestine," I insisted that the mere idea of a canon, particularly a modern one, is antithetical to how I see Arab culture (2014). Western modernity is intertwined with the idea of the canon. As the Euro-American modern age unleashed its technological and artistic revolutions, its intellectuals raced to define the most influential works. Modernity is not necessarily concurrent in the Arab world. Broadly, in Arabic, literature is divided in many ways historically, but also in terms of typologies, categories, and genres. Presently, there are national canons and ethnic canons. We speak of Kurdish, Arabic, and Persian poetry in the core geographical region of the Middle East. Here, these canons are determined along linguistic, perhaps nation-state lines.

Najjar: Early Maronite Christian playwrights were from the same geographic area in Lebanon. Their Maronite Christian background was the identity that held that group together. There was also the rise of various newspapers in Little Syria which were representative of other Syrian sects, and these papers also included poems and plays. Therefore, these Syrian literatures were arising at the same time, and they were forming a kind of Syrian immigrant canon. When Kahlil Gibran and his fellow colleagues formed The Pen Group, which espoused the philosopher-poet ideal, they were contributing to the Arabic literary renaissance, which was also taking place in the Levant and North Africa. It was the beginning of Arab American literature, though at the time Gibran, Mikhail Naimy, and Ameen Rihani would not have labeled themselves in that way.

Al-Saber: This multiplicity of aims is visible in Palestinian and Egyptian cultural histories as well. In both of these national contexts, for example, authors struggled against the occupation of the British mandate on the one hand, and Ottoman superiority on the other. But dreams of self-determination as a collective goal held the population together. A desire for nationalistic cohesion led writers, thinkers, and intellectuals to self-group not only in terms of aesthetic and literary styles but also in political coalitions that formed to achieve national goals. Since conceptions of Arabness are divergent in the Arab nation-state context, we must ask: must we bring these characteristics with us to the Americas as we form our canons here? Why should the canon in this geographical site be different?

Najjar: I think that's why the Middle-Eastern-American moniker has become the more prominent one now. Some are now embracing "Middle-Eastern-American," which is presenting new problems with inclusion of South Asian American writers. Aren't they Middle-Easterners as well? How do we contend with geography foisted upon us by the Western powers? Many plays emerged from the Arab world in the post-World War I period, based on colonialist interventions and nationalisms. However, it is different for different populations. For Palestinians, the 1948, 1967, and 1973 periods are extremely important; for Lebanese it might be the post-1943 independence that is the focus, while for Egyptians it might arise after the 1979 peace treaty with Israel was signed. By contrast, the Americas have a different timeline, so the events that affect Arab Americans took place during different periods such as the various waves of migration, the wars that the US has fought with Arab nations, and specific events such as 9/11. Therefore, how do we have two simultaneous canons occurring in two different parts of the world, and yet we have two different timelines that are wholly dependent upon one another?

Al-Saber: The historian necessarily addresses this canonical conundrum with the basic questions first. Just as we do with any problem, we have to determine the criteria and the available evidence. What is the period and geography of the investigation? What constitutes the range of primary sources? What makes something Arab American as opposed to Arab? That question haunts the identity of every immigrant artist. In my case, I see myself as Arab, despite my presence in the West. You and Jamil Khoury have identified an American context that embraces an "identity plus," a hybrid, which is a definition that I disagree with. I don't accept the existence of a hyphenated identity as its own separate entity. I admit to my desire to provoke rather than illuminate here, but

Americans and Arab Americans must consider a process of identification that is determined by the "and," not the hyphen: Arab and American, not Arab American. I believe that the so-called Arab American identity is simply American. The exclusion of Arabs from the American canon is xenophobic, while the exclusion of Arab Americans from the American canon is racist. Why should you go along with the master's definition of Arab Americans as non-Americans? By creating such a canon, you effectively endorse white American exceptionalism.

Najjar: Unfortunately, the canon *is* the currency by which one gains legitimacy in the Western academy. Those without a canon become *personae non gratae*. It's not ideal, but it is necessary because the rules of the game were set by the European powers, adopted by the Americans, and have become the only means by which any group can have a voice. Arab Americans write from an English perspective, and really as a translation, as a sort of bridge, between American audiences, non-Arab audiences, and Arabs who hold on to a long and proud history of Arabic literature and culture. It strikes me that the Arab American is a person either born in the Middle East or in the diaspora, but the primacy of language and experience is not necessarily Arabic. Do they believe that Arabic is their central language and the ideas flow from there, or does it come from an English, Anglophone ideal? Or a Francophone ideal? Or Spanish? Or Portuguese? However, there are those who write in multiple languages, so then how do we categorize them? It's highly problematic, and I can't pretend to say that I have a definitive answer.

Authorship

Al-Saber: The identity of the plays, the canon, the playwright, a type of theatre, and the artists involved must be located in reception, not origination. If the Arab American actually is defined by language, the primary language, then the identity of a canon lies within the originator or the author. The canon of Arab American theatre constitutes authors who self-identify as Arab but barely speak Arabic. Locating the canon's definition in the act of cultural communication or self-translation places the identity of the canon in the audience. Here, I suggest that who you are speaking to becomes the defining criteria for what makes a hyphenated identity in the theatre. An Arab American canon is fundamentally defined by the non-Arab audience that the playwright might desperately want to convince of a particular perspective ultimately for the purpose of gaining respect, inclusion, or assimilation. You might see the canon as a "speech act." Does Arab American theatre happen in the mind of the audience or is it what happens in the air between the performer and the audience member?

Najjar: Let's explore two examples: Ajyal Theatrical Group in Dearborn performs plays in Arabic using Arabic idioms and humor, and incorporating Arab performance styles including dabke dance and zajal poetry. When they travel, mostly Arabs go to see them. Arab American writers like Yussef El

Guindi, Heather Raffo, or Betty Shamieh write in English and most of the audiences that attend their plays are non-Arabs. Their plays do not contain much (if any) Arabic, do not incorporate Arab performance techniques, and rely on Euro-American theatre techniques. Few Arabs go to these plays. I've come to the realization that Arab American writers are translating the Arab experience for non-Arabs in America. In general, Arabs are not interested in that translation because they live that experience every day.

Al-Saber: These examples demonstrate that geography is a suspect criteria. If periodization and geography fail, then we must return to language. The classic and widest definition of "Arab" is "someone who speaks Arabic." That's it. You can be a Kurd and an Arab; a Persian, or Iranian, and Arab; A Turk and Arab, because you speak Arabic and you count it as a primary language for you. But then, if we accept language as the arbiter, then we have a problem here: Arab American drama is written in English, and if English is a defining language, then it is English or Anglophone or American drama.

Najjar: In a sense, but it works with Arabness, and within an Arab-centric identity. Ultimately, this is an identity that one must adopt, or it might be adopted for them. These identities and labels are ones that are both a blessing and a curse; a blessing when the community accepts these writers as their own and herald their work, a curse when they are "pigeonholed" and not allowed to write about anything but that identity. These writers are usually not fully accepted by the mainstream, so these writers must accept their hyphenated identity if they wish to have any career whatsoever. As they continue to write these works, they become categorized, anthologized, and yes, canonized. So this process is one that unfolds over time, and with that unfolding a canon eventually emerges. Some embrace the moniker "Arab American" but others find it constricting. Let me ask you, Samer, do you consider yourself Arab or Arab American?

Al-Saber: I completely and entirely operate in the United States, but I am not Arab American. I am not even American. I recently received my Green Card, and yet it is very easy for me to be defined as Arab American in the way I live here and operate as an artist-scholar. How many identities can a canon hold and still be considered unique and discrete? The problem here is that there are accepted canons but there aren't accepted criteria to create canons. Does a canon have to have an ethnic glue that holds it together? A geography? A national heritage? No canon is pure.

Najjar: We are imposing these categories upon people, but scholars have done this forever. We are creating these categories, but the question is: "is it right, is it fair, and is it correct?" Ultimately, we need an umbrella term to encompass these writers, and Arab American (for better or worse) is the one that was created, and the one that we inherited.

Al-Saber: What benefit or advantage do we get out of these impositions, as you say? Some are enamored by the idea of the canon and seek to be at the forefront of being the individuals who define it as directors, playwrights, scholars, and intellectuals. If we are of the same mindset that these categories are problematic, why do we keep doing it?

Najjar: I may be generalizing, but most Americans have very little conception of what the Middle East is historically or geographically. There are twenty-two nations that comprise the Arab world. Can we have representation from all of these places? Some might have a general idea of what's happening, or perhaps they think everyone in the Middle East is Muslim, or that it's a region beset with conflict. I think the onus is upon us of Arab descent to be translating the experience to them, especially in the academy. By creating these multiple canons, we expose those who have little or no understanding of the Middle East to the diversity of nationalities, identities, religions, and languages. Therefore, why not have an Arab American canon, an Iranian American canon, a Turkish American canon, and so on? Is that ultimately a bad thing?

Al-Saber: Naming an act, category, or phenomenon preserves it. Perhaps creating a coalition of what these phenomena are may save them. One example is in the English canon where the Shakespearean canon saved Shakespeare.

Najjar: What I find interesting about Shakespeare is that there were many of his contemporaries that were included in anthologies of Elizabethan and Jacobean theatre, but he became a canon of his own. Shakespeare festivals rarely produce works by Marlowe, Jonson, or Webster. Therefore, Shakespeare's canonization as a singular playwright overrides any canonization of his contemporaries.

Al-Saber: The collecting and archive-building happened because of his contemporaries. The canonization of Shakespeare happened through the attempt of the British Empire to civilize all the nations they've colonized. The canon was chosen as the ideal representation of English literature, something to aspire to, of which Shakespeare was of utmost importance.

Najjar: Shakespeare's works were the means by which the British could claim their greatness: "Look how great our greatest writer is; you should know this writer; you should emulate this writer, and anyone who is not this writer is, frankly, a nonentity."

Critical Intervention

Al-Saber: It's time for us to discuss the idea of using the master's tools to dismantle the master's house (Lorde 1984). Do we use canonization to dismantle Shakespeare? Does canonizing Arab American drama lead to the deconstruction of American theatre as a supremacist institution?

Najjar: Arabs and Arab Americans have been on the outside of this discussion for a very long time. We didn't have anthologies of plays, theatres of note, classes, and academic departments like others had. We were the outsiders gazing in. However, the master's tools are now becoming available. Why shouldn't we utilize those tools in order to bring these ideas to life? This canonization of theatrical literature has become another tool we can utilize to change and deconstruct the American theatre which, as the saying goes, has been dominated by "dead white men." And now that Middle Easterners can write, anthologize, and create theatrical productions from their perspective, they are in a position to challenge the status quo in a way they never were before. In other words, we must create alternate canons of our own until the mainstream allows us to be a part of their own.

Al-Saber: At a certain point in time, canons must be dismantled because they have outlived their usefulness. This viewpoint would take on an activist dimension. In a way, the canon becomes a method for activating resistance. For example, we create a canon of Palestinian plays that are all about being steps toward liberation. If liberation is achieved, and a new stage in Palestinian life, culture, and heritage has begun in the future, does the present canon become a form of historical documentation? Canons are discrete and time-limited. They have a narrow temperament and a limited temporality embedded within them.

Najjar: Abolitionist plays in the United States were very important literatures during the age of legalized slavery, yet now they are read as historical artifacts. The Western canon allows for only one representative play from other cultures, which is better than nothing I suppose. The problem with the Anglo European/American canon is that it's been fixed. Now we are saying it's time to examine alternate canons. How do we reform the canon with a multiplicity of voices? There are many with vested interests in limiting the canon and a reticence in allowing new voices. Academics of color have been agents of change since the Civil Rights Movement, if not before. We see this at the level of theatre history classes whether it means including more women, more people of color, and voices from other world cultures. Change is slow because this occurs on a case-by-case basis, and not systematically.

Al-Saber: To anthologize is not necessarily to canonize, but it is impossible to canonize without anthologizing. Contemporary theatre canons emerged from drama departments in the early twentieth century. They are quintessentially euro-centric and defined by literary criteria, which conceive of plays as drama as opposed to performance. This canon can only be fixed because its ontology is perceived as textual, a thing rather than an act. Traditional canons do not contend as much with exhibits of bodies, places, and cultures. The canon being conceptualized as something beyond text in the theatre is compelling, particularly in the context of the Arab repertoire, which runs as far in the past as antiquity. If canons remain limited to text, in inanimate anthologies, Arabs in and outside the American context are more likely to be excluded. Text necessitates some act of linguistic or behavioral translation, and a medium to preserve it.

Najjar: Anthologies, especially English anthologies of plays, tend to only have room for a few "foreign" plays; the majority are "classics" with, perhaps, one Arab play. I embrace Arab American anthologies and publish them as a means of making our work visible. If we did not do so, I believe we would continue to remain unknown and anonymous. Or course, in Arab theatre, the performance of dance and music is paramount, so even if you translated a play text from Arabic to English, how would you translate or collect dance or a style of song?

Al-Saber: The written text is so much easier to collect than the body. Anthologizing is an act of textual organization. But look at Diana Taylor's Hemispheric Institute and its massive archive. Which do you assign? Both, the textual and visual collections, are anthological. There is a preference for students to buy an anthology, read the play at home, and discuss in class. The formulation of the canon in terms of distribution and dissemination as primarily text is a prison. There are ways to break this anthological prison, but the dramatic canon, in particular, has been colonized by textual privileges in the form of a thick brick-like object.

Function

Najjar: In your scholarship, you write about Arab plays and productions, but I wanted to see these plays! I don't have the texts, I don't have the play performances on video, so I am relying on your excellent exegesis. All I am left with is the ability to perhaps track down the play and read it now that the performance is over. However, we do not have access to many of these plays in English, so we must wait until a translator publishes a translation before English speakers/readers can experience the play at all. This process could take decades and, by then, the necessity of these plays may have faded and their efficacy diminished because they become historical texts, not current works dealing with current topics.

Al-Saber: A convenient way to anthologize is to collect plays written in English. The ease of collecting these plays suggests that the ambassadorial mission of "non-western" theatre isn't accomplished to the same extent. The Arab American identity has the most access in the United States because the plays were written originally in English. In contrast to the often collective outcome of canon formation, to anthologize is to collect with purpose. It is a unique and specific act. Locating a series of plays and covering topics meant to serve a misrepresented group is difficult enough. The massive project—of translating a play and finding dramatic equivalence in English, and carrying a whole cultural and idiomatic baggage—is truly difficult.

Najjar: This is terribly complicated for Arabic, specifically. How does one write a play and, once it's written, how is it translated into a medium that will be comprehensible to a British or American audience? These are difficult issues and major reasons why Arab plays have not been widely disseminated. Countless Arabic plays remain untranslated. Even if you are a highly proficient translator, Arabic plays are metaphorical, lyrical, poetic. Teaching these translated plays is a challenge. Even the best translators will have to go through somersaults to communicate what's being said.

Al-Saber: In teaching Arab theatre in an Anglophone context, we both have experienced similar struggles in the classroom. Sometimes, a play has a sentence or an idea that is taken for granted in the original context, but we have to spend an hour explaining it. In such a scenario, we stop being artists or professors, and become cultural consultants. In order to propose a canon, we must recognize a body of literature as serving a particular function. How do you deal with this problem in the American classroom for example? By teaching works in the classroom, we are taking the first step toward canonization, aren't we? Let me present you with a challenge: how do you come up with a canon of Arab theatre with the givens we have today? Why do you do it in the first place?

Najjar: Currently we have an assortment of Arab plays in English translation that are accessible. There are collections like Badawi's *Early Arabic Drama* (1988), Jayyusi's *Short Arabic Plays* (2002) and *Modern Arabic Drama* (1995, with Allen), Al-Azraki's and Al-Shamma's *Contemporary Plays from Iraq* (2017), Dodgson's *Plays from the Arab World* (2010), and Saab and Myers' *Modern and Contemporary Political Theatre from the Levant* (2018), for instance. With these collections, students can read major Arab playwrights to gain a conception of what these plays are about. They can talk about the issues the plays present even if some are not "great" translations. At the very least we can read these plays and understand what these playwrights were contending with.

Al-Saber: So you teach these plays as snapshots of Middle Eastern history?

Najjar: I always tell the students that, if we were reading these plays when they were written and/or performed in Arabic, we might have foreseen the terrible events that are plaguing the Middle East today. However, by the time they have been translated decades after their productions, we are experiencing them in the aftermath of these events. It is a bit of a fool's errand because there is so much material and so little time. I can only contextualize what I can in a two-hour class, so it's very difficult. How do you teach these plays? What has been your experience with these plays in translation?

Al-Saber: I have been trying to deal with it in terms of questions that are unrelated to area studies and the region itself. For example, I teach a course called "Performing Arabs" where we study the Arab American canon of plays but the whole class is all about casting. Students in the class consider whether they are able to play a particular role or not. Then, we would put a scene on its feet in the classroom and the students have to confront whether playing an "Arab" character is possible for them. By looking at the Arab American canon as a casting problem, I end up teaching it. I find that it has more interest in the student body than teaching a class called Arab American Theatre. I also teach a class about Israel and Palestine, where the goal is examine the politics of occupation. It's a culture and conflict course where I only teach Palestinian and Israeli plays, in lieu of a course on Israeli or Palestinian theatre.

Najjar: I teach a Middle Eastern theatre class and I have a Arab American theatre class. For the former, I try to get the plays that were written in Arabic, Farsi, Turkish and other languages from the region that are in English translation. I use plays written in English by Americans of Arab descent for the Arab American class. In both cases, I have seen students really respond positively because we discuss the politics, the history, and the social conditions that led to these plays. For my Israeli-Palestinian theatre class, students usually have very little conception of what's happening in this conflict, and these classes offer a great way of exploring this history. These classes show students that this conflict is happening to real people, and they humanize a political situation in a way that students can understand. I believe that is a powerful act of transference.

Al-Saber: I want to circle back to something I mentioned earlier. A canon has to have a criteria that is invented by us for a particular purpose. This purpose can be transcended to the point where a canon can lose efficacy. Thus, canons are not unitary and cannot be fixed for too long. A canon is basically a body of works with a particular criterion along aspects of language, geography, and periodization that is necessarily temporally restricted. But fundamentally, a canon must have a declared purpose, otherwise it's ideologically suspect and perhaps insidious. A canon can outlast its purpose and when we are conscious of this ironic ontological situation, we have to let it go.

Najjar: Every canon speaks to its own age. Arab American theatre in post-9/11 America specifically addresses the conditions of Arab Americans including governmental persecution, surveillance, and societal suspicion. These plays offer perspectives of Arab Americans and of Arabs living in the Arab World. They are a view into a hyphenated culture that has been ignored and erased for many decades. These playwrights are embracing their Arabness and telling stories from their perspective. This particular canon is forming as we speak, so it will be for historians to decide if these works are a fully formed canon, or a collection of works that addressed a specific historical moment. Ultimately, a canon is helpful only if it serves its purpose.

Al-Saber: You've taken on the question of Middle Eastern theatre as a category, from various perspectives, and you include Turkish, Armenian, Israeli, and Arab theatre within this definition. In your writing, I've seen a tension that I haven't been able to reconcile. If we consider the Middle East in terms of ethnicities or nationalisms, and then compare it to the Arab world, are we putting populations that are not even close to being in the same size and geographic presence in direct comparison in a way that may not be fair? For example, you could categorize the region's theatrical context as Turkish, Iranian, and Arab. This would constitute the vast majority of theatre in the Middle East. But then, if you add minoritarian languages, you would have to seek the representation of millions of speakers of Armenian, Hebrew, Aramaic, and Amazigh, among other languages, in addition to the many other ethno-religious groups. How many plays must a community produce to be a significant producer of the Middle Eastern canon? Everyone has the right to representation and self-representation, but I am asking the question about canonicity here. How do you deal with this question of balancing scope, range, size of geography and population, as well as questions around colonization, when you are contending with a Western concept like the Middle East?

Najjar: We might need to give up on that ideal because it is impossible. We may have to give up on the notion that we are able to represent everyone, because, for instance, I don't know of any major Kurdish plays that have been translated into English at this point. I would love to represent the Kurds, the Yazidis, the Ismailis. I don't know plays that do that. Even if they exist, have they been translated? It is what I call a "sin of omission," which is to say that because the plays are not translated, we omit them from the curriculum. A class like Middle Eastern Theatre is terribly selective based on the materials that are available in translation. That, frankly, is a terrible way to create a canon but when you are dealing with so little, you must work with what you have. So, for the time being, our "canon" must, unfortunately, remain unbalanced in favor of plays in English translation, and there are too few of those at this time.

Al-Saber: Your statement makes me feel a certain sympathy toward the individuals who created canons that we consider oppressive. So, when you say, "I want to but I don't have the material," you make me wonder about oppressive, imperialist, settler-colonial, white-supremacist, and Euro-centric canons. As we fight against these so-called exclusionary canons, I wonder if their creators struggled with access as some of us might today.

Conclusion

After much debate, we returned to some of the original questions that started our inquiry. They are not dissimilar to the inquiries of those Oriental Studies departments of old. When these deeply racist and supremacist departments were attempting to understand the Other, what were they attempting to achieve? Why weren't they translating plays? How did they choose to form the canons that became staples of Orientalism? Were they conscious of their supremacy or not? Is it possible that we are somehow replicating some of their methods? Present-day academic institutions in departments of theatre and performance studies and well-meaning regional theatres, unconsciously perhaps, express a need for diversity in their curriculums, but lack a similar global expertise, which may translate into poor judgment or lack of articulate criteria. What we have tried to accomplish in this discussion is to examine the problems we face today, and to be transparent about the fact that we are wrestling with the notion of "canon." Our primary criticism centers on the persistence of contemporary Euro-American canons rather than the availability of materials or lack thereof. We may not have the canon we desire at this time, but at the very least, we'll keep anthologizing.

Works Cited

Al-Saber, S. 2014. "Arabic Facts in Palestine: Clashing Hybridities in Transnational Cultural Production." *Theatre Research in Canada / Recherches théâtrales Au Canada* 35, 3. Retrieved from https://journals.lib.unb.ca/index.php/TRIC/article/view/22392.

Barakat, Halim. 1983. *Days of Dust*. Washington, DC: Three Continents Press.

Lorde, Audre. 1984. *Sister Outsider*. Berkeley: Crossing Press.

Najjar, Michael Malek. 2015. *Arab American Drama, Film, and Performance: A Critical Study, 1908 to the Present*. Jefferson, NC: McFarland and Company.

9 Your Heritage is Safe Here: Defining Three Indigenous Theatrical Canons

Jay B. Muskett and Jonah Winn-Lenetsky

In this chapter, we argue that a Native Theatrical Canon is of vital importance and relevance today for Native and non-Native scholars and for students studying theatre and Indigenous performance. This Canon must also be understood as supplemental to and just as significant as the Western Canon. In order to approach this concept, it is also necessary to look at how the Canon has historically been understood and specifically at the Western Canon, that lofty colonial concept that has come to define the humanities and especially theatre in the 20th and 21st centuries. Therefore, we give a brief history of the Western Canon through the theories of Harold Bloom as a contrivance of Western literature and finally propose how we can reimagine a canon by and about Indigenous performance through the interplay of three intentional lists. The irony and inadequacy of using such a neo-colonial device as the Canon to decolonize it through an Indigenous reappraisal are not lost on us, but it can be repurposed as the site of collective memory and identity. Additionally, it is the predominant form through which cultural legacy is transmitted in the academy and is important to the task of enlightening mainstream audiences about Indigenous performance. We will also argue for the necessity of reading and deconstructing another problematic canon, one made up of works about Indigenous people by non-Native playwrights, novelists, and filmmakers. We are approaching this project from very different trajectories and experiences. Here we would like to introduce ourselves and explain our relationship to the Native Canon project.

Jonah Winn-Lenetsky: I have only discovered the rich tapestry of Native theatre as an adult. I am a non-Indigenous ally, who is committed to the power and relevance of Native theatrical traditions and contemporary iterations of Indigenous performance. I believe that Native theatre has the unique power to speak directly to the community and to engage it in ceremonial practice. As Hanay Geiogamah describes, "In ceremonial theatre approaching the audience as part of the community, or tribe, is a key component. The community members thus become direct participants in an issue, a debate, a form, a theatrical context" (Geiogamah 2011). This direct and meaningful engagement with audiences really speaks to me, especially as it engenders a powerful sense of ritual and community within the performance event. Raised Anglo, gay, and Jewish in Santa Fe, New Mexico, I have always had the sense of being an outsider in my own community. From being

DOI: 10.4324/9781003031413-9

called a "kyke," to a "fag," to a "stupid jew," I found myself silenced as a child. I found performance as a teenager and it gave me an outlet, where I could find my voice and others like mine. That said, my education was also sorely lacking in alternatives to the "Western Canon." When I discovered the range and power of Native theatre that was not being taught in traditional theatre programs, I became frustrated. I feel it is my obligation as a scholar and educator to make sure that Native stories and playwrights find their way to the curriculum of every major high school, university theatre program, and theatrical training program. Additionally, I think it is important to teach and deconstruct the misrepresentations of Indigenous peoples throughout US and European theatre history.

Jay B Muskett: The majority of my life I have been trying to define and inform people, both Native and non-Native, of my "Indianness," which for most of my life remained this unexplainable shifting label that I was constantly being measured against. Indianness was something that haunted me yet I couldn't put my finger on exactly what Indianness was until I stumbled upon professor, educator, philosopher, and real-life Indian, Vine Deloria Jr., who best explains what Indianness is in his Indian manifesto, *Custer Died for Your Sins*:

> Our foremost plight is our transparency. People can tell just by looking at us what we want, what should be done to help us, how we feel, and what a "real" Indian is really like. Indian life, as it relates to the real world, is a continuous attempt not to disappoint people who know us. Unfulfilled expectations cause grief and we have already had our share […] Because people can see right through us, it becomes impossible to tell truth from fiction or fact from mythology. Experts paint us as they would like us to be. Often, we paint ourselves as we wish we were or as we might have been. (Deloria 1969)

Deloria Jr. eloquently encapsulates "Indianness," which has misrepresented me and deluded me in that I had thought it was something to strive for. Indianness was more than just a label, it was a measuring device given and then passed among other Natives which acted as a banner. It was something to be proud of, even if we didn't know what it was. We just knew it was us, more than them. This need to measure, this need to gauge and compare, extended beyond that of our groups, it extended most effectively internally to oneself, and for myself, it was something I was never able to live up to. Little did I know, I wasn't meant to. Why? Because they would never let me. The "they" are the oppressive majority of artists who continue to perpetuate the myth of what it is to be Indian through artistic liberties that dehumanized the Indigenous population and replaced real life with a fiction. Real Indians no longer existed, instead what was constructed in their place was the romantic notion of who they were. Thus Indianness was created. As such there was no need to seek out the real thing, that would be a letdown. Best stick to the idea and it is this idea of Indianness that still holds relevance within the sacred space of the theatre.

Discovering theatre was like returning home and as it turned out it filled that missing element of my life. The combination of sacred space, ceremony, ritual, and performance spoke to the heart and soul of my being as they filled a vacantness that I didn't recognize was there. It felt right in a body that felt wrong. I found as an actor that my Indianess was not dictated by anyone else and I was free to be the Indian I wanted to be, the only problem was that there were very few of those roles I could naturally fit into as I was too red for any of Shakespeare's leads, as well as those of Chekhov, Ibsen, O'Neill, Williams, or Miller. My brief time treading the boards consisted of roles that split duties between stagehand and what I used to joke about as exclusive cameos, moving across the stage to hand someone a prop or announce dinner. Frustrated, I moved to the other side of the pen and page.

Being the creator of my own performance I found there was an expectation that I had to write about Indian life, after all, I was Indian and still alive, so I thought I was well suited for the task, but as I began to write, that whole mess of Indianness began to creep up and dominate my thoughts and a realization hit me. I didn't know how to be Indian. The most authentic Indian I knew was my dad but there was an unspoken and unseen barrier he felt necessary for my benefit. He believed I needed to leave some of that Indianness behind so as to make me more competitive within the colonial system. I looked at the television for a brief moment and saw how they represented Indianness, then quietly shut it off and sold my tv. Well, ten bucks richer but not a step closer, I began to despair. I had been playing Indian all my life, I didn't know how to actually be one.

I studied and read as many plays involving Native Americans as I could. It was a short journey and what I found was confusing at first, but the more I made my way down the rabbit hole the clearer and more infuriating things became. What I found was that there were a number of plays that supposedly represented me in various ways. These plays spoke "about" Indians while I was looking for authenticity about "being" Indian. I finally knew what I was looking for as I compiled my own Canon, but the list remained small and divided.

A Brief History of the Canon, Punctuated by Eurocentrism and Calcification:

Before we can propose a new type of Canon that decolonizes the process of canonization, it is important to examine the extremely problematic and biased nature of the Western Canon we have inherited. The Canon emerges from a colonial legacy of Western imperialism, where cultural values can be distilled into a list of core writers and philosophers. As an Imperialist project, the Canon allowed European thought and aesthetics to be reified and exported and in the US this took the form of classical studies and the humanities in the late 19th and early 20th centuries.

The humanities have begun to shift and recognize the problem of deifying specific intellectuals. Even the word Canon itself is the literal act of sainting someone in the Roman Catholic Church. So in essence, the humanities have embraced Catholic doctrine to create an aesthetic religiosity. So, what is the good of a concept such as canonization at all? Additionally, if the works of the Canon are considered essential to the formation of the liberal subject and for the development of academics and artists, but that same Canon is completely void of Native and Indigenous artists and is sorely lacking in artists of color at all, can it be resuscitated for a more adequate and inclusive purpose? We will argue that there is some benefit to supplementing the Canon as scholars and artists working in Native theatre, however, we must first deconstruct the monolithic assumptions that undergird the Western Canon and the ways that traditional higher education reaffirms that Canon.

There is currently only one Indigenous-focused, Native-serving art college in the country and this is indicative of how few resources and how little recognition on a national level are directed toward the development of Indigenous artists doing work for Indigenous communities. This seems woefully inadequate given that the Native population of the US is approximately seven million people. In order to develop a Native Canon and a more robust education in Native performance, it is essential that more recognition is given to contemporary Native performing. This can only really be accomplished if Native playwrights and performers are equally valued and studied in theatre education. This is why it is so urgent that a Native canon is given space alongside the Western Canon.

For Harold Bloom and other defenders of the traditional Western Canon, Postmodernism and Multiculturalism represent the "politicization" of aesthetics, a vaunted and holy category. For him, the Canon is constructed of a great Euro-American past, one that is diminished by the introduction of texts by historically marginalized authors and should not, therefore, be opened up to rigorous revaluation and updating. He sees such attempts to redefine and broaden the Canon as an assault on aesthetic value. As he argues, "the flight from aesthetics among so many in my profession [...] reduces the aesthetic to ideology [...] Against this approach I urge a stubborn resistance whose single aim is to preserve poetry as fully and purely as possible" (1994: 17–18). But what are these aesthetic values that undergird Bloom's philosophy and aversion to ideology? This sense of aesthetic purity and authority stems from a fallacy that art and ideology can be separated. He goes on to argue that, "Things have however fallen apart, the center has not held, and mere anarchy is in the process of being unleashed on what used to be called the 'learned world'" (1994: 1).

Bloom's position is a threatened one. Bloom seems to be arguing for a continuance of the status quo. When he lists authors that exemplify his Canon they include Homer, Tolstoy, Dante, Wilde, Aristophanes, and Shakespeare (and the list goes on), but lack almost entirely authors from the Global South, Women, or BIPOC writers. In a particularly telling example, he lists Maya Angelou as an example of a poet who will likely be inducted into the Canon, but that he feels should not be, along with "all the other instantly canonical achievements that flood our academies" (1994: 16). Another telling passage from his book argues,

> The compeers of these skeptics sometimes go farther and question even Shakespeare [...] Originality becomes a literary equivalent of such terms as individual enterprise, self-reliance, and competition, which do not gladden the hearts of Feminists, Afrocentrists, Marxists, Foucault-inspired New Historicists, or Deconstructors. (1994: 20)

Shakespeare here stands in for the unassailability of the traditional Western Canon. Indeed, all these people Bloom terms "Feminists," "Afrocentrists," etc., seem to threaten the Canon not because they value inclusion and multiculturalism and oppose racism, sexism, and classicism, but because they do not value the purely aesthetic. So then the Canon for Bloom should be based solely on aesthetics. But what is the basis for those aesthetics? Are they not also grounded in the same Euro-American and Neo-Colonial ideology that Bloom argues has no place in canonical thought? Harold Bloom is not alone in his defense of the Western Canon as it was historically figured. Allan Bloom's (no relation) book *The Closing of the American Mind* undoubtedly influenced Harold Bloom's claims that "abandoning the Western canon had dumbed down universities, while the 'relativism' that had replaced it had 'extinguished the real motive of education'" (A. Bloom qtd in Donadio 2007). The idea that aesthetics need to be anchored to an old, heavy European or Anglo-American past is what we argue against by suggesting that a multiplicity of canons emerge from Native performers and writers and therefore demand a different approach than the Western one proposed by Bloom.

Hanay Geiogamah gives us a beautiful alternative to Bloom's Canon by proposing an Indigenous Canon, based on Indigenous histories, lifeways, and aesthetics. A Canon that allows for traditional Native Performance, while also making room for non-traditional Indigenous theatre, which also includes ceremony, spirituality, and ritual as primary components of Indigenous aesthetics and performance (Geiogamah 2011).

For Bloom, the Canon occupies a place of elevated depoliticized aesthetics. However, aesthetics are always political and always ideological. Nowhere is this more true than Native performance which has been repressed: first through material genocide and then through a slow cultural genocide, where US government policy has attempted to erase Native cultural identities in part through the prohibition of performing sacred rituals, songs, and dances. Therefore, any expression of Indigenous performance is a political act, for the sheer audacity to perform, live, and make art in the face of such pervasive cultural oppression. Bloom would argue that Native performance would only deserve a place in the Canon if it valorized Western aesthetics and that any attempt to question this is an ideological intrusion. It is particularly telling that his shorthand example of a truly elevated literary critic seems always to be Oscar Wilde, who he argues was "always right about everything" (Bloom 1994: 16). This is the same Wilde who valued aesthetics far above politics. In the subtext of this argument, we see Bloom's shadow argument, that politics has no place in art and that there is an objective set of cultural works that should be valued above all others.

A Native Canon can and should serve a different primary function than the Western Canon has served. If the Western Canon is a system of fixing and valuing a codified system of aesthetics, the Native Canon, though also espousing cultural values, is instead not based predominantly on aesthetics. Aestheticism itself is a narrowly European concept of refinement of form and style. Instead, a Native Canon centers the wisdom, philosophies, ceremonies, life-ways, and culture of survivance. While for Bloom, the Western Canon is purportedly apolitical and divorced from culture, though we know this not to be true, the Native canon still engages with politics as a central concern. For Bloom, to politicize the Canon is to dissolve it. What this argument fails to recognize is that the Canon is already politicized. The apolitical Canon acts as a neocolonial device designed to sanitize and smooth difference and divergent thinking from the arts and humanities. The Native Canon should acknowledge the diverse and relevant aesthetics of North American tribal arts without asking that politics be put aside. In many cases, the value of a work might primarily be its political implications or the conceptual arguments it makes. Additionally, Native aesthetics often serve important ceremonial purposes that may not be immediately readable or translatable to Anglo audiences. If we use Diane Glancy's *The Woman Who Was a Red Deer Dressed for the Deer Dance* (1995), for example, it does not easily fit within Western theatrical traditions. The play serves as a ceremonial conversation between a girl and her grandmother about the deer dance. It does follow Aristotle's unities but is lacking in drama and conflict, which in many Indigenous traditions are not a central aspect of story structure. However, it is also an excellent example of Indigenous ceremony within a contemporary Western theatrical context and it represents Indigenous characters and ceremonies, intended for an Indigenous audience. It is therefore a crucial piece of theatre for a Native Canon.

To take a very different example, *Power Pipes* (1999) by Spiderwoman Theater also does not fit within Western canonical conventions but is a very contemporary blending of Indigenous ceremony and language with a "One Woman Show" format. This play would also have an important place within a Native Canon because it utilizes ceremonial aspects, Kuna language, and regalia. Additionally, it is again by and about Indigenous peoples and intended for a largely Native audience. As yet another example, *The Independence of Eddie Rose* (1986) by William S Yellow Robe has a typical three-act play structure, but powerfully renders the lives of Native peoples on an undefined Northwestern Reservation in the 1980s. The play adapts the modern realist form and could easily be compared to *Death of a Salesman*, or *True West*, but its subjects and intended audience are Native folks struggling to survive in a colonized society. All of these works must be included in a Native Theatrical Canon. While one work adheres to strictly Western Theatrical conventions but centers Native subjects and issues, the other two evade those conventions in favor of Native ceremonial aspects. All three have an important role in elucidating the scope and complexity of Native performance and belong in a Native Canon, or as we will propose, one of three Native canons.

If we think of the Western Canon as one of exclusivity, then we can imagine a Native Canon as one of inclusivity. If the Canon project entails a cementing of history and knowledge, the Native Canon allows for a ceremonial unfolding. By breaking it into three spiraling lists that are open to flux and interpretation, the Native Canon opens up new pathways for thought and new (and old) ways of performing. Jaqueline Shea Murphy gives us a possible basis for an Indigenous North American Canon when she argues that one of the primary values of Indigenous art is based on collective memory and in knowledge sharing:

> what enables this "collective memory" to be shared across time and place is not a shared Indigenous bloodline or gene. Rather, what connects Aboriginal peoples from the Arctic to South America is a similar experience of colonialism and land loss, and a common relationship to and understanding of land and to the animals that share it. This relationship is passed from generation to generation. (Shea Murphy 2007: 226–227)

As Shea Murphy eloquently outlines here, victims of inherited trauma through Colonialism, forced diaspora, and cultural oppression urgently need a space for the reclaiming of memory, history, and communal identity. Our hope is that a Native Canon can serve all of those purposes for Indigenous communities, while also laying the foundations for anyone interested in studying, or creating, Native theatre.

The Three Canons of Native Performance

When we speak about the Canon of dramatic works within Native American Drama, we are speaking of three actual canons, the *Oral* or *Pre-colonial* Canon, the *Assimilated*, and the *New Indigenous Aesthetic*. When two cultural entities clash and come together and one culture benefits from the persecution of the other with the intended goal of extending colonialism, there is an attempt to replace and eradicate the Canon for the good of the colonial view. Such is the case with the Native American Dramatic Canon.

American theatre existed before the European invasion. However, it was perceived and practiced in very different ways. The ideas of drama, performance, ceremony, and ritual are not interchangeable. They must be viewed with specificity and respect, as they point to a way of being to everyone involved. A Navajo storyteller during the winters would travel from community to community performing the drama of creation through ritual narratives that involved an audience who were gathered to listen, observe, and learn the ways of the people. The narratives are not the ceremony but the gathering of the people themselves. Sacred spaces arrived and departed with the people.

Birgit Däwes writes in her essay *Performing Memory, Transforming Time*, "many works have been forgotten or lost, so that the historiography of indigenous North American drama requires accurate research and a multiplicity of sources and voices" (Däwes, 2013: 4). The first canon, the *Oral Canon* which is better represented as the *Pre-Colonial Canon*, is a victim of the repeated repression, dismantling, and replacement of Indigenous culture, which effectively destroyed any aspect of personal and communal identity. Deloria states,

> While the thrust of Christian missions was to save the individual Indian, its result was to shatter Indian societies and destroy the cohesiveness of the Indian communities [...] Christianity destroyed many Indian religious practices by offering a much easier and more practical religion. (Deloria, 1969: 102)

What Deloria refers to as "easier" and "practical" encompasses the realization that it was easier to feign conversion and give up such practices than passing on the narrative storytelling. Within the family unit, personal ceremonies such as the Navajo Kinaalda (The Navajo Puberty Ceremony celebrating maturity of girls among the Navajo is held generally on the fourth night after the first evidence of the maiden's entrance into womanhood. On the first morning following the moment of this change in life the girl bathes and dresses in her finest clothes (Carey 2010) and other coming of age ceremonies that welcomed individuals as contributing members into the whole of the tribe were among the first to go. Other ceremonies such as the blessing way or the Pueblo feast days evolved to include colonial and Christian ideology on the surface as a way of subterfuge. The intention of Christian and colonial practices was to separate individuals from the community. Sarah Bryant-Bertail writes in her essay included in the compilation *Native American Performance and Representation*, "At base it was the Indians' communal culture itself that had to be controlled, even though this amounted to an annihilation to their historical identity" (Wilmer and Bryant-Bertrail 2009: 58).

Taking away ceremonies that connected one to the community effectively took away the connection to the self. Because of this, a dependency was developed; Deloria points out, "Indians have come to believe that their problems were soluble by conformity to white culture" (Deloria 1969: 265). It's important to note that some ceremonies and aspects of the Oral Canon survive, however, and that which is left serves as a reminder of how wide the disconnect is between contemporary Indians and their ancestors. The loss of performances that make up much of what was the Oral Canon points to a significant loss for Indigenous communities. It was a loss of the spiritual life that contributed to a crisis of identity and stripped away any allusion to personal development, purpose, and choice. Indianness was thus opened to interpretation.

The second Canon, or the *Assimilated Canon*, is the attempt to fill in the void created by the eradication of the *Oral Canon*, largely by nonnatives. Their attempt served to erase actual identity and replace it with the colonial ideological view of Indianness that spawned the ignoble images such as the "noble savage" and the "white savior." Both film and theatre have been used to create and maintain this misrepresentation, to confuse and blend indigenous identity as a means of control. Practices such as redface and the stereotyping of Indigenous peoples as primitive or savage hold captive the Indigenous narrative. Maria Lyytinen in her essay "The Pocahontas Myth and Its Deconstruction" states, "Theater and Film have been effective media in spreading the colonial imagery of Indians" (Wilmer and Lyytinen 2009: 84). Nowhere was this more apparent than in film. Jacquelyn Kilpatrick writes in *Celluloid Indians*,

> To get to the genesis of Native American stereotypes requires investigating the artistic language that has propagated them. Human consciousness and art, including the arts of literature and by extension cinema, do not result from or even come into direct contact with the real world but rather represent its languages and discourses. (Kilpatrick 1999: 1)

The replacement of Native culture by nonnatives is direct misrepresentation meant to justify white cultural mores that skew, distort, and outright mislead the Indigenous culture while also reaffirming its replacement. Kilpatrick states,

> During the 1960's, for a growing segment of society, particularly the younger generation, the idea of a "mythical" people who valued "unity" and lived in shared communities [...] and who were (apparently) naturally at peace was very attractive [...] and produced a longing to "be" American Indian. (Kilpatrick 1999: 66)

Plays such as Arthur Kopit's *Indians* (1968) and David Mamet's *November* (2008) distort the image of contemporary Native Americans to a romanticized unattainable concept or sideshow spectacle whose dignity is stripped away and at play's end is fully assimilated. The other approach, as in the case of Tracy Letts's *August Osage County* (2008), is one in which the Native character is used only as a prop and storytelling device for the convenience of the plot. The Cherokee character in Letts' play only has close to a genuine moment with another character as a means of contrast, and by play's end suddenly becomes this deus-ex-machina figure who stops the near-rape of an underage girl. The entire arc ultimately dehumanizes her as she is nothing more than a convenient device for the story and is never approached or seen as an actual human being. All of these plays and ones like them, written by non-Natives, approach Indianness as metaphor and story device which acts as a means of washing away and avoiding the truth of contemporary Indian life. In fact, the whole idea of Indian life is illusionary as these writers contribute to the control-based Assimilated Canon which set up these detrimental tropes with the underlying idea that it is better to situate the Indian in a place where they can be controlled. Whether imaginatively or in reality, the colonial force at play intentionally does so as a way of demonstrating colonial authority.

The third Canon, *The New Indigenous Canon*, consists of the many Indigenous playwrights that are treading new aesthetics as they reestablish what was lost. These plays represent the modern struggle and celebratory life of the contemporary Native American in all its various forms. Each of these plays redresses the wound of violently being stripped of identity and purpose, while the best of them not only reignites the individual's conviction but also moves the audience member onto the path of understanding, acceptance, and growth, while healing both spirit and mind. It is in this instance that once again the coming together of the people is a reflection of ceremony.

Many Indigenous bodies of work go unnoticed or are dismissed altogether due to the non-Aristotelian elements the plays follow, which seem to disqualify the works for production by many theatres. Geiogamah's *Body Indian* (1981), for instance, does not follow the traditional view of what composes a play by blending both time and space into one singular constant moment that the characters can't escape or grow from. The scene shifts from the relative safety of the trap house in which its inhabitants seek refuge to drink the world away, and is bombarded by the loud, invasive, and oppressive sound of a train that haunts the protagonist as it passes out on the train tracks that hobbled him. The cacophony also serves as reminder to the others that it's only a matter of time before one of them also suffers the same fate. The main character knows the eventual outcome of his path and sets forth a plan of action that the other characters take advantage of despite the implied doomed resolution, which is the loss of the money that would pay for rehab. The character is left in despair yet the play leaves open the possibility that he will succeed. There is always hope.

Writers such as Hanay Geiogamah, Thomson Highway, Rhianna Yazzie, Ty Defoe, William Yellow Robe Jr., Larisa Fasthorse, Mary Kathryn Nagle, and many others who are considered canonical refuse to conform to the tropes of European aesthetics. Instead, their focus is to reclaim an Indigenous aesthetic that was stripped away so as to reassess and bridge the gap that has widened not only between cultures but also within the individual self that is the direct consequence of the *Assimilated Canon*. They hope to capture the essence of the *Oral Canon* while at the same time reestablishing the sacred space within the Indigenous bodies, who can finally see themselves represented more than just through the stereotypical Western lens. Through writing their stories, their way, the focus changes from what "has happened" to "what could happen." This is the growth, which history has denied the

Indigenous people, and is what Indianness is about: the ability to see the development of the self outside of the influence of colonial projection and influence.

The establishment of a new Indigenous aesthetic is important because it acts as a voice that challenges, rebukes, the assimilated aesthetic while re-establishing the necessity of Indigenous thought and identity. The oral record of ceremonies and rituals was full of symbolism amongst actualities. These performances encompassed the story that is indigenous. The Indigenous Canon is the link to Indigenous identity which comprises the necessity of connection to others and more importantly to the personal self. How this is achieved is through the connection of the people with the land.

Vine Deloria Jr. states, "Land was the means of recognizing the Indian as a human being" (Deloria 1969: 7). Once again, the Indian who is using this mindset must step from behind the curtain of invisibility and claim their space which has been denied them, only this time it is the stage space, the sacred space of performance and ceremony in which the very essence of Indian life begins and is sustained.

All three canons crucially construct the reality of the modern Indigenous identity. The production of Native theatre is the reestablishment of the Indigenous narrative. A lot has been systematically lost and it is only by returning to the essence of what those ceremonial performances hinted at that Indigenous people can feel safe and rooted and secure, knowing that the heritage that encompasses their entire being is safe within the hands, ears, mouths, hearts, heads, and actions of the people.

Works Cited

Bloom, Allan. 1987. *The Closing of the American Mind: How Higher Education Has Failed Democracy and Impoverished the Souls of Today's Students*. New York: Simon and Schuster.

Bloom, Harold. 1994. *The Western Canon*. Orlando: Harcourt Brace, & Company.

Carey, Harold Jr. 2010. "Kinaalda - Celebrating Maturity of Girls among the Navajo." *Navajo People*. Accessed on 30 November 2020. http://navajopeople.org/blog/kinaalda-celebrating-maturity-of-girls-among-the-navajo/

Däwes, Birgit. 2013. "Performing Memory, Transforming Time." In *Indigenous North American Drama: A Multivocal History*, edited by Birgit Däwes, 1–15. Albany: State University of New York Press.

Deloria, Vine. [1969] 1988. *Custer Died for Your Sins: An Indian Manifesto*. Norman, OK: University of Oklahoma Press.

Donadio, Rachel. 2007. "Revisiting the Canon Wars." *New York Times*, 16 September. Accessed on 16 October 2020. https://www.nytimes.com/2007/09/16/books/review/Donadio-t.html

Geiogamah, Hanay and Darby, Jaye, eds. 2000. *American Indian Theater in Performance: A Reader*. Los Angeles: UCLA, American Indian Studies Center.

Geiogamah, Hanay. 2011. *Ceremony, Spirituality and Ritual In Native Performance: A Creative Notebook*. Los Angeles: UCLA, American Indian Studies Center.

Gisolfi D'Aponte, Mimi, ed. 1999. *Seventh Generation: An Anthology of Native American Plays*. New York: Theatre Communications Group.
Kilpatrick, Jacquelyn. 1999. *Celluloid Indians: Native Americans and Film*. Lincoln: University of Nebraska Press.
Shea Murphy, Jacqueline. 2007. *The People Have Never Stopped Dancing: Native American Dance Histories*. Minneapolis: University of Minnesota Press.
Wilmer, S. E., and Sarah Bryant-Bertail. 2009. "Old Spirits in a New World." In *Native American Performance and Representation*, edited by S. E. Wilmer, 40–60. Tucson: University of Arizona Press.
Wilmer, S. E., and Maria Lyytinen. 2009. "The Pocahontas Myth and Its Deconstruction in Monique Mojica's Play: Princess Pocahontas and the Blue Spots." In *Native American Performance and Representation*, edited by S. E. Wilmer, 78–94. Tucson: University of Arizona Press.

Appendix

Examples of Traditional Native Performances open to the public
Crow Fair, Montana
Gathering of Nations, Albuquerque NM
Intertribal Ceremonial, Gallup NM
Pueblo Feast Days, New Mexico
Sundance, South Dakota
Writers Whose Work Make up the New Indigenous Canon
(This is by no means an exhaustive list, but is a good place to start)
Cheechoo, Shirley
Chitto, Dillon
Clements, Marie
Defoe, Ty
Fasthorse, Larissa
Geiogamah, Hanay
Glancy, Diane
Gomez, Terry
Highway, Thomson
Howe, LeAnne
Gordon, Roxy
Nagel. Mary Kathryn
King, Bruce
Luna, James
Miguel, Gloria
Miguel, Muriel
Reinholz, Randy
Yazzie, Rhiana
Yellow Robe Jr., William
Places to catch Contemporary Native Theatre
Amerinda (American Indian Artists) Inc. (NYC)
Centre for Indigenous Theatre (Toronto)

Dark Winter Productions (Alaska)
Debajehmujig Theatre Group (Ontario)
Gordon Tootoosis Nīkānīwin Theatre (Saskatchewan)
NAC Indigenous Theatre (Ontario)
New Native Theatre (Minneapolis)
Oklahoma City Theatre Company's Native American New Play Festival
Raving Native Productions (Twin Cities)
Red Eagle Soaring (Seattle)
Safe Harbors Indigenous Collective (NYC)
Spiderwoman Theater (NYC)
The Eagle Project (NYC)
Thunderbird Theatre (Kansas)
Turtle Theatre Collective (Twin Cities)
Two Worlds Theatre (New Mexico)
Voices at the Autry Museum of the American West (Los Angeles)
Western Arts Alliance (Portland)

10 "Frenemies" of the Canon: Our Two Decades of Studying and Teaching Disability in Drama and Performance

Ann M. Fox and Carrie Sandahl

Carrie Sandahl: What is the value of disability in canonical dramatic texts? And what can canonical dramatic texts do for disability? As canons form and re-form, how do we keep things flexible? How do we have some common structure, but create flexibility within that? Let's talk about this: hopefully, we can raise questions, make observations, point others to useful sources, and begin avenues of exploration that are only seeds at this point. The point is not to be revisionist, but expansionist: the field is wide open and there's so much to do!

Ann Fox: Our conversations on disability in the dramatic canon go way back—when did we first meet? Maybe at an Association for Theatre in Higher Education (ATHE) Women and Theatre Program Conference in the mid-1990s, when we were in graduate school? I know that we first spent time together at the National Endowment for the Humanities (NEH) Summer Institute on Disability Studies in 2000. We spent six weeks at San Francisco State University with other academics, led by the feminist disability scholar Rosemarie Garland-Thomson and the late disability historian Paul Longmore. Your anthology *Bodies in Commotion: Disability and Performance* (Sandahl and Auslander 2005) was still a few years off. Over the past 20 years, our approaches to disability in drama and performance have become quite organically complementary.

Sandahl: Yes, that NEH Institute is where we really got to know each other as scholars. We bonded as the "theatre people" of the group and had many side conversations about how emerging ideas in disability studies might apply to performance in general and drama more specifically.

We've had very productive areas of agreement and disagreement that have pushed me to think more complexly. For instance, let's take the dramatic canon: those works of drama that are repeatedly anthologized, taught, and staged across generations of theatre classes: everyone from the white, European-derived tradition (e.g., Ibsen) to people who we consider are becoming canonized (e.g., Tony Kushner). Early on, I dismissed disability representation in the dramatic canon as not much more than damaging metaphors and stereotypes that serve as what David Mitchell and Sharon Snyder called "narrative prosthesis" (see Mitchell and Snyder 2011). In their formulation, narrative depends on disability as a metaphor for a problem to be solved, and this problem is most often solved by the disabled character's death, cure, rescue from censure, or disability's revaluation. Even though Mitchell and Snyder write about ways modernist authors have complicated narrative prosthesis toward a more expansive view of disability, I was just over it. I was tired of these metaphors being applied to me as a physically disabled woman in public spaces, including everyday interactions and on the stage.

You gently but firmly pushed back with textual analysis and historical context that I couldn't dismiss. Following your lead, I have encouraged students to sit uncomfortably with what I've come to call "representational conundrums," which are paradoxes or puzzles unique to disability representation (Sandahl 2018).

Fox: The work we do represents two different, but complementary directions. We need to pay attention to disabled performers and theatre artists (like Ryan Haddad or the late John Belluso) who are making new disability-themed work; we also need an examination of how disability might have worked to influence canonical authors (e.g., Tennessee Williams). So I'm always asking: can literary disability studies help us understand the ways in which disability has existed in modern and contemporary drama over time in ways that did not emerge from disability culture or was not written by authors who identified as disabled? I've even started to write about this as a kind of "adaptive activism" (see Fox: forthcoming). By "adaptive activism," I mean theatre that reveals the embodied, relational, economic, and social aspects of disability in ways that counter ableism but which might not strike an audience as overt disability advocacy. For example, take Stephen Karam's *The Humans* (2015). It was wildly successful, but most reviewers emphasized that it showed the plight of a downwardly-mobile American middle class. But disability is all over the play! A character is about to be fired because of her chronic illness; her parents are caring for her grandmother with dementia because there's no money for any kind of home support. Those parents have arthritis and back pain after years of physical labor; they face being uninsured in a country without universal health care. Yet no reviewers discussed how disability and class are deeply intertwined.

Sandahl: I agree with your run-down here and love the term "adaptive activism." I want to add a couple more assumptions that guide canon formation. First is assuming that being nondisabled is "universal," and, therefore, the audience is too. By that logic, a play about disability is too narrow or not relevant to a general audience. But we both know that disability itself is a universal experience—through relationships or personally if you live long enough (as disability activists like to say). *The Humans* is a perfect example of this—we see disability as it impacts a family across different generations. It irks me that the default audience member is thought of as nondisabled because theatre is not made accessible to many of us who are actually disabled! Perhaps we'd be more universal if we could get in the door, find a seat, and have accommodations like American Sign Language interpretation. Until disabled people are literally in the audience, we won't be considered part of the "general" audience.

A second assumption that guides canon formation is more mundane—the cost of buying books, which can be prohibitively expensive. When I was teaching in a theatre program, I hesitated to ask students to buy additional plays not in the anthology because buying single plays (or at the time photo-copying single plays for 100+ students in a large lecture course) was prohibitively expensive. To address this, the theatre faculty would assign an anthology that could be used across courses from early theatre history to contemporary drama. This was mostly before we could upload full texts to a content management system like Blackboard. Our ability as teachers to make our anthologies easily and inexpensively (and within copyright) might provide more flexibility to engage with the canon productively. Speaking of traditionally printed play anthologies, they often don't contain politicized disability drama (like the Belluso plays you mentioned). By "politicized," I mean work that takes social, cultural, and historical conditions into account, rather than taking for granted that disability is an individual pathology. Aside from the financial issue, there are few plays by contemporary disabled playwrights in general and even fewer of them have been published and made available for production.

In the absence of published and produced work by politicized disabled playwrights past or present, I agree with you that we can turn to the canon for clues to how disability was—and is—understood through its use as metaphor. Looking at metaphors of the past might give us an understanding of potential historical meanings of disability that had to have affected the lived experience of disabled people in those time periods (see Sandahl 2018). Sometimes we can cross-reference those metaphors with some of the new disability histories that have come from a disability studies perspective. I'm thinking about, for the European context, *A History of Disability*, which the French philosopher Henri-Jacques Stiker wrote in the mid-90s, and, for the US context, *A Disability History of the United States* by disability studies historian Kim Nielsen, published in 2012. These are just two examples, but texts like these might help us find ourselves in the dramatic canon, as you suggest, and in disability metaphors. By reading canonical plays in the context of their contemporary disability metaphors, we understand how disability might have been used as a narrative device, performance convention, and clue to the actual lives of disabled people from the play's era.

Fox: And we also have undiscovered disability histories about canonical authors that might inform our analyses. I mentioned Tennessee Williams earlier. Other critics argue that his sister's lobotomy might have influenced his depiction of Laura in *The Glass Menagerie* (1944). I think that's true, though not in the sense that she is made pitiable to create a limping metaphor for Rose Williams's intellectual disability. As I've written elsewhere, I think in this play and others like *Suddenly, Last Summer* (1958), Williams is making a pointed critique of the medical model. So the notion that disability must always be cured and the medical establishment always knows best is directly challenged (see Fox 2004 and 2016). Williams's grappling with the forces of stigma, medicine, and biopower appears in his work repeatedly.

Sandahl: What might we make of the fact that homosexuality in Williams' time—in the 50s—was classified in the Diagnostic and Statistical Manual as a psychiatric disorder? Was Williams, then, considered disabled in his day? How might he have experienced psychiatrization and how might this experience have shown up in his use of metaphor? (See Robert McRuer (2006) for a full discussion of how able-bodiedness and heterosexuality are co-constitutive.)

Fox: And think of the other canonical works that may simply never have been read in terms of disability! Edward Albee's work is full of it. If we're sticking to American playwrights here, just think of Eugene O'Neill, Arthur Miller, Cherríe Moraga, Marsha Norman, or Anna Deavere Smith, to name a few; disability appears in their plays in significant ways. Other scholars and performers are revealing this about a playwright like, say, Samuel Beckett: for example, Michael Davidson's analysis of *Endgame* (see Davidson 2019), or Jess Thom's amazing performance of *Not I*, framed as a narrative about and imbued with her Tourette's (see British Council Arts 2017). While disability culture has moved beyond the canon to become its own thing, it's important that we not simply see disability presence as disabled people reacting to nondisabled people.

Sandahl: Agreed. And we can't do all this work with the small (albeit growing) numbers of disability drama/performance scholars. In addition to the literary metaphors that we discussed earlier, other topics that desperately need attention include the history of disabled theatre practitioners, the link between medicine and actor training (such as rehabilitation practices and actor training, see Sandahl 2005), the accessibility—physical, financial, educational, and attitudinal—of our stages and audiences spaces, the role of marketing and reviews in creating and reflecting audience expectations of disability representation, social policy's link to educational and training opportunities for disabled theatre artists. (See Patrick McKelvey's work for a foray into the topic of disability employment in theatre (2019).) And we need to teach the canon to deconstruct it, don't we? Perhaps we can teach canonical work, but not as much of it? Or pair canonical texts with work that references it? For example, I spend so much time explaining a parody's canonical references that the parody loses its punch. An explained joke is simply no longer funny. Perhaps the fact that a parody loses its oppressive referent is a sign that it's no longer a necessary critique. I don't have an answer. Might we need a more balanced approach?

Fox: Yes, I think we do need that kind of balanced approach. You and I were in graduate school at a time where it was very fashionable—at least from a feminist perspective—to bash the canon. But you can't critique the canon if you don't know what's in it! And works that have been canonized can be very moving, and still have deep resonance for us today, even if we also understand they can be problematic. But we can also bring new—and forgotten—works to light as we teach traditional ones. This is as true for disability works as it is for anything else. I will say, though: I still hate Strindberg. A lot.

Sandahl: I like *Miss Julie* (sorry). Brings up a point about whose tastes get to inform the canon.

Fox: Ha! Exactly. We could argue *Miss Julie* shows a really important and interesting way in which a disability reading helps us uncover the play's misogyny (i.e., she is "hysterical" because she is menstruating).

Sandahl: Bringing up how disability intersects with gender makes me think of other productive intersections. We can apply a disability studies lens to canon formations that are emerging in the theatre history of groups that, historically, have been left out (and, well, still are). For instance, minstrelsy. How did the intersection of Jim Crow's disability (e.g., his "crippledness"), Blackness, and maleness inform the development of minstrelsy—in terms of ideology, choreography, and enduring legacy? Scholars have raised the issue of Jim Crow's disability, but in a way that throws disability under the bus (e.g., his crippledness as an example of the egregiousness of the stereotype—disability makes the representation *even worse*). What if we interrogated the disablement of Black men in the era and how this relates to the representation's popularity among white audiences? (See John Nickel (2004) for a place to begin on the intersections of race, gender, and disability in representations of black disabled men in American film.)

Fox: Maybe because we as disability scholars are used to living in the tension (say between categories like "disabled/nondisabled") it feels easier to live liminally like this.

One of my concerns, however, is that disabled people get grief from both directions. Disability is part of new canons being shaped: plays featuring communities that have been traditionally oppressed are getting acclaim—an amazing thing. So for example, Martyna Majok's *Cost of Living* (2016) features disabled main characters who are played by disabled actors, but disability also intersects with issues of class, race, and isolation. Yet for every play that casts a nuanced look at the social, relational, and economic aspects of disability like *Cost of Living*, there seems to be another that still rests on the same old ableist imagery to advance an otherwise progressive message. Consider the ending of Lynn Nottage's *Sweat* (2015), for example, where disability becomes the punishment for racial and class discord. I was livid when I saw how audiences wept at the end when they saw a newly-disabled character limp out, the innocent victim of others' anger who now has a traumatic brain injury because he tried to stop a fight. Nottage made space for people to feel good about feeling sorry for the disabled character, using him as a cheap shortcut on the way to her call for social justice; he's nothing more than the ghost of racial injustice present. So we also need to hold contemporary drama that advocates for social justice accountable for how disability exists in the vision of inclusion and diversity for which it advocates (see Fox 2020).

Sandahl: And do we take the identity of the playwright into account in the shaping of the canon? Martyna Majok is an ally and, from what I've heard, not disabled herself.

Where are the disabled playwrights who are telling these stories? Furthermore, what does it mean when she disavows disability in interviews? What I mean by this is comments like the one she told an interviewer when asked about her interest in writing about disability: "I don't think I'm examining disability. I wrote a play about class and yearning and loneliness and the journey towards connection with other human beings in America that happens to feature two disabled characters" (Marks 2018). Sure, the play has provided opportunities for professional actors with disabilities, but why undermine the power of these opportunities for our community by writing about disability while at the same disavowing it?

I know you have found a lot to discuss in Majok's play about disability (see Fox 2018). Whether or not she owns it, the play is about disability AND class AND yearning AND loneliness. These issues are intersectional and uniquely inflected by disability in the play.

Fox: Absolutely! I think it becomes especially important for her—or any playwright who writes meaningfully about the intersectional nature of disability—to own that, especially given that many, if not most, reviews of plays that feature disability tend to trade in disability stereotypes as it is. And her denial perpetuates the notion that disability is something we shouldn't discuss.

Sandahl: We don't have enough published disability-centric plays and criticism. I've been wanting to put together an anthology of solo disability pieces. Victoria Ann Lewis (a.k.a. Vicki) and I started that project once, but then life got in the way. We really don't have enough publications of playtexts or performance documentation.

Fox: I need to remember, as much as we know, there is so little actually published for others without our personal connections to discover. Luckily there's a new anthology coming out from John Michael Sefel (Sefel et al. 2020); we need more of this kind of work!

Sandahl: And Vicki's anthology (Lewis 2006) features Charles Mee—a well-known disabled playwright who doesn't talk about his work in terms of disability—so an anthology that's disability-centric or includes "disability-adjacent" works can also help us reframe what we're even calling "disability."

I feel like people don't buy anthologies as much but pick and choose and post to Blackboard. We need a way to do this that's clearly within copyright. We need to be able to easily make our own anthologies. Many publishers have articles or chapters you can download without buying the whole book or journal. Or e-books in the library. This was a bigger problem before e-publishing. Let's embrace the way instructors are always mixing and matching source material for their classes. And make it affordable.

Fox: I love this: a sort of DIY anthology, which seems so in the spirit of access and disability workarounds.

Sandahl: Maybe taking an intersectional approach to disability would give instructors a way to incorporate a disability analysis into works they already teach. You and I have talked about how, for example, the anthology *Contemporary Plays by Women of Color* edited by Perkins and Uno (1996) has so many plays that feature disability, including Glenda Dickerson and Breena Clarke's *Re/membering Aunt Jemima: A Menstrual Show* (1992), Cherríe

Moraga's *Heroes and Saints* (1992), and Kia Corthron's *Come Down Burning* (1993), for example.

Even if a play isn't "about" disability, disability representation is everywhere. Remember this was revelatory and almost our mantra at the NEH seminar? So true. It's everywhere.

Fox: You can't unsee it. And disability encompasses so many kinds of experiences besides obvious physical disabilities, many of which are featured frequently on stage: addiction, cancer, and mental illness, to name just a few. In the essay you wrote for the 2018 issue of *The Journal of Literary and Cultural Studies* we co-edited, you talked about asking your students: what is the work this representation is doing? My students and I often make use of the red-light, yellow-light, and green-light system you devised as a shorthand for thinking about representations.

Sandahl: My light system (red for words to almost never use, yellow for use with caution, and green for words that are almost always ok to use) has been a way to capture how language is context-dependent, rather than to prescribe "good" and "bad" disability words. I'm not in a theatre and drama department anymore, so I haven't had as much opportunity to teach plays. And when I do, my classes are more geared toward learning about disability through the arts and creating disability art. Most of my students—the undergraduates anyway—are in applied health or the social sciences. I miss the deep disciplinary engagement about theatre and drama with students who are steeped in the field. By "steeped in," do I really mean knowledgeable about a shared canon? Yikes, I think I might. Help! I need to reflect on this. How do you approach the dramatic canon in your teaching?

Fox: There are some canonical texts that are vital to teach but also breathtaking in their complexity approached in a new way. For example, Ibsen does a fascinating job exposing the lie that immorality corrupts the body in *A Doll's House*. By the time Torvald wants to send Nora away so she won't corrupt the children, we understand her forgery as deeply ethical—she was saving her husband's life within an economic system that would not legally allow her to borrow the money for his care, and within a patriarchal system in which she had to preserve his masculine pride.

Sandahl: And Torvald's disability—his illness—launches the entire narrative.

Fox: I can't believe I never thought about that! And Nora has been a resourceful caregiver, to say the least. One might even argue that she confides in disabled Doctor Rank because she sees in him a kindred spirit; they are both outliers in this normate world of moral hypocrisy. Torvald's bloviating speech about Dr. Rank after he dies affirms our disdain for the kind of normalcy Torvald espouses (doubly ironic, given his own illness—although he clearly sees himself as re-normalized because he was cured). And yet, the doctor dies, and does seem to embody the notion that the sins of the parents are visited on the children (since he dies of syphilis contracted because of his father's infidelities). Even if we can't resolve this contradiction, we can deploy canonical texts to deepen conversations around disability about which we care a great deal.

Sandahl: It would be interesting to think about Dr. Rank's disability in terms of sexual morality. His "spinal tuberculosis" is coded language for end-stage syphilis. Ibsen's representational strategy of using disability as a eugenic cautionary tale reminds me of the American "hygiene film," *The Black Stork* from 1917. In that eugenics-era film, audiences are warned against loose women who will infect otherwise-upstanding men with sexually transmitted illnesses. These men will then infect their wives who will give birth to disabled progeny. Not only does the film portend these births, but it argues for euthanizing disabled infants. Sexual immorality = disability = death. Taken together, *The Black Stork* and *A Doll's House* paint a stark picture of the ideological environment in which disabled people in Eurocentric countries lived.

Fox: The canon, of course, still plays out on the stages where our students perform and direct. I would pose these questions to any theatre department caught between having to stage the canon and their own concern about how to represent disability:

- Have you sought out and cast disabled students, even if they don't match your image of what virtuosity looks like?
- Have you thought about cross-ability casting?
- Have you tried to avoid plays that use disability as an out-and-out destructive metaphor?
- If the work you are doing features a disability that could be depicted in a hackneyed way, have you sought out acting, directing, and design choices that might reframe it?
- Have you refrained from simply shrugging and saying "It is what it is; I can't change the script"?

In some ways, it's very situational. I've had a student approach me because he thought I could help him make connections in the disability community so he could be all Method and shadow someone to play the "village fool" character he was playing. Instead, I gave him literature about the dramaturgy of disability. He ended up doing a really good job finding space in his acting choices to resist what the role called for in the hackneyed script. That might on the surface feel like a failure, but I actually saw it as a quasi-victory. That young man not only intervened into the portrayal through his own performance but now hopefully when he goes on to perform/direct, will approach the presence of disability in a more nuanced and thoughtful way. So the results are mixed. Ideological purity isn't always possible.

Sandahl: I've had similar situations. Although, I do think some disability representation is beyond rehabilitation. For instance, I don't think there is much one can do with a character like Tennessee Williams' Brick in *Cat on a Hot Tin Roof*. Brick's injury and subsequent wheelchair use—and all the stereotypes that go along with them—are central to the plot. Or consider a bit more recent example such as Marsha Norman's Jessie in *'night Mother*. Without Jessie's epilepsy and resulting suicidal ideation *as* the plot's action, there is no play. Jessie's suicide only makes sense as an act of empowerment *because of* stereotypical disability metaphors.

It's one thing to read and discuss these canonized plays when you can spend time with the material in the classroom, but it's another to stage it for a general audience. I guess I'm still strident here. You might need to convince me a bit more about how an actor can make choices that hold any sway over the sedimented meanings of canonical disabled characters. Over the course of my career, I've had a fair number of students ask me how to respectfully embody a disabled character. Or they want to know about the technical aspects of performing disability. Surely, there is technical skill involved, but disability experience resonates far beyond the limp, the wheelchair, the American Sign Language, the crutches, the wayfinding cane…blah, blah, blah. It's a lived experience that is always political, and fully human in ways that are rarely articulated in the play texts themselves. And this brings us back to the pipeline problem. If we don't have disabled actors, directors, practitioners, then we don't have disabled people who can produce new disability plays. I wonder if it gets to be a choice between producing identity-specific work or the canon.

Fox: I do think there are disruptive stagings to be found if we approach the canon carefully. I think of Jill Dolan's essay about Wendy Wasserstein where she acknowledges she needed to shift her understanding of feminism to appreciate Wasserstein (see Dolan 2008). There are opportunities for interventionist stagings in canonical work if we make use of disability. (Deaf West and their work is an obvious example, but so is Sam Gold's 2017 production of *The Glass Menagerie*).

Sandahl: I try not to hate on the canon. You're right. The tone is off. Maybe we can have a love-hate relationship with it. Maybe we can be frenemies with the canon?

Fox: That's it exactly! I want to be frenemies with it! Or maybe amicable exes!

Sandahl: I like amicable exes! Co-parents?

Fox: Why not? But the all-or-nothing approach feels binaristic and limited/limiting.

Sandahl: True.

Fox: It also seems pretty depressing to contemplate rejecting everything that came before in the interest of being neo-futurists. And it's not like the "future" isn't flawed in itself; it would be the height of irony—not to mention arrogance—to replicate the chronological chauvinism underscoring the idea that newer is better. Disabled people have to negotiate a world that can't imagine they have a future in it—just look at how society would rather talk about technological advancements that erase disability than making disabled people's lives easier through access and accommodation. The future isn't necessarily better! So I just can't quit the canon quite yet!

Sandahl: Right, and not after I spent eight years of grad school learning it! And 11 years teaching it at Florida State University without totally rejecting it. Maybe because my training included both canonical and noncanonical work, it seems hasty to do away with the canon. And, then there's prelims I did in theatre history, literature, and theory from the Greeks to the present. I have to admit, the discipline of learning a canon helped me understand why things are the way they are to better address the terms of the oppressor. Ok, I'm flip-flopping all over the place here. I'm a frenemy of the canon, for sure. Oh, I need to re-read Jill's writing about Wasserstein that you mention.

Fox: I actually used her work in a piece I wrote about the avoidance of disability in drama as a field (see Fox 2015). I found her arguments really resonant for me. She observes: "Perhaps it is now time to acknowledge the potential of looking inside [rather than on the political and artistic margins] as well, and to address feminism as a critique or value circulating within our most commercial theatres" (Dolan 2008: 435). I think we can also say something very similar to disability, particularly in the way I have tried to approach it.

Sandahl: Yes. This is why I wanted to have this conversation with you because over the years you've done a lot to convince me of the value of disability imagery in canonical texts.

Fox: Thank you! I never want to be an apologist for ableism, but I do think that with disability in canonical works, there can be nuance. Interestingly, I think my grad training had a lot to do with that. I came of age as an academic, like you, in the 1990s when edgy feminist performance was in vogue. Yet I found the in-between spaces and the less obvious feminism interesting—why I wrote on early 20th-century playwrights Sophie Treadwell and Rachel Crothers, among others. I have learned a great deal from you about the significance of disability performance and disability culture—and particularly a disability performance culture that speaks to the community itself.

Sandahl: I don't ever see you as an apologist, just being a clear critical voice. Another thing about when we were in grad school is that so much of the feminist work spoke back to the canon. We're a good team. Maybe we could start the dialogue about when you and I talked about "territory" at NEH and ATHE. The field of disability and performance was truly wide open. I recall you, Petra Kuppers, and I kind of divided it up at first. You were gonna cover modern drama, I was gonna cover new disability theatre, and Petra Kuppers was going to cover performance art. Am I remembering correctly?

Fox: I think that's absolutely right. You and Petra clearly were working on disability performance and I was so new to the field that for me, it made more sense to use this amazing new lens to look at the work I loved. And so I've written about how disability applied to dramatic literature ever since. And I think you, Petra, and I have had our own areas of the field but have also been very open to understanding how each other's work informs our own. We all criss-cross territories now. I'm writing about adaptive activism in plays that have met with recent acclaim on Broadway: plays like Amy Herzog's *Mary Jane* (2017), Mike Lew's *Teenage Dick* (2018), and *Cost of Living*; I've also made forays into other kinds of visual representation like curating and graphic medicine. Those were completely unexpected directions for me, but they've brought me a lot of joy! Both bring disability studies to audiences I might not otherwise encounter doing literary disability studies. And they have also been ways for me to practice my own kind of disability arts. (I even made a comic about an experience with injury!)

Sandahl: We're also both doing creative work in disability arts. You have become known for your curation of disability art exhibitions. The film *Code of the Freaks* (2020) that I collaborated on with Susan Nussbaum, Aly Patsavas, and Salome Chasnoff is out in the world!!! I will shamelessly self-promote the film here to theatre professors. It does the work of breaking down how disability has been represented in film, and, in most cases, it applies to theatre as well. We had the educational setting in mind when we made the film. My hope is that the film will be shown as an overview so as to pave the way for more complex discussion—beyond the tired tropes of disability—as a semester progresses (Figures 10.1 and 10.2).

Fox: I am so excited about *Code of the Freaks*! It's a completely smart, elegant way to make several important points about disability representation clear at once. I'm excited about my most recent project, too: I'm collaborating again with a brilliant curator, Jessica Cooley, who is responsible for bringing me into curatorial work in the first place. We're working with the Ford Foundation Gallery in New York City to bring an online and in-person exhibition, *Indisposable: Structures of Support after the ADA*, to life. With disability as the binding thread, it will explore how the support structures for life (health insurance, housing, food security, and education) are insecure at best for far too many people. COVID-19 and the continuing effects of white supremacy expose an ideological landscape where some

Figure 10.1 The actor Mat Fraser in the documentary *Code of the Freaks* (2020)

lives, particularly those living at the intersection of disability, queer, and BIPOC communities, are deemed disposable. We want to emphasize this and explore the many ways in which crip existence, knowledge, support structures, and creativity *are* indisposable, as are, of course, disabled lives.

Sandahl: I feel like we're coming to a close here—now that we've resorted to hawking our own work—but I want to throw in one more thing. I've found that when people don't know canonical texts, they often don't understand works that speak back to the canon. Such as *Annie Dearest* or *Scary Lewis Yell-a-Thon*, which are parodies by Mickee Faust Theatre of *The*

Figure 10.2 *Teenage Dick* by Mike Lew at Theatre Wit (2020). Directed by Brian Balcom. From left to right, performers MacGregor Arney (RICHARD) and Tamar Rozofsky (BUCK).

Miracle Worker and *The Jerry Lewis Telethon*, respectively. When I show these films to my students, I have to show them the source materials first because they are too young to remember the original. Again, the power is taken away from the punch when you have to explain it. What about the new play *Teenage Dick* that revises *Richard III* from a disability perspective? Do audiences need to know the original to get the play? What do we lose when we lose the canon? Are we throwing the baby out with the bath water? (Figure 10.2)
Fox: That's exactly right. I'm currently teaching *Teenage Dick* but I have to pair it with *Richard III*. If we throw the canon out, we lose the sense of what works like Lew's are responding to. Plus we also lose a disability history we need to know, whether Helen Keller (and William Gibson's *The Miracle Worker*) or Jerry Lewis's telethons.
Sandahl: Ah, yes. So much more work for all of us to do.

Works Cited

British Council Arts. 2017. "Edinburgh Showcase 2017: 'Not I by Samuel Beckett' by Touretteshero and Battersea Arts Centre." YouTube, 28 January. Accessed 20 July 2019. https://www.youtube.com/watch?v=Bwv8riGhOcw.

Chasnoff, Salome 2020. dir. *Code of the Freaks*. New York: Kino Lorber.

Davidson, Michael. 2019. *Invalid Modernism: Disability and the Missing Body of the Aesthetic*. Oxford: Oxford University Press.

Dolan, Jill. 2008. "Feminist Performance Criticism and the Popular: Reviewing Wendy Wasserstein." *Theatre Journal* 60, 3: 433–457.

Fox, Ann M. 2004. "'But, Mother—I'm—crippled!' Tennessee Williams, Queering Disability, and Dis/Membered Bodies in Performance." In *Gendering Disability*, edited by Bonnie G. Smith and Beth Hutchison, 233–252. New Brunswick: Rutgers University Press.

Fox, Ann M. 2015. "Fabulous Invalids Together: Why Disability in Mainstream Theater Matters." In *Disability, Avoidance, and the Academy: Challenging Resistance*, edited by David Bolt and Clare Penketh, 122–132. New York: Routledge.

Fox, Ann M. 2016. "Reclaiming the Ordinary Extraordinary Body: Or, The Importance of *The Glass Menagerie* for Literary Disability Studies." In *Recasting Modernism: Disability Theatre and Modernism*, edited by Kirsty Johnston, 129–152. New York: Bloomsbury.

Fox, Ann M. 2018. "Staging the Complexities of Care: Martyna Majok's *Cost of Living*." *Journal of Literary & Cultural Disability Studies* 12, 2: 145–160.

Fox, Ann M. 2020. "Disability, Drama, and the Problem of Intersectional Invisibility." In *The Routledge Companion to Literature and Disability*, edited by Alice Hall, 290–302. New York: Routledge.

Fox, Ann M. Forthcoming. "Making Disability Activism Adaptive: Redefining Health and Healing Through Art." In *Health and Healing in Culture and Literature*, edited by Jeff Howlett, Defne Ersin Tutan, and Gözde Kılıç. Wilmington, DE: Vernon Press.

Lewis, Victoria. 2006. *Beyond Victims and Villains: Contemporary Plays by Disabled Playwrights*. New York: Theatre Communications Group.

Marks, Brian. 2018. "Immigration Crises, Through a Polish Lens: Martyna Majok's 'Cost of

Living' at the Fountain." Accessed 20 July 2020. https://thisstage.la/2018/11/immigration-crises-through-a-polish-lens-martyna-majoks-cost-of-living-at-the-fountain/

McKelvey, Patrick. 2019. "A Disabled Actor Prepares: Stanislavsky, Disability, and Work at the National Theatre Workshop of the Handicapped." *Theatre Journal* 71, 1 (March): 69–89.

McRuer, Robert. 2006. *Crip Theory: Cultural Signs of Queerness and Disability*. New York: New York University Press.

Mitchell, David T., and Sharon L. Snyder. 2011. *Narrative Prosthesis: Disability and the Dependencies of Discourse*. Ann Arbor: University of Michigan Press.

Nickel, John. 2004. "Disabling African American Men: Liberalism and Race Message Films" *Cinema Journal* 44, 1: 25–48.

Nielsen, Kim E. 2012. *A Disability History of the United States*. Boston: Beacon Press.

Perkins, Kathy A., and Roberta Uno, eds. 1996. *Contemporary Plays by Women of Color: an Anthology*. New York: Routledge.

Sandahl, Carrie, and Philip Auslander, eds. 2005. *Bodies in Commotion: Disability and Performance*. Ann Arbor: University of Michigan Press.

Sandahl, Carrie. 2005. "The Tyranny of Neutral: Disability and Actor Training." In *Bodies in Commotion: Disability and Performance*, edited by Carrie Sandahl and Philip Auslander, 255–268. Ann Arbor: University of Michigan Press.

Sandahl, Carrie. 2018. "Using our Words: Exploring Representational Conundrums in Disability Drama and Performance." *Journal of Literary & Cultural Disability Studies* 12, 2: 129–144.

Sefel, John Michael, Amanda Slamcik Lassetter, and Jill Summerville, eds. 2020. *At the Intersection of Disability and Drama: A Critical Anthology of New Plays*. Jefferson, NC: McFarland.

Stiker, Henri-Jacques. 1999. *A History of Disability*. Ann Arbor: University of Michigan Press.

11 The Uses of Awe

Rinde Eckert and Ellen McLaughlin

In which Ellen McLaughlin and Rinde Eckert discuss the Western canon as it applies to their work in theatre and opera as writers and performers. Both are playwrights who have also worked in music theatre as performers and librettists; Rinde is a composer as well. They have each written plays based on canonical work (Eckert: Dante—*The Gardening of Thomas D.*; Herman Melville—*And God Created Great Whales*; McLaughlin: Virginia Woolf—*Septimus and Clarissa*), and both have made extensive use of classical Greek sources. McLaughlin has written adaptations of numerous Greek plays, some of which are collected in *The Greek Plays Plays*; her most recent offering was The Oresteia, which premiered at the Shakespeare Theatre Company in Washington, D.C., in 2019.

Ellen McLaughlin: When we talk about the canon, it seems to me that we are always asking a question the Greeks were fond of asking: "What do we owe to the dead?"
Rinde Eckert: Or maybe the question is, "What do the dead have to teach us?" We're always weighing the need for reverence for our ancestors against the desire to expand and innovate.
McLaughlin: When did the idea of the canon come into being? It has to be a modern idea. I've always been struck by the idea that in the Renaissance, for instance, a man who sought to educate himself and could read Greek and Latin had a good chance of being able in his lifetime to read everything in those languages that was available in print. Now the sea of work available to the literate is so overwhelming that there is no human possibility of reading even a good fraction of it. So decisions are made in the culture, presumably in academia, to sort through the overabundance and come up with what are defined as essential works.
Eckert: I think the idea of the canon, at least in Europe, has to begin in the end of the eighteenth century with the opening up of the great palaces—the democratic notion of public art coming into being with the fall of monarchy. The Louvre, after all, is just a palace, a previously private collection, opened up to the public. Great libraries that had been accessible only to one wealthy family are made public, and public universities come into being.

DOI: 10.4324/9781003031413-11

McLaughlin: And with that, the idea is not only that great works should be accessible to the many but that the many need to be taught why those works are worthy of study. There's the sense that the canon has to be formulated so that you can develop a curriculum—which is the idea of a liberal arts education. It's not for artists who are making new work so much as it's to educate the members of the public, who are going to appreciate that work or not according to what they have learned.

Eckert: But it was concerned with training artists as well. In Europe, artists start to be trained by academies to study the canon thoroughly so that they can then go out into the world knowing what their legacy is—what has already been done in their fields. The institutions are there in large part to preserve a heritage of thought and teach it. When you talk about the flooding of culture with the expansion of the printed word, and then recordings and videos and now the unimaginable size of what's available—the library of human culture—one of the things that's lost is a sense of the common. Shakespeare could refer to folklore, stories, and shared history. He could make biblical allusions that he didn't have to explain, knowing they would have meaning for his audience. But now, do we all share a body of lore anymore? What stories do we have in common? The canon at its best has given us a way to sort and navigate through the material and set aside the detritus in order to figure out what's important.

McLaughlin: Ideally, it serves to give us common stories. Allusions that are useful in making sense of things. We need Clytemnestra and King Lear.

Eckert: Ahab and Don Giovanni.

McLaughlin: But then, I don't know whom I mean when I say "we" in that way.

Eckert: Yeah, who's the "we" we're referring to?

McLaughlin: We speak as two middle-aged white artists who both received extensive education in the Western canon at a time when that canon consisted almost exclusively of dead white male artists. I didn't even read the works of many dead white *female* writers—much less those of contemporary women of color—in school. It was largely outside of college that I read those writers.

Eckert: And yet you were an Afro-American studies major for a while there at Yale.

McLaughlin: Well, growing up in Washington, D.C., I fell in love with jazz early on. I spent an awful lot of my time in high school trying not to get carded in jazz clubs and soaking that music in. So when I had the opportunity to study it, I did.

Eckert: Yes, I was listening to jazz classics early too, and Jimi Hendrix, and whatever blues I could get my hands on. I consider Hendrix part of the musical canon, as Duke Ellington is, and Billie Holiday. I was also listening to Ravi Shankar a lot. There wasn't much available in the sixties by comparison to what we can hear now, but I was doing my best to open up my ears to the vast world outside the Western canon. But the Western classical world was pretty consuming. Part of the issue here is that the Western canon was written down. The great music of India, by contrast, was passed down by hand and ear. The great gamelan music was taught by imitation as well. So if you're in the middle of Iowa in the sixties and not very worldly in the first place—a suburban white boy—you're not going to have any idea what the wider world has been doing and for how long. One could enter the mind of Bach through the score. And the library had those scores. (In my case they were in my parents' piano bench.)

McLaughlin: That's the problem with a reliance on, well, *paper,* meaning a reliance on libraries. It limits one to what can be written down, when so much that informs us and drives the culture is not anything you're going to find in a library.

Eckert: Look, before the age of recordings, if you wanted to enter into the mind of some great composer of ragas, you were out of luck. Availability of sources makes a difference. If you have to know someone who knows someone who knows what's important to hear and how and where to find it, you're less likely to expand your notion of the canon outside the boundaries of the available culture.

McLaughlin: American culture is steeped in influences that can't be understood in terms of recordings or the written word. African influences are essential to the way American music developed, of course, but African story forms are no less important in determining the difference between the way Americans tell stories and the way, say, Europeans do. And American folk traditions, which aren't readily accessible in libraries, also include Native American structural ideas. These aren't aspects of the culture I was ever taught in school, but I could feel them working in me nevertheless. I think one of the reasons the Greeks are so central to the canon as it's taught is that they *can* be taught. It's amazing to have this literature one can actually *read* that was written two thousand years ago.

Eckert: Right. And that's the problem. We have very few examples from that period of performance pieces from any other place in the world. Japanese Noh theatre is only about 650 years old, and Bunraku goes back to about Shakespeare's time. Shadow puppetry in India probably goes back to the third century B.C.E. but was not codified in any rigorous way. African theatrical form was rich and profound but could not be translated or transcribed in any way. It had to be handed down, witnessed, *felt* to be understood.

McLaughlin: Again, it's the crucial difference between a literary tradition—like that of the Greeks—and an oral one when it comes to ancient sources.

Eckert: So we are faced now with the need to revise the canon in the wake of movies and video recordings dating back a mere hundred years. Since our Western institutions were set up to deal with the history of Western thought and the texts and scores of antiquity, those institutions have been slow to adapt to the changing nature of documentation and the epistemology necessary to analyze and teach based on a visual or aural record. But the work goes on.

McLaughlin: I have to believe that a far more diverse canon is being taught now than was the case when we were in college.

Eckert: The limiting of the canon to one's familiars is not necessarily a choice but a matter of circumstance and probability. That said, many of us are trying to expand our horizons. It never happens fast enough, but the circumstances we find ourselves in are not surprising or necessarily voluntary, given both human nature and fate.

McLaughlin: It's important to cop to each of us having a different idea of the canon because of our educations, and that initially we are limited by what we were exposed to while growing up. We are all formed by those influences, at least until we take over our education and search out our own ideas of essential cultural works—which I'm finding is a lifelong endeavor, expanding my personal canon.

Eckert: It's what you have to do if you are going to be an artist in this world who can speak with any usefulness to the moment.

McLaughlin: Which leads me to the idea of what a canon, however, defined, is there to do. Which, I would say, is to provide a culture with common stories. I think we need them, but I suppose I could just say *I* need those stories; they have helped me immeasurably in making sense of the world.

Eckert: But what you're talking about is more than a personal need. In making art, an artist wants to be able to make references to common stories and characters—ways of making sense that have lasted—because, without those shared sources, it's so much more difficult to communicate.

McLaughlin: Exactly. Well, for instance, I wasn't raised in any system of religious belief. I don't know any holy book well and never attended any place of worship during my childhood, so there is a wealth of literature—ritual structures and so forth—that is largely lost on me. I've played catch-up over the years in order to be able to partake of all kinds of art and understand what's being evoked, but these aren't my stories. They don't, for one thing, have any spiritual heft for me because I'm not a believer, but also, because I came to them late, they just aren't known to me in the way that lore that is part of a child's upbringing is known and felt.

Eckert: Which is probably why you're so clued in to Greek mythology. You came across it in childhood and it was a kind of indoctrination into meaning.

McLaughlin: Yes! *D'Aulaires' Book of Greek Myths* was the first book I was able to read to myself. It went in deep.

Eckert: Well, as I've always said, you're basically a pagan.

McLaughlin: I am! But yeah, there is a lot to be said for a common culture and a pool of shared references. Those are hard to come by now, when we're all stuck in our separate cultural silos with our earbuds in so no one else can hear the music, and while we read our ebooks, which makes it impossible to see what anyone else is reading. (I really miss being able to sneak looks into the books people are reading on the subway. Sometimes that led to the kinds of great conversations with strangers that you just can't have anymore.) I often think of what you've said about the Beatles—that when they were walking around Liverpool in their adolescence, dodging the bomb craters and rubble that were still very much in evidence through the fifties, what they were hearing on the streets was American jukebox music, early rock and roll, and rhythm and blues; but also sentimental favorites from the Second World War on the radio, and coming out of the pubs would have been the sound of sing-alongs, ballads, and English folk songs, and then there was music-hall stuff, not to mention hymns sung in the churches, Sousa marches at the bandstand ... all these influences bleeding into their consciousness. And it all shows up in their music, but with a great sense of play and innovation.

Eckert: Right. And that's what comes from being able to work from a common musical language. Part of the joy of listening to the music is hearing all the richness—influences high and low and everything in between—that they are working with. And when it comes to the weight of the past, they know where they come from, but they aren't constrained by it. There's love for all that came before, but there's also humor and the overriding desire to make something new.

McLaughlin: Which reminds me that your understanding of the nature of canons is different from mine in that it's specifically linked to your upbringing in a family of opera singers and voice teachers, which means that you've been reckoning with the canon of Western *music* all your life as well as with the literary canon. You also trained as an opera singer in the graduate program at Yale during the seventies, and have gone on to compose and perform new work in the medium. Though you have a deep understanding of the form, and serious skills as a singer, in particular, your work as an artist has been largely outside the opera world's traditions.

Eckert: Well, I grew up inside the opera world and have a great love of it. But the institution of opera has ossified the form and set up strict controls on what can be done with it. It's a misunderstanding of the use of the canon. So you're forced to be iconoclastic if you make new opera because no one inside is acknowledging the problems of the opera canon as defined by its major institutions. Which leads to blowback; you're treated as if you are being disrespectful, working against the canon somehow.

McLaughlin: Whereas playwrights are expected to reimagine established texts. It's, after all, what the classical Greeks were doing themselves: constantly reworking the myths, remaking them to suit the needs of the times.

Eckert: Well, no playscript is as codified as a musical score. And when it comes to the Greeks, we have the advantage of *not* knowing how the plays were performed originally.

McLaughlin: Yes, they're old enough to be unfettered by any definitive tradition of performance. We have some clues from the remains of the theatres and from artwork of the time depicting masks and so forth, but much of what happened in those performances is still a mystery. From the music—most, if not all, of the performance was sung—to the style of the acting to any sense of the movement, since much of it was danced, we just don't know. So we can guess but we can't get doctrinaire, because all of that knowledge has been lost. We can see the beauty of the texts, and we know that the plays in performance had extraordinary power, but we don't know how they were done. And that's really helpful when it comes to making new work.

Eckert: Right, whereas classical music is rich in detail on how it's supposed to be performed. A score gives you everything—from how fast things need to be to all kinds of indications of nuance. We still have the instruments that classical music was composed on hundreds of years ago, and modern instruments are not so different. No matter what you do, a violin is still a violin. It has to be, or it won't make the sound you are looking for.

McLaughlin: The organs Bach played on are still in the churches he played them in.

Eckert: So what happens in the classical music world is that the first response to new work is comparative. Whatever you've done doesn't compare to, you know, *Beethoven*. Well, of course it doesn't. But comparisons aren't useful when it comes to new work.

McLaughlin: It's this notion of "greatness." Which is really a way of talking about what we have been taught—what we understand because it has been part of the culture for so long.

Eckert: It's what we already know. We know how to listen to Beethoven because we've had hundreds of years of listening to it. If you sit in your room and stare at the wallpaper long enough, you can see subtleties there. Your grandfather's face is not the face of a stranger. You know the depths and beauty of that face in a way that you can't about someone you're seeing for the first time. We've been staring at Beethoven's face for centuries.

McLaughlin: When I've gotten bad reviews, I've taken comfort in remembering some of the most disastrous opening nights in history: [Anton] Chekhov's *Seagull* in St. Petersburg …

Eckert: *Waiting for Godot* [by Samuel Beckett] at the Coconut Grove in Florida…

McLaughlin: *The Rite of Spring* [by Igor Stravinsky] in 1913 in Paris, for god's sake.

Eckert: So many of the essential works that make up the canon had hard births precisely because they defied tradition, whereas much of the work that didn't and received great praise at the time has been forgotten. When the canon is seen as sacrosanct, it's a no-win situation. The art form can't progress. It's stultifying.

McLaughlin: It seems to me that when we are dealing with the canon as artists, it's a matter of balancing the need to progress against knowing what's worked in the past. We study the canon out of a desire for rules—looking for structures that have grandeur but also provide flexible ways of shaping meaning and organizing power by giving it form.

Eckert: But there is a difference between structural forms and structural

systems, and that's where the use of the canon becomes trickiest. In terms of form, in the music world, the sonata form dominated music for centuries—
McLaughlin: Just as the sonnet form did in poetry—
Eckert: And the most important form in twentieth-century music is the blues. These are forms that admit extraordinary variety in terms of what you can make with them. They shape but don't determine. The problem is when you have a *system*. For instance, one canonized system that gained a kind of stranglehold on modern classical music was serialism, [Arnold] Schoenberg's 12-tone technique, and its scions, which became the darlings of the academy because they yielded so well to analysis and were so teachable, but weren't great for music because they couldn't generate much worthwhile new work (particularly work with emotional range). It's not that there's anything wrong with these systems, particularly for a few great composers, but when a system or system-think dominates the curricula of academe, it produces teachers and critics who mistake complexity for sophistication. And then we lose our grasp on forms that might better serve the creation of new work.
McLaughlin: Yeah, so when we talk about the uses of the canon and the dangers of it, we're talking about how ideas of time-tested structure, *form*, can be liberating—the tragic form in Greek classical literature or the sonata form in music—because such forms give themselves over to infinite variation, as opposed to a *system* like serialism, which is far more rigid and constraining and which, if you attempt to use it to make something new, only reinforces itself and mostly demonstrates that you will never do it as well as the people who created it. The canon can inspire us to respond to the past in our own ways or it can work to intimidate and silence us.
Eckert: If we experience art only in the hushed safety of academe, we forget how radical it is. It wasn't meant to be read, it was meant to be lived through.
McLaughlin: Museums are useful. So are libraries. But there's a difference between a theatre or an opera house and a museum.
Eckert: If the only encounters with the past we're ever allowed are ones in which we are obligated to worship the greatness that is no more, then how does the culture progress? Sure, it's great to study and revere this work, but we also need to challenge it, make it ours, *use* it to understand who we are now. And though there's comfort to be found in knowing how long these things have survived, how well they have held up, you can't lose sight of how shocking some of them were when they first appeared.
McLaughlin: Yes, I'm always struck by just how disturbing Greek plays are. How at the center of each one there is an unthinkable thought, a terrible image that is designed to jolt us into a struggle with the ethical conundrum that the play circles and tries to resolve but can't. There is nothing tidy, nothing settled, at the end of a Greek play. These aren't nice pieces of literature you sit with your glass of sherry and savor; they bleed all over the floor if you try to bring them inside the house.
Eckert: I've found the Greeks a great counterforce to other parts of the

canon because of their freedom from any obligation to psychological realism. Those works aren't slices of life or a window into the kitchen.

McLaughlin: The idea of the Greeks as standing in opposition to the canon is ironic, right? Since they are so often held up as examples of the origin of the Western canon—the great source for everything that followed.

Eckert: Yes, the Greeks may be the basis of much of the work that came after. But even if the artistic descendants of the ancient Greeks borrowed certain formal ideas from those sources, they often failed to recognize other key elements that give that work its real power. You have to return to the original sources to be reminded of what made them seminal to begin with. To my mind, the power of Greek theatre lies in its poetics. That theatre is not interested in ordinary conversation or psychological realism, just as Shakespeare was not interested in ordinary conversation. His characters are not masking their intentions through politesse; they are trying to grapple with inner truth through poetic expression. His characters, like those of the Greeks, use language with panache and poetic extravagance.

McLaughlin: I think of the Greek plays as being written with primary colors. There is a level of abstraction, but the characters aren't types; there isn't anything generic about them. They are specific to themselves. They are aspects of the human that are not so much recognizable as identifiable as parts of the self. You don't think "That's just like Aunt Agnes." You think "Is that what I have in me?" The abstraction isn't intellectual; these are embodied truths.

Eckert: There are no easy victories of sentiment in these canonical works. They demand patience and attention from their audiences. We aren't being spoon-fed or comforted by "normal" conversation, the anodyne mannerisms of common life. When we lose hold of the poetic, something is lost from art; we have to return to work that still had faith in it. This is one of the reasons to return to canonical work over and over: to remind ourselves of the power of the poetic in a world increasingly preoccupied with surface, sentiment, and solace.

McLaughlin: Yes, and I think another misunderstanding that arises when the Greeks are positioned as, well, the "founding fathers"—and I do mean that ironically—of the Western canon is that they become solely the property of white culture, as if they were the original dead white guys, the Greats. But the power of their plays for me has always been in their mystery, flexibility, and adaptability, which are due to their abstraction and their very age. Because they are just so damn *old* and because the religion they are steeped in is no longer practiced by anyone, they belong to no one culture; they belong to all human beings. One of the most provocative versions I've ever seen of a Greek play was the *Yup'ik Antigone*, created by Yup'ik Eskimo in Alaska back in the eighties and performed in their own language. And I've always thought that the most successful adaptation of all was Lee Breuer's *Gospel at Colonus*, also performed in the eighties all over the world, which recast Sophocles' *Oedipus in Colonus* as a gospel ritual, a Pentecostal sermon in which the myth is told as a kind of Christian parable. Four professional gospel singing groups performed all the characters, along with a large choir and a few actors. For the first time, I understood the way the plays had originally been produced in the context of religious festivals. And it made perfect sense at last of the Greek notion, central to the ancients, that the only way we can ever learn what we need to know and be purified into joy is through suffering. It's a difficult concept to grasp, but it was the lived truth of that theatre experience. It was something I could never have understood through any dutiful attempt to reconstruct some idea of ancient theatre. It was profoundly Greek, as far as I was concerned, and there wasn't a white person on stage.

Eckert: Yeah, it was stunning. And I think the Greeks of the classical era would have understood it completely.

McLaughlin: One of the things that's most valuable to remember about the Greeks is that they were absolutely committed as a culture to the creation and investigation of the new. The great festivals that were the centerpiece of pan-Greek culture and were attended by people coming from across the country were all the equivalent of new-works festivals. The days-long marathons of plays—trilogies of tragedies followed by satyr plays—were all new. People weren't coming hundreds of miles to see something they'd already seen; they were coming to see brand-new work. *That was the point.* Greeks took the ancient stories they shared as a culture and remade them so that those stories might be understood in the context of the times the Greeks were all living through, addressing their plays to the issues of the moment. Making the plays and attending them, as a people, were how the Greeks made sense of their experience as they were in the midst of it. Which doesn't mean that the theatre, other than comedy, was overtly political; it wasn't. But the tragedies were written to speak to their moment, the concerns particularly of the people of Athens as they navigated through its most turbulent century. The point is that this was an entire populace that was devoted to new theatre; indeed, the audiences would have been disappointed to see anything other than new work. (And truly astonished to think that if people go to the theatre these days—and both of us are painfully aware of how few people see even one play a year—they are far more likely to see something old than anything new.)

Eckert: If you think about how money is spent now, that new work is always put in competition with old, established work and always loses because no one wants to go to anything unfamiliar—they think it's not a good bet—what would have happened to Greek theatre if it had been put in competition with itself?

McLaughlin: Yeah, everyone yelling, "Why can't you just put on *Oedipus* again? We liked *that* one!" No, they went to the theatre the way I often feel I do: I go because I want help in figuring out my life as I'm living it. There is a pressing need.

Eckert: And you can feel it in the plays—the urgency, the sense of a society's needs being met with art.

McLaughlin: The Greeks have given me courage and size, which I dearly wanted. Grappling with their work in any way will force you to put your money where your mouth is. You can't make neat little plays that don't attempt anything they can't handle if you're dealing with the Greeks, and I've found that liberating. Scary in the right way.

Eckert: I think that dealing with the Greeks released you from the obligation to write tidy, strictly naturalistic work, much as you might admire that when it's done well. There's an exhilaration to the ambition, the chutzpah, of the Greeks. There is an understanding of what theatre is supposed to do, which is to change the air we breathe. You wanted to engage with that and so the Greeks led you where they did.

McLaughlin: But I think that you have walked a similar path and dealt with the same desires by way of your lifelong relationship to the opera. Your whole upbringing and education drew you to opera—the size of it, its ambition, what it can do emotionally. But you are not interested in writing another [Giacomo] Puccini opera. That's been done, and it's wonderful, but it's not what you want to do with your time, because you're dedicated to making something new. You know how it was done; you've been inside these great works as a singer and you have analyzed them from without as a student of the form; you know why the opera works when it does and how it creates its peculiar, enduring intensity and beauty—but you take what you've learned and bring it to bear on entirely new experiments with the form. You borrow ideas of structure, but there is a playfulness and insouciance there since you're taking advantage of the form's flexibility even as you revel in its particular power and theatrical heft. You're not hampered by the rules passed down.

Eckert: Well, this gets back to whether you are drawn to a form or confined by a system. People get hung up on definitions. Opera is *this* and it can't be *that*. If you say, for instance, that an opera has to include an orchestra, or you need singers who sing in this particular way, and if you diverge from that, it's not opera, then you've embraced its limitations rather than its potential. You're bound by a set of rules, a system. But the origins of opera lie in combining disparate elements; it's a generous, inclusive, and highly eclectic form rather than one that's rigid in its fundamentals. What makes it exciting is precisely its all-encompassing reach—the way it's an amalgam of dance, singing, instrumental music, and theatrical effect. It's an extraordinary form if you don't get hung up on what turn out to be useless and meaningless limitations.

McLaughlin: The trouble comes when the canon becomes, well, *canonical*, religious. The canon is a measure of what we can achieve, but it must be a usable measure rather than a means of silencing innovation.

Eckert: Innovation always vies with tradition, but that struggle ultimately creates a seed of change. The best progress is made when tradition is honored but is absorbed. There is a prophecy embedded in any great work, the felt need for the next thing, the necessary revolution.

McLaughlin: But it's a balance, right? There's the notion of the anxiety of influence, the necessary struggle every artist goes through when creating the new while feeling the weight of the past, the great artists whose work determined so much of their aesthetic and whom they revere.

Eckert: Well, that's the thing. Reverence—awe—is important. If you'd never felt it, why would you want to make art in the first place? But there are limits to reverence; there comes the point when you have to transcend it in order to take your own work as seriously as you take the art that inspired you to do it.

Works Cited

Breuer, Lee. 1989. *Gospel at Colonus*. New York City, NY: Theater Communications Group.

D'Aulaire's, Ingrid and Edgar Parin. 1964. *D'Aulaire's Book of Greek Myths*. New York City, NY: Bantam Doubleday Dell Publishing Group, Inc.

Eckert, Rinde. 2006. *Orpheus X and Other Plays*. New York City, NY: NoPassport Press.

McLaughlin, Ellen. 2005. *The Greek Plays*. New York City, NY: Theater Communications Group.

"Yupik Antigone: Sophocles' Play in Yupik." 1984. Adapted by David Hunsacker and Perseverance Theater. Accessed 14 October 2020. https://www.youtube.com/watch?v=6GBSZj75pUE.

Part III
Fluid Approaches

12 Toward and Away: The Dramatic Tension of a Queer & Trans Canon

Finn Lefevre

There are probably as many definitions of queerness as there are queer people. As a sexual and gender identity it serves both as an umbrella term encompassing many identities and as a label specific for a single person's identity. This plurality is important to my understanding of queerness, as is its stubborn refusal to be rendered intelligible through language. It is, and can be, many things, but for the purposes of this project, a personal favorite is: gender and sexual identities which exist outside, or in opposition to, the cisheteropatriarchy.

Queer theory also has its favorite definitions, common threads including the ability to make the non-queer seem strange, the inability to fit within the constraints of cisheteronormative society (Rinaldi 2015: 85), or "whatever is at odds with the normal, the legitimate, the dominant" (Halperin 1995: 63). This chapter employs queer theorist José Muñoz's definition of queerness as the horizon: queerness as existing always in the reaching toward something that does not quite fit in our present universe, pushing back against our current boundaries. His queerness definition "is a formation based on an economy of desire and desiring. This desire is always directed at that thing that is not yet here, objects and moments that burn with anticipation and promise" (Muñoz 2009: 26). It is desire and dissent that guide this chapter's exploration of a queer and trans canon. A canon—canons—not yet here, but burning with promise.

Desire and dissent are irrevocably linked. Desire for dissent, for some of us, is borne of anxieties of assimilation, of fear of irrelevance through normalization: "Without antipathy, is there just apathy? Without something to fight against, does the once edgy avant-garde of queer theatre disappear?" (Small 2018). Queer theatre-makers (such as Shakina Nayfack, Kate Bornstein, Tim Miller, Jill Dolan) have often argued that not all LGBTQA + theatre is *queer* theatre, that queer theatre must push back against tradition both in form and content. Small cautions that this queer dissent should let go of the old tropes, even if the social world has not caught up: "Today's queer theatre need not be reactionary vis-à-vis an intolerant America—it should instead strike out on its own as a force for political alternatives, resistance, and utopia" (Small 2018).

DOI: 10.4324/9781003031413-12

His words push back against the fear that a queer canon must always exist in relation to the traditional canon.

By that definition, a queer canon is unreachable, and yet always reaching. It pushes back against the boundaries of the traditional canon while pushing forward into an imagined queer future. It is in this space that a queer canon resides, in the push and pull, the tension between visibility and legibility, between desire and dissent. This tension "embodies a resolute despair due to a feeling of exclusion from mainstream society and a paradoxical desire to remain out of it" (Badenes 2015: 33).

Queer canons make their home in this paradox. We, as queer and trans theatre-makers, are pulled ever toward canonizing projects just as we push away from their call for stability, assimilation. This chapter aims to unpack the tension between these impulses, the desires, and powers that pull us toward and push us away from a queer canon.

Definitions of a trans canon are harder to find. For this project, I am defining a trans canon as performance pieces conceived/written/performed by and about trans people (taking inspiration from W.E.B. Du Bois's "Krigwa Players Little Negro Theatre" essay, 1926). Trans theatre exists here in relation to queer theatre, in that not all trans theatre is *queer*, just as not all LGBQ + theatre is queer. This paper then will refer primarily to "a queer canon" inclusive of trans works that also queer form/aesthetic/structure, though it is occasionally necessary to separate for clarity.

Finding the queer in the traditional canon

The trademark of the traditional academic canon is its stability. Some authors may come and go as works once considered new or avant-garde become normalized to the point of a classic. But usually, a few familiar names haunt us no matter which anthology or syllabus we encounter. Canons can't, by nature, include every existing work. They are the works that stand the test of time, works that tenaciously hold the public's respect, never wavering in value.

A queer canon, then, can queer the very idea of canonization through its instability, its impermanence. Trans theatre is especially in motion, as is transition, the very concept of *trans*. It is not, and should not, be captured and made a permanent fixture the way Shakespeare has— though I'd love to picture a world where dozens of colleges produce *Hir* (Mac 2016) or *Sagittarius Ponderosa* (Kaufman 2021) every season.

Any stable canonizing projects for queer theatre (anthologies, syllabi, season selections, etc.) necessarily mark themselves in one specific moment of queerness. What was transgressive at that moment will someday, and possibly even through canonization itself, become naturalized. A queer canon today will be queer theatre history tomorrow, and a new canon—or several—will emerge. Despite this paradox, canonize we do, and probably always will.

Philosopher Umberto Eco referred to this as an effect of our human need "to make infinity comprehensible" (Beyer and Gorris 2009). But the desire to canonize queer performance has an additional impulse behind it—to make *ourselves* comprehensible, at least within the structures of the traditional canon.

Before grad school, *Angels in America* was the only play I ever saw by an explicitly queer playwright on a syllabus. I've never been assigned a play by a trans playwright. Most of the expensive anthologies I purchased for my classes included no queer or trans authors, some had no images of queerness at all. These absences were daunting for me as a budding queer and trans dramaturg, staring into a future in theatre and deciding if I belonged. In *Meditations on a Queer Canon,* Michael Lipkowitz writes that we seek out works which "reflect our souls back at us" (2012: 12). When queer and trans authors are absent from our textbooks and our syllabi, our students lose out on this experience. They might, as I did, question their own place in theatre and higher education. As civil rights activist Marian Wright Edelman poignantly said, "you can't be what you can't see" (qtd in Newsom 2012).

Even more dangerous than these silences, however, were the moments of recognition I did find within the traditional canon. Queer and trans people have yearned for representation so deeply that we subsist on queerbaiting and tropes. As Heather Love argues, "longing for community across time is a crucial feature of queer historical experience" (Love 2007: 37). Many of the small moments of queerness I've found within the traditional canon are, at best, woefully outdated and willfully cis white male-centric, and at worst perpetuate violent stereotypes. The images I saw in school of gender or sexual non-conformity ended in the restoration of status quo or humiliation and death; *Twelfth Night* (1602), for example, offers both a return to gender norms for Viola and humiliation at gender non-conformity for Malvolio. And yet *Twelfth Night* is also the perfect example of queer attachments in the traditional canon. The gender-bending, cross-dressing, and queer pairings make the text a touchstone, and despite the tropes described above, *Twelfth Night* persists in this role.

Teaching classics like these comes with real-world consequences that educators and theatre-makers must attend to (as described by Miss Major, Cece McDonald, et al in *Trap Door* 2017). Trans women of color are particularly misrepresented, the trope of the "surprise trans woman" budding up in works like *Come Back to the 5 & Dime, Jimmy Dean, Jimmy Dean* (1976) or *M. Butterfly* (1988). These images seep into the mainstream, where actual trans women experience the consequences of "trans panic," a connection I have written about previously (Lefevre 2021). Continuing to present material with this trope without unpacking its real-world impact reifies and normalizes this conception of trans women.

Activist/artist Tourmaline describes the link between visibility and violence as an effect of the limitations and assumptions of work created by cisgender artists about trans subjects. Cisgender creators, Tourmaline argues, might be spreading more images of trans people than ever before, but these images are often not accurate, and come with little attention to the material impacts:

> While trans visibility is at an all-time high, with trans people increasingly represented in popular culture, violence against us has also never been higher. The push for visibility without it being tied to a demand for our basic needs being met often leaves us without material resources or tangible support, and exposed to more violence and isolation. (Tourmaline)

Plays by cisgender heterosexual playwrights dominate the traditional canon; their distance from queer experience is strikingly visible in the use of queer lived experiences as plot points and props. The trans reveal trope is only one of many ways this canon misrepresents queer experience. Plays like *Tootsie* (1982) make a joke of trans identity. Djuna Barnes's *The Dove* (1928) and LeRoi Jones's *The Toilet* (1967) reinforce images of sexual repression and shame bursting forth into violence. Lillian Hellman's *The Children's Hour* (1937) is part of a long legacy of plays reinforcing consequences for being discovered as queer. Tropes like "bury your gays," the "closeted homophobe," and the "flamboyant feminine villain" dominate.

The continued teaching of these problematic pieces (especially without more trans-aware critique) reinforces harmful stereotypes. But to ignore all these pieces or separate them into an historical canon is to perpetuate the idea of a "bad gay past" (a la Heather Love's *Feeling Backward* (2007)) and imply a neoliberal progression in which we look only at our past as shameful, less queer, and thankfully over. To erase our queer theatre history is to sever ties with our ancestors. But these are not ideal ancestors. "In attempting to construct a positive genealogy of gay identity," Love argues, "queer critics and historians have often found themselves at a loss about what to do with the sad old queens and long-suffering dykes who haunt the historical record" (2007: 32). What of the Bricks (*Cat on a Hot Tin Roof* (1955)) and the Mrs. Danverses (*Rebecca* (1939))? Or Irene in *The Captive* (Édouard Bourdet (1926))? My attachments to these characters intermingle with my frustration at the tropes and stereotypes they reinforce.

Even the more overtly queer pieces that skirt the academic canon carry these same difficulties. In *The Boys in the Band* (1968), Michael laments, "If we could just learn not to hate ourselves quite so very much," and that quote could easily sum up the entire ethos of the play (Crowley 1968: 111). This play reinforces the trope of the depressed gay man, but it's also the first play that showed me the possibilities of queer friendships on stage. I am still haunted by seeing Angel sing "Contact," as she dies in *RENT* (1996), but I also carry her spirit with me in a long line of non-explicitly stated (though fanon—fan accepted canon) trans characters through whom I crafted and came to understand my own identity. Do we throw out all the works that showcase shame, self-loathing, and violence? Do we mark them as historical canon, museum pieces of queer theatre past? To ask more generations of queer and trans theater students to find themselves in these tropes feels akin to academic hazing: my generation had to pull barely visible queer threads from between the cracks of Ibsen or Molière, so the next generation should as well. I don't want that for my students, and I don't want that for the field of theatre.

This instinct to separate canons into "the past" and "the present" falls short when developing a queer canon. Citing Broadway and off-Broadway as his main objects, theatre critic Christian Lewis argues that there are two distinct queer canons being presented: an "older gay theatrical canon" designed to subtly educate primarily cishet audiences, and a newer, queerer canon of contemporary texts with an updated politic and geared more for younger queer audiences. This sentiment is echoed across several other discussions of the queer canon, divided not always temporally but sometimes by intended audience (queer or cishet) or if the representations are positive or negative. But each of these divisions is built around binaries. If being non-binary has taught me anything, it's that the world is full of false dichotomies, that even spectrums insist that in order to be more of one thing you must be less of another. This is antithetical to queerness.

The language of queerness and transness is ever-evolving. The absence of overt/recognizable trans language in older texts often precludes them from consideration in a trans canon, but contemporary scholars and artists are finding themselves in these historical works anyway. In "Diversifying the Classical Canon," Barbara Fuchs contends that just as important as finding and crafting a contemporary canon is reintroducing silenced voices into classical canons (Fuchs 2016). I recently consulted for a colleague, Harley Erdman, on his translation of the Spanish Golden Age play *La Serrana de la Vera* by Luis Vélez de Guevara (1613). The original text never uses language of gender identity or transness. Those words didn't even exist in 1613. And yet, the title character asserts: "If you think that I'm a woman,/You're very much deceived:/I am very much a man" (Vélez de Guevara and Erdman 2019: 59). This line is one of many in which Gila describes an identity that would today be read as transmasculine. Erdman took it as his responsibility to both fairly translate the original text and also make visible the threads that connect Gila to contemporary trans characters.

Without the ability to dig into historical plays and pull out previously unnoticed gender non-conformity, a trans canon is limited to those works where transness is explicitly named and understood within a cisnormative society. This modernization of transness distances trans people from our own cultural legacy: "trans people remain largely historically isolated, adrift on the sea of history, with little access to knowledge of where we came from and who got us here" (Page 2017: 135). To ignore classic works then is especially harmful to trans theatre, as it reifies a common problematic discourse, "framing trans people as new, as a modern, medicalized phenomenon only now coming to light in the topsy-turvy post-gay marriage world" (Page 2017: 135). The traditional canon offers anchor points in history for trans theatre-makers. Moments of gender exploration. Character attachments.

Even *M. Butterfly*'s Song Liling is finding a new place among trans reconciliations with the canon (Seid 2015). A trans canon must make space for discovery of these historical attachments, if only to say that at the time this canon project was developed, the way we view transness made these figures feel like kin. I'm not suggesting, as Michael Lipkowitz does, that we *owe* anything to the canons of our past (Lipkowitz 2012: 11). But maybe these canons owe us. Maybe the traditional canon owes us an opportunity to reexamine it through a queer lens. Maybe these texts owe us a chance to see ourselves.

The traditional canon does give too much weight to history, haunting our stages with well-worn pages, but a queer canon need not hold the same power. Instead, we might take inspiration from projects like *Callisto: A Queer Epic* (2016), which collages stories and source materials of queer past, present, and future into an interrelated web of queer becoming.

How we teach these materials is just as important as which texts we choose. If undergraduate education programs intend to expand their syllabi and seasons to include queer work, their classes must support this expansion through the tools of analysis they provide. Play analysis courses that break up texts into beats and scenes, objectives and obstacles, cause and effect, limit themselves to framework that may not serve queer texts. The form itself needs a queer lens as much as the content. Analytical texts that break plays down into traditional conventions and structures (like *Backwards and Forwards* 1983) are unprepared to analyze plays whose form itself is queer. The frequent use of Aristotle's *Poetics* and its influence on contemporary play analysis reinforces a traditional plot structure and prioritizes linear time, which serves to discredit the creativity of queer temporalities.

A higher education program hoping to do justice to queer and trans works must also contend with the gaps in their analytical frames, acknowledging that these tools have been developed to analyze structures of the traditional canon. These courses would benefit from pairing plays with analytical texts intended to unpack that particular form: E. Patrick Johnson, et al's *Blacktino Queer Performance* (2016), for example, offers in-depth analysis of the aesthetics formed by this subset of queer artists, a rare collection that focuses on the intersection of Black and Latino identities within queer theatre. *Queer Dramaturgies: International Perspectives on Where Performance Leads Queer* (2015) offers analytical tools and case studies from dramaturgs working in a variety of queer performance modalities. The *Methuen Drama Book of Trans Plays* (2021) might be the first trans theatre anthology to date, and alongside the plays themselves, it offers critical analyses by trans theatre-makers utilizing gender theory, trans theory, and more.

In addition to queer theory and queer critical analysis, queer canons should also be explored through non-academic lenses. Adapting Cirus Rinaldi's project in "Queering Canons," these programs must also employ embodied research, valuing experiential knowledges alongside theoretical texts, and imagining a "co-involvement" between the material and its analyst (2015: 87). Some existing texts already do this kind of sensory work: Eleanor Fuchs's

"Visit to a Small Planet" is a personal favorite analytical tool that interrogates the physical and social world of a play, divorcing it from our own world, and acknowledging that the world of each play operates in its own unique way with its own perceptions of time, movement, weather, etc. (Fuchs 2004). Queer playwright Maria Irene Fornés was also known to employ embodied methods of creation, research, and analysis (Memran 2018). Her own writing was often sparked by moments of embodied work in rehearsal spaces, and to analyze it without embodied knowledges would be a disservice. A queer pedagogical approach, then, would include "teaching and learning in acknowledgement of our bodies as whole experiential beings in motion, both inscribed and inscribing subjectivities" (Perry and Medina 2011).

Queer Canonizing Projects

In "Where are all the bisexuals?: Understanding the grey areas of LGBTQ representation," Emily White laments the lack of bisexual narratives and characters on the stage, stating, "there is really only one well-known and popular play that prominently features bisexual characters: Diana Son's *Stop Kiss*" (White 2015). Her argument is solid, but her word choice is most critical: she is looking not for *any* play that features bisexual characters (or a simple New Play Exchange search would solve her query), she is looking for one that is "well-known and popular." White's essay echoes how much legibility is tied directly to visibility, and for better or worse the projects described below are included because of that visibility.

It isn't that these canonizing projects are better or more researched, but their position as places/events/objects of power authored by voices recognized and accepted makes their impact more legible. Alisa Solomon, in her essay "Gay Theatre Gets Hammered by the Canon, Again" strikes back at *New York Times* journalist Jesse Green's attempt at creating one such canon (2018). Solomon argues that Green "makes a point of acknowledging that '[his] canon' may differ from others', though he blithely ignores the glaring difference: Only his glints off the glossy pages of a *Times* publication, helping to establish the record" (Solomon 2018). So much of the tension of a queer canon is who gets to set this record. Here, canons are explicitly connected to archives, to the way we record history. While a theoretical queer canon is only limited by one's imagination, the study of that canon is limited to the texts we write down, publish, anthologize, put on our syllabi, and teach. Queer archivist Jamie Ann Lee likens this to the way Judith Butler defines gender performativity in *Gender Trouble* (1990): the process of archiving naturalizes knowledges, making invisible the hands and choices that crafted the archive (Lee 2015: 75–76). Similarly, plays are considered part of canon not because of some mysterious inherent value, but by individual actions repeated over time. Practice, or in this case canonizing, does not make perfect. It makes permanent.

The least permanent of these canonizing projects are the festivals. Companies such as La MaMa, Theater Offensive, National Queer Theater, and the DC Center produce festivals each year. Though these festivals most closely mimic the ephemerality of other live performances, festivals serve to establish significance and value. Often tackling a yearly theme, the festival organizers are responsible for reading more plays and proposals than will ever reach an audience, narrowing it down to a handful. Each company has its own criteria for selection, usually an answer to one of the most common questions of dramaturgy: "why this play here and now?" This innocuous question allows small committees to decide what it means to be relevant, what is important in queer theatre today. The individuals in these rooms are not mysterious unknown forces, and yet their ability to sway the landscape of queer theatre is immeasurable. These festivals will be documented and the plays noted, while hundreds of other pieces fade into the background.

Similarly, queer theatre companies must acknowledge the platform they have and its impact on canonizing projects. Trans Theater Lab has taken up this responsibility, naming that they are using their visibility to make space for more trans playwrights to tell our own stories. Companies like National Queer Theater and 20% Theater Company focus their labors on underrepresented voices and narratives. Several companies, such as SNAP! Productions and About Face Theatre center community education in their missions, creating a queer canon accessible to cishet audiences. Each of these companies has the power to create their own vision of a queer canon through season selections and new play development/creation.

Even more impactful than queer theatre companies, I argue that anthologies and academic texts can be the longest-lasting and most influential canonizing projects. The names alone can tell you a lot about common threads in these projects: *Places, Please! The First Anthology of Lesbian Plays*; *Forbidden Acts: Pioneering Gay & Lesbian Plays of the 20th Century*; *Staging Gay Lives: An Anthology of Contemporary Gay Theater*. And the list goes on, divided nearly every time by gender. Identity spaces can be important, but the near-constant binary gendering of these anthologies is disruptive to a queer canonizing ethic. Beyond the binary reinforcing, these texts have also been critiqued for their inability to represent the community fully, an admittedly unwieldy challenge for a small anthology. Jill Dolan recognizes the weight of this challenge, noting that Kate McDermott, editor of *Places, Please!*, cannot be expected to represent the entirety of lesbian playwriting in one anthology, but that she still chose "such a one-sided, reductive sampling of lesbian experience, and such a uniformly classical-realist selection of writing styles that the anthology is hardly representative at all" (Dolan 1987). *Forbidden Acts* received criticism for its inclusion of several cishet authors, and *Staging Gay Lives* was critiqued for its centering of white masculinity. None of these texts feel like a queer canon in 2020, but each of these texts are taught yearly.

Despite academia often being the source of canonizing projects, the barriers and borders of academic knowledges can stand in opposition to the ethics of a queer canon. As Mel Chen explains, "the internet must be acknowledged as a potent archiving resource; even as it is understood to be transient, 'non-credible,' 'unreputable,' 'unofficial,' and 'disordered'" (Chen 2017: 151). It's impossible to ignore that these labels are so similar to the definitions (and my lived experience) of queerness. That knowledges can be devalued for their accessibility is also deeply concerning. Those qualities may in fact be what makes the internet so well suited for queer archiving. Chen argues that critical archive theory has made space for new ways of imagining the archives, but the work can be pushed further:

> A queer of color approach to the archive requires a genuine receptivity to the material effects of archival sources in skewed or odd relation to state archives. This includes new media, including internet forms. Those that have been relatively democratized offer us new architectures of access and of archive-building. (Chen 2017: 152)

Modern media have made space for queer performers to connect with a canon differently; listicles, blogs, and digital platforms like Zoom make sharing queer performances more accessible, especially those ephemeral arts which rarely make it into printed text.

These spaces have also democratized critique. A critique of the male-dominated industry already, The Kilroys List premiered in 2014, compiling a list of plays by "women, trans, and non-binary authors." The List's initially tenuous explanation of their inclusion of trans identities (which has since been clarified and updated), alongside the desire to create a trans-specific canon inspired a response project: The Killjoys lisT. The lisT was spearheaded by trans playwright and academic Joshua Bastian Cole, and was the first time I ever saw a collection of trans plays listed together.

Canonizing a Queer Body (of) Work

One of the most common assumptions about a theatrical canon is that it consists of texts. If a canon is only composed of text-based theatrical works, queer performances that exist in ephemeral, non-text forms will be left behind. A queer canon should be inclusive of drag performances, autodramas, experiential projects, cabaret, solo shows, and all the other kinds of queer performances that don't make it into the written canon.

Written archives lack the tools to record these works. Performance descriptions only go so far, leaving out the sensory and experiential components of performances. Images leave out the movement, the sound, the texture. With each attempt to produce a tangible archive of a queer canon, more of these gaps emerge.

The solution is not as simple as learning new archival methods to document, disseminate, and canonize these works. Queer archivist Michael Conners Jackman asks that we honor those works which exist only in the body or are temporally locked, suggesting that "resistance to documentation must be understood as the prerogative of artists for whom performance is neither future-oriented nor intended to be reproducible" (Jackman).

Alternative methods of sharing these works already exist; friends share stories in the oral tradition of spilling tea at a kiki, a drag queen passes traditional knowledges (and tucking tips) to her drag daughter in the greenroom, a trans elder helps a newly out trans girl find her voice. As queer people, we have always found ways to share our knowledges, our lived experiences, our cultural products outside the academy and in the margins of the historical record. We invented whole languages (such as Polari) to share knowledge without detection. We carry in our bodies the muscle memory of old choreography, the taste of hairspray after setting our face, the scars of binding or tucking with ace bandages instead of nylon, the hum of a few notes from some 80s ballad, the goosebumps from the first time we saw someone who looked like us survive the end of the show.

Queer archivists have already started exploring ways to connect our queer knowledge sharing to archival work. The link lies in our ability to reimagine archival bodies, to reimagine the body *as* archive, experiencing, interpreting, holding, sharing (Lee 2015: 74–75). Taking up Lee's thesis, this more expansive body (of) work queers the limitations of archiving the traditional canon. Queer canons can be found in more than books; queer canons exist in the body of queer performers, but they also exist in rehearsal halls, in dressing rooms, in night clubs, chipped teeth, and makeup pallets.

Claudia Nolan, a friend and colleague, recently wrote an essay examining dramaturgy through the lens of fungi (2020). Above the soil, fungi appear in clusters: a grouping here, a whole patch there, one lone little toadstool. Below the soil, she explained, was an entirely different story. Mycelial networks—interconnected filaments hundreds of miles long—offered underground, complex pathways for knowledge and resources to be shared. This is how I envision a queer canon existing, growing, connecting. Above the surface, there are the festivals, anthologies, blogs, syllabi, and visible canonizing projects. Below the surface, queer communities spread their own stories, connect plays with readers who'd adore them, and share resources and methods. A web of queer communications would tangle and weave the visible canons together with all of those works that cannot, and maybe should not, be archived in the same way.

This process was visible in my own work with Queer&Now (a queer and trans performance collective). A queer canon consisting of drag, physical theatre, and dance theatre was critical to our aesthetic and discourse. Several words and moments from this unofficial canon made their way into our lexicon as shorthand. The way a student of the traditional canon might say "this scene feels a little *Romeo and Juliet* to me," or compare the DMV to *Waiting for Godot*, folx in Queer&Now would reference moments from our canon to communicate inspirations, ideas, connections, or questions. Sasha Velour's rose petal reveal to Whitney Houston's "So Emotional" on *RuPaul's Drag Race* (2017), for example, may not appear in queer play anthologies, but it survives as drag canon. So do Busy Drag Queen, the "park and bark," and fan codes. These stories were shared through YouTube videos watched together on the floor of the rehearsal hall, gifs passed back and forth in the group chat, memories of unrecorded experiences re-performed by its witnesses, second-hand remembered choreo taught to each other during breaks. There was no drag archive, no anthology of house shows to turn to in our research, but there was the collective knowledges of the dozen or so queer and trans artists in our company.

A queer canon is a slippery thing. It yearns for connection to the past but aches at the way the past haunts it. It strives for inclusion and rails against assimilation. A cohesive queer canon, then, might be as impossible as a cohesive queer community. On the surface, it may seem fragmented and messy when compared with the curated perennials of the traditional canon. But, like the fungi, queer canons need not be visible and legible to be real.

Within, around, and through this queer canon, trans canons might also bloom. Trans theatre-maker Emma Frankland facilitated a 2019 Stratford Festival workshop titled, "Toward a Trans Canon." Despite the title, it seems Frankland and her collaborators were just as torn between the desire to create and the impulse to destroy canons. Participants in the workshop came to following the conclusion:

> Perhaps trans identity is too diverse to be gathered together in the idea of one canon? Rather than move towards the idea of a singular canon, we realized we need many [...] They interlink and crossover, creating beautiful spiraling patterns, Venn diagrams of intersecting violence and joys, but something specific about the trans experience is that, on some level, one must experience it alone. (Frankland 2020)

I agree with Frankland that each of us experiences transness in our own way, and in that way, we craft our own canons. Each of us individually crafting these canons, however, becomes a massive collective dissent. And collective dissent is at the core of trans history. After all, the Stonewall Rebellion wasn't a solo show.

Works Cited

Badenes, Guillermo. 2015. *"Contemporary American Queer Drama: Pushing the Limits to Remain at the Borders."* PhD diss, Universidad Nacional de Córdoba.

Beyer, Susanne, and Lothar Gorris. 2009. "SPIEGEL Interview with Umberto Eco: 'We Like Lists Because We Don't Want to Die,'" *SPIEGEL Online*, 11 November 2009. Accessed 30 September 2020. https://www.spiegel.de/international/zeitgeist/spiegel-interview-with-umberto-eco-we-like-lists-because-we-don-t-want-to-die-a-659577.html.

Chen, Mel Y. 2017. "Everywhere Archives: Transgendering, Trans Asians, and the Internet." In *Trap Door: Trans Cultural Production and the Politics of Visibility*, edited by Reina Gossett, Eric A. Stanley, and Johanna Burton. Cambridge, MA: The MIT Press.

Congdon, Jessica, ed. 2012. *Miss Representation*. New York, NY: Virgil Films. DVD.

Crowley, Mart. 1968. *The Boys in the Band*. New York: Farrar, Straus & Giroux.

Dolan, Jill. 1987. "Places, Please! The First Anthology of Lesbian Plays Kate McDermott." *Theatre Journal* 39, 1: 120.

Frankland, Emma. 2020. "Toward a Trans Canon." *Howlround Theatre Commons*, 26 May. Accessed 1 October 2020. https://howlround.com/toward-trans-canon.

Fuchs, Barbara. 2016. "Diversifying the Classical Canon." *Howlround Theatre Commons*, 2 April. Accessed 2 October 2020. https://howlround.com/diversifying-classical-canon

Fuchs, Elinor. 2004. "EF's Visit to a Small Planet: Some Questions to Ask a Play." *Theater* 34, 2: 4–9.

Halperin, David M. 1995. *Saint Foucault: Towards a Gay Hagiography*. Oxford: Oxford University Press.

Jackman, Michael Connors. n.d. "Hole in the Dark: Archiving Queer Performance." *Eastern Edge Gallery*. Accessed 4 October 2020. https://easternedge.ca/retroflex/hole-in-the-dark-archiving-queer-performance-essay-by-michael-connors-jackman/.

Lee, Jamie Ann. 2015. "A Queer/ed Archival Methodology: Theorizing Practice Through Radical Interrogations of the Archival Body." PhD diss, University of Arizona.

Lefevre, Finn. 2021. "Schrödinger's Dick: The Transgender Reveal Trope in *Boy Meets Girl*." In *Beyond Binaries: Trans Identities in Contemporary Culture*, edited by Lamothe, John C; Rachel Friedman, and Mike Perez. Washington, DC: Lexington Books.

Lipkowitz, Michael. 2012. "Meditations on a Queer Canon." In *The Midway Review*, 7, Winter: 5–12.

Love, Heather. 2007. *Feeling Backward: Loss and the Politics of Queer History*. Cambridge, MA: Harvard University Press.

Mac, Taylor. 2016. *Hir*. New York: Dramatists Play Service.

Memran, Michelle, Jennifer Fox, Melissa Neidich, Max Avery Lichtenstein, and Maria Irene Fornes. 2018. *Maria Irene Fornes: The Rest I Make Up*. Women Make Movies.

Muñoz, José Esteban. 2009. *Cruising Utopia: The Then and There of Queer Futurity. Sexual Cultures*. New York: New York University Press.

Neidich, Melissa, ed. 2018. *Maria Irene Fornes: The Rest I Make Up*. New York, NY: Women Make Movies. DVD.

Newsom, Jennifer Siebel, Regina Kulik Scully, Oprah Winfrey, Rosie O'Donnell, Condoleezza Rice, Lisa Ling, and Nancy Pelosi et al. 2012. *Miss Representation. [Videorecording]*. OWN Documentary Club. Virgil Films.

Nolan, Claudia. 2020. "Mycelial Dramaturgy: Unseen Connections." Dramaturging the Phoenix: an online essay collection by Literary Managers and Dramaturgs of the Americas, LMDA.org, 29 April.

Page, Morgan M. 2017. "One from the Vaults: Gossip, Access, and Trans History-Telling." In *Trap Door: Trans Cultural Production and the Politics of Visibility*, edited by Reina Gossett, Eric A. Stanley, and Johanna Burton. Cambridge, MA: The MIT Press.

Perry, Mia, and Medina, Carmen. 2011. "Embodiment and Performance in Pedagogy Research: Investigating the Possibility of the Body in Curriculum Experience." *Journal of Curriculum Theorizing*. V27, 3: 62–75.

Rinaldi, Cirus. 2015. "Queering Canons. Methodological Heteronormativities and Queer Inquietudes." *Revista Latinoamericana de Estudios Sobre Cuerpos, Emociones y Sociedad* 7, 18: 83–94.

Seid, Danielle. 2015. "Transfiguring the Asian Trans Femme: Revisiting Racial Castration and David Henry Hwang's *M. Butterfly*." *Proceedings of the 113th Annual Conference of Pacific Ancient and Modern Language Association, 6-8 November*. Portland, OR.

Small, Zachary. 2018. "LGBTQ, Emphasis on the Q." *American Theatre*, 1 January. Accessed 8 November 2020. https://www.americantheatre.org/2018/01/09/lgbtq-theatre-emphasis-on-the-q/.

Solomon, Alisa. 2018. "Gay Theatre Gets Hammered, Again." *American Theatre*, 23 March. Accessed 12 September 2020. https://www.americantheatre.org/2018/03/23/gay-theatre-gets-hammered-by-the-canon-again.

Tourmaline. n.d. "Trans Lab Theater - About." Accessed on 2 October 2020. TransTheaterLab.org.

Vélez de Guevara, Luis, and Harley Erdman. 2019. *The Mountain Girl from La Vera = La Serrana de La Vera*. Aris & Phillips Hispanic Classics. Liverpool, UK: Liverpool University Press.

White, Emily. 2015. "Where are All the Bisexuals?: Understanding the Grey Areas of LGBTQ Representation." *Howlround Theatre Commons*, 28 July. Accessed 2 October 2020. https://howlround.com/where-are-all-bisexuals-understanding-gray-areas-lgbtq-representation.

13 Dancing With/Out the Canon

Hannah Kosstrin

Introduction

I begin in the body. What I am about to explain is entrenched in kinesthesia, or body knowledge. Kinesthesia is intimately tied to cerebral knowledge but is often under-acknowledged as its own source of knowledge production in the otherwise-logocentric academy. The material evidence of how canonical entities persist in and through the body has implications for how we understand the canon in the dance field, and how we address, revise, thwart, or perpetuate it. Canonical status is imprinted in our kinesthesia through legacies of colonialization, and so refusing it is a long process of repatterning and redirecting. We must reckon with this residue in order to reimagine kinesthetic epistemologies of knowledge production, particularly in dance and performance fields. In this essay, I write from the body in order to show how embodied knowledge is part of, and affected by, canonical discourse.

The canon in my body comes from the Laban systems of movement notation and analysis, Labanotation/Kinetography Laban and Laban Movement Analysis (LMA). Labanotation is conceptually similar to music notation: it includes symbols on a staff that show where dancers' bodies go in space and time. LMA is an index of movement-based theoretical rules to quantify and define movement patterns. I deeply studied the Laban systems during all of my undergraduate and graduate degree programs, and I continue to use them in my work. These codified practices define a system for how to quantify and notate movement. They are one of the central tenets of the Euro-American concert dance canon, which is generally understood to be the lineages of ballet and modern dance as they grew out of the courts and theatres of Western Europe. These systems are rooted in German expressive dance practices of the early and mid-20th century, alternately labeled *Ausdruckstanz*, *Neue Tanz*, and Weimar dance (see Elswit 2014), which defined modern dance in Europe and then in the United States, England, Japan, China, British Mandate Palestine, India, and many other places where German dancers traveled. The Laban systems trained me to index movement in my own body and to see it in other people's bodies in a specific way that engenders a fine level of detail.

DOI: 10.4324/9781003031413-13

Something that always drew me to this work is that it is embodied theory: in order for the concepts to manifest, practitioners must perform them fully through the body in a way that connects kinesthetic with cerebral reasoning. These systems undoubtedly provided me the tools to evocatively describe movement in my scholarship the way I do.

As a dance historian invested in understanding the kinesthetics as well as the events of the past, moreover, reading a Labanotation score of a concert dance work like Anna Sokolow's *Rooms* (1954) or Bebe Miller's *Prey* (2000) gives me a small thrill of feeling as though I am in the rehearsal room, learning the dance alongside the cast who learned it at the time a notator wrote the notation score since notators are generally in the studio, learning, and recording in real-time. Understanding history through the body in this way, however, demands recognition for assumptions about shared ethics of whose movement we embody, implications for embodying other people's movements, and a necessity to address how the notation system itself contains harmful biases that affect the work. Implications of using the Laban material, which is kinesthetic-knowledge-dependent, entwine material with theoretical stakes for the canon, specifically when reckoning with its Nazi residues.

The Laban systems' progenitor Rudolf Laban's relationship to the Nazi party was rarely a topic of discussion when I was a student. When this topic arose, the narrative followed a protection project that went something like this: Laban fled the Nazis like everyone else and he was a great man. Thanks to the work of scholars like Lilian Karina and Marion Kant (1996; 2003) and Susan Manning (1993; 2006), we know that Laban and his student Mary Wigman actively subscribed to the ideals of the Nazi party (not to mention Laban's long-practiced misogyny from his days at the artist's colony he ran in Ascona, Switzerland in the 1910s, and the way he treated his women students like Irmgard Bartenieff who further developed his theories with little credit). As a student, when I raised points about Laban's Nazism, people I respected instructed me to quietly put it in a footnote. My moment of enlightened crisis occurred in graduate school when I presented a conference paper in which I used LMA to analyze Jewish choreographer Anna Sokolow's solo *Kaddish*, an elegy for the Holocaust set to the Jewish mourner's prayer. I am forever grateful to the Jewish dance historian who took me aside and said something to the tune of, "I find it interesting that you are using the work of a Nazi to analyze a Holocaust memorial." In that moment, everything changed. My canonical education, which I fought so hard to fulfill even when things did not fit, was a power play of smoke and mirrors—and its problems landed.

It took me many years to figure out what to do with the Laban work. I could not reconcile using it because of these implications. And, because it had fallen out of favor in the field of dance studies as a mode of analysis, pursuing it did not seem worth it. It became clear to me how colonized my seeing was: how I see dance (by "see" here I mean analyze or write movement description) remains driven by Laban-informed taxonomies because I had deep training in those systems. As I looked around me, particularly in the dance departments where I was teaching, my colleagues still used Laban-based language in modern/contemporary movement practice and composition classes—space, weight, time, flow, posture, gesture, space hold—without labeling it as such. Celebrating figures like Laban as geniuses is an explicit way of upholding damaging parts of the canon, which many practitioners have reduced. But, letting these figures' work become an unspoken part of the concert dance fabric without naming it as such or reconciling what it means to continue to use it implicitly perpetuates this power dynamic.

In the discussion that follows, I argue that a revisionist approach to the canon can engender practices of equity for teaching dance histories. My embodied experience influences my assumption that the canon is present, and it persists; we decide to uphold or refuse it. I teach through a revisionist mode to shift the paradigm. A revisionist model addresses multiple parts of a historical moment by revising established narratives. Revisionist history relies on counternarratives to give a fuller picture of the history than has been told through more canonical means. With the phrase "revisionist mode," I point to dance scholarship from the late 1990s and early 2000s that undressed the stories of canonical figures or inserted marginalized histories into dominant conversations (see, among others, Graff 1997; Dixon Gottschild 1996; Foulkes 2002; Manning [1993] 2006; Manning 2004; Shea Murphy 2007; Srinivasan 2012). I believe there is value in building a narrative that purposefully engages equity of representation in terms of race, ethnicity, gender, sexuality, class, nation, and ability, and engaging students in conversations about the "whys" of the choices. I am invested in how a revised collection of conversations, constructed with aims for equity in terms of representation of people and practices, and providing students with what they need to engage with the material, can remap students' understanding of the world. All dance practices have pasts, presents, futures, and other ways of engaging temporality. When coursework represents a range of experiences, students think these examples are significant. Yet, we must also recognize how revised histories' biases still privilege some lineages over others due to the power structures that elevated these people, enabled these forms to circulate, and decided who or what should be there or not.

Dance Studies, the Body, and the Academy

The historiography of the academic field of dance studies offers a nexus for patterns of establishing and revising the canon. Dance studies is the pursuit of dance as a cultural phenomenon. As an interdisciplinary field, dance studies encompasses dance history, ethnography, literature, and theory engaged through embodied practice, creative endeavor, and intellectual discourse. Although scholarship on dance existed earlier, the current field (sometimes called critical dance studies or new dance studies) gained traction during the mid-to-late 1990s, out of many theoretical turns in the 1980s and 1990s: multiculturalism, critical race theory, feminist theory, postcolonial theory, and poststructuralism, among others. The 1990s represents a watershed moment in dance scholarship and a turn away from earlier efforts separating historical and anthropological inquiry largely along Western and non-Western lines as scholars invested in newer theories drove the charge (see, for example, Foster 1986; Savigliano 1995; Albright 1997; Martin 1998; Dixon Gottschild 1996; Chatterjea 2004). These kinds of studies catalyzed more critical modes of analyzing dances than the longstanding colonialist separations between "dance history" (humanities-based studies of Euro-derived dance practices for the concert stage), "dance anthropology" (social science-based studies of all other kinds of dance), and "dance criticism" (performance reviews).

Because of this history, the field of dance studies has been a site of both progressive and conservative epistemologies. As such, its struggle with and troubling of traditional scholarship (including the idea of canons and the assumptions rooted in canonization) is particularly pertinent. On the one hand, dance studies has challenged older models of teaching in higher education. For example, dance departments tend to respect practitioners as faculty members in tenure-track positions to the same degree (and sometimes more than) traditional scholars. And, as a female- and non-binary-dominated field, gender equity has always been core to academic missions in dance. On the other hand, when dance faculty sought to legitimize the field in the academy as they separated dance into academic departments out of their previous locations in physical education programs, they adopted some traditional structures that resembled longer-established academic disciplines like English or history through the expectation of knowledge production including: the publishing of articles and books; the primacy of Western dance histories, genres, and aesthetics as subject matters for inquiry; and the structure of conferences and other academic gatherings.

The reciprocity between dance histories and creative practices should be examined in ideological and practical terms at the site of students' education to address the canon. Dance departments feature a unique relationship between practitioners and scholars in the academy: scholars are often in the same departments as practitioners (like theatre but not like art and, often, music) and work toward common goals by bringing different strengths to the table. Despite dance's relatively un-entrenched position in the academy, the canon of Eurocentric dances from ballet, modern, postmodern, and contemporary concert dance genres, not explicitly but often narrated as a white European to predominantly white American trajectory, became entrenched. Canonical discourses assigned these genres value that was not similarly offered to popular dance forms (see Dodds 2011). Dance practices outside the above trajectory and off the concert stage became structurally marginalized. Many dance departments are restructuring curricula to address these inequities (see, for example, Kwan 2017 and O'Shea 2018), and/but there is still much work to be done at the interstices of dance studies and practice pedagogy, and the canon.

My Body, My Canon?

It is hard to rationally separate out problems when we recognize that we embody them. I was angry for not realizing that my Jewish body, and the way that I see and analyze dance, was colonized by the Laban systems and, arguably, by their accompanying Nazi ideals or at least their kinesthetic residue. I cannot unlearn or unsee these modes—because who can say what I do definitely is or is not Laban when it is all so deeply kinesthetically entrenched? The workings of white supremacy are embedded in these systems. I am not talking about the valid criticisms of some practitioners' use of the Laban systems related to examining dance practices through another's cultural lens, but those are issues too.[1] I am talking about if you reach your right arm into the Laban position "forward high"—hand shooting straight from your shoulder into the space in front of your forehead, fingertips reaching, palm facing down—it is a Nazi salute. "Forward high" is a basic direction of the arm in Labanotation and central to the Laban movement scales in LMA (which follow the same concept as music scales), and the "default" palm facing is down, i.e., this position. One could argue that fascist ideological kinesthetics remain in these practices.

One tension I address when teaching dance history and Laban vocabularies is reconciling our embodied histories with the horrors of their practices. Then, where do we fit? If it is in my body, is it mine? What is my responsibility for it? If I am a white student learning Africanist dance practices, I need to actively parse and be accountable for what it means to learn someone else's history, particularly the embodied historical and contemporary practices of subjugated people, through my more dominantly-privileged body (see, for example, Scott 1997 and Johnson 2012: 40–70). If I am a Jewish student recognizing that my body has been trained in the same systems used to propagate Nazi ideology for the purpose of extinguishing other Jewish people's bodies, how do I reconcile that kinesthetic residue in my very being? How do I separate my kinesthetic knowledge from myself in order to practice ethically? It is unresolved.

One of the things I struggle with in my teaching is what to do with the material in the Laban systems of notation and movement analysis, because I still teach it. I have discussions with my students about its kinesthetic residue, and how to engage its usable parts, which I do think it has. To begin, I tell students about this history and its embodiments—and instruct them to turn their palm to the side and soften a gentle bend in their elbow as a default position for "forward high" of the arm. We interrogate the cultural assumptions of the systems, what the systems do well, and what they elide. In a sense, my act of performing this work to reclaim it starts to challenge its history. By purposefully re-embodying this work from an anti-racist stance, we can reclaim some of the usable parts of these movement analysis systems without propagating their attendant trauma. For me, this means that as a Jewish practitioner I recondition an analytical movement system previously used in the service of government projects designed to identify Jewish people by their physical characteristics and measurements (a kind of movement analysis) before eliminating those people. So, where it gets tricky is when we have to decide what we do with this kinesthetic inheritance. This is the reason that I gravitate toward revisionist history in thinking about the canon.

In many instances, I cannot avoid needing to know what came before in order to explain why we do not do it this way anymore. Because canons persist, regardless of whether we want them or not, we need to teach in such a way as to rework ingrained narratives and assumptions with alternative ones or with critical thinking—especially when many of our students come to us having been told stories by their dance teachers that uphold canonical attitudes, or they think if they are not learning a specifically-delineated set of facts and figures they are not learning the so-assumed "real" history. I take care to avoid repeating damaging narratives and omit much material from my own schooling altogether so as not to reproduce the hierarchies I aim to dismantle. I do this work by carefully curating the readings and viewings I assign in addition to the ways I facilitate conversations in class.

Revising for Representation: Historiography and Hierarchies

I always tell my students that people build the field. Some of these people's voices are given more weight than others, at different points in time, depending on what is valued in any given moment. Whether or not one agrees with who holds the power in these discourses, it is important to know what they are to ascertain where one is in relation to them. When I craft syllabi, I make decisions about what content the students will learn. I view that content as opening doors to other conversations that students direct with their curious inquiry. Is this curation a form of canonization? In a sense, yes—I am directing the content for students to learn over the course of a term. If mine is the one dance history class they take, its series of encounters build what many of them consider the narrative of "dance history." No matter how many times I tell students that a syllabus represents the choices I made for what appears on it, they think that the materials came forth from some magical index for the particular topic of the course. But in general, no—curation is not canonization. I make choices based on field trends and what I think is right, but in the end my syllabus is an "n" of 1. Nevertheless, the way that we teach our students influences what and how they learn. We can think of this power as networked or hierarchical—but our students' learning experiences, which is where the rubber hits the proverbial road when it comes to the canon, are determined by our choices. Our job is to disrupt.

Some students find revisionist history challenging because they want to know why the history needed to be revised, or why others have deceived them with the powerful and obscuring narratives of the canon. Such questions lead to fruitful discussion, and beg the question of how students would conceive what it means to be human if they perceived this material as a series of narratives dependent on different points of view and not an established narrative that we dismantle. A curated collection of content in any given course acts as touchpoints or landmarks, each acting as a portal for further inquiry. Recognizing how power structures work and why certain works are on any given list at any given time goes hand in hand with attending to why other works are not on those lists. My intent here is not to reify what came before, but to build on change that has begun. To this end, the following historiography outlines a series of canonical revisions to provide context for ways that the field of dance studies has revised its own hierarchies over the past twenty-five years. I outline it as a way to understand what has come before so that we may move forward.

For generations, "dance history" referred to the study of courtly and concert dance practices originating in Western and Northern Europe and migrating to the United States. These lineages were directly affected by how white dance critics in the *New York Times* and *Dance Magazine* canonized certain dancers into the modern dance and ballet pantheon (Morris 2006). Conversations in the Black press, Jewish press, and leftist press, not to mention those in the Midwest or on the West coast, were not as influential in defining the pantheon as were those in the Northeast. In the eyes of "dance history" that engendered a dance canon, dance practices that occurred off the concert stage, in Black or Jewish venues, or in the Global South, were relegated to the realm of anthropology or "cultural dance." Joann Keali'inohomoku famously asserted in 1970 that all dance forms bear the markers of their historical and cultural contexts, and thus all dance is *encultured*. Her specific example that showing how ballet is an ethnic dance form upended colonialist labels that separated dance practices into high and low art and culture. Despite Keali'inohomoku's corrective, many people still use the racist terms "cultural dance" or even "ethnic dance" to refer to dance practices within the old rubric. Indeed, Ananya Chatterjea argues that these biases remain in contemporary dance on global stages: if a dance looks contemporary, she says, that means that there are aesthetic and compositional elements in it that resonate with Euro-American practices (2013). The distinction between the concert stage and the popular presents another point of contention. In "When is Contemporary Dance?" SanSan Kwan lays bare contestations over the term "contemporary" as university dance departments use it (a chronological outgrowth of "modern" dance, a predominantly white American dance lineage that dates to the 1920s and focuses on a spiraling torso, a weighted relationship with gravity, and bare feet) versus how commercial dance and reality television use it (emotive dance sequences with highly technical virtuosic skills), and the dissonance first-year university dance students experience if they come to college expecting the commercial version of contemporary dance and find the former (2017).

While dance studies has skirted the so-called dead white men project, the field has participated in similar reifications of Euro-American lineages as it has long struggled with demonstrating how dance is an important mode of inquiry because of the intellectual primacy of the same dead white men. In "Roots/Routes of Dance Studies," Janet O'Shea identifies a theoretical and methodological shift in dance scholarship between the late 1980s and early 2000s that determined the contemporary field of dance studies. Prior to this turn, dance scholarship focused on artists' biographies in feminist actions to write women into history; during and after it, dance scholarship featured interdisciplinary investigations examining dance within its social context (2010: 1). O'Shea outlines four developments that grew into the field of dance studies: examining dance as part of a political consciousness; a shift from dance observation to poststructuralist analysis; attention to practitioners' lived bodily experiences; and rethinking the act of dance reconstruction from a practice of resurrecting dances from archival sources to rendering them through critical acts of embodied analysis (2010: 3–13). Similarly, in "Dance Studies/Cultural Studies," Gay Morris addresses how, by the early 2000s, dance studies took on the interdisciplinary concerns of cultural studies regarding the social and political interpretation of cultural phenomena through the body (2009). Unlike cultural studies, she argues, dance studies has its own methods in addition to borrowing from other fields that center theory in moving bodies, which, she predicts, will prevent dance studies from facing cultural studies' demise. Dance studies has produced revisionist or corrective histories in monographs and anthologies for the past twenty years that challenge ingrained racisms and elisions associated with a pantheon of choreographers and dance styles that were previously considered part of a canon (Dixon Gottschild 1996; Jackson 2000; Foulkes 2002; Manning 2004; Shea Murphy 2007; Kowal 2010). Understanding dance studies' historiography and disciplinary methods help address the ways we can rethink our approach to the canonical.

One place this power dynamic appears is in the language we use to discuss dance practices. The American and British academies dominate the field of dance studies. As a result, many examples come from the American context and mirror the ways generations of students learned dance history. By doing dance studies in the 21st century, we inherit centuries of institutionalized practices established to subjugate people of color and immigrants who phenotypically deviate from dominant Eurocentric aesthetics and practices that we must actively refuse. In the United States, dance critics have been the arbiters of taste by separating dance into categories of art and not-art. Predominantly white critics' opinions since the early 20th century, and those of the choreographers they upheld, determined what became an American dance canon. This lineage crystallized during the Cold War when the United States rose as an imperialist superpower. The US government carved the world into capitalist and communist against the backdrop of the Civil Rights Movement and, later, the second-wave feminist movement at home. Impresarios like Sol Hurok toured thousands of "national" dance companies from around the world who performed Euro-legible versions of their local practices, alongside African American artists like Katherine Dunham, under banners of exotic sensationalism, at the same time the US State Department sent American choreographers abroad under strict aesthetic parameters to win hearts and minds in the name of capitalism (Kosstrin 2020b; Bench and Elswit 2019; Shay 2002; Croft 2015). Within this language, "modern dance" stood for "art," which was code for whiteness, considered universal in nature, into which audience members could emotionally insert themselves, whereas labels like "Negro dance," "Jewish dance," "ethnic dance," and, later, "cultural dance" marked the performances as not-quite-art and instead a specific ethnographic experience based on the performers' race, ethnicity, and narrative content (George-Graves 2010; Perpener 2001; Manning 2004; Rossen 2014; Sherrod 2014; Kowal 2020). Beyond revising this history, we must change the ways we language our work so our definitions reflect the values of the work instead of relying on undoing harmful assumptions, which just reinforces old problems.

Of course, we make new hierarchies. There are lists of scholars and conversations with which a person claiming to be conversant in dance studies needs to be familiar—replete with discriminations of why certain voices stand out. Some of these conversations are necessary to know so that we do not repeat their problems; some are necessary to know because they are significant for one reason or another at a given point in time. And, there are sub-lists for subfields. There are choreographers, dances, dancers, and movement practices one should know about to be a well-informed practitioner or scholar depending on one's area of expertise. These lists are intimately tied to current conversations, which in turn reflect the values of the people participating in them. A lot of what is important is based on context. Like colonialism, the canon remains embedded; it undergirds what we do even as we refuse it. Since a "canon" points back to the process through which Catholic saints are assigned, we must also break from a predominantly Christian worldview to consider different kinds of cultural literacies.

The choices we make when we teach, and when we cite scholars in our published work, matters. What matters also is how we use this material. For example, how do we use dance and dance studies to teach students how to be curious? How do we teach students the skill of being able to figure out context from something unfamiliar in order to have an informed conversation about it? How do we teach students to have challenging conversations and understand that there are many answers? When we bring these questions to bear on curricula, moreover, we must address students' holistic experiences in their studio (composing, practicing) and studies (ethnography, history, theory) work so that everyone has access to participation in a common conversation (see, for example, Monroe 2011 and McCarthy-Brown 2017). These actions demonstrate to students the ways they can understand how thinking critically translates across their movement practice classes, composition process courses, and dance studies pursuits. Even as I advocate for a revisionist model that aims for equitable representation, I also strive to implement modes of approach that pair with different kinds of evidence to fully realize this model.

Conclusion/Moving Forward

There is not one set of information that everyone must know. But, it is important for students to understand the histories of the dance practices they study. Such inquiry gives them a sense for what came before them in the tensions they embody, and in what it means for their bodies to have certain codifications embedded. This knowledge helps them place themselves in relation to others who undertook similar endeavors, which is why broad representation is important. It lets students build on this information, find role models, or reject these elements altogether, but ultimately such training does not let them think they are the first person to make a dance with chairs, as Sokolow did in 1954 in *Rooms* and scores of others did before her and since. It is also important for students to learn the histories of dance practices that they do not themselves practice so that they know what is out there beyond their own experience and where their knowledge meets new knowledge. For similar reasons, it is important to be familiar with some of the main threads of the arguments, and the people who wrote them, in the fields with which departments and students align.

In theory and practice, we must address the choices we make as educators, even when we think we are not making choices. It is crucial to be mindful of how our non-choices, to just do something because it seems it has always been done that way, are also choices. It is also necessary to recognize how some non-choices are choices others have made for us, and how we address the kinesthetic colonization in our own bodies after it has taken up residence. For example, how are people and practices that have historically been Othered out of some dance history classes actually foundational ways of understanding dance practices and histories and not tangential to them? This shift allows us to recognize inclusion and equity as essential to understanding this material and not an external effort. I am invested in providing students the tools they need to comprehend dance as a way to understand what it means to be human. By teaching through questioning and introducing students to work that opens conversations, we give them the tools to investigate and to access a wide variety of topics. To this end, teaching our students *how* to think and not just *what* to think creates opportunities for us and our students to make connections that empower them to spur social change.

Thanks to Nadine George-Graves for productive conversations that shaped this essay.

Note

1 For example, leading Labanotation practitioner Ann Hutchinson Guest (2005: 5–8) and Laban Movement Analyst Irmgard Bartenieff (1980) make claims about the universality of the Laban systems. With the late-1990s postcolonial turn, these attitudes rightfully came under suspicion in the field of dance studies. See also Kosstrin 2020a.

Works Cited

Albright, Ann Cooper. 1997. *Choreographing Difference: The Body and Identity in Contemporary Dance*. Middletown, CT: Wesleyan University Press.

Bartenieff, Irmgard, and Dori Lewis. 1980. *Body Movement: Coping with the Environment*. Langhorne, PA: Gordon & Breach.

Bench, Harmony, and Kate Elswit. 2019. "Dance Touring and Embodied Data: Some Approaches to Katherine Dunham's Movement on the Move." *Current Research in Digital History* 2. doi: 10.31835/crdh.2019.12

Chatterjea, Ananya. 2004. *Butting Out: Reading Resistive Choreographies Through Works by Jawole Willa Jo Zollar and Chandralekha*. Middletown: Wesleyan University Press.

Chatterjea, Ananya. 2013. "On the Value of Mistranslations and Contaminations: The Category of 'Contemporary Choreography' in Asian Dance." *Dance Research Journal* 45, 1: 4–21.

Croft, Clare. 2015. *Dancers as Diplomats: American Choreography in Cultural Exchange*. New York: Oxford University Press.

Dixon Gottschild, Brenda. 1996. *Digging the Africanist Presence in American Performance: Dance and Other Contexts*. Westport, CT: Greenwood Press.

Dodds, Sherril. 2011. *Dancing on the Canon: Embodiments of Value in Popular Dance*. London: Palgrave Macmillan.

Elswit, Kate. 2014. *Watching Weimar Dance*. New York: Oxford University Press.

Foster, Susan Leigh. 1986. *Reading Dancing: Bodies and Subjects in Contemporary American Dance*. Berkeley: University of California Press.

Foulkes, Julia. 2002. *Modern Bodies: Dance and American Modernism from Martha Graham to Alvin Ailey*. Chapel Hill: University of North Carolina Press.

George-Graves, Nadine. 2010. *Urban Bush Women: Twenty Years of African American Dance Theater, Community Engagement, and Working It Out*. Madison: The University of Wisconsin Press.

Graff, Ellen. 1997. *Stepping Left: Dance and Politics in New York City, 1928–1942*. Durham: Duke University Press.

Guest, Ann Hutchinson. [1954] 2005. *Labanotation: The System of Analyzing and Recording Movement*. New York: Routledge.

Jackson, Naomi. 2000. *Converging Movements: Modern Dance and Jewish Culture at the 92ndStreet Y.* Hanover, NH: Wesleyan University Press/University Press of New England.

Johnson, Jasmine Elizabeth. 2012. "*Dancing Africa, Making Diaspora.*" PhD diss., Berkeley: University of California. UC Berkeley Electronic Theses and Dissertations.

Karina, Lillian, and Marion Kant. [1996] 2003. *Hitler's Dancers: German Modern Dance and the Third Reich.* Translated by Jonathan Steinberg. New York: Berghahn Books.

Keali'inohomoku, Joann. 1969–1970. "An Anthropologist Looks at Ballet as a Form of Ethnic Dance." *Impulse Magazine*: 24–33.

Kosstrin, Hannah. 2020a. "Kinesthetic Seeing: A Model for Practice-in-Research." In *Futures of Dance Studies*, edited by Susan Manning, Janice Ross, and Rebecca Schneider, 19–35. Madison: The University of Wisconsin Press.

Kosstrin, Hannah. 2020b. "Whose Jewishness?: Inbal Dance Theater and Cold War American Spectatorship." *American Jewish History* 104, 1: 31–58.

Kowal, Rebekah. 2010. *How To Do Things with Dance: Performing Change in Postwar America.* Middletown, CT: Wesleyan University Press.

Kowal, Rebekah. 2020. *Dancing the World Smaller: Staging Globalism in Mid-Century America.* New York: Oxford University Press.

Kwan, SanSan. 2017. "When Is Contemporary Dance?" *Dance Research Journal* 49, 3: 38–52.

Manning, Susan. [1993] 2006. *Ecstasy and the Demon: The Dances of Mary Wigman.* Minneapolis: University of Minnesota Press.

Manning, Susan. 2004. *Modern Dance, Negro Dance: Race in Motion.* Minneapolis and London: University of Minnesota Press.

Martin, Randy. 1998. *Critical Moves: Dance Studies in Theory and Politics.* Durham: Duke University Press.

McCarthy-Brown, Nyama. 2017. *Dance Pedagogy for a Diverse World: Culturally Relevant Teaching in Theory, Research, and Practice.* Jefferson, NC: McFarland & Company, Inc., Publishers.

Miller, Bebe, chor. 2000. *Prey.* Labanotation score by Valarie Williams, 2005. New York: Dance Notation Bureau.

Monroe, Raquel L. 2011. "'I Don't Want to do African… What About My Technique?': Transforming Dancing Places into Spaces in the Academy." *The Journal of Pan African Studies* 4, 6: 38–55.

Morris, Gay. 2006. *A Game for Dancers: Performing Modernism in the Postwar Years, 1945–1960.* Middletown: Wesleyan University Press.

Morris, Gay. 2009. "Dance Studies/Cultural Studies." *Dance Research Journal* 41, 1: 82–100.

O'Shea, Janet. 2010. "Roots/Routes of Dance Studies." In *The Routledge Dance Studies Reader*, 2nd ed., edited by Alexandra Carter and Janet O'Shea, 1–15. Abingdon and New York: Routledge.

O'Shea, Janet. 2018. "Decolonizing the Curriculum? Unsettling Possibilities for Performance Training." *Brazilian Journal on Presence Studies 8*, 4:750–762.

Perpener, John O. 2001. *African-American Concert Dance: The Harlem Renaissance and Beyond.* Urbana: University of Illinois Press.

Rossen, Rebecca. 2014. *Dancing Jewish: Jewish Identity in American Modern and Postmodern Dance.* New York: Oxford University Press.

Savigliano, Marta. 1995. *Tango and the Political Economy of Passion.* Boulder: Westview Press.

Scott, Anna Beatrice. 1997. "Spectacle and Dancing Bodies that Matter: Or, If It Don't Fit, Don't Force It." In *Meaning in Motion: New Cultural Studies of Dance*, edited by Jane C. Desmond, 259–268. Durham: Duke University Press.

Shay, Anthony. 2002. *Choreographic Politics: State Folk Dance Companies, Representation, and Power*. Middletown, CT: Wesleyan University Press.

Shea Murphy, Jacqueline. 2007. *The People Have Never Stopped Dancing: Native American Modern Dance Histories*. Minneapolis: University of Minnesota Press.

Sherrod, Elgie Gaynell. 2014. *Dance Pedagogy of Katherine Dunham and Black Pioneering Dancers in Chicago and New York City from 1931–1946*. Lewiston, NY: The Edwin Mellen Press.

Sokolow, Anna, chor. 1954. *Rooms. Labanotation score by Ray Cook, 1980, repr. 2003*. New York: Dance Notation Bureau.

Srinivasan, Priya. 2012. *Sweating Saris: Indian Dance as Transnational Labor*. Philadelphia: Temple University Press.

14 What Do We Do with the Musical Theatre Canon?

Stacy Wolf, with Masi Asare, Rob Berman, Randall Eng, Eric M. Glover, David Savran, Georgia Stitt, Brandon Webster, and Sarah Whitfield

Asking the Question

Stacy Wolf

What do we do with the musical theatre canon? I posed this question to eight artists and scholars across identities and institutional locations. The challenge of an action—what do we do?—underlines musical theatre's ubiquitous presence as a living and relevant theatrical genre in US culture. For many people, musicals are the only theatre they know, the only theatre they have experienced as participants or as spectators. For many people, musicals ARE theatre.

The musical theatre canon is unique in the theatrical ecosystem for a number of reasons. First, it emerged and is constituted and revised at the intersection of art and economics. Shows gained entry to the canon when they both succeeded financially on Broadway and earned critical acclaim. Rodgers and Hammerstein, whose 1943 *Oklahoma!* came to define the very terms of the traditional musical theatre canon, were forthright in their desire to "elevate" popular and commercial entertainment to the status of art. They and their peers, including Leonard Bernstein, Frank Loesser, and Lerner and Loewe, for example, defined "good musical theatre" as built on a story, formally integrated with (supposedly) seamless transitions between speaking and singing and between movement and dance, and featuring character-specific music and lyrics. These (and other) formal conventions came to serve as the benchmarks for artistic achievement. As Raymond Knapp writes, "[T]he deck has been stacked from the outset, since the very notion of a canon, particularly a critical canon, presupposes some supporting notion of integration that attaches to its individual entrants" (Knapp 2020: 477).

At the same time, musicals are commercial products, which aim to make a profit. Once a show enters this marketplace, it accrues value by a long run, by the distribution of cast albums and sheet music, and most of all, by licensing touring productions, regional productions, and amateur productions at community theatres and high schools. In other words, Broadway musicals are a mainstream and commercial form of performance, thus the shows collected in its traditional canon are situated at the intersection of art and entertainment, of artistic achievement and audience appeal.

Even as formal conventions, commercialism, and the concomitant conventional representations of race and gender organized one aspect of the canon, changing audience tastes, easy access to musicals on the internet, and the proliferation of fans as critics challenged both the form and the content of musicals, expanding what had been the traditional canon.

Second, the musical theatre canon is relatively young, with origins in the early to mid-20th century. And because the launching pad for a musical's canonicity is Broadway, which consists of only 41 theatres in a single neighborhood in New York City, the musical theatre canon is smaller and more hegemonic than other theatrical canons. This dynamic, too, is changing, as more musicals are following the route of *A Chorus Line*, *Fun Home*, and *Hamilton*, being developed at not-for-profit theatres. Still, musicals are ridiculously expensive to produce—even small and minimalist shows—which limits the repertoire.

Third, academia's imprimatur, which confirms intellectual value when scholars write about and professors teach a genre or subject, only dates back to 1997 with the publication of Geoffrey Block's *Enchanted Evenings*, the first scholarly study of musicals in their entirety (as opposed to a strictly musicological approach), which he wrote to use as a textbook in his classes (Wollman forthcoming). Block, first in an article on the canon in 1993, and then in his book, aimed to navigate "the alleged conflict between temporal popularity and lasting value and the selling out, again alleged, not of tickets but of artistic integrity" (Block 1993; Block 2009: 5).

The notion that musicals, including the music and lyrics, script and performance, deserve scholarly attention and a place in academia is still not accepted in many universities. Elizabeth L. Wollman points to a number of issues that hampered the study of musicals. First, that the canon was formed by the theatre industry and fueled by commercial aspirations; second, that copyright issues prevented distribution and therefore, widespread study (Reside forthcoming); third, that the adjacent fields of theatre and music and dance held disdain for popular and commercial entertainment forms; and finally, that musical theatre's multiple genres make it extraordinarily complex to study (Wollman forthcoming). That said, musicals that are taught and written about tend to be canonical and to reinforce their own value.

Finally, and most importantly, musical theatre's living breathingness—the fact that thousands of musicals are produced and performed each year—means that the canon is reproduced on bodies and in voices across gender, race, class, geography, and age. High schools (and increasingly, elementary and middle schools), colleges and universities, repertory and community theatres produce shows from the (ever-changing) canon repeatedly. Musical theatre is enacted as a local, community-based practice, not just one that lives on Broadway (Wolf 2020). This living, passion-inducing, transformative genre reinforces whose stories matter in our culture. People understand themselves through representation; for musical theatre, their connection and identification happen through participation and intense fandom, too. Unlike (some) other theatrical canons, then, the musical theatre canon has widespread effects.

All of these forces—economic, aesthetic, chronological, geographical, intellectual, and performative—and the people who serve as gatekeepers—including theatre owners and producers, composers and lyricists, critics, scholars and professors, teachers and directors, to name a few—participate in and perpetuate musical theatre's canon. Raymond Knapp argues that there are many canons for different uses and contexts and publics: "performing, critical, and teaching canons" (Knapp 2020: 477). As we'll see in the essays that follow, there are many things we can do with the musical theatre canon.

Thirteen Ways of Looking at a Canon (With apologies to Wallace Stevens and a nod to the Cole Porter list song)

David Savran

I

Since the construction of a canon attempts to legitimize a narrative about the development of an art and an academic field, let's remember that for a very long time musical theatre was considered mere entertainment, throwaway art. Therefore, we want to stack the canonical deck with serious, Pulitzer Prize-winning oeuvres by the Gershwins, Rodgers and Hammerstein, Frank Loesser, Stephen Sondheim, and Jonathan Larsen, all culminating in *Hamilton*, which (thank God!) has rescued the art from the jaws of irrelevance.

II

Since canons are really about popularity, let's choose the musicals that have enjoyed the longest runs on Broadway. We'll end up with a motley and not terribly appetizing crew, but nobody can argue with popularity.

III

Because canons should reward artistic excellence, let's construct a canon that rehabilitates the many musicals that have not had a fair shake in the crude, vulgar, dehumanizing factory known as Broadway. Let us, therefore, rescue undervalued or obscure works by acknowledged masters such as Kurt Weill, Leonard Bernstein, Jerome Moross, Stephen Sondheim, Adam Guettel, and Jeanine Tesori.

IV

Canons should be constructed to redress the many—and unforgivable—injustices resulting from the United States' original sin, slavery. Therefore, we should privilege works by and about Black and brown US-Americans (from *Shuffle Along* to *A Strange Loop*) as well as musicals (like *The Cradle Will Rock* and *Ragtime*) that illuminate the systemic, genocidal inequities that have long structured US society.

V

In the 21st century, the Broadway-style musical has become the global theatrical lingua franca. As a result, any canon that aims for catholicity but excludes original musicals from (among others) South Korea, Germany, Brazil, India, Austria, and South Africa is a joke.

VI

Canons should permit a re-evaluation of the many flops that have littered the Great White Way. Flops (such as *A Doll's Life*, *Carrie*, and the LaChiusa/Wolfe *The Wild Party*) tell us more about the art and the business of musical theatre than all the successes combined.

VII

Discussions of canonization usually acknowledge the importance of vaudeville, but tend to minimize the contribution of another singularly inventive, tuneful, and globally-circulated precursor, operetta. Let us reevaluate and revalue operetta as the musical's glorious forerunner—and alter-ego.

VIII

Because musicals can never be fully understood by means of scripts, scores, or cast recordings, let us canonize works that circulate widely via movies, television, pirate videos, and YouTube.

IX

Because musicals can never be fully understood by means of scripts, scores, or cast recordings, let us canonize works we can see live on stage—whether Broadway, civic light opera, summer camps, or high schools.

X

Canons are delivered to avid students in the form of syllabi. Therefore, we should design courses that mix what they think they know with what they don't know, while drawing attention to the sometimes brutal patterns of exclusion and the unacknowledged hierarchies of taste that always attend canon construction.

XI

Let us canonize the musicals we love.

XII

Fashioning a canon is a way of constructing the historical present. Let us, therefore, canonize work that relates to climate change, migration, civil war, epidemics, and the resistible rise of neo-fascism.

XIII

Canons are constructed not only with an eye on what is, but also on what should be. Let us remember that the historical mission of musical theatre has been to build community, to make happy endings, and to envision—and bring into being—a better world. Construct a musical theatre canon to fulfill those ends.

Preserving and Challenging the Traditional Musical Theatre Canon

Rob Berman

As the music director of the *Encores!* series at New York City Center for the past 14 years, I have had the pleasure of conducting over thirty-five, one-week-run, staged concert productions of vintage Broadway musicals, from Cole Porter's *The New Yorkers* (1930) to the relatively more recent *Grand Hotel* (1989). There was a scholarly, historical, and musicological mission when *Encores!* began in 1994: to present shows with significant theatre scores—featuring their original and complete orchestration—that probably would not receive a full-scale Broadway revival. In fact, an early nickname for the series coined by some of its founders was "Flops by Tops."

The 2020 season, cut short by the coronavirus pandemic, included Jerry Herman's *Mack & Mabel* (1974), a short-lived show which introduced several enduring theatre songs, including "I Won't Send Roses" and "Time Heals Everything," but has never been revived on Broadway, and *Love Life* (1948), a rarely performed piece by Kurt Weill and Alan Jay Lerner that is widely credited as the first so-called "concept musical." *Encores!* avoids titles from the traditional canon and rather complements and shadows that canon. For instance, *Encores!* produced a Rodgers and Hammerstein critical and commercial failure, *Pipe Dream* (1955). While a clumsy adaptation of John Steinbeck's novel *Sweet Thursday*, *Pipe Dream* features a lush and melodic score worth hearing played with its full orchestration.

In 2021, *Encores!* is at a crossroads. By definition, *Encores!* produces musicals from the age of the traditional canon, the so-called "golden age" when musicals were mostly written by and performed by (and for) white people. Over the years, the series has taken seriously issues of representation and diversity, producing a number of musicals that featured mostly or all-Black casts, such as *St. Louis Woman*, *House of Flowers*, *Purlie*, *Lost in the Stars*, and *Cabin in the Sky*, as well as casting shows non-traditionally that originally featured all-white casts. With new artistic leadership as of 2020, *Encores!* will select more recent works and stories that center BIPOC characters, such as *The Life* (1997) and *The Tap Dance Kid* (1983), and will employ more BIPOC actors, directors, and designers.

These shifts in priorities are necessary and due, but as a music director and as someone who has loved the sound of classic Broadway shows my whole life, I also believe the music of the golden age of Broadway has great value and should not be lost.

From my highly specialized (and privileged) perspective of the conductor's podium, there is a visceral thrill that is hard to describe when I have led orchestras and casts through performances of shows such as Frank Loesser's dense and rich *The Most Happy Fella* or Lerner and Loewe's enchanting *Brigadoon*. When a large Broadway orchestra digs into a classic overture, I hear excitement and possibility of what is yet to come; it is a purely American phenomenon.

The music of Broadway for much of the 20th century was in fact the soundtrack of American life. It supplied the great American songbook with hit after hit. The songwriting skills of Jerome Kern, Rodgers and Hart, Irving Berlin, George Gershwin, Leonard Bernstein, Jule Styne, Stephen Sondheim, and many others were unparalleled, and all of these writers—white men—were also outsiders, whether immigrants, Jewish, or gay. Many, like Oscar Hammerstein II and Yip Harburg, were politically progressive and brought those values to their work. These are the folks who created the great original American art form that is the Broadway musical.

The works that make up the traditional canon, such as *Guys and Dolls, West Side Story, A Chorus Line*, and *Sweeney Todd*, have endured because of the appeal and theatricality of their music, their well-crafted lyrics, vivid characters, and the humanity and emotion contained within the stories they tell. Audiences and critics alike have responded to these shows with praise and enthusiasm; they have achieved both commercial and artistic success in their original productions as well as many revivals across the country, not to mention thousands of amateur productions in schools and community theatres. These musicals (and their music) have seeped into the culture at large.

The works of the traditional canon are strong enough to withstand various interpretations and re-interpretations. "Revisals," such as Daniel Fish's 2019 *Oklahoma!*, reveal new truths about the musical itself as well as about American history. A 2019 national tour of Lincoln Center's *My Fair Lady* revival drew packed houses across the country. Let's grapple with these shows' complexities and argue about how they should be cast and who should tell these stories. Let's acknowledge and challenge the conditions under which they were created and reinvent ways to present and perform them. Let's continue to learn from the works and not discard them.

In, But Not Of

Eric M. Glover

All musicals by and about Black people happen to reside simultaneously in the middle and on the edge of the canon of great musicals. Even though Pauline Elizabeth Hopkins's *Peculiar Sam* (1879) is the first musical by a Black person ever, George Gershwin's *Porgy and Bess* (1935) remains a synecdoche for Black musical theatre in theory and practice. A powerful concurrence of factors, including but not limited to epistemology and historiography, contributes to why students know Gershwin's musical and not Hopkins's musical. If Black musical theatre writers are not included in research and teaching on musical theatre history, then the glaring omission further perpetuates a narrative that Black musical theatre writers do not matter. However, students of African American languages, literatures, and cultures and those of drama and performance must experiment with more sophisticated approaches to the American musical.

bell hooks's *margins as a space of radical openness* guides my approach to the US musical in and out of a classroom. Based on hooks's premise that Black people ought to be judged on our own terms philosophically, she recommends that Black people apply our marginality toward creating new ways of seeing material conditions: "It [marginality] offers to one the possibility of radical perspective from which to see and create, to imagine alternatives, new worlds" (2015: 149). It is important to me that absorption into a white universal canon cease to be a metric by which scholars judge a Black artist's value. For example, Eubie Blake's, Hopkins's, and Charlie Smalls's musicals do not increase or decrease in value whether or not white scholars exclude their musicals in research and teaching on musical theatre history. Choosing the margins as a political philosophy compels reflexivity about how we know what we know and why we respect who we respect.

The presence of the Chitlin Circuit (culturally specific venues that have historically catered to Black people) belies a myth that Broadway, Off-Broadway, and regional theatre are the province of the US musical. When Langston Hughes and Jobe Huntley's *Tambourines to Glory* introduces gospel music in 1963 on Broadway, they beget heirs to a "gospel musical" by their activity and influence all over the world. Everybody from Tyler ("Madea") Perry to David E. Talbert is indebted to Hughes and Huntley for their help in making their urban musicals (the preferred term among artists for gospel musicals) successful. By looking at Hughes and Huntley's *Tambourines to Glory* alongside Talbert's *Mr. Right Now!* (1999), students see the ways in which Talbert builds on Hughes and Huntley's characters, events, and given circumstances dramaturgically. Unlearning white supremacy by learning more about urban musicals helps students rethink where roots and routes of the US musical begin and end.

Researching and teaching biographies of Black artists who participated in white musicals is another way to learn more about the canon from a different perspective. I'd be rich if I had a nickel for every time that a white person told me that they did not know Hughes wrote the lyrics for composer Kurt Weill's *Street Scene*. A damnatio memoriae approach to Leonard Bernstein, Marvin Hamlisch, John Kander, and Jerome Kern also erases the Black stars who gave each role body and voice. When I teach *West Side Story*, *A Chorus Line*, *Cabaret*, and *Show Boat*, I introduce students to Elizabeth Taylor, Candy Brown, Barbara Alston, and Jules Bledsoe, among others, as "cocreator" (Kirle 2005: 2). As such, these Black artists belie a myth in everyday life and live performance that the canon is the sphere of white artists only.

hooks reminds me that a single syllabus is not the sum total of musical theatre history but a starting point for theory and practice. If instructors were to free ourselves and our instruction from well-worn teleological narratives of musical theatre progress, then students would also interrogate the causes by which canonicity arises along with the purposes canonicity serves. I find it worthwhile to have a discussion about what we look for when we see musicals when marginality is what frames a discussion. Allowing that Gershwin is no more valuable than Hopkins because he is much more well-known than she is, marginality asks what is at stake in being included in the musical theatre canon. Consequently, what students think an American musical is continues to have precedence over why an American musical is included in the canon at all.

The Musical Theatre Canon and the Women It Overlooked

Georgia Stitt

A canon is a display of power. Some collective body of like-minded individuals has decided what's relevant, what's impactful, and what deserves a place in history. The inclusion of a person's work in the canon means that over time it was seen, studied, evaluated, affirmed, and anointed. But a canon is reactionary; it responds to culture rather than informing it. Consider the same phenomenon as it occurs in language. If enough people use the word "y'all," eventually it shows up in the dictionary. But a single person or group of people can't force language to change.

A problem with the canon is really a problem with the culture it reflects.

I was quoted in a 2018 *New York Times* article by Michael Paulson titled, "The Problem with Broadway Revivals: They Revive Gender Stereotypes, Too." In the article, in response to the announcement of an upcoming season that included revivals of *Carousel*, *My Fair Lady*, *Kiss Me Kate*, and the premiere of the new musical, *Pretty Woman*, I said, "It's frustrating that … people seem to want to throw their energy into old properties where women have no agency. And then there is the real scarcity of women on the creative teams."

These two statements are not unrelated.

At Maestra Music, the not-for-profit organization I founded in 2017, we built a Timeline of Female Composers on Broadway. We cited shows from 1899 (*Sister Mary*, with songs by Cissy Loftus) to the present (*Hadestown*, which opened in 2019 and was composed by Anaïs Mitchell). I did not know until we began researching how few women composers were produced between 1940 and 1970 during what we call the "Golden Era" of musical theatre. Maestra's team has identified only three female composers in those thirty years of Broadway history. Their names are Anna Russell, Marian Grudeff, and Mary Rodgers. Arguably, Mary Rodgers is the only one of the three whose work has entered the canon.

If you look at the musicals of the Golden Era, you'll recognize women characters as ingenues, brides, prostitutes, whores, mothers, crones, and comedic sidekicks. It's rare to find a musical that passes the Bechdel test, a system of measurement named after American cartoonist Alison Bechdel that considers whether at least two named women in a work of fiction speak to each other about something other than a man. The egregious absence of women's musical authorship in the most formative era of the musical theatre is certainly a canon-shaping piece of information. What additional female archetypes might have emerged in classic musicals if the women who were composing them had been produced at the highest level? (If you suspect women weren't writing musicals, that's the canon at work. Just because you haven't heard of Kay Swift, Trude Rittman, or Nancy Ford does not mean they weren't there).

"What do we do with the musical theatre canon?" We must regard it with skepticism, question its gatekeepers, and do everything in our power to make sure the voices of our time are heard and archived.

You see, if you take the stance that revivals are bad and shouldn't be produced, then you are removing from our theatrical vocabulary two kinds of important experiences. First, revivals can recreate something from a bygone era, like the 1995 revival of *Hello, Dolly!* that still starred the legendary Carol Channing and used the same 1964 original set design. And second, revivals can offer historical perspective, like the 2019 revival of *Oklahoma!* that deconstructed every creative element as a commentary on 21st-century politics of race and gender.

Must we retire a show that has become offensive in its old age? One could argue that no one ever again needs to see *The Mikado*, written in a time when imperialism was celebrated and casual racism was exploited for humor. But you can't make *The Mikdao* not-have-existed, and its place in theatrical history seems secure. Is the experience of seeing this show educational? Entertaining? Nostalgic? Provocative? Does it matter, if people buy tickets? Who gets to be the arbiter of value, the censor of out-of-date ideas, the gatekeeper of acceptability? Ultimately, that's the canon.

In order for the canon to evolve, as it inevitably will, the stewards of this generation's work must insist upon producing more voices of women and people of color. An investment in these writers, categorically overlooked for so long, will yield new stories, characters, actors, and audiences.

Canonical Show Tune Conventions

Masi Asare

Implicit in any possible canon of musical theatre are the canonical writing practices that mark shows as musicals in the first place. The way I learned it in the BMI Lehman Engel Musical Theatre Workshop in the early 2000s, there were "rules" to which one should adhere—or at best, strong encouragement to comply—for dramaturgical success in writing musicals. Founded by and named for the late Broadway conductor, this New York-based workshop at the music copyright organization BMI has, for over five decades, educated musical theatre writers and composers on industry writing practices. As we were instructed, writers must be able to create an "I Want" song, a comedy song, a torch song, a "charm song," a love duet—and know which kinds of songs should be matched to the voices of which kinds of characters. That big, conflicted ballad deep in the second act? It should go to a major character. Similarly, don't give away your big love duet to the secondary couple; it goes to the leads. Traditionally, the 11 o'clock number, that showstopper as the musical nears its close, is often sung by a minor character.

As Diana Taylor has established, any archive—and a fixed collection of canonical works may be taken as an archive—exists in tension with the ephemerality of repertoire (Taylor 2003). Of interest here is a repertoire of *kinds of songs* that musical theatre writers and composers both create and situate in appropriate dramatic moments such that the performance is understood as a musical. Each song delivers—shapes and is shaped by—the scenario of a dramatic situation; audiences expect to encounter familiar scenarios when they go to see a musical. "Something's stopping me from this dream I have" is an "I Want" song. "I've got some jokes, keep that tempo snappy," a comedy song. "My lover has left me but I'm still holding out hope": torch song, likely blues-edged. "Scary things are afoot but let's keep the mood light and look how fun I am": charm song. As a unit of repertoire, Taylor writes, "The scenario structures our understanding. It also haunts our present… We've seen it all before" (Taylor 2003: 28). While taken for granted, show tune conventions have their own affective, gendered, and racialized histories. The operative question for musical theatre writers is: how will we move among, with, and beyond the established repertoire of canonical musical theatre writing practices?

As a writer and composer, I do love a good "I Want" song. But I will never forget being admonished, very kindly, by Broadway lyricist Lynn Ahrens that the protagonist only gets *one* "I Want" song per show in which she throws forward the full force of her dreams for the future. So I cut the second song that was a double beat, a joyful but excessive reiteration. There is only so much dreaming a musical theatre heroine is allowed before she must take action.

I also strongly resisted, for years, writing love songs in musicals, reluctant to rearticulate the passive acquiescence of female characters that such songs seemed, to me, to call up. I preferred to write fight songs, where characters who may have great love or admiration for one another and nonetheless have an all-out, lusty disagreement in song, sometimes in counterpoint. My anti-love song arc has been firmly reversed, however, since joining the creative team for a beautiful musical with a double wedding at its center, and I am grateful for multiple women of color collaborators on that project and our conversations about how to ensure that female characters have their own drives, desires, and resistances in song—and not just canonical tunes of lovelornness and acquiescence.

I also think quite a bit about musical style as a function of character, and in relation to racialized characters. This has the potential to thwart troubling conventions, such as the utilitarian gospel number late in the show that performs a sense of uplift but generally in service of white characters and storylines. It's a convention that Michael R. Jackson has powerfully invoked and upended in his musical *A Strange Loop*. And this is why the work of female writers/composers and musical theatre writers of color is especially needed—to contribute additional nuance to how the repertoire of musical theatre song conventions may be revoiced, situated, and extended.

Drowning Narcissus

Brandon Webster
The people watched as Narcissus stared into the pool of water. In line with what would become a "great-tradition" in 1 person shows, the world grew embarrassingly tired of waiting for something to happen. Narcissus had become relentlessly boring, and deeply unsatisfying. The author feared harsh critique and needed to wrap the story, so he made sure Narcissus dissolved,

or evaporated, or wasted away, or committed suicide, or whatever elegant-but-tragic ending comes to white men who waste time and resources; and the world moved on. Only one remained with a grievance: The pool of water. A victim of what would become white culture—For it had been deeply misused like a tool; passive and neutral, instead of feared, and respected as elemental. With no author to tell its story, and no audience to hear it, the pool of water was left with a new truth: it should have drowned Narcissus for misunderstanding it as a mirror.

It's not difficult to figure out how to solve these larger and more oppressive parts of US Musical Theatre. The Canon, as a reflection, elevation, and celebration of what's assumed to be the best of US Musical Theatre has been crippled by a deep Racism, Misogyny, and Xenophobia, while loudly boasting a mediocrity that is fundamentally and uniquely American. A glaring celebration of US White Supremacy, The Canon tells a contrived and duplicitous story of the history of white music in theatre while erasing the very existence of musical storytelling in non-white cultures and communities. This manufactured history is further reified by the canon; and in a world where a truer history of storytelling with music in theatre is available, one has to wonder why this canon is still used as a measuring stick.

The American Musical Theatre Canon fails every non-white student who comes in contact with it, in spite of the fact that it's used as the primary tool for training and education, both as musical history and pedagogy. At best non-white students are removing a part of themselves to access the work, or damaging their voice to create an "acceptable" sound. But far too often, non-white students are deemed incapable, based on their performance of work from a Canon that wasn't designed for them. In fact, The Canon, among many other systems, was designed to keep non-white folks, including our students, off of the American stage, which is good reason to simply discard it.

We don't have to keep bemoaning AND uplifting the problem. We could just… drown Narcissus. Which is not to say that we won't have a Canon, or to say that we don't need a Canon, but to say that it doesn't have to be THIS one. And I think, in developing a new Canon, it can truly do more, and it must if Musical Theatre is to grow.

100 years of exploring what white music in stories has to offer has distilled white storytelling into the best it can be. After all of the theft, suppression, oppression, gaslighting, and dis-inclusion, the "Old American Musical" flamed out quickly, with startlingly less growth than one would expect for a 100-year run. On one hand, the lessons learned from the old American musical have made clear that there is a tried-and-true recipe to making a musical; but that double-edged truth also shines a light on the probable existence of many other unexplored recipes and ways to put together stories told with music. Whether by the death and creation of an entirely new genre, or the radical change of the old genre, the future of the American Musical Theatre lies in the exploration of new recipes; and from that exploration and excavation should come a better, more effective Canon.

An ENTIRE world of storytelling waits outside of the walls of what we imagine theatre can be. In that world, storytelling with music is infinite with possibility. In that world, the canon is not just a reflection of something beautiful, static & tragic. This Canon, deliberately developed and re-compiled with education, performance, and mastery in mind from conception, is an ultimate guide for storytelling with music, celebrated for its efficacy, accessible, flexible, everchanging. Not a reflection of what has happened in some twee recollection of a time that was oppressive to everyone but white men, but a collection of songs from new works that are a deep promise in manifesting the world of theatre that we want to live in, that we want our children and students and peers and friends to live in.

Refusing the Musical Theatre Canon: Burn the House Down

Sarah K. Whitfield

We tactically refuse. We say enough. We dissent. We "burn the fucking house down" (Lloyd Malcolm 2018: 82). Because we cannot go on like this.

In my Introduction to *Reframing the Musical: Race, Culture and Identity*, I address how the story of the musical revolves around the canon. It has led to a set of male, mostly white "people, places and events [being] privileged as more important, more worth remembering and paying attention to than others: public discourse around the musical has minimized, ignored and erased the contributions of many marginalized people" (Whitfield 2019: xii). Like other popular culture canons, the musical theatre canon is intertwined with US national ideologies, enmeshed with nostalgia, with White Western ideals of identity, heterosexuality, and normate bodies. It has been formalized by power structures that have asserted exacting copyright control over original texts, revealing an unwillingness to move away from script and score as a "regulatory reliquary," as W.B. Worthen memorably positions it (2008: 12). The canon is perpetuated by university curriculums, by amateur and commercialized theatre production, publishing, public broadcasting, and wider public discourses. Attempts to dismantle the canon are hampered by the reluctance of gatekeepers to risk conceding power and space (or money, always money). But we say, enough.

If we are serious about refusing the canon, we have to start by showing reverence to and attending to the work of Black women artists and philosophers who have imagined ways out of the mess; futures beyond white supremacist, white hegemonic, paternalistic and heterosexual dominant ideologies and assumptions. Audre Lorde's invocation, often quoted and still profoundly relevant, calls us to attend to the idea that "the master's tools will never dismantle the master's house. They may allow us to temporarily beat him at his own game, but they will never allow us to bring about genuine change" ([1984] 2019: 18). Clearly fueled by the work of Lorde, Black feminist activist Legacy Russell proposes dismantling the system through her Glitch Manifesto:

> The first step to subverting a system is accepting that that system will remain in place; that said, **the glitch says fuck your systems**! Your delineations! Your determinations as imposed upon our physicality! The glitch respectfully declines second rank to common convention. (emphasis in original, 2012)

Elsewhere, Russell notes if Lorde's argument holds "then perhaps what these institutions [need] is not dismantling but rather mutiny in the form of strategic occupation" (2020: 25). Russell enacts refusal; inhabiting glitches *in* the system ruptures the system itself.

The call to mutiny is seductive, but we may need to address uncomfortable and complex truths about how we have wielded and benefitted from "the master's tools" in the canon before we get to join in the riot. Here, I note my identity as a white, cis, bisexual+ disabled woman. Although white women composers and lyricists have been minimized in the musical theatre canon, (performers have been better remembered), white women benefit from white supremacist structures. Kalwant Bhopal considers how in education, for example, "White privilege and a hierarchy of oppression has resulted in a discourse of denial in which gender as a competing identity has been given greater significance and prominence compared to race" (2020: 807). Even if white people have other minoritized identities that the canon disregards, the overriding privilege of whiteness cannot be discounted. More pressingly, it has compounded erasures of Queer and disabled PoC.

If we are to embark on a mutinous refusal to accept the limitations of the system, led by the insightful revolutionary vision of thinkers like Russell and Lorde, we have possibilities. We might strategically occupy canonical works, demystifying nostalgia to reveal what we are so dangerously nostalgic about. We might delight in its glitches, breaking the canon by refusing to obey its strictures about permitted bodies. We could invoke a form "where white people are willing to be sidekicks to Black superheroes" (Galella 2019: 15). Some of us might structurally survey the damage the canon has done to our field, to the form. Some of us could use our skills to revisit and uncover what was missing, consider the processes of production as well as the product. We would unleash voices that have been waiting for too long to be heard.

Expanding the Canon

Randall Eng

If we accept the existence of the musical theatre canon and its outsized impact, then the most important thing we need to do with the canon is to grow it. Part of this means bringing in lesser-known works from previous eras. And much of it means developing, supporting, and producing new work.

The canonical works of musical theatre are an incredibly rich set of pieces. They have been preserved, documented, studied, re-interpreted, emulated, and have given joy, solace, and meaning to generations of audiences. But unsurprisingly, given the historical context in which they were written and produced, they represent a narrow range of viewpoints. If musical theatre wants to remain in conversation with the multifaceted world that we live in, the canon needs to not only reflect that world but be rooted in it. It will take time to achieve this, but the quickest and most urgent path is through the full-hearted embrace of creative new work.

Much of this new work needs to be written by artists of color and others whose perspectives or aesthetics are absent in the existing canon. Over my 20 years of teaching musical theatre writers, I have watched our student population (and the kinds of stories they are compelled to tell) diversify more and more. The richness of their work points towards a more inclusive, more representative future for musical theatre. But for that future to come to pass, the field must act with purposefulness and commitment. It must embrace the work of writers of color and others who can evolve the canon to a place that speaks more directly to the world we live in.

None of which is to say that the existing canon need to be set aside. These hardy works have much to say to us today. There is so much about the canon that speaks to me, and though characters like Curly or Mama Rose or Sweeney Todd may look different than a middle-aged Chinese American from Staten Island, I know their struggles and pain and triumph, as we all do. These great works speak universal truths, and many argue that if they happen to be written by a narrow slice of creators, it's not a problem because everyone can relate to the stories that they tell regardless of personal background.

But this universality cuts both ways. Sure, people of color will find their way into the canonical works; they've spent their whole lives having to find points of identification within white mainstream culture. Yet there are equally universal experiences to be had within shows that come from other points of view. Bookwriter/lyricist/composer Kirsten Childs, for example, reflected on her breakout musical, *The Bubbly Black Girl Sheds Her Chameleon Skin*, "People used to come up to me, and they'd say, 'That's my story.' And they weren't all black women. They were white men. Black men. White women. Asian men" (Isenberg 2000). Making room in the canon for a more diverse set of creators doesn't mean carving out niches for other groups to have their place—it means enlarging the set of experiences, perspectives, and stories that everyone can connect to.

When we do revive works from the canon, it's important to grapple with the context not only in which they were written (and when they were set), but also the context in which they are now being presented. Recent revivals of *Oklahoma!* (2019, dir. Daniel Fish) and *Porgy and Bess* (2011, dir. Diane Paulus) show that when visionary adapters are given relative freedom by rights-holders, canonical musicals can withstand the same kind of artistic license that we take with Shakespeare or Sophocles. These productions speak differently to contemporary audiences than traditional revivals, asking different questions and guiding us to different conclusions. And in doing so, they help illuminate the value of the canon itself—the centering of works that can hold up to some de-centering.

If there's one message I could convey to producers, audiences, critics, and scholars, it would be this: Have faith in writers, both old and new. The canonical shows are written well enough that they don't need protective barriers around them. As well, we must embrace the fact that today's writers have as much to say to us as the Golden Age writers had to say to their contemporaries. There are so many writers creating shows right now of intense beauty and depth, reflecting and engaging with the multicultural world outside and inside our doors. Give them a chance to speak, let the canon breathe, and the rewards will be immense.

Works Cited

Bhopal, Kalwant. 2020. "Confronting White Privilege: The Importance of Intersectionality in the Sociology of Education." *British Journal of Sociology of Education* 41, 6: 807–816.

Block, Geoffrey. 1993. "The Broadway Canon from *Show Boat* to *West Side Story* and the European Operatic Ideal." *The Journal of Musicology* 11, 4 (Autumn 1993): 525–544.

Block, Geoffrey. 2009 [1997]. *Enchanted Evenings: The Broadway Musical from Show Boat to Sondheim and Lloyd Webber.* 2nd edition. New York: Oxford University Press.

Galella, Donatella. 2019. "'Superman/Sidekick': White Storytellers and Black Lives in *The Fortress of Solitude* (2014)." In *Reframing the Musical: Race, Culture and Identity*, edited by Sarah Whitfield, 3–16, London: Red Globe Press.

Greenberg, Shoshana. "The Maestra Timeline." Accessed 28 January 2021. https://maestramusic.org/timeline/.

hooks, bell. 2015. *Yearnings: Race, Gender, and Cultural Politics.* New York: Routledge.

Isenberg, Barbara. 2000. "All of Her Heart and Soul." *Los Angeles Times*, 18 June. Accessed 11 January 2021. www.latimes.com/archives/la-xpm-2000-jun-18-ca-42023-story.html

Kirle, Bruce. 2005. *Unfinished Show Business: Broadway Musicals as Works-in-Process.* Carbondale: Southern Illinois University Press.

Knapp, Raymond. 2020. "Canons of the American Musical." In *The Oxford Handbook of the Operatic Canon*, edited by Cormac Newark and William Weber, 475–490. New York: Oxford University Press.

Lloyd Malcolm, Morgan. 2018. *Emilia.* London: Oberon Modern Plays.

Lorde, Audre. 2018 [1984]. *The Master's Tools Will Never Dismantle the Master's House.* London: Penguin Modern.

Paulson, Michael. 2018. "The Problem with Broadway Revivals: They Gender Stereotypes, Too." *New York Times*, February 22. Accessed 23 January 2021. https://www.nytimes.com/2018/02/22/theater/gender-stereotypes-carousel-my-fair-lady-pretty-woman.html.

Reside, Doug. Forthcoming. *Fixing the Musical: How Media Technologies Shaped the Musical Theatre Canon*. New York: Oxford University Press.
Russell, Legacy. 2012. "Digital Dualism and the Glitch Feminism Manifesto." *Cyborgology*, 10 December. Accessed 8 December 2020. https://thesocietypages.org/cyborgology/2012/12/10/digital-dualism-and-the-glitch-feminism-manifesto/.
Russell, Legacy. 2020. *Glitch Feminism: A Manifesto*. London: Verso Books.
Taylor, Diana. 2003. *The Archive and the Repertoire*. Durham, NC: Duke University Press.
Whitfield, Sarah. 2019. "Introduction." In *Reframing the Musical: Race, Culture and Identity*, edited by Sarah Whitfield, xi–xxxii, London: Red Globe Press.
Wolf, Stacy. 2020. *Beyond Broadway: The Pleasure and Promise of Musical Theatre Across America*. Oxford: Oxford University Press.
Worthen, William B. 2008. "Antigone's Bones." *TDR: The Drama Review* 52, 3: 10–33.
Wollman, Elizabeth. Forthcoming. "Musical Theater Studies: A Critical View of the Discipline's History and Development in the United States and United Kingdom." *Music Research Annual*.

15 Canons in Motion: Japanese Performance, Theatre History, and the Currents of Knowledge

Jyana S. Browne and Jessica Nakamura

As scholars of Japanese performance, reassessing the canon means confronting multiple entrenched bodies of knowledge. It may seem as if our specialties—early modern popular performance for Jyana and postwar and contemporary theatre for Jessica—are firmly within the field of theatre and performance studies. We both trained at theatre and performance studies graduate programs. Yet throughout our careers, we have felt the pull of several fields—theatre and performance studies, Japanese studies, and Asian studies more broadly—each with its own set of canons.

Our different institutional perspectives require us to negotiate multiple canons. Jyana is housed in an East Asian Languages and Cultures department, where she is the specialist for premodern Japan; she teaches courses on Japanese performance, literature, and cultural studies as well as advanced reading in modern and classical Japanese. Jessica is housed in a Theatre and Dance department, where she is the Asian theatre specialist in a globally-oriented curriculum; she teaches courses in Asian theatre and performance, Asian American theatre, and the history of directing. Before her current position, Jessica taught theatre history as the only faculty member with a PhD in a small Theatre and Dance department.

Our institutional positions defined our writing process. We began with a series of conversations about the ways in which we encounter knowledge production. We soon identified a theatre history canon for undergraduates and a theoretical canon for graduate training, as well as various canons on the side of Japanese studies. The origins and effects of these canons have been historically determined, reflective of the connection between canon formation and systems of knowledge. The overwhelming association between canons and text manifest in our conceptions of "theatre," "Asian theatre," and "theatre history." For Japanese performance, this association ignores performance forms that may not leave textual remains and brings scripts and playwriting to the center of forms that have historically privileged acting and live performance. The canon is also reliant on what has been translated for the English-reading public. English-language Japanese performance scripts not only reflect the preferences of their translators, but they also determine a canon, reinforcing ideas of Japanese theatre simply by what is available or not.

DOI: 10.4324/9781003031413-15

Our many canons are also historically determined by Western performance history. Our undergraduate classes covered global performance forms through the influence of Asian theatre on Western directors, including Antonin Artaud, Bertolt Brecht, Peter Brook, and Ariane Mnouchkine. The effects of Asian theatre on the field through the lenses of these directors cannot be underestimated. Structural, aesthetic, and other formal elements from Asian forms reverberate in theatre and dance performance work today. These same directors, however, perpetuated misconceptions about Asian performance in their writings. The canonization of these writings, including Artaud's *The Theatre and its Double* and Brecht's "Alienation Effects in Chinese Acting," has made these misconceptions difficult to dislodge (See Savarese 2001 and Tian 1997).

These historical factors are some but not all of what continues to determine the canons we aim to challenge and revise. What emerged over our conversations are the ways in which the effects of the traditional theatre history canon and its limitations can be felt well beyond the classroom. We realized how much canon formation not only determines our undergraduate students' understandings of Japanese theatre but also influences theatre production, graduate training, the development of scholarship, and the field itself.

Our chapter stages our virtual conversations to reflect the ways in which we experience multiple canons. Because we reside between canons in our teaching and research, we argue for the value of actively negotiating canons. As we explore below, our canons already influence each other while they obscure their own mechanisms of knowledge production. It is critical, then, to intentionally direct these currents of knowledge so they converge and flow together. Putting canons in motion will innovate teaching, scholarship, and ultimately understandings of theatre and performance in our fields.

Our Canon(s)

Jessica Nakamura: When I think of the "theatre canon," the first thing that comes to mind is my undergraduate education. I learned a theatre history canon composed mostly of plays and predominantly from the West. I encountered this canon again as a graduate student for my first comprehensive exam at Stanford (a list of 150 plays).

Jyana S. Browne: Me too. I had seen various genres of Japanese performance growing up thanks to my father, but I had almost no exposure to Asian dramatic forms in my undergraduate or graduate education. In college, Asian forms were only included when they were an important influence on Western theatre. My graduate training largely replicated the same theatre history canon, although Asian and other "non-Western" works snuck into student presentations and postcolonial theory syllabi.

Nakamura: When our graduate training reiterates our undergraduate education, it can reinforce what "theatre" is. Here we see a connection between canonicity and the production of knowledge or at least the shaping of our understandings of theatre. By our experiences with the theatre history canon, theatre is defined as text-based and predominantly Western.

There's another canon in graduate training, the theoretical canon. I rarely see any theories that originate from outside the West. And I feel the need to be well-versed in Western theory (and history, for that matter) to join in the scholarly conversation. So this bias affects my scholarship all the time.

Browne: This is one of the thorniest issues for scholars of Asian performance. As a field, theatre and performance studies encompasses a broad temporal and geographic range, so our common theoretical canon brings us together. However, the Western focus of the theoretical canon perpetuates a troubling practice of using Western theory as the sole method to analyze Asian materials.

From the Japanese studies side, there are additional canons, in my case, principally the Japanese literary canon, which US-based scholars inherit from scholars in Japan. For many centuries, the Japanese literary canon was composed of classical poetry from anthologies such as the *Collection of Poems Ancient and Modern* (*Kokinwakashū* c. 905) and prose works such as *The Tale of Genji* (*Genji monogatari* c. 1000). The canon expanded in the nineteenth century with the national literature movement (*kokubungaku*) and the theatre reform movement, which recategorized drama as literature and cast puppet theatre and kabuki playwright Chikamatsu Monzaemon as Japan's "Shakespeare" (See Lee 2002: 183–184, 188). While the canon has continued to incorporate new works, the 19th sense of the classics persists.

Nakamura: As you explain it, Western influences shape the very idea of a literary canon in Japan. While we're focused on canons in the US, the case of Japan illustrates the ways in which Western influence determines knowledge production elsewhere on a number of levels.

Thinking more about canons of Japanese theatre in the US, I wonder if we could add a canon of Japanese performance forms? I work on contemporary Japanese performance, and US scholars are always asking me for my thoughts on butoh, even though it's one of many postwar experimental performance movements.

Browne (laughing): I believe it. Butoh was my entry into Japanese theatre.

As scholars of Japanese performance, we're pulled between these canons—an undergraduate theatre history canon, a graduate theoretical canon, a Japanese literary canon, and a canon of Japanese performance forms. Graduate students who want to study Japanese performance usually have to choose between attending a Japanese literature program (which will privilege honing linguistic and text analysis skills) or a theatre and performance studies program (which will develop their theoretical and analytical engagement with performance but rarely provide a rich contextual understanding of Asian theatre). Each discipline emphasizes a different canon: the Japanese literary canon in the Japanese literature program and the theatre history canon in the theatre and performance studies program.

Nakamura: And that leaves no program to address the Japanese performance canon! We started by discussing the many canons we experience: theatre history, theoretical, Japanese literary, and Japanese performance. These canons are already in motion, influencing and informing each other. While what is defined as knowledge about performance changes from canon to canon, the production of knowledge is related to the interplay between canons, including how we define what counts as theatre and what constitutes scholarship. From a theatre department perspective, if part of our work is to educate future artists, what students learn about Asian theatre affects production too, determining the aesthetics, structures, and other dramaturgical forms that students have in their vocabularies for performance making.

Problems with Canon(s)

Nakamura: When the different fields of theatre and performance studies and Japanese studies develop their own canons, they appear distinct from each other. Although, as we discussed, they're interrelated. This false sense of separation elides the problems inherent in each canon, what each privileges and ignores.

The theatre history canon ignores so much Asian performance, which is not at all reflective of our or our students' experiences. You've spoken about your exposure to Japanese theatre growing up. I'm from Hawaii and saw Asian performance throughout my childhood. Each quarter, I have students who want to see a broader range of performance than what can be found in the theatre history canon. Some of these students are eager to have their own cultures reflected on stage.

Browne: Even students who haven't seen live performances often have seen and heard elements of Japanese performance in video games, anime, manga, and other media. Many students have "ah-ha" moments in class when they realize why a character in a video game has a particular movement style or costume. They've been absorbing images and soundscapes shaped by Japanese performance, they just didn't know it.

Nakamura: Our vantage point as researchers caught between canons can provide fresh perspectives on canon formation. As someone who works on Japanese theatre, for instance, it's clear that a major issue with the theatre history canon is that it not only ignores a number of global performance forms but also it overwhelmingly emphasizes play text. Japanese theatre–traditional forms *and* experimental postwar theatre movements that do not rely on textual remains–can call attention to these deficiencies. In Japanese performance, not only do we have forms that don't use scripts, like butoh, but we also have forms like kabuki in which scripts are secondary to the performance.

Browne: The Japanese literary canon in the US also has a problematic association between text and canon by focusing on literary analysis of scripts rather than a holistic analysis that includes performance elements. The emphasis on textual study gives a false impression that dramatic texts are stable.

Nakamura: On the theatre side of things, the main examples of Japanese performance in the theatre history canon are scripts of traditional theatre forms. This gives the incorrect impression that Japanese performance is composed solely of traditional theatre forms and these forms are fixed in the past. These inclusions reinforce an imperialist logic of the non-West as residing in the past, behind the West on a linear historical trajectory (See Chakrabarty 2000).

Browne: Since we're teaching in English, we are limited to the plays in translation and videos with English-language subtitles. While I have experimented with students doing live translation alongside an unsubtitled video, I usually opt for videos with subtitles. The students already have so much to take in: the physicality of the performance, the intricate costumes, and the musical and sonic elements. It's overwhelming to add in an unfamiliar linguistic register. Most of the videos available (particularly those with subtitles) showcase the national theatres with all-male casts and end up reinforcing narratives about how Japanese theatre is, and always was, "all-male" when in fact there are long traditions of female performance in a range of performance forms, as scholars such as A. Kimi Coaldrake, Loren Edelson, and Katrina Moore have documented for noh, kabuki, and bunraku, respectively.

Nakamura: Here is where available translations determine both the theatre history canon and the Japanese literary canon in the US. Translation becomes an issue where we start to see how so many other things factor into canon formation. When the canon privileges text, it favors language. Older, clunky English translations of play texts may make translated work seem less poetic, its language less worthy when compared to that of Shakespeare, Marlowe, and O'Neill. Or part of the reason why so many people know about butoh and not about the other excellent experimental postwar theatres is that butoh, as a dance form, does not require translation of text.

Browne: The limited availability in English of certain plays also impacts how the canon is discussed in scholarship. For example, the two plays most widely circulated and read in English by Chikamatsu are *Love Suicides at Sonezaki* (*Sonezaki shinjū*) and *Love Suicides at Amijima* (*Shinjū ten no Amijima*). Their familiarity leads to mistaken assumptions. I see these plays referred to as "representative" love suicide plays (*shinjūmono*) when they only seem to be representative because they have been anointed as exemplars by the canon. In fact, they are interesting mainly for their innovation. Other less well-known plays from the genre would be more representative, but most people don't read them.

Nakamura: Speaking of scholarship, the Western focus is a major limitation of the theoretical canon in graduate training. This issue has been well documented: in an essay by Mitsuhiro Yoshimoto, "The Difficulty of Being Radical: The Discipline of Film Studies and the Postcolonial World Order" from 1991, Yoshimoto laments the one-way direction of Western theory and non-Western case studies, asserting "while Western critics as subject can analyze a non-Western text as object, non-Western critics are not allowed to occupy the position of subject to analyze a Western text as object" (Yoshimoto 1991: 124). Even in scholarship about global performance forms, I rarely see theories that originate from outside the West.

Browne: I agree Yoshimoto's ideas still resonate today. Perhaps one exception is Japanese roboticist Mori Masahiro's 1970 theory of the uncanny valley (*bukimi no tani*). Mori posits that human affinity for non-human objects grows as the objects become more human-like until a certain point at which the object becomes creepy in its resemblance to the human, provokes revulsion, and falls into the "uncanny valley." Mori's essay has had a huge impact beyond robotics in performance, puppetry, film, and media fields.

Nakamura: Mori's a good example. The application of his theory in the West parallels the ways in which Western theatre artists integrated elements of Asian performance forms for their own purposes while also altering the original source. In her recent book, Jennifer Robertson comments that Mori's *bukimi no tani* would more accurately be translated as "valley of eerie feeling" (2017: 153). She notes that, excepting scholarship on Ishiguro Hiroshi's androids, Mori's theory "is largely a preoccupation of Anglophone scholars representing a spectrum of disciplines" (157).

In most instances we see US scholars applying Western theory to Asian case studies. When Western theory is applied elsewhere, we get what Kuan-Hsing Chen describes as the "familiar complaint: the West is equipped with universal theory; the rest of us have particularist empirical data; and eventually our writings become a footnote that either validates or invalidates Western theoretical propositions" (2010: 226).

Browne: Chen makes such an important point for our field because he highlights how theoretical approaches and scholarship from outside the West are marginalized in the Western academy. You opened this section by pointing out how canons obscure what is privileged and ignored. We frequently see the ways in which canon formation results in fixed ideas of performance, of tradition, and of archival form. Since we're negotiating multiple canons, we can see how the frictions between canons make the limitations more apparent and open new possibilities.

Teaching within and across canons

Browne: Teaching offers us an opportunity to highlight limitations in the canons, intersections between the canons, and possibilities for alternative canons. Since we are teaching at the confluence of streams of knowledge usually kept separate, we have to come up with creative solutions.

Nakamura: A canon, whether theatre history or Japanese literature, can provide much needed historical context, so putting canons together can yield new historical understandings.

Browne: Absolutely. Working within the Japanese literary canon helps students see the intertextuality of Japanese cultural production across performing, literary, and visual arts. For example, the Dōjōji story progresses from a narrative picture scroll (*emaki*) to a noh play, and later a kabuki dance piece. Students often have little knowledge of the cultural context for Japanese theatre. Studying texts that allude to previous works in the canon leaves room for a deeper examination of the performance since we don't need as much class time for background context. So I often find myself creating pairings or trios for students.

Nakamura: Intertextuality is immediately clear in a Japanese literary canon, and it is less so in a canon focused primarily on Western theatre. In an undergraduate course on Japanese theatre, students can see this textual lineage, whereas you have to take a deeper dive in Western theatre history to show students, for instance, that *Hamlet* has precursors.

Browne: Do you feel the need to advocate for the Japanese plays on your syllabus compared to the plays students expect to see, like *Hamlet*? My institution has few Asian performance offerings, so my classes might be the only times they'll encounter Japanese theatre. I allot time to advocate for both the significance and the awesomeness of what we study.

Nakamura: This idea of cultural advocacy is key. When I teach my lower-division Asian Theatre course, I want to augment the theatre history canon by trying to cover as many forms as possible. At the same time, I'm always confronted with the fact that this logic of coverage is a trap: based on what's available, I can't cover all important Asian theatre forms, let alone in a ten-week quarter.

Cultural advocacy and coverage reflect the ways in which an idea of a canon cannot be avoided. When you teach these thematic courses, do you feel that the undergraduates crave a canon? I organize my lower-division Asian Theatre course thematically around definitions of the performer, but I always receive comments from students about wanting a clearer linear trajectory.

Browne: I teach different acts of *Chūshingura* in all my classes and then students write in the evaluations that they wished we studied more "famous" plays. *Chūshingura* is the most famous Japanese play! One strategy I use to get around their resistance to plays they don't recognize as part of the canon is to have them engage directly with the "canon" through public humanities projects, such as editing Wikipedia. For such a project in a class on modern and contemporary Japanese theatre, when the students first looked at Wikipedia, the comparative lack of information on Japanese theatre artists led them to conclude that these artists were less important than their Western counterparts. A student noted that one Lady Gaga song had an entire Wikipedia page whereas many of the Japanese theatre artists didn't even have an entry. Our class Wikipedia project built more content for the site. More importantly, the students learned that they could use existing tools to advocate for the artists they find significant.

Nakamura: That's a great example because you show how our classes themselves can create knowledge. It makes me think about the ways in which the canon may be inescapable: If we are providing the only "theatre history" or "Japanese theatre" or "Asian theatre" course that undergraduates will ever take, does this mean that syllabus creation goes hand in hand with canon formation? And should we think of ourselves as (re)creating a canon or potentially creating an alternative canon? If so, how do we not replicate the problems of the canons as we've discussed them?

Browne: I see benefits in creating alternative canons in our courses. Alternative canons can address entrenched ideas. Take, for instance, the portrayal of prostitution in early modern Japan. Many of the materials available in English, such as anthologies of primary sources, present prostitution through the male gaze and thus uncritically reiterate the patterns in the primary materials. Since I assemble my own materials, we can read the accounts of visits to the brothels and view the woodblock prints alongside Amy Stanley's *Selling Women: Prostitution, Markets, and the Household in Early Modern Japan* (2012) and Julie Nelson Davis's *Utamaro and the Spectacle of Beauty* (2007). The students are able to develop a much more complex understanding of the primary materials through learning about the working and living conditions of the prostitutes and the representational tactics in the visual, prose, and theatrical works.

Nakamura: Another benefit to creating alternative canons in our courses is that we can highlight the importance of embodied knowledge in the study of theatre. We do this when we teach the material conditions and production elements of Japanese performance. I also have students get on their feet and learn various aspects of the forms themselves. In my Japanese Theatre course, I devote some time to the general stance and movement patterns in noh, kyogen, and kabuki. I'm familiar with this material from training in traditional Japanese Dance (*nihon buyō*) at University of Hawaii at Manoa. Because training for traditional performance forms takes decades, part of my instruction is to teach students about training practices, including the fact that I am not an expert in dancing *nihon buyō*—my teacher at UHM, for instance, has decades of experience and permission from her school to train students. I also accompany my instruction with video clips, and one of the assignments asks students to replicate a sequence of movement from a play we've studied.

Browne: That's a wonderful way to give your students access to embodied knowledge of Japanese theatre. We need to push beyond treating text as the primary record of performance to incorporate the knowledge transmitted through the body, choreography, sound, rhythm, and visual culture.

As we've discussed, when we organize our courses, we are confronted with the limitations of existing canons. We also create our own canons, so part of our work is to be transparent with students about how syllabi and classroom practices shape the production of knowledge. By making the process of knowledge production clear to our students, we empower them to step into and navigate these currents of knowledge themselves.

Productive Intersections

Nakamura: Because the effects of the theatre history canon and the Japanese literary canon play out in graduate training and then the development of separate scholarly fields (theatre and performance studies and Japanese studies), the question becomes one of how we intersect canons. We've started to talk about how we negotiate between canons in our classes, but how can we actively put them in dialogue with each other?

It's not enough to include kabuki on a theatre history syllabus. Throughout the history of performance, we've seen what happens when global performance forms influence Western artists and, as we've discussed, inaccurate information about these forms becomes embedded within the theatre history canon.

Browne: Yes, and the focus on artists like Meyerhold and Brecht elides the ways in which Japanese artists were influenced by Western theatre forms in the early twentieth century. Then, we have Japanese artists like Suzuki Tadashi, who were inspired by Western forms that later inspire Western artists. When we don't acknowledge how complex this history of global performance flows is, we treat Asian theatre as if it is "raw material" for the West.

Nakamura: Absolutely! Instead of viewing Asian theatre as "raw material," separated from its cultural contexts, we need to reevaluate *how* we discuss this material.

I think about this acutely in a theatre department: some of the students I'm educating will be future theatre artists. I feel a responsibility to expand their theatre history canon as it has reverberations in American theatre practice and in turn what appears in a theatre history canon in the future. If artists have led the charge in putting their different cultures (and corresponding canons) in conversation, can we look to them for inspiration?

Browne: An excellent case of an artist putting two canons in conversation is Shi-Zheng Chen's production of *The Orphan of Zhao* at the Lincoln Center Festival (2003). Chen was born in China and trained and performed in flower-drum opera (*huaguxi*) before moving to New York and collaborating with experimental artists, such as Meredith Monk. For *Zhao*, Chen brought in classical Chinese opera (*kunqu*)-trained actors who had appeared in the US premiere of his acclaimed and controversial *Peony Pavilion* (1999) as coaches to the American actors. Together, they developed a new performance style that integrated the precision and physicality of Chinese opera with the emotional depth of American-style realism. It was a fascinating, beautiful production.

Nakamura: I think of the artistic work by my students as an argument for bringing these canons together. In my Japanese Theatre course, I assign a creative final project. One year, a student wrote a Black Lives Matter play in the style of Japanese noh. In the play, the *shite* main character was the ghost of an African American man, and the *waki* secondary character was the policeman who murdered him. Like *Atsumori*, a noh play that shows the meeting between the ghost of Atsumori and the man who killed him in battle, the drama of the student's play was not based in conflict but on the dialogue between the two men, the living person listening to the perspective of the ghost. Using noh dramaturgy, the student had created something unique that also brilliantly commented on police violence and the need to listen. The student's play demonstrated her deep knowledge about noh that developed out of class discussions about noh's dramaturgy *and* its historical contexts, not because it was put on the syllabus as an example of Japanese theatre.

Browne: Your example is wonderful because it points out how intersecting these canons in a deliberate way is productive. We can break new ground artistically through these intersections. The same can be said for scholarship. We are seeing more scholars acknowledge the flows between canons in their research. Satoko Shimazaki's *Edo Kabuki in Transition* is one recent work that combines rigorous engagement with performance, meticulous reading of primary sources, and careful construction of context. Shimazaki restores the performances themselves as the heart of kabuki and reminds us, "That to some extent, the very idea of the play is an illusion; that we have access to only a fraction of the masses of printed materials that once gave form to Edo kabuki; that it was not scripts and authors who mattered but the audiences' memories of the theatre, inscribed on the bodies of actors" (Shimazaki 2016: 275). I hope as more scholars move intentionally between canons that the theatre canon will become more global and the Japanese "literary" canon will embrace the non-textual aspects of performance.

Nakamura: You bring up one of the areas in which putting canons in conversation is not only productive but necessary to move forward as we negotiate various fields in our research. Similarly, SanSan Kwan's *Kinesthetic City* (2013) on Chineseness, the cityscape, and choreography connects spaces and dance companies, historically situating contemporary work in political and social histories while also developing "choreography" as a rich analytical lens.

Browne: Kwan's work shows how reevaluating geographic designations challenges past divisions and correspondingly, conceptions of the canon. And we're seeing new work that disrupts the East-West binary to acknowledge Oceanic flows, for example in Diana Looser's *Remaking Pacific Pasts* (2014), Afro-Asian flows in Will Bridges's *Playing in the Shadows* (2020), and Atlantic flows in Sean Metzger's *The Chinese Atlantic* (2020).

Nakamura: These flows, along with the slightly earlier concept of the "transpacific" as a critical site, illustrate that when we reconceive of geography, we rethink what makes up sites of knowledge and knowledge producers in multiple fields: theatre and performance studies, Japanese and Asian studies, and Asian American studies (See Son 2018 and Mok and Bahng 2017).

Browne: Some new anthologies stage a dialogue between Japanese and Western scholars to give space for a multi-directional flow of ideas, for example, *Media Theory in Japan*, edited by Marc Steinberg and Alexander Zahlten (2017).

Nakamura: A lot of exciting work is happening, but there is still much to do. In the Steinberg and Zalten anthology, they tackle the unidirectional flow of theory from a media studies point of view, starting with the unidirectional translation of Western theories to non-Western locations. And there's been work in Asian studies and cultural studies more generally that applies Kuan-Hsing Chen's "Asia as Method" that uses "the idea of Asia as an imaginary anchoring point" to move beyond a West/Other binary (Chen 2010: 212). I struggle with this question still in theatre and performance studies: how might some kind of theoretical framework be applied back to Western case studies, to reverse the unidirectional flow of theory? And how can I begin to address this in seminars for my department's graduate program in theatre, dance, and performance studies?

To take on this unidirectionality involves adding material to challenge the makeup of existing canons, but it also involves thinking about how we analyze performance.

Browne: Challenging this "unidirectional flow" is a substantial hurdle for our field. One strategy I use in my scholarship is to return to the performance texts to uncover the theory encoded in the plays' metatheatrical scenes. Chikamatsu's *Souvenirs of Naniwa* (*Naniwa miyage*) is well-known for articulating his ideas on performance, but no one has given the metatheatrical scenes in his plays robust consideration despite their deep exploration of the audience-performer relationship. Perhaps these scenes are given less attention because they are in plays that remain untranslated into English.

Nakamura: Your strategy is so important. Not only are you integrating artist writings into your analytical framework, but you're also introducing an English-language readership to these ideas.

In my book (*Transgenerational Remembrance* 2020), I develop a theoretical framework based on Japanese philosopher Takahashi Testuya's concept of response-ability and the noh ghost. But the difficulty also comes in Japanese materials—Takahashi is a scholar of Derrida, so most of his references are in the Western philosophical tradition. Takahashi talks about the Asia-Pacific War past as ghostly, but he references *Hamlet* and not noh, so I add in noh, which I argue is better suited to a dialogic relationship with the past. But I keep wondering if there are other ways in which we can expand our repertoire of theory. We are developing theoretical frameworks based on Asian sources for Asian case studies because we're specialists on Japan. Can these frameworks be used for non-Asian case studies? In other words, is there a way to try to move this flow the other way?

Browne: Overall, we're calling for more deliberate engagement across canons in teaching, research, and theatre practice. Not only should we disrupt the "unidirectional" flow of knowledge, but ideas such as the "Oceanic" and "Afro-Asian" highlight how currents of knowledge circulate together across time and space. Our teaching, scholarship, and practice must find a way to engage with the dynamism of these canons that are already in motion.

Canons in Motion

Nakamura: As we've discussed throughout, our perspectives require us to negotiate between canons, and this negotiation reveals both the limitations with existing canons and the benefits of intersecting canons.

From our experiences, we see canons as in flux, so we argue for putting them in motion–what we describe as the intentional engagement of canons. We've discussed strategies we've used or seen in teaching and research. But we want to stress that canons are shifting, and so we cannot rely on a particular strategy to work time after time.

Browne: In fact, such concrete strategies may hinder the development of ideas. Any fixed approach risks replicating canon formation and ossifying into its own canon. Further, since the problems with the canon are so entrenched in multiple levels of our fields, we need to be open about how we revise them.

✶✶✶✶✶✶

Putting canons in motion is thus not a set of concrete strategies. Instead, we encourage our readers to develop their own methods based on active and ongoing engagement with canons. We see "canons in motion" as a holistic shift in thinking about the production of knowledge that extends into our pedagogy, scholarly inquiry, and artistic practice through four approaches:

First, canons in motion acknowledges and promotes a multi-directional flow of ideas. Currents of knowledge move in a variety of ways: between East and West, within Asia, and beyond current geographic understandings. Recent scholarship has reevaluated currents of knowledge, and we advocate for continuing this work. By putting canons in motion, we recognize and develop the complexity of existing flows and contemplate where other currents may move.

Second, canons in motion strive for greater transparency in the production of knowledge. This means considering how syllabi, research methods, and theoretical frameworks are constructed. When we actively put canons in motion, we make the mechanisms of our existing canons visible, allowing us to identify their limitations. In teaching and scholarship, we must recognize, discuss, *and* demonstrate the ways in which the production of canons are built on and replicate knowledge biases.

Third, canons in motion understands that flows of knowledge are always moving. Even when we try to disrupt existing canons, we can create new ones with their own limitations. We must embrace change while being self-reflexive. We must be attentive to innovations in scholarship, and we must listen to the questions and provocations of students and artists.

Finally, canons in motion recognizes that the production of knowledge occurs throughout our work: in our teaching, research, and participation in larger questions in our field. We must consider parties in these areas as co-conspirators in canon formation. This also means that we are all responsible for canon formation. Our call for canons in motion invites our fellow scholars, artists, and students to journey with us into these uncharted waters: let us develop new tools, new work, new methods, and ultimately new forms of knowledge.

Works Cited

Bridges, Will. 2020. *Playing in the Shadows: Fictions of Race and Blackness in Postwar Japanese Literature*. Ann Arbor: University of Michigan Press.

Chakrabarty, Dipesh. 2000. *Provincializing Europe: Postcolonial Thought and Historical Difference*. Princeton, NJ: Princeton University Press.

Chen, Kuan-Hsing. 2010. *Asia as Method: Toward Deimperialization*. Durham: Duke University Press.
Coaldrake, A. Kimi. 1997. *Women's Gidayū and the Japanese Theatre Tradition. The Nissan Institute/Routledge Japanese Study Series*. London: Routledge.
Davis, Julie Nelson. 2007. *Utamaro and the Spectacle of Beauty*. Honolulu: University of Hawaii Press.
Edelson, Loren. 2009. *Danjūrō's Girls: Women on the Kabuki Stage*. 1st ed. *Palgrave Studies in Theatre and Performance History*. New York: Palgrave Macmillan.
Kwan, SanSan. 2013. *Kinesthetic City: Dance and Movement in Chinese Urban Spaces*. New York: Oxford University Press.
Lee, William. 2002. "Chikamatsu and Dramatic Literature in the Meiji Period." In *Inventing the Classics: Modernity, National Identity, and Japanese Literature*, edited by Haruo Shirano and Tomi Suzuki, 179–198. Stanford: Stanford University Press.
Looser, Diana. 2014. *Remaking Pacific Pasts: History, Memory, and Identity in Contemporary Theater from Oceania*. Honolulu: University of Hawaii Press.
MacDorman Karl, F., Kageki, Norri, and Mori, Masahiro. [1970] 2012. "The Uncanny Valley." *IEEE Robotics and Automation Magazine* 19, 2: 98–100.
Metzger, Sean. 2020. *The Chinese Atlantic: Seascapes and the Theatricality of Globalization*. Bloomington: University of Indiana Press.
Mok, Christine and Bahng, Aimee. 2017. "Transpacific Overtures: An Introduction." *Journal of Asian American Studies* 20, 1: 1–9.
Moore, Katrina L. 2014. *The Joy of Noh: Embodied Learning and Discipline in Urban Japan*. Albany: State University of New York Press.
Savarese, Nicola. 2001. "1931: Antonin Artaud Sees Balinese Theatre at the Paris Colonial Exposition." *TDR* 45, 3: 51–77.
Shimazaki, Satoko. 2016. *Edo Kabuki in Transition: From the Worlds of the Samurai to the Vengeful Female Ghost*. New York: Columbia University Press.
Son, Elizabeth. 2018. *Embodied Reckonings: 'Comfort Women,' Performance, and Transpacific Redress*. Ann Arbor: University of Michigan Press.
Stanley, Amy. 2012. *Selling Women: Prostitution, Markets, and the Household in Early Modern Japan*. Berkeley: University of California Press.
Steinberg, Marc and Alexander Zahlten, eds. 2017. *Media Theory in Japan*. Durham: Duke University Press.
Tian, Min. 1997. "'Alienation-Effect' for Whom? Brecht's (Mis)interpretation of the Classical Chinese Theatre." *Asian Theatre Journal* 14, 2: 200–222.
Yoshimoto, Mitsuhiro. 1991. "The Difficulty of Being Radical: The Discipline of Film Studies and the Postcolonial World Order." *Boundary 2* 18, 3: 242–257.

16 The Kids' Table: Cross-institutional Treatment of the Canon and the Un-canonizable Nature of New Work

Charlie Dubach-Reinhold and Melory Mirashrafi

Welcome

There is a dissonance between the theatre taught in undergraduate classrooms and the theatre performed on stages across the country. While the transition from an undergraduate setting into a full-time career is jarring regardless of one's field, theatre in the United States suffers from a particular cross-institutional inconsistency when it comes to the treatment of the canon. The realm of new play development and dramaturgy proposes a distinct set of challenges, given that its purpose is to create work that has not yet entered the canon—to innovate—yet it relies on an understanding of historical theatrical traditions as a shorthand for communication. This composition seeks to illuminate *why* this theatrical shorthand is valued in new work, specifically at large institutional theatres, and its connection to the teaching of and relationship to the canon in undergraduate institutions.

Meet your Players

Melory Mirashrafi and Charlie Dubach-Reinhold: two guinea pigs from two different incubators of theatre education, deposited into full-time positions in literary departments of large, non-profit LORT theatres on opposite coasts. In an alternate reality, perhaps they were twins separated at birth. In the current reality, they are two individuals interested in having a conversation about how the canon shaped (or didn't shape) their undergraduate experiences and currently impacts their work as early career theatre practitioners. The conversation will take place in two sections:

1. a casual, reciprocal interview covering individual backgrounds, experiences, and initial thoughts
2. a conversation sparked by the prompt: *In what ways do we commodify theatre?*

Welcome to the kids' table.

DOI: 10.4324/9781003031413-16

Part I: Speed Dating, or, An Informal Interview

Charlie Dubach-Reinhold: Hello! Who are you? How did you arrive at a career in theatre?

Melory Mirashrafi: I grew up thinking that a career in theatre wasn't for me. I'm a first-generation Iranian-American Muslim, and was on-track to be pre-med until my junior year of college, when I was asked to develop and assistant direct a new adaptation of Shakespeare's *Romeo and Juliet* blended with one of its predecessors, Nizami Ganjavi's epic poem *Leyli va Majnun*. That production completely shifted my understanding of new play development and dramaturgy: to give people the tools to curate their own stories. This wasn't a novel discovery, but for me it was the first time I felt that I could bring my culture, family, religion, and bilingualism into a rehearsal room and feel like it was helping me instead of holding me back. After that I knew I wanted to make theatre, but more importantly, I knew why. I switched majors and decided to pursue dramaturgy and new work. I wanted to be at the source of all the gatekeeping in US theatre because it was such a mystery to me. It still is. What got you into all of this?

Dubach-Reinhold: I also confess to premedical studenthood. I slowly transitioned into theatre: I kept accidentally-on-purpose taking theatre classes instead of premedical ones, and my extracurricular activities became my academic activities. Around the same time that I discovered performance studies and the concept of performativity, I came out as transgender and experienced the performative nature of gender firsthand. From then on, theatre, gender, and trans and queer studies were inextricably linked in my mind. I also realized my penchant for collecting information and being able to "write good" translated well to dramaturgy. I applied to the large LORT theatre that served as a second home for me in high school and *bam!* there I was, prepared to research and totally unprepared to see behind the liberal façade of theatrical institutions.

Mirashrafi: Could you describe your undergraduate institution? Was the canon valued and taught? Were "new plays" taught?

Dubach-Reinhold: I attended a medium-sized, elite research university on the West Coast. Our theatre department was erudite in the extreme. It had a peculiar proclivity for Brecht—he was our one-man canon. We didn't solely perform his shows, but plenty of the shows we did were deeply connected to his work. I never explicitly studied the "avant-garde" but that perfectly describes the preferred aesthetic of the vast majority of the professors. I entered during a growth spurt—my freshman year, my major's graduating class was four, and the year behind me graduated over twenty. Many new students wanted to enter the professional theatre world rather than the academic one, and a dramatic shift toward that kind of preparation began. New plays were previously never taught and rarely highlighted, but during my final year, our department hired a prominent playwright from the New York scene in the 2000s and 2010s, and the shift solidified. Rather than beginning with the old stuff (sorry, Brecht!) and working forward, new plays—and especially student-written work—exploded onto our robust extracurricular and curricular theatre scenes.

Mirashrafi: I can't say I've ever been a part of anything "elite" in my life. I went to a very small college in the Pacific Northwest, with an even smaller theatre department that emphasized technical theatre and design. Only two required courses focused primarily on reading and talking about plays: a year-long "Theatre History" course, and "Play Reading and Analysis." The graduating class in my major was three people, all of whom were queer students of color. We did not have a single on-staff professor or director of color (there were some visiting instructors), and for the most part that was reflected in the work we were expected to read and perform at the institution. Super white. My senior year they hired a new professor who really wanted to shake things up, and it was met with a *lot* of pushback from the older faculty members.

Dubach-Reinhold: How does your college experience compare to your work after graduation? How did your workplace approach the canon—was it valued or referenced?

Mirashrafi: After graduating I worked at a large, LORT, regional theatre on the east coast. While the staff and audience base were majority white, the artistic department was less so—although my non-white-cis-male coworkers were still at the bottom of the food chain, both in terms of structural position and salary. My title was "Literary Apprentice," and I was one of three people in a literary department under the umbrella of an artistic department. I did dramaturgy for shows, attended artistic staff meetings, and was integrated into the daily tasks of the literary and artistic staff. [It is worth mentioning that all this vastly shifted after the coronavirus pandemic.] The theatre's programming was split between new and canonical work, with one space specifically dedicated to presenting new plays and several new play workshops throughout the year. The canon was referenced often but not in a patronizing way, and my supervisor would often give me plays to read that might be helpful for me to understand a piece that we were working on. I loved how my workplace and relationship with my supervisor felt at times like a "live" classroom. What about you?

Dubach-Reinhold: At my large LORT regional theatre on the west coast, the artistic department was entirely cisgender, heterosexual white women except for me (white, transgender) and the directing fellow. This theatre boasts something incredible: a new works development program including an exploratory laboratory during the summer months dedicated only to supporting artists at any point in the process. To the executive administrators, it's a waste of money. To the literary department, it's the ultimate incubator of creative growth and genius. The selection process runs through a director, with input from the department on hundreds of applications. You can only imagine the bias in selecting. In deference to this, we have explicit, spoken emphasis on selecting writers of color and especially women. In this process and in my day-to-day, my colleagues placed a large emphasis on familiarity with a certain body of plays. This canon consisted primarily of older white men, and also some ladies, like Caryl

Churchill, Paula Vogel, and Lauren Gunderson. A common interaction during my time:
Me: "Who's that?"
Supervisor: "You haven't read [insert play by elderly or fairly recently dead white man here]? Oh my god!"
But we didn't actually talk about these plays. We just referenced their titles when discussing new work, as either a shorthand for a style of theatre or as said shorthand combined with "but the [insert demographic here] version." Such trivializations appear in speeches at promotional events and in materials—someone could be "the Black Beckett" or do a "Sarah Ruhl play, but transgender." These references were unsophisticated and primarily social. They were only made in agreement—*ah yes, we both understand this*—and could leave me and the other young (nonwhite, queer) member of the department out of the conversation. Referencing the canon in new works situations ends a discussion. Where there might have been a conversation untangling the various structural, character-based, and prose variations within a work, there instead arose a simple definition based upon plays with which most of the people in the room were familiar.
Mirashrafi: What does the canon mean to you?
Dubach-Reinhold: I know we are supposed to think of a theatrical canon as though it exists singly and universally, but I can't conceptualize that. The places where I made theatre all have their own versions of what might be called a canon. At my university, it was time period- and style-specific: Brecht and his era dominated the conversation. That canon changed only at the whim of the professors, and their whims moved slowly. Conversely, at my theatre, our canon was anything of the now. We stayed on top of popular performances at regional theatres across the U.S.—I spent hours scouring regional theatre websites and the back pages of *American Theatre*, watching as shows old and new popped up again and again. You?
Mirashrafi: When I think about the canon I think about reading a diary from middle school. It might give you some essential truths about yourself, but usually it's embarrassing, reductive, and leaves out anything that didn't directly apply to the bubble of your life. Canon comes from the Greek "kanon," meaning yardstick or measuring device, and I think that's spot on. It's the tool we have right now for measuring the "best" or most iconic work we've done throughout history, but unfortunately, it also is like history in that it's designed to support those already in power.

Part II: Commodification and the Canon

Mirashrafi: I think our generation ("Gen Z") is obsessed with commodifying every aspect of our lives. We're economically doomed, so the constant need to produce consumable material feels completely pervasive. Non-profit regional theatres and undergraduate classrooms, which also feel a bit doomed sometimes, have this commodification mindset too. In classes, everything is done with the intention of constructing a package that will be marketable to the professional world, from practical skills to knowledge of theatre history and plays.

Unsurprisingly, while the things considered "marketable" in the classroom are not necessarily so in the professional world, they're still used as a baseline indication of your value and ability to succeed in the field—"classic" and "canonical" plays, European history, and so on. In the world of new work development and dramaturgy, plays are often not yet categorizable, and so fluency in the canon goes from being a tool to being a litmus test. When discussing a new play, it's common to hear statements such as, "This is so Chekhovian!" or, "This character is just like Hedda Gabbler…," statements that create a common reference to describe how one might be interpreting a play. In many cases, establishing a shared vocabulary, or common language is great; however, if understanding one thing is dependent on the understanding of something else, then that interpretation is permanently tainted. This process of referencing past works to understand new ones is great for pushing along the development process (which the commodification mindset says is good), but can become problematic when dealing with new work by and about underrepresented people, in large part due to the whiteness, heteronormativity, Eurocentrism, and maleness of most "common reads." New play development is designed to be as streamlined as possible, but I propose that efficiency is not necessarily a friend of new plays—at least not when it comes to reading and comprehension. The process of developing, reading, talking about, and evaluating new work should be slower, more deliberate, and more interested in coming up with defining terms that come from within the work and its specific history.

Dubach-Reinhold: Your description of efficiency as the enemy of new plays hits the nail on the head for me. I want to add to that an exploration of another covert form of commodification: that which disguises itself as intellectual pursuit. As you describe, canonical fluency certainly dominates a selection process, and its efficiency lends itself to the commodification of this artistic endeavor. Canonical fluency also relates to the ability to articulate taste, and an elitist culture within large regional theatres. My literary department terrified other departments within our theatre precisely because we were making money for our intellectual rigor and artistic taste—we got paid for our big brains. When we invited people into our office they would remark on how intimidating it was to enter the room full of books and the people whose words were printed in the program, no matter how fun we are as people and at opening night parties. I am still parsing the difference between elitism and having your labor in the institution be based on your ability to perform intellectual work as defined by our education system.

At my institution, an academic elitism replaced the emphasis on "marketability" that you describe, but had the same effect that you describe in building the foundation for our ability to pass the "litmus test" for future job possibilities. The interest of articulating the aesthetic of a performance—its meaning as social or political critique—was overshadowed by the ability to attach it to a historical name (Brecht, Beckett, Chekhov). In that environment, the conversation was dominated by canonical reference, and it stayed shallow. The danger of elitist conversation is insularity, and both were encouraged. The commodity here is not monetary, but related to social capital. Particularly the academic social capital that enables better recommendations, higher grades, greater networking ability, or the ability to complete an honor's thesis. All of which eventually lead to a better chance at capital gain. The commodity is the ability to intellectualize about the canon rather than the work's ability to engage an audience.

At the theatre I faced ridicule—lighthearted, but still ridicule—when I admitted to unfamiliarity with a big canon name. My lack of knowledge about Thornton Wilder's *Our Town* elicited incredulous laughter, and called into question my ability to evaluate a play based on it, despite the fact that many of our audience members may not be familiar either. The particular efficiency of canonical reference that you describe not only dilutes a conversation, but also creates a space that dismisses the input of the canonically deficient. I have watched this (along with a deliberate or unintentional bias away from work that seems too "out there" but is actually just from a non-white, non-normative perspective that a selection committee doesn't have, but a more diverse audience might) sway play selection processes in favor of works by straight, white, cis, able-bodied men. In both my academically-minded (read: elitist, know-it-all) undergraduate institution and academically-minded (read: avant-garde, deeply contemplative) large regional theatre, marketability sat below the surface, couched in erudition, upheld by bias.

Mirashrafi: Everything you're saying about the way that knowledge of the canon serves the early-career theatre practitioner is so true. Something that I think about often, as someone who is foremost interested in developing new work, is the *treatment* of young theatre-makers, particularly underrepresented artists and academics who deal heavily in and study canonical work as opposed to new work. If you're not white and you study Shakespeare, for example, you suddenly become an "exceptional minority," and a diversity checkmark craved by the theatre and theatre-adjacent community. The underrepresented Shakespeare scholar is placed on a pedestal for engaging with classical literature in nuanced and complex ways, and while there's absolutely no problem with doing so, the instant legitimacy and air of respect granted to Black and brown (for the sake of the initial example) classical scholars and performers is a perfect example of the way one can commodify talent and identity by dealing in work that is considered "valuable" by the white and wealthy American theatre. This is particularly true if that means adding a "diverse" lens to the work, for example, "queering" a Shakespeare that everyone knows. Too often, the question seems to be: How do we keep the things that we love, and stay politically relevant? How do we change as little as possible about the work that we already know, but participate in theatre that is "diverse?"

It's worth noting that someone like me, who's been schooled exclusively in smaller, underfunded, rural or suburban, and often public schools, has had exposure to the canon not necessarily because it's the most accessible, but because it's the most available. Lots of "canonical" work is in the public domain (free), and has vast distribution due to frequent publishing and performance. That means the canon then becomes the most easily *available* work for institutions with tight budgetary restrictions or limited pathways to finding alternative material, even if that work is some of the least *accessible* in terms of language, demographics, lifestyle, and beyond, to the students, audiences, and artists who then engage with it. Big-budget theatres in densely populated, wealthy, white parts of the city often have more avenues to produce and support new work, and can therefore afford to perform that work for their audiences, which are typically also white and wealthy. Smaller theatres with smaller budgets are often in Black and brown neighborhoods and rural or suburban locations. The result of this phenomenon is that theatres with the money to commission new and diverse work end up having the least number of people in their audiences who look and live like the people represented in their programming. The smaller, lower-budget theatres, then, are forced to do more work in the public domain, more well-known work because it's cheaper, and there's more and easier access to it.

Dubach-Reinhold: Talk to me about queering Shakespeare, yes! I was convinced that I had to get a degree in Shakespeare or Early Modern Drama to be able to critique it through a transgender studies lens, because I knew no Shakespeare scholar would take my writing seriously if I didn't follow their exact path. I fell into the trap of attempting to dismantle only with "the master's tools" (Lorde 1984). I believed that to make scholarly claims they would take seriously, I must be trained like them. Which undoubtedly unconsciously affects my thinking.

To expand on your description of the smaller theatres' limited pathways to non-canon work, I want to elucidate how the networks of influence that connect big-budget theatres to playwrights' agencies play a role in turning smaller theatres to works in the public domain. Many of our shows were chosen because of close personal connections to playwrights, and when a big theatre puts on the show, a moratorium on that show (legal or otherwise) is created around the entire region. Licensing and rights negotiations are absolutely brutal, even in well-resourced theatres, and hinge upon the tenuous professional contacts of folks working at the theatre.

Fortunately for me, my supervisors couldn't wait to introduce me to key players in this web of new work development and pre-canonical play selecting. With the name of a big-budget theatre behind me, I could cold email folks and request scripts and connections and partnerships. And this is how the elitism of the new works world thrives. This networking—like any networking—skews toward the white, affluent, and traditionally charming. And so our version of "the best" of new works is automatically biased toward works that are normative, or works that might showcase diversity but continue to smooth the feathers of the audiences. Influence over where a new work is sent stays among a select group, and the best plays go to the highest-budget theatres.

One might argue that this is a good thing that the best new plays should go to the theatres that can produce them the best. But who dictates "the best" play? Those voices that disrupt and confuse old white people are relegated to tiny incubators, while those that smooth the feathers of this elite are paraded around the large circuits. And "the best" theatre? Our metric is that of capital—of the number of shiny toys, the experience of those involved, perks like free coffee from a sponsor. This measure leaves out the appropriate cultural competency and fluency for a show, the level of comfort within the room that all the theatremakers feel, a lack of racist microaggressions and sexist comments, the interest in engaging new (read: nonwhite, not rich) audiences, the emphasis on education and training, the equity of pay within the organization, the transparency of the administration—I could go on.

Mirashrafi: It's fascinating to hear about the way different theatres process and work through new scripts and submissions! I worked at two LORT theatres directly after undergrad--one had a similar model to what you're describing (picking through piles of new plays, or rather, making an intern do it), but the second had a different approach: They would look at the types of plays they were aiming to produce (for example, plays by Muslim women), and then specifically comb through plays that fell within that constraint in order to fill a slot in the season. Upon first glance I liked that approach, because instead of focusing on the sea of new plays, they approached (part of) season planning with a goal in mind, or a voice to highlight. I wonder often, as you mentioned, about gatekeeping and who gets to choose what work is "good." Ultimately, I think that if you're reading without a specific agenda, you'll edge toward whatever work you personally think ticks that box (informed by your personal biases, education, taste, etc.), but categorizing plays by "type" can also box out voices that might not yet be categorically recognizable…so, I wonder if theatres choosing to develop and perform the voices of underrepresented *and local* playwrights might be a better model—reaching out instead of in, and seeing what their greater community already has to offer.

Touching on your point about new work: I think new work development programs might be in direct juxtaposition to the process of canonical programming. I really like the concept of a theatre investing in playwrights whose voices they believe in. Recently, I led a workshop called "Canning the Canon," in which the goal was to discuss and define with a diverse group of educators, students, and fulltime practitioners the benefits and drawbacks of the canon, ending with a structured debate: should the canon be "canned" (a la *What the Constitution Means to Me* as Heidie Schreck debates whether or not to scrap the constitution). Ultimately, the affirmative (abolishing the canon) won with the argument that the canon should be abolished through defunding—pouring season money, instead, toward developing and producing new work by and for underrepresented artists and audiences. Making the choice to "defund and abolish" the canon was such an interesting conclusion, particularly with the surge in abolitionist rhetoric in the mainstream as a result of the 2020 Black Lives Matter movement. What might a season look like if it promised to make zero money off of work by white men, or work published before the public domain cut-off date?

Dubach-Reinhold: I love presenting a cultural project to shift away from the overrepresentation of cis white male playwrights as defunding the canon! So much to be said about applying the same structural lenses to various social ills so that folks can understand how everything is connected—and supported by capitalism and the drive to ensure the longevity of an organization over the moral, ethical, and social project of its programming.

A project like The JUBILEE begins to do exactly that. Over 60 theatres pledged to join this "yearlong, nationwide theatre festival featuring work generated by those who have traditionally been excluded—including but not limited to artists of color, Native American and Indigenous and First Nations artists, women, non-binary and gender non-conforming artists, LGBTQIA2 + artists, Deaf artists, and artists with disabilities" by programming only shows that fit this criteria (The JUBILEE 2018). Unfortunately, it was scheduled for the 20/21 season, and many of the shows were cancelled. The JUBILEE framed their program in a non-castigating way, the way I've found most effective in communicating with reticent upper management and artistic direction at theatres. Positively framing this sort of intervention as jubilation, excitement, and joy, goes a long way toward convincing those who are currently in power to become involved. As I've learned, hell hath no defensiveness like a cis white artistic director accused of cultural insensitivity, racism, transphobia, etc., in their season planning process. As we fight for larger systemic changes in theatre—including the replacement of a heavily cis white male artistic directorship cohort—we must push for short-term solutions. The JUBILEE not only frames the centering of marginalized voices as exciting, but provokes the question: what would it take to do this every year? What would you have to let go?

I agree that a "type" might be problematic, especially when that "type" refers to an identity. That boxes out not only identities that are often overlooked, but also intersectional ones, or identities that are based on what one might call an "experience" rather than an identity category of race, gender, class, etc. I had a conversation recently with a fellow theatre artist who posits that the next step beyond fulfilling the "types" of identities that are currently underrepresented—which is a first step that so many theatres have yet to take—might be searching for plays and forming ensembles (already diverse and run by marginalized folks) who share a particular experience that we don't see as an optics-based identity onstage, but still informs the work. I already see this beginning. For instance, in a production of Jocelyn Bioh's *School Girls, or, the African Mean Girls Play*, the director, a first-generation Ghanaian immigrant herself, insisted on extra outreach to actors who were not just Black, but African—and particularly first-gen immigrants or the children of first-gen immigrants—to bring the perspective of that cultural experience, in addition to the optics of Blackness, into the rehearsal room and performance. What might it mean for an ideal theatrical landscape to not just be able to find theatremakers to fulfill specific identities, but to have those as the given, to be able to highlight specific experiences? If all of those in the room had a shared understanding that does not have to be explained by one person speaking up for an experience or identity. Can we move beyond tokenization?

From my perspective in the literary world, new works programs are a fantastic place from which to support this shift. The mindset of, "*I know this person, I trust this artist,*" still dominates many selection processes, but the open submission model at my theatre does allow for the new and unexpected (to the cis whites who read the submissions) stories to be proposed and developed. The model of unfinished scripts feels important as well—you don't have to have a full script to be chosen for development. The "no-strings-attached" aspect of the program emphasizes the not-pipeline nature of truly diverse development as well: don't just invest in a play if you think it's going to make you money. The program gives exposure and time (two things that our community and profession trades on and lacks) as well as actual script development. This is what large theatres can offer—their names. Their names mean so much more than they believe. And it's not just names—what else can they offer that will encourage a system that actively resists exclusion, subtle racism, insular networking, and other issues, now? I'm talking about affirmative action, absolutely. We value equity in this house. Theatres don't understand how much more they have to offer, and how their choices in programming and new works development—all choices, down to the individual hire—have the ability and opportunity to radically shift the canon.

Mirashrafi: I'd love to highlight something you mentioned: Institutional memory. The institution at hand of course being the American theatre, the default of which is white, heteronormative, cis, male, able-bodied, and so on. So much of the canon is dependent on memory—the ability to recreate work that is integral to (Western) culture in order to preserve its universal truth, quality, or novelness. I'm thinking of the printing press. I'm thinking of "literacy." Often a canonized play or playwright will be the first of its kind—for example, Henrik Ibsen is permanently stamped in history books because he's considered the "father of modern drama" (Martin 2015: 7)—the goal for so many contemporary playwrights and new work development programs, then, is to achieve canonization and memorability through crystallization in the written word, because the economy of the American theatre depends on a play having repeatability, that it has a life after its premiere. Theatre performed in the United States bends toward producing new work, however most premieres do not get a second performance, much less solidified in print. Diana Taylor writes in her book *The Archive and the Repertoire: Performing Cultural Memory in the Americas* that "The writing = memory/knowledge equation is central to Western epistemology [...] Instead of reinforcing memory or providing an analogy, writing becomes memory itself" (Taylor 2003: 24-25), elaborating upon an ideology very present in the American theatrical psyche: that the goal of writing is to find a place within a greater memory: to canonize. As noted in the title, Taylor's suggestion is to categorize memory into two parts: archival, or written, made up of "documents, maps, literary texts, letters," and so on as a way of keeping records, and the repertoire, which holds embodied memory in the form of "performances, gestures, orality, movement, dance, singing—in short, all those acts usually thought of as ephemeral, nonreproducible knowledge" (Taylor 2003: 19-20). Taylor's shift in the way we might consider memory is fascinating to me in terms of how we might rethink new work development in connection to the canon. Should the goal of all new work development programs be to solidify a script that might live on in the archival memory, or rather to participate in the creation of an embodied memory contained in the repertoire? Perhaps the canon as a concept is not problematic because of its preservation of the written word, which will always favor white, Western, and cis male modes of knowledge, but rather because it is incomplete; the canon has no embodied counterpart, as the archive has to the repertroire.

In a similar vein, I love new work development programs accepting unfinished plays! It falls in line with the philosophy of not necessarily using written language as the baseline for evaluating a play. I wonder, too, how the ultimate goal of reaching a performance (or a "performable" script) impacts that evaluation process. Embracing "unfinished" scripts opens up the possibility of bringing experience and embodiment into a story. As I was reading your thoughts on the submission process, I also found myself fixating on "the cis whites who read the submissions." This brings into focus my reason for wanting to work in dramaturgy and literary management: radically shifting the gatekeepers of theatrical programming in the United States. So often, theatres program an entire season of new plays by and featuring Black and brown artists, however the people making choices are almost all, if not completely white. How we evaluate plays can change, but until the people selecting plays shift, there will be very little difference on US stages on a systemic level. The power structures at work in the development and production process will be upheld, because the hand that curates the "memory" of the institution is heavily implicated in the erasure and oppression of the people from whose labor it profits.

Dubach-Reinhold: How drastically could the field—and by extension, the future canon—shift if we made changes to the building blocks of institutional memory? The ability of artistic directors and literary departments across the country to select plays that will take off is held up as paramount. Could we sharpen the stick that pokes them and suggest specific changes?

Conclusion

Despite our vastly different undergraduate and postgraduate experiences, certain throughlines are clear: the use of the canon as a litmus test in the professional world, a push toward commodification of one's self and knowledge that takes advantage of underrepresented theatre-makers in particular, and the dissonance between those creating new work, those choosing new work, and those sitting in its audiences. In response, we wonder: how is an aspiration toward canonization, performing the canon, and perpetuating its worth, driven by capitalism? How might we decentralize, reshape, and throw open the doors of new work development, leaning into a dramaturgical process that brings new work into the communities from which its stories are taken and repackaged?

The gate to throw open in the process of creating a canon is clearly, to us, the new works development programs that at once incubate ideas and playwrights. We agree on the objective of the opening—to widen the field, uplift marginalized and local artists, and change the direction of the future canon by moving away from voices who have dominated the space for so long. We see that the great barrier to the effectiveness of these programs is capital, particularly in funding distributions within the theatrical institutions that contain these programs, which are often set up to oppose supporting marginalized work and playwrights with financial gain. This false dichotomy justifies all that we have discussed so far, particularly when large regional theatres are choosing their main seasons. A larger set of conceptual and social shifts must take place in the theatrical world—some already in motion through initiatives such as #weseeyou, the online movement sparked by the testimonial letter addressed to "White American Theatre" by a group of BIPOC theatremakers, which helped propel conversations about and accountability measures for anti-Black sentiment within theatres across the country (We See You 2020). By implementing #weseeyou demands—for example, "the majority of writers, directors and designers on stage for the foreseeable future be BIPOC artists"—new works programs could be a highly effective path to equity (We See You 2020). Not only could they be, they should be.

Considering the avenues through which we select, talk about, and give value to new work is essential in moving toward a less myopic and exclusive theatre across the country. As early-career practitioners and scholars, we're told so often that we have to play within the system; do what we're told, listen and learn, and wait until we have power to try and make any change. We challenge this notion. In fact, it's dead to us. If we, as young people, must constantly handle being told the "brutal truth" (and we must, to survive in educational and work spaces), then institutional theatre and academia can handle the same. We might not be able to overturn the top–down power structure of the American theatre and its many institutions overnight, but we do have the power to choose how we talk about the canon with our students and peers. We do have the power to give new plays the time, space, and resources they need during the evaluation and development process. We have the power to examine our programming, think about who it's by, who it's for, and then, who it's *really* for.

Works Cited

Lorde, Audre. 1984 "The Master's Tools Will Never Dismantle the Master's House." In *Sister Outsider: Essays and Speeches*, edited by Audre Lorde, 110–114. Berkeley, CA: Crossing Press, 2007.

Taylor, Diana. 2003. *The Archive and the Repertoire: Performing Cultural Memory in the Americas*. Durham, NC: Duke University Press.

The JUBILEE. 2018. "Join the JUBILEE." Accessed 31August 2020. https://jointhejubilee.org/.

We See You. 2020. "We See You, White American Theatre." Accessed 1 November 2020. https://www.weseeyouwat.com/.

Part IV
Departures and Re-visions

17 Rethinking the Canon through the Digital

Miguel Escobar Varela and Derek Miller

The Canon Wars, the cultural battles of the 1980s and 1990s that forced a reckoning with the white supremacist, patriarchal, imperialist literary heritage that had defined a proper education, were in one essential sense about scarcity (Dolan 1997). Time—on the syllabus; in our lives—is short, and therefore we must choose what to assign and read and what to ignore. Scarcity haunted the Canon Wars because scarcity converted all arguments into some version of, "Well, if I have to teach *that*, then I won't have time for Shakespeare!"

However disingenuous this argument may have been, the proposition that we cannot teach all things at all times is, of course, so obvious as to seem trivial. But it is not trivial. The Canon Wars are a special, explicitly politicized case of cultural artifacts' eternal battle for survival. All cultural history engages only a subset of the past. Even the best canon can be but part of the whole. Art is abundant; time for that art is scarce.

Modern digital tools and analytic methods offer us an opportunity to think better about the dynamic interaction between abundant art and scarce canons. Digital technologies do not resolve the problem of scarcity: what we teach can never be fully commensurate with the artistic universe we seek to understand. But if approached with the right balance of curiosity and skepticism, digital methods help us to think better about the problem of scarcity itself.

This chapter begins by describing theatrical canons as a kind of sample of theatrical works—but a particular kind of bad, skewed sample. We then turn to three different ways to use digital technologies to reconsider the canon, both to contextualize it better and to amend it. First, quantitative studies of theatre allow us to explore the precise nature of the canon's shortcomings as a representative sample of theatrical activity. Second, digitized texts—playscripts, but also manifestos, financial records, and more—expand the accessibility of non-canonical works and thus make it easier to teach outside the canon propagated by anthologies. Third, digitized performances integrate the complex interpretive history of theatrical productions into the seemingly rigid canon passed down only in playscripts. Finally, we offer a brief view of the canon as currently taught in the United States by drawing on a quantitative analysis of contemporary syllabi.

DOI: 10.4324/9781003031413-17

Digital tools and methods do not resolve the challenge of representing—on a syllabus, in a season, in an anthology—the full complexity of theatre history with a small set of cultural artifacts. But they can help us think better about that problem and show us the nature of what we do not yet understand. These new techniques and sources of evidence can enrich conversations about the politics and histories of canons, as well as teach us about the import and impact of canonicity itself

The Problem: Canons Are (Bad) Samples

A theatrical canon samples from the population of theatrical works. We rarely think of canons as samples. Unlike biological or financial samples, canons are anything but random. Natural or social scientists randomly select samples from a population and subject them to statistical analyses so as to describe the whole. Generations of audiences, readers, and artists elevate canonical works through a combination of prestige and popularity; they represent not all plays, but the best plays. Precisely because they are not random, canons represent strangely the population from which they arise. In other words, canons are bad samples. Canons skew our view of the population with respect to three aspects of the works they represent: survival and success, authors and themes, and forms.

First and foremost, canons misrepresent both the survival and the success of works in the population. The population of plays includes lost plays and extant plays that were contemporary mediocrities or failures. Canons represent neither of these categories. The population of existing plays is much smaller than the population of all plays once produced. The extant Greek tragedies, for instance, are but the tip of a proverbial iceberg of Athenian drama lost to centuries of forgetting and catastrophe. Early Modern English drama included vast numbers of works now knowable only as a title or vague plot summary.[1] Canonical works can only include those plays fortunate enough to have survived the passage of time. But how well, if at all, do canons represent lost plays?

Survival and success interact closely, of course: many plays survive largely through their constant reproduction, that is, because of continuing demand. But of course many existing works are now marginalized or forgotten, whether they once won acclaim and later fell out of fashion (such as Voltaire's tragedies), or never won any esteem at all. Canons are particularly antithetical to the latter class of play, the vast sea of works still extant but never admired, the endless, churning chaff of cultural production. Canonical works represent this population only insofar as they stand *ahead* of their contemporaries—which is not the same thing as standing *for* their contemporaries. Canonical works are thus unusual because they both survive and win long-term success.

Second, and relatedly, canons structurally oversample for works by dominant cultural producers that reproduce hegemonic ideologies. Colonialism, imperialism, patriarchy, heteronormativity, and white supremacy all increase the chances for success of plays by white, male "genius" authors at the expense both of works by non-white, non-male authors and of works made collaboratively. Culture's relationship to power may be antagonistic at times, but cultural reproduction occurs only when acceded to by power. The Canon Wars, which fought to elevate works by excluded authors, were in one sense about the social and political shortcomings of canons as samples.

Third and finally, canonical samples distort our formal understanding of plays. This is true with respect to generic diversity among productions and with respect to the forms the plays themselves take. The generic skew is clear: our canon is a high tragedy canon, with a smattering of cleanly plotted comedies mixed in. Canons do not reward generic mixing (burlesque) or period-specific forms (afterpieces). Yet works of such generic in-betweenness and formal idiosyncracy proliferate in theatre history. Canons also privilege dramatic literature. Theatrical forms that depend on physical acting and improvisation rarely achieve canonicity. Such generic exclusions tie closely into the political exclusions noted above. Non-traditional genres and non-verbal genres systematically undermine popular, non-elite forms, and tend to be particularly central to performance traditions outside of Europe and North America.

Assessing how canons misrepresent plays' internal structures proves more difficult. On the one hand, many canonical works represent the apotheosis of a particular formal style: Congreve's *Way of the World* can stand in for Restoration comedy. In such cases, canonical works convey clearly what their discarded contemporaries express with less certainty: the apotheosis of a form. Canonization thus by definition obscures formal muddiness, the groping-into-being that most forms perpetually undergo. On the other hand, canonical works also often represent a break with formal traditions, a break that may disguise norms or grant undue credit for purported innovations. *Oklahoma!*, for instance, has been lauded for inaugurating the integrated musical. Yet as many scholars have explained, few of *Oklahoma!*'s supposed novelties were truly new at the time (Block 2011). Moreover, while the integrated musical now stands as the essential form of Broadway in the 1940s and 1950s, many shows in the same period continued to follow the supposedly superseded musical comedy form that had dominated the 1930s (Stempel 2010: 409–58). Thus canonical works misrepresent contemporary productions by being more formally coherent and sound than most works and either (a) more distinct than most works, or (b) less distinct than the process of canonization has led us to believe.

Canons are thus poor samples of the population of theatrical works. They oversample for success and survival, for dominant ideologies, and for formal innovation and/or coherence. Most plays are not as successful or formally well-defined as great canonical works. And although many non-canonical works reproduce dominant ideologies, canons do so often to the exclusion of all other perspectives.

Given these problems, what is to be done? The following sections describe three ways in which digital methods and tools can help us remain attuned to canons' shortcomings as samples.

Solution #1: Quantitative Analysis

Quantitative analysis based on large cultural data sets can help us better understand precisely how the canon distorts theatrical history. Using data in this way, we rely on it not to settle questions about canonicity or to explain canonical disproportion but to help us reckon with systemic imbalances. In one famous example of this thinking from the art world, The Guerrilla Girls, an anonymous collective of feminist artists, brought attention to sexist bias in museums through interventions that combined statistics, visual artworks, and performances. Their famous poster entitled "Do women need be naked to get into the Met. Museum?" reports that "Less than 5% of the artists in the Modern Art Section are women, but 85% of the nudes are female" (Guerrilla Girls 1989). This intervention spurred conversations about the cultural forces that shape museum collections. Educators might similarly use data and statistics to start conversations about representation and bias in the theatrical canon.

To take a simple example, imagine an influential, widely-used anthology of canonized plays from a given time period. Of those collected plays, 1% are by women. Taken at face value, the anthology suggests that women contributed only marginally to this theatrical culture. If, however, data show that women wrote a full 30% of plays in this period, we can both critique the anthology's choices and reckon with the scale of its underrepresentation.

Indeed, we can do more than notice this disparity: we can use this knowledge to critique the process of canon formation itself. For instance, imagine that, of the *existing* plays from this period, only 10% are by women. We now have three data points to compare: the historical population of plays (30% by women), the existing population of plays (10% by women), and the canonical sample (1% by women). Rather than simply observe the small number of women playwrights in our anthology, we can now tell a story about canonization, exploring how women-authored plays first disappear from print and then were left out of the canon.[2]

Our critique can extend even further, to encompass the data and the categories that define it. The statement that "30% of plays were written by women" raises questions about what a play is and what defines a woman writer. "Woman" might be too large and ill-defined a category to capture the range of voices we wish to consider. Yet by pointing to women playwrights as an under-represented category, we call attention to the act of categorization and begin thinking consciously both about whom canons represent and about how canons represent them.

This approach uses data not to provide answers, but to prompt discussion and reflection about representation and imbalances in both canons and artistic production generally. The canon thus becomes not a fixed object of study, but something readers themselves transform, either through building new canons, or adding to the world of theatre data. Noe Montez has done the latter with *Wikiturgy*—a portmanteau of "Wikipedia and dramaturgy"—projects, for which students write Wikipedia entries on underrepresented Latino/a theatre artists in the US (Montez 2017). Using Wikipedia has the advantage of leaving a record for other students to use in the future, thus transforming data-driven criticism of the canon into action.

Data can also help us assess canonical works' claims to formal innovation. Tools from stylometry—the computational analysis of style—can allow us to investigate such claims. Studies might explore how and whether canonical works indeed represent a break with tradition. Ted Underwood's scholarship on science fiction, for instance, trained computers to identify works from the mid-20th century that belong to the genre. He then applied that same model to works from the 19th century, finding that the computer retained a high degree of accuracy in identifying Jules Verne and H. G. Wells as proto-science fiction writers (Underwood 2019: 35–44). A similar study of, say, musical comedy and operetta might help us better understand the continuities and discontinuities between those forms.

A third use of data might explore how canonicity impacts performance history, as well as how canons operate in different periods and across different geographies. We can gather data to answer questions such as:

- are canonical works more likely to be performed than non-canonical works?
- is there a global theatrical canon?
- how have canons changed over time?
- are certain features of canonical works more likely to be challenged or reproduced by new generations of artists?

In all of these cases, digital scholarship that describes the mass of theatrical production—production calendars; performance databases; catalogs and lists—allows us to situate the skewed canon within the richer, if still uncertain context of the population. That population then serves both as an object of cultural inquiry in its own right, and as the background against which we can better understand the canonical sample.

We must reiterate that although data can force us to rethink canonicity in many ways, we must not put undue faith in data. Data-driven work still requires careful attention to bias in databases and in the sources from which they derive. Documents that had specific purposes at the point of their creation easily become data, put to purposes never originally envisioned by their creators. For example, a dataset of performances might be assembled from records of ticket sales or promotional posters. This is a valid use of historical materials, but one must be wary of the interpretive decisions by which posters become performance datasets (see Vareschi and Burkert 2016). Similarly, data are always partial. The universe of plays from any given historical period and geographical area can be almost unfathomably large; extant and reusable records will always be limited. One of the most comprehensive records of historical performances is the *Comédie-Française Registers Project*. But even that company's unusually systematic, bureaucratized record-keeping falls short: in a full run of annual performance registers from 1680 to the French Revolution, the register for the season 1739–1740 is sadly lost (Biet et al. 2015).

Large datasets provide a sense of scale, offer a view of the sample in relation to the population and enable comparative, synthetic studies. All of these affordances create opportunities for a rich discussion about canonicity and its problems. Educators designing or critiquing curricula and syllabi, working with their students in a classroom, can use quantitative studies and other data-driven analytic methods to put the canonical sample into the context of the theatrical population. This approach can, in turn, become a form of collaborative research rather than passive learning.

Solution #2: Digitized Texts

Plays themselves have also joined the dataverse in digitized forms. Expanded access to scripts—always contingent, of course, on a reader's own technological access and knowledge—can fundamentally alter canons in two important ways. First, greater access allows canonical texts to appear in more varied forms, including digital facsimiles or multimedia formats that make canons available for diverse scholarly approaches. Second, such access diminishes the importance of print anthologies in defining a set of teachable plays. Large collections of digital playscripts—whether paywalled (Bloomsbury's *Drama Online*) or open access (*Drama Corpora Project*; *The Internet Archive*; *Project Gutenberg*)—offer more freedom of choice for students as well as instructors, even if they don't fully resolve the imbalances in representation mentioned earlier.

The wider online availability of plays in a variety of formats means that we can explore how canonical works were constructed, and the histories of how they were inscribed into the canon. The British Library's *Shakespeare in Quarto*, for example, enables users to compare digital facsimiles of different versions of Shakespeare's texts, thus connecting Shakespeare studies to book history and helping students with limited access to archives consider the complex relationship between print and performance. Digital archives also enable us to examine the histories by which specific texts became canonical. *A Global Doll's House*, for instance, investigates how Ibsen's most famous play came to be inscribed in the global theatrical canon (Holledge et al. 2016). Using the *Ibsen Stage Performance Database*, Holledge and co-authors used digital tools to show that the play's success owed much to specific genealogies of transmission, always subject to complex political and historical contingencies. Tracing the history and politics of how works become canonical is not a new endeavour; book history, for example, has a long tradition of considering similar questions. But data and digital methods provide new ways of seeking answers to these questions. Digital archives—especially when they include multimedia records, as discussed in the following section—enable us to consider the many ways in which canonical works are interpreted in print and then challenged in performance.

An increasingly digital world also encourages greater freedom in selecting and constructing the texts we teach. No longer must we rely on a small handful of large, expensive anthologies. Sources ranging from expensive, facsimile-based sites such as *18th-Century Collections Online* (ECCO) to the scanned volumes of *HathiTrust* all democratize access to play texts—at least those in print and out of copyright. Instructors now have more freedom to let students choose from among, say, ECCO's vast catalog of Restoration drama. Such sites help us rethink canonicity by presenting for study a larger sample of plays than ever before.

Some of these texts even come with a scholarly imprimatur, selected and edited according to clearly stated principles. *Plotting Yiddish Drama*, a project that collects scholarly play synopses, does not include full play texts, but gathers a wealth of nearly forgotten dramatic narratives for study. Digitized, well-edited plays represent an area where students can make a particularly important contribution. Armed with some basic editorial principles, classes might work together to create simple Text Encoding Initiative-compliant plays that expand the online canon.

While many readers benefit from digital facsimiles and other complex online media, simple, transcribed texts remain tremendously important. The vast possibilities offered by the Internet are not really unlimited. Not only paywalls but also low bandwidth data access or weak computing power keep some of the most sophisticated resources out of reach for many learners across the globe. To make the Internet's potential as a non-canonical, comprehensive theatre library a reality, scholars must expand the supply of curated texts, and produce all texts with support for "minimal computing," which lowers the computational cost of engaging with the wealth of available materials (Gil 2015).

Solution #3: Digitized Performances

Digital technologies help non-print materials to circulate, too. Images, audio, and video are all more widely available through digital platforms than they have been in analog forms. The wealth of such materials may help us to expand the canon to works with a primarily non-textual performance tradition. But, equally importantly, digitized performances offer a view of how performers put the canon to work. Insofar as canonical works remain relevant because they inspire responses in performance, video recordings become essential tools for demonstrating how artists interpret the same text in widely different ways. This multiplicity of views simultaneously dismantles the supposed stability of canonical works and demonstrates their generative capacity.

The *Asian Shakespeare Intercultural Archive* (A | S | I | A), a collection of video recordings of Shakespeare's texts as interpreted by leading directors and theatre companies in East and Southeast Asia, encapsulates these possibilities (see Yong and Yip 2020). The A | S | I | A video collection shows the complex relationship between Shakespeare as avatar of European culture and colonialism and the actual use so many artists have made of his plays. Artists working across vastly different theatrical traditions have appropriated and reinvented Shakespeare's works for their own purposes in order to speak about their local issues and histories. To recognize this aspect of canonicity, how canons simultaneously assert hegemony and become objects of resistance, we need only explore A | S | I | A's performance archive. There we find the canon expressing not textual solidity and singularity, but fluidity and polysemy in performance. This phenomenon, while not new, comes into sharp relief when exploring digital performance archives. Such archives re-articulate the usefulness of canons by demonstrating the range of non-canonical interpretations they can inspire.

Digital resources can also redirect attention to theatrical cultures that rarely feature in mainstream academic discourses. Examples focused on contemporary practices include the *Cuban Theatre Digital Archive* and the *Hemispheric Institute Digital Video Library*. Audiovisual resources are also useful for exploring non-textual canons. The actor training materials in the *Routledge Performance Archive* or Paul Allain's *Physical Actor Training: An Online A-Z* both offer access to a rich array of performances and performance techniques.

A third use of audiovisual resources is to call attention to lesser-known non-textual canons from around the world. As an example consider Javanese *wayang kulit*, a form of puppetry that has been performed for over a 1,000 years and that is still the most respected theatrical form in Java, Indonesia. The seven- or eight-hour *wayang kulit* performances are partially improvised, based on the *balungan* (literally "skeleton") of the story (see Escobar Varela 2019). The *wayang kulit* canon includes these skeletal storylines, but also textual formulas, movement techniques, musical conventions, and other aesthetic rules.[3] Textual materials alone fail to convey the complexity of these materials. Only audiovisual resources, such as the multimedia version of Bernard Arps' *Tall Tree, Nest of the Wind*, can document and present how performers invoke and reinterpret the *wayang kulit* canon (Arps 2020).

The availability of web resources that discuss and present theatrical canons from different theatrical traditions can help usher in discussions about canons' cultural and historical specificity in performance. Multimedia performance resources expand our understanding of canons as something put to use by performers, while also offering primarily non-textual forms as essential parts of theatre history.

Open Syllabus

Having seen three ways in which digital tools and methods transform our thinking about the canon, let us return to a possibility raised earlier, namely using quantitative analysis to explore which works we actually canonize through our teaching. The Open Syllabus Project, which aggregates books assigned on English-language syllabi, gathered primarily from automated crawls of university websites, offers a data-driven glimpse of canonical theatrical texts (Karaganis et al. 2019). For texts classified as "Theatre Arts," the 25 most commonly assigned on syllabi from the United States are:[4]

Rank	Text	Author
1.	Theatrical Design and Production	J. Michael Gillette
2.	Oedipus Rex	Sophocles
3.	Theatre	Robert Cohen
4.	Backstage Handbook	Paul Carter
5.	Respect for Acting	Uta Hagen
6.	Poetics	Aristotle
7.	Scene Design and Stage Lighting	W. Oren Parker
8.	A Raisin in the Sun	Lorraine Hansberry
9.	A Midsummer Night's Dream	William Shakespeare
10.	Stage Makeup	Richard Corson
11.	Acting One	Robert Cohen
12.	Hamlet	William Shakespeare
13.	Death of a Salesman	Arthur Miller
14.	Audition	Michael Shurtleff
15.	Backwards and Forwards	David Ball
16.	The Art of Theatre	William Missouri Downs et al.
17.	Practical Handbook for the Actor	Melissa Bruder
18.	Angels in America	Tony Kushner
19.	A Doll's House	Henrik Ibsen
20.	Tartuffe	Molière
21.	A Streetcar Named Desire	Tennessee Williams
22.	Living Theatre	Alvin Goldfarb, Edwin Wilson
23.	The Importance of Being Earnest	Oscar Wilde
24.	History of the Theatre	Oscar Gross Brockett
25.	Waiting for Godot	Samuel Beckett

The most striking aspect of this list is how few plays are on it: a mere 11 out of 25 texts. Among the plays, few surprises: with the exception of Hansberry's *A Raisin in the Sun*, the most frequently assigned works are all by white men, representing a handful of pre-20th century classics alongside a thin list of high-canon American dramatists plus Beckett. In other words, the canon often assumed to determine our teaching in the aggregate, does, indeed, determine our teaching in the aggregate.

What, though, to make of the other texts? Dominating the list we find not plays but volumes about the craft of theatre: how-to books about technical theatre, directing, and, of course acting. A smattering of history textbooks and a pair of formalist theories of play interpretation (Aristotle's *Poetics*; David Ball's *Backwards and Forwards*) join them. A quantitative glimpse at the syllabus-created canon redirects the problem of canonicity away from plays and playwrights and toward texts about theatre-making.

Without expounding too deeply upon the implications of this surprising canonicity, we must acknowledge how all of the challenges inherent in canons resurface in slightly different forms when the canon consists of these practical guides. We can ask questions such as:

- what acting/audition theories or stage techniques are canonical?
- what economic/managerial forms of theatrical production do these texts reproduce?
- what models of theatre-making do they exclude or marginalize?

Unfortunately, digital technologies may offer less support for disrupting these practical theatre canons than they do for canons of plays. Because these canons attempt to pass on knowledge that comes only from embodied experience, that is, from performance, such knowledge is less likely ever to find its way into the digitized archive.

The availability of syllabi as data can also help us better understand how we are teaching certain texts and trace developments over time. For this reason educators should contribute data on their courses to shared repositories whenever possible.[5]

Consider, in addition to the Open Syllabus Project, other sources of evidence for how canons are constructed in theatre studies curricula: for instance, in undergraduate student theses, or in published scholarship. "The canon" is not exactly equivalent to "dominant scholarly trends," but the connections between these two deserve attention. A discussion on canons and their roles might also consider canonical conceptual frameworks and canonical scholars. Extending our focus has the danger of making an analysis of canons too wide and diffuse to tackle at all, but canonicity as a concept is embedded in larger academic practices. Recognizing this wider canonicity is crucial for any project that seeks to bring attention to imbalances in canons, and to change how future canons are constructed and analyzed.[6]

What's Next

Digital technologies thus offer a host of new ways to expand and critique canons and canonicity. Canons are mere samples of theatrical activity. The digital age allows us to analyze, archive, and access far more of that theatre than was ever possible. These affordances transform canons from skewed representations of theatre history to tools for thinking about theatre historiography. We can and should use quantitative studies and digitized archives of plays and performances to make the analysis of canonical works and canons an active project in our classrooms. In this way, we put the canon to work for us, to help us teach and understand both the larger history of art and the history of exclusions that built the canons we still rely on today.

These digital tools do not, however, entirely resolve the canon's problems. We cannot simply point to a digital archive or offer a quantitative analysis of theatrical production. Digital information is also constructed by humans, and like canons, subject to the same biases that go into our anthologies. This glimpse of canons in a digital world should above all encourage the reader to take action in their classroom to build and disseminate new canons and canonical works. Share your syllabus online; create transcriptions of undigitized works; make images and videos to capture local performance traditions. Such efforts to increase the variety, quality, and accessibility of theatre history in all of its forms will never make canons obsolete, but they can shed a critical light on the concept of canonicity. We need a critical mode of interrogating the canon and its problems. Digital methods can help us to reinvent how we think about canons and, more importantly, to reimagine our relation to theatre knowledge more generally.

Notes

1 The Lost Plays Database (Knutson et al. 2018) attempts to catalogue references to plays no longer extant.
2 A more detailed account of how canons depend on surviving texts can be found in Bode 2020.
3 The Javanese equivalent to the canon is *pakem*, a word covering a slightly different semantic space, as it refers not to a specific set of texts of known authorship, but to canonical versions of storylines.
4 Field designations derive from texts, not courses. The data here thus represent the most widely assigned theatre arts texts, whether assigned in theatre classrooms or in those of other disciplines. For more on Open Syllabus methods for data gathering and analytic possibilities, see https://blog.opensyllabus.org/about-the-open-syllabus-project.
5 To share your syllabi with The Open Syllabus Project, review the submission information at https://blog.opensyllabus.org/share-syllabi/.
6 For more on the relationships between canons and academic discourse see Low and Wynne-Davies, 2006.

Works Cited

Allain, Paul. 2018. *Physical Actor Training: An Online A-Z*. Accessed 11 August 2020. https://www.dramaonlinelibrary.com/video?docid=do-9781350997189&tocid=do-9781350997189_5794178143001/.
Arps, Bernard. 2020. *Tall Tree, Nest of the Wind: A Study in Performance Philology [Digital Edition]*. Accessed 11 August 2020. http://pintubahasa.com/ttnotw/P6-1_video.html.
Biet, Christian et al. 2015. *The Comédie-Française Registers Project*. Accessed 11 July 2020. https://www.cfregisters.org/en/registers/.
Block, Geoffrey. 2011. "Integration." In *The Oxford Handbook of the American Musical*, edited by Raymond Knapp, Mitchell Morris, and Stacy Wolf. Oxford: Oxford University Press.
Bode, Katherine. 2020. "Why You Can't Model Away Bias." *Modern Language Quarterly* 81, 1: 95–124.
Cuban Theatre Digital Archive. Accessed 11 August 2020. http://ctda.library.miami.edu/.
Drama Online. Accessed 11 August 2020. https://www.dramaonlinelibrary.com/.
Dolan, Jill. 1997. "Advocacy and Activism: Identity, Curriculum, and Theatre Studies in the Twenty- First Century." *Theatre Topics* 7, 1: 1–10.

Eighteenth Century Collections Online. Accessed 11 August 2020. https://gale.com/ecco/.
Escobar Varela, Miguel. 2019. *Digital Wayang Encyclopedia*. Accessed 11 August2020. https://villaorlado.github.io/wayangnetworks/html/lakons.html.
Fischer, Frank et al. 2019. *Drama Corpora Project*. Accessed 11 August 2020. https://dracor.org/.
Gil, Alex. 2015. "The User, the Learner and the Machines We Make—Minimal Computing." 21 May. Accessed 11 July 2020. http://go-dh.github.io/mincomp/thoughts/2015/05/21/user-vs-learner/.
Guerrilla Girls. 1989. *'Do Women Have To Be Naked To Get Into the Met. Museum?'* Accessed 11 August 2020. https://www.tate.org.uk/art/artworks/guerrilla-girls-do-women-have-to-be-naked-to-get-into-the-met-museum-p78793.
HathiTrust. Accessed 11 August 2020. https://www.hathitrust.org/.
Hemispheric Institute Digital Video Library. Accessed 11 August 2020. http://archive.hemisphericinstitute.org/hemi/en/hidvl/.
Holledge, Julie et al. 2016. "A Global Doll's House: Ibsen and Distant Visions." In *Palgrave Studies in Performance and Technology*. London: Palgrave Macmillan.
Ibsen Stage Performance Database. Accessed 11 August 2020. https://ibsenstage.hf.uio.no/.
The Internet Archive. Accessed 11 August 2020. https://archive.org/.
Karaganis, Joe et al. 2019. *The Open Syllabus Project*. 26 June. Accessed 11 July 2020. https://opensyllabus.org/.
Knutson, Roslyn et al. 2018. *Lost Plays Database*. Accessed 11 August 2020. https://lostplays.folger.edu/.
Low, Gail Ching-Liang and Wynne-Davies, Marion. 2006. *A Black British Canon?* London: Palgrave Macmillan.
Montez, Noe. 2017. "Decolonizing Wikipedia through Advocacy and Activism: The Latina/o Theatre Wikiturgy Project." *Theatre Topics* 27, 1: E-1–E-9.
Plotting Yiddish Drama. Accessed 11 August 2020. https://web.uwm.edu/yiddish-stage/plotting-yiddish-drama/.
Project Gutenberg. Accessed 11 August 2020. https://www.gutenberg.org/.
Routledge Performance Archive. Accessed 11 August 2020. https://www.routledgeperformancearchive.com/.
Shakespeare in Quarto. Accessed 11 August 2020. https://www.bl.uk/treasures/shakespeare/.
Stempel, Larry. 2010. *Showtime: A History of the Broadway Musical Theatre*. New York: Norton.
Text Encoding Initiative. Accessed 11 August 2020. https://tei-c.org/.
Underwood, Ted. 2019. *Distant Horizons: Digital Evidence and Literary Change*. Chicago: University of Chicago Press.
Vareschi, Mark and Mattie Burkert. 2016. "Archives, Numbers, Meaning: The Eighteenth-Century Playbill at Scale." *Theatre Journal* 68, 4: 597–613.
Yong Li Lan et al. 2015. *Asian Shakespeare Intercultural Archive*. Accessed 11 August 2020. http://a-s-i-a-web.org/.
Yong, Li Lan and Roweena Yip. 2020. "Teaching with the Asian Shakespeare Intercultural Archive (A|S|I|A)." *Research in Drama Education: The Journal of Applied Theatre and Performance 25*, 1: 8–25.

18 *Antigone* is Dead, Long Live *Antigones*!

Adaptation, Difference, and Instability at the Heart of the Traditional Western Canon

Rachel M. E. Wolfe

When I was in grad school, I set out to study adaptation and tripped over the canon.

I wanted to study how the same stories got retold over the greatest possible span of time and place, so, naturally, I turned to the Greeks. They were, I had been told, the inventors of theatre (though class prep research I have since done has revealed that theatre was independently invented several times in several places)[1] and had spawned adaptations in hundreds of societies from ancient Rome to contemporary Peru. Between the love of Europe for the drama of the Greeks and the expansive colonization those countries practiced, Greek theatre had made its way all over the world, offering my studies of adaptation more than 2000 years and a global scope. The fact that this lined up precisely with the Eurocentric canon was, of course, both cause and result of this epic spread. Basically, in trying to find the greatest wealth of material for comparative retellings, I got railroaded right into the center of the canon.

Adaptation, as both a process and a product, turns out to be inextricably linked with canon formation. While many different scholars have attempted to define adaptation, fittingly enough, with numerous minor variations,[2] the core that everyone seems to agree on is that adaptation is a process whereby a person who is not the first author of a story retells that story with some variation—and the resulting story is then also called an adaptation. Both process and product contribute to canon formation because the works that are the most studied and the most widely read spawn the most adaptations, and these adaptations in turn spread knowledge of those works even more widely, entrenching them even more firmly into the canon. The plays, novels, and stories that we all think of as being the most canonical are not just the ones that are most frequently assigned by teachers, but rather (or also) the works that are most widely adapted: the ones you know from watching the film, or reading that satirical reinterpretation, or which had that obvious reference in the video game you played growing up (now that you think about it).

Many scholars of adaptation studies even go so far as to pinpoint adaptation as the driving mechanism of canon formation, biologist Gary R. Bortolotti and adaptation theorist Linda Hutcheon famously arguing in a co-authored paper that the cultural adaptation of telling old stories in new ways is an equivalent process to the genetic adaptation that underlies natural selection in biology (Bortolotti and Hutcheon 2007). Their argument, in a nutshell, is that the success and survival of a story in the cultural realm requires adaptational change to ensure both its spread and its staying power. Julie Sanders, in her book *Adaptation and Appropriation*, makes the obvious links between this idea and canon formation explicit, arguing that the more widely adapted a work is (or, in other words, its success in spreading and staying) the more firmly entrenched in the canon it becomes, such that "adaptation becomes a veritable marker of canonical status; citation infers authority" (Sanders 2006: 9). The canon, therefore, is made up of stories that have successfully adapted, and without adaptation the canon would not exist.

This is basically the way that current scholarship on adaptation and the canon situates this relationship: adaptation as a driving mechanism for canon formation. It's simple. It's easy to grasp. But I have found adaptation more complicated than this, its relationship to canon formation less straightforward and somewhat more insidious. I offer this chapter in dialogue with this common assumption of the interdisciplinary field of adaptation studies. Using the case study of Sophocles's *Antigone*, I push back against the popular conception of the Eurocentric "traditional canon" as monolithic and unchanging by exploring the complexities of adaptation—a force that does not merely preserve the canon, but constantly alters it. While I do not dispute that adaptation contributes to canon formation, the idea that it does so by making knowledge of a given work more widespread is the part that I contend with, and all on account of that one little word, "a." Adaptation, spawning new works by its very function, resists definition in the singular; and yet, that is routinely, unthinkingly, how we use it.

There is a persistent assumption underlying discussions of adaptation and its place in canon formation: adaptation = preservation. When Bortolotti and Hutcheon introduced their homology, they did so with the following succinct statement: "both [biological and cultural] adaptation are understandable as processes of replication" (Bortolotti and Hutcheon 2007: 444). The rest of their article goes on to describe adaptation as a mechanism of survival for both organisms and narratives, adopting the terminology of evolutionary biology to theorize how literary adaptation enables narratives to outlast their original cultural contexts. Not limited to Bortolotti and Hutcheon nor even just to scholarship, the idea that adaptation preserves the essential spirit of a work surfaces time and again in the descriptions of adaptors and theatre practitioners talking about their work. Beth Piatote, a member of the Nez Perce tribe who adapted *Antigone* to discuss the importance of repatriating Native American remains, ties together several of the strands of rhetoric that surround ideas of adaptation, preservation, and canonicity succinctly in an interview about her play:

> The question that was with me is like, 'Why can people understand these concepts of universal literature, like *Antigone*, that's supposed to deal with

these universal problems of the living and the dead… Why can the same people who can understand that great classic literature, not understand how native people feel about ancestral remains?' (quoted in Brice 2018)

What Piatote reveals in this quote is a belief that the messages about the relation of the living to the dead that she sees in *Antigone* are also the messages that other people see, and that in adapting this work she is preserving those "universal" messages and carrying them forward. Her use of terms like "universal literature" are a method of signaling canonicity for a lay audience who may not be familiar with terms like "canon" and "canonization," and she uses them to imply a similarity between her own adaptation and Sophocles's that is tantamount to preservation. This assumption, espoused either consciously or unconsciously by adaptation theorists and theatre practitioners alike, ignores difference at the center (within the traditional Western canon) even as we celebrate difference on the margins (the new expansions of the canon that create space for previously excluded authors like Piatote). It is this faulty assumption which positions us to view the canon—especially the traditional Eurocentric canon—as stable, unitary, monolithic, and timeless; the very qualities implied by the word "universal." Even as we seek to expand the canon through the ever-increasing inclusivity begun by postcolonial and gender studies and rapidly expanding to every sort of identity field, we cannot fundamentally excise the ethnocentrism at its heart until we tackle this assumption head-on.

In an ironic twist, I believe we can begin to tackle the assumption that to adapt something is to preserve it through a more thorough engagement with Bortolotti and Hutcheon's biological homology, despite their notions of preservation contributing to the issue. The tension inherent in Bortolotti and Hutcheon's theory, unexplored by the authors themselves, is that the homology with evolutionary biology implies not only preservation, but also loss. As they put it: "Organisms act as vehicles for genes; the literary texts or the stage performances we call **adaptations** are the vehicles of narrative ideas—that is, their physical embodiment in some medium" (Bortolotti and Hutcheon 2007: 447, bold in original). In Bortolotti and Hutcheon's biological theory of cultural adaptation, the external adaptive form that a story takes is what enables it to survive in a given cultural context, but each new form contains (or, one might say, preserves) a core "narrative idea" that is passed from adaptation to adaptation the way that genes are. The thing that is easy to overlook here is the attendant process of loss that accompanies both genetic and narrative adaptation. The new vehicle does not simply preserve the genes or narrative ideas that used to be contained in a different vehicle; it preserves *some* of them by combining them with new stock while discarding others. I have 46 chromosomes, 23 from my mother and 23 from my father. My mother and father each had 46 chromosomes. That means that each of them, in gifting me 23 chromosomes, had to throw out 23 (and that's not even taking into account things like crossover processes and random mutations). To say that I, as a new vehicle, preserve the genes of my mother is a partial truth at best; I preserve some of her genes unaltered, some altered, and fully half of them not at all. And that's only the difference of one generation! Over many generations, the number of genes I preserve unaltered from any given ancestor becomes fewer and fewer, to the point where it vanishes into statistical insignificance. The case for the preservation of "narrative ideas" is even less straightforward, as there is no simple natural mathematics that can allow us to make such precise estimations of how much has been preserved versus how much has been lost. In addition, the entire thing is immensely complicated by the fact that "ideas" are completely subjective and largely culturally determined, such that the same narrative read by two different cultures is likely to yield entirely different ideas even if the narrative itself has barely been altered—or even preserved entirely untouched.

Despite their awareness of these facts as they apply to biology, and their attendant treatment of adaptation and source text in the roles of descendent and ancestor, respectively, Bortolotti and Hutcheon dedicate little attention to the loss factor when it comes to cultural adaptation; primarily, I suspect, because Hutcheon (like most scholars of adaptation) focuses primarily on adaptation across medium rather than across culture. Adaptation studies, as an interdisciplinary field, traces its origins back to George Bluestone's 1957 groundbreaking study, *Novels into Film* (Bluestone 1957). Its theorists have consequently largely been drawn from literary and film scholars, and its subjects virtually always treat the transition from novel into film; though since Linda Hutcheon's own groundbreaking monograph, *A Theory of Adaptation*, the media have branched out to include other storytelling mediums like television, theatre, graphic novels, video games, and even theme parks (see Hutcheon 2006). Having a plethora of additional media, however, has not changed the focus on medium-to-medium adaptation, as Hutcheon defines adaptation in this work specifically by what she calls "transcoding," which "can involve a shift of medium (a poem to a film) or genre (an epic to a novel), or a change of frame and therefore context: telling the same story from a different point of view, for instance, can create a manifestly different interpretation" (7–8). Despite the inclusion of this last category, the examples that pepper Hutcheon's foundational work virtually all feature a shift in medium, making the shift in context, at best, an afterthought. Privileging a change in medium rather than a change across time or space, adaptation studies has, metaphorically speaking, been looking primarily at the transfer from mother to daughter, in which a full 50% of the "genes" are preserved. As a theatre scholar looking at canonical adaptation across vast swaths of time and space but within the medium of theatre, my own studies of the Greeks have been literally and figuratively more focused on the relations between distant ancestors and their heavily altered descendants, in which significant preservation cannot be assumed. And yet, surprisingly, distressingly, it *is* assumed, with startling regularity, by scholars and theatre practitioners alike, particularly when it comes to the canon.

There is a strong tendency when discussing adaptations of canonical stories—especially within production companies who pen and stage live theatrical productions—to emphasize similarity over difference and to lay claim to artistic and cultural genealogies *not as genealogies*, but rather as time capsules. Consider these rhetorical flourishes in the press release for an Australian production of *Antigone* explicitly described as "a new contemporary adaptation of this ancient play":

> Creon in Antigone [*sic*] refuses to bury the body of his nephew for his crimes against his own community. In the United States', [*sic*] *two-and-a-half-thousand years later*, the state officially refused to put the corpse of its Boston Marathon bomber in American soil… Antigone, a child of war, like too many in our world, asked a burning moral question *thousands of years ago that remains* too difficult for us to answer even to this day." (Sport for Jove Theatre Co. 2016, emphasis added)

The use of the time scale is employed here to emphasize similarity, not difference. The invocation of the great span of time that has passed invites us to marvel at the continuity of human sentiment and thought, not the particular cultural contexts that make ancient Thebes or contemporary Boston unique. Even as this press release repeatedly uses the word "adaptation" and credits adaptor Damien Ryan, the advertising places a heavy stress on the antiquity of Sophocles's version that posits adaptation and source text as contiguous.

The common rhetoric of theatrical marketing when it comes to adaptation rests on the idea that the fact of adapting a story or artistic work over a long span of time constitutes the preservation of that work—and such marketing routinely downplays or outright ignores its recombination into a new work. Read or listen to any interview with a director of Greek tragedy—any Greek tragedy—today and you will hear the same mantra: this 2,500-year-old story speaks to the present day. These characters are struggling with our common humanity, with issues that are just as relevant now as they were in the Golden Age of Athens. *Antigone* is about civil disobedience in the face of an oppressive government that tramples on individual rights (see the studies of contemporary productions contained in Tiefenbrun 1999 and McDonald 2009, as well as the direct comments of Voutsa 2016). Or maybe it's about the pain of being a woman who loses her male relatives in war, whether official or unofficial (this was the approach taken by the recent productions *Antigone of Syria*, documented in Auger and Azzam 2018, and Classical Theatre of Harlem's carefully crafted Black Lives Matter version of *Antigone*, reviewed in Collins-Hughes 2018). Hell, it might even be about the continuing relevance of the right to give one's kin proper burial; after all, that's how Beth Piatote harnessed it in her stirring adaptation, *Antíkoni*, performed in the Hearst Museum of Anthropology about the continued exhibition of Native American remains by museums despite calls by tribes for their repatriation (see documentation in Brice 2018, paired with the example of Piatote's rhetoric above). The central

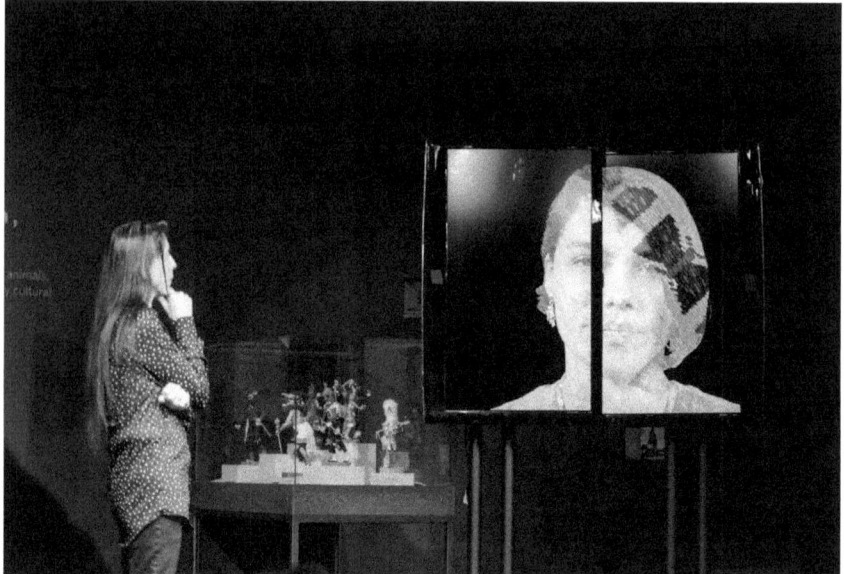

Figure 18.1 In this scene from *Antíkoni*, the title character (Fantasia Painter) appears before Kreon (Phillip E. Cash Cash) in a state of digital transfiguration. The staged reading took place in the Hearst Museum of Anthropology at UC Berkeley, which holds more than 9,000 ancestral remains, the largest collection outside of the Smithsonian. Photo credit: Irene Yi.

message might change from production to production, adaptation to adaptation, but the thing that's the same is this narrative of continuing relevance. This narrative assumes that we use Sophocles's *Antigone* to explore these contemporary concerns because they are already *in there*; he knew way back when, and the very fact that these concerns appeared in this ancient play is cited as proof that they are universally human, relevant across time and space—note how frequently the words "relevant" and "universal" pop up just in the titles of articles in my reference list below. The place of Sophocles's *Antigone* in the canon is rhetorically justified by its continuing relevance to this day, while at the same time contemporary directors and adaptors can capitalize on its status as a canonical work to bring attention to the messages they deem most relevant. Symbiotic.

But do these plays, both adaptations and productions of *Antigone* and other ancient stories, really conform so easily to modern concerns? Classical studies of these texts in their ancient Greek cultural contexts tell us that *Antigone* is about the conflict created when the rule of law (specifically pre-democratic tyrannical law with a singular head-of-state) clashes with proper religious observance (of specifically ancient Greek religion)—and moreover, that Antigone herself is not even the protagonist, but rather that the story asks us to examine the position of the tyrant Creon (see Foley 2001 and Meinel 2015, among others). In fact, the deeper one dives into studies of ancient Greek culture and religion, the more evidence one finds that there is a significant disconnect between a historical approach to Greek tragedy and the rhetoric that is used to tout its continuing relevance. Classical scholars who take the historical approach write about the particularities of Greek belief systems, social structures, and cultural obsessions, pointing out their differences from our own. Froma I. Zeitlin, for example, in her book *Playing the Other: Gender and Society in Classical Greek Literature*, contends that Antigone and other female characters written and played by men for a male audience in an unapologetically male society

> are never an end in themselves… Rather, they play the roles of catalysts, agents, instruments, blockers, spoilers, destroyers, and sometimes helpers or saviors for the male characters (Zeitlin 1996: 347)

This analysis is a far cry from the Antigone-as-empowerment-symbol image the character routinely gives off in contemporary productions, and undercuts her modern status as the titular protagonist. Similarly, Helene P. Foley examines "The Politics of Tragic Lamentation" in a chapter that links Antigone's speeches with Solonic laws that curtailed the power of public mourning and funerary rights—a legal and cultural context specific to ancient Athens and wholly alien to most theatre companies and audiences who interact with the play today (Foley 2001: 21–29 and 31–33). In perhaps the most difficult of all to summarize, Fabian Meinel weaves a complex tapestry of ancient Greek cultural associations between boundary transgression, civic space, corpses, and ritual pollution to argue that "dissolution of the body's boundaries and transgression of civic boundaries go hand in hand" in *Antigone*, a read that focuses primarily on the "expanding" corpse of Polynices rather than Antigone *or* Creon, and would be a rare focus indeed in modern productions (Meinel 2015: 113).

Contemporary adaptors and practitioners of Greek tragedy in production, on the other hand, are more likely to write triumphantly about the ability of these ancient stories to speak directly to our own (very different) belief systems, social structures, and cultural obsessions. Marianne McDonald, writing about contemporary Irish adaptations of several Greek tragedies (including multiple versions of *Antigone*), looks at the particulars of the English colonization of Ireland in order to argue that

> Ireland is England's… Antigone, who in the face of insufferable odds, does not falter, but retains a sense of justice (McDonald 1997: 58)

And, more broadly, that "in these Irish plays, the particular is also enhanced by the universal" (70), with Ireland's colonial history and the content of Greek tragedy standing as the particular and universal, respectively. For McDonald (and, presumably, the many adaptors she treats), the figure of Antigone is used as a mirror in which the politically oppressed may view their own faces, a "universal" whose character traits and circumstances may easily metonymically stand in for contemporary analogues including all forms of justice—even those that do not share the specifics of the word's religious and cultural value in the ancient Athenian context. Bryan Doerries, likewise, has made a major splash in both classical and drama therapy circles lately with his tellingly-named monograph *The Theatre of War: What Greek Tragedies Can Teach Us Today*. While Doerries barely addresses *Antigone* (except to discuss her status as a teenager; Doerries 2015: 11) on account of his primary concern with warrior narratives as therapeutic tools for veterans, his general attitudes about the applicability of ancient scripts to modern concerns—perhaps best exemplified in his chapter title "PTSD is from BC"—is quite representative of the way Greek tragedy is used by practitioners, whether in the realm of drama therapy or the commercial theatre. And, of course, the mere title of J. Michael Walton's *Euripides Our Contemporary* speaks for itself (Walton 2009).

This rhetoric of similarity, which I refer to as "the myth of still relevant," pervades our artistic attitudes toward classical drama, disguising differences where they exist and contributing to a narrative of continuity in Western culture from the Greeks to the present. Fundamentally, what this myth asserts is that we extract meaning from ancient plays using contemporary interpretations—that is to say, the meaning was in the original to begin with, needing only to be uncovered by the modern production. I assert that the process works in the opposite direction: contemporary productions take the bare-bones plot points of ancient works and layer currently relevant meanings over them, creating—rather than preserving—a work that speaks to the present society. Canonical Greek plays do not "still" speak to us because they contain universal truths, but rather because adaptation has sufficiently changed them to fall in line with specific and subjective truths espoused by the target audience.

The fact of the matter is that while classical plays like *Antigone* may be unproblematically asserted to comprise part of the traditional Western canon, they only do so because of significant adaptational change—and not just the kinds we usually consider to be within the definition of that term, either. Leaving aside for the moment clearly changed adaptational variants like Femi Osofisan's *Tegonni: An African Antigone* (Osofisan 2007) and other modern adaptations which employ different character names and (occasionally) plot points than the source text, the scripts that we consider to be "original" and on which we confidently print "by Sophocles" are already extremely different even from their earliest surviving forms. Lacking spaces between words, often fragmentary, and written in a dead language, ancient Greek scripts are different on a fundamental linguistic level from the versions you and I read in our schoolbook anthologies (a major driver of canonization if ever there was one).

Given the number of linguistic and artistic choices a translator must make in order to turn Sophocles's actual script into something intelligible to the English reader, it would be more accurate to refer to the *Antigone* in the perennially popular Norton anthology as the *Antigone* of Robert Bagg rather than the

Figure 18.2 Writing along the fibers. Content: Sophocles' *Antigone*. From the Papyrus Manuscript Fragments Collection, Kelvin Smith Library Special Collections, Case Western Reserve University.

Antigone of Sophocles (Gainor et al. 2018).[3] On my office bookshelf stand the *Antigone*s of Hugh Lloyd-Jones (Sophocles 1994), David Grene and Richmond Lattimore (Grene and Lattimore 2013), and Robert Fagles (Sophocles 2014), all of which are billed as the *Antigone* of Sophocles (I mean, look at what I had to put in my parenthetical citations!) and not one of which is officially considered an adaptation, despite significant differences between them.[4] The things we think we know as the canonical *Antigone* of Sophocles are nothing more than Roachian effigies,[5] simulacra variously and eternally signaling the absence of an original we can never reclaim. Sophocles's words, not only written in ancient Greek but composed as lyrics to go with musical notes and dance moves long since lost and divorced from the "dance culture" (in the words of Zarifi 2007) that gave them meaning and relevance, *even in the absence of translation* constitute no more than the bare skeletons of full productions.

These skeletons, which we have inherited and twisted into our foreign tongues, cannot possibly bear more than a shadow of a resemblance to their ancient forms, even in the most diligent attempts at historical reconstruction. Sir Peter Hall has been given a great deal of credit as the most historically accurate modern director of Greek tragedy, religiously using masks; employing composers of verse, dance, and music to all go together; featuring all-male casts without assigned characters; and even staging his productions on the remains of actual ancient Greek theatres—but even he admits that, divorced from the civic and religious context the Athenian audience brought to the productions, his versions cannot possibly hope to replicate the ancient originals. As he puts it in a transcript of a scholarly conversation at the Getty:

> I shouldn't think we can get near it [the experience of attending the original plays]. I mean, how could we?... And I don't think *that's* the point. I think the point is, we find out as much as we can about how they did it and why they did it, and then we try to find equivalents for our audience (Hart et al 2003: 142, emphasis in original).

Despite being hailed as the master of historical accuracy in staging Greek tragedy, Hall's rhetoric in this passage and others very much stresses the relationship of his plays to now, and speaks to his attempts to find modern parallels for irretrievable states of being and modes of thought. The masks that we create are only guesses at what ancient masks might have been like, our music and dance composed afresh in an attempt to recapture a spirit none of us has ever known, and the ancient stages we can still perform on are no longer the vibrant civic spaces of yesteryear but crumbling museum pieces for the artistically elite.

Theatre and adaptation scholar Katja Krebs has eloquently made the case for all productions being, in some sense, adaptations, as even a second production of a play written last year will be notably different from the first, on account of the various artistic choices that must be made in the creation of a new staging (Krebs 2014). If we accept this principle—and certainly I do—we can assume an even greater degree of unavoidable change when the original and new productions are separated by roughly 2,500 years. The artistic choices made in staging the new production will be different not only on account of the personal tastes of the theatre practitioners involved, but also on account of the radically different cultural context they inhabit. The trappings of material culture (clothing, scenery, props, and gesture) will exhibit as much change as the linguistic context. Like translation, production caters to the common assumptions of the target culture, not the source.

Having twisted and rearranged the bare bones we have inherited through translation, and then fleshed them out through the processes of staging, we finally clothe these reconstituted bodies in our own contemporary interpretations. The numerous contemporary *Antigones* listed above are each solidly grounded in the issues of the present day and time, often with remarkable specificity. To give some additional examples, Grupo Cultural Yuyachkani used their production of *Antígona* to explore themes of witnessing and survivor's guilt in the wake of the Dirty War in Peru.[6] Wang Mo-Lin turned the same story into a transnational commentary on state massacres of civilian protesters in his *Andigangni*, drawing specific parallels to the 228 Incident in Taiwan, the Gwangju Uprising in South Korea, and the Tiananmen Square protest in China (see Ho 2013). These productions, like the civil disobedience, Syrian Civil War, postcolonial Irish, Black Lives Matter, Boston Marathon bomber, and indigenous repatriation *Antigones* covered earlier, are explicitly about modern events and designed to speak to modern audiences. In each case, the story of Sophocles's *Antigone*, this bare skeleton, is subjected to vast differences of interpretation based upon the receiving culture's own assumptions, concerns, and desires. Once this barebones structure has been draped in these inescapably modern trappings, there can be no question that the resulting figure has an infinitesimal chance of looking like its original form. The new play is no clone—it is a distant descendent at best. And yet these twisted and reassembled shapes, clothed in the garments of our own contemporary cultures, are routinely referred to in terms that foreground continuity, similarity, and invariance[7]—they are, in a very real sense, the poster children for "the myth of still relevant" and the interrelated idea that to adapt something is to preserve it.

I view the widespread practice of staging classical drama (and touting it as timeless) as more akin to Lawrence Venuti's notion of "fluent translation" than to preservation (Venuti 1986). Intelligibility across languages that the receiving audience member does not speak is impossible, so the translator creates a new thing that bears some resemblance to the old, but has necessarily been greatly changed in order to render it intelligible to the new audience. As Venuti puts it in the article where he introduced the concept of fluent translation, "The Translator's Invisibility," "translation is the unstable reconciliation of two different, often conflicting, sets of cultural determinations" (Venuti 1986: 209). Reconciling these different sets of cultural determinants involves constant decision-making by the translator; work which, Venuti argues, is rendered invisible in the most marketable type of translation: the type which capitulates wholly to the target culture in vocabulary and syntax and aims to appear as though it had been written in the target language to begin with—or "fluent translation" for short. In a later book, *The Scandals of Translation: Toward an Ethics of Difference*, Venuti describes such fluent translations as "domesticating translations that assimilate foreign literary texts too forcefully to dominant values at home," reinscribing those dominant values in the process (Venuti 1998: 5). Readers, not required by fluent translations to confront differences between their own cultural worldviews and those of the source culture, may be fooled into thinking that the translation is an accurate representation of the foreign original, and that therefore the dominant values they see in the fluent translation are universal or at least cross-cultural when they were, in fact, added by the translator and are unique to the target culture. Fluent translation, Venuti argues, creates the illusion of "a transparent window through which authorial psychology or meaning can be seen"—when in fact, meaning is radically destabilized by its removal from the socio-historical-linguistic context or "chain of signifiers" in which it was originally written (Venuti 1986: 188).

"The myth of still relevant" enacts the same process, but with translations across time rather than (or, in this case, in addition to) translations across language. As with Venuti's notion of fluent translation, "the myth of still relevant" allows receivers of the new work (the translation, the adaptation, or, to borrow Michel Garneau's term, the middle-ground "tradaptation"[8]) to fool themselves into thinking that their own cultural assumptions map 1:1 to an objective reality that is known and accepted by all cultures; with the further implication that those assumptions are therefore universally true across vast swaths of time and space—the idea that forms the lynchpin in defenses of the traditional canon. This culturally insular worldview, and the unintentional ignorance it generates, encourages us to view the adaptation and the source as fundamentally the same, to ignore and cover up difference, and to erase the work of the translator/adaptor/receiving culture which has substantially altered the work from its previous state. Unable to see the differences between the visible adaptation and the invisible source, contemporary consumers of the canon conflate descendent and ancestor and view them as one and the same. "The king is dead, long live the king," only with the first part erased. The Inka, son of the Sun, has always ruled the empire, and the fact that he has been many different men recedes in our consciousness to the point of irrelevance.

The "traditional Western canon" has a long history of being defended by claims of universalism. The fact that certain works have "survived" so long has been offered as proof of their timelessness and ability to speak to all cultures across time and space—as many of the quotes and book titles already mentioned in this chapter can attest. But when we look at adaptation not as a mechanism of survival but as a means to *create* relevance in new contexts, this customary position becomes harder to maintain. If we refocus the discussion away from "finding" meaning in ancient texts and toward *adding* meaning to old narrative structures, we make equality between traditional and new canons more conceivable. Once we accept that all meaning is determined by the target audience and not by the source, we demystify the staying power of canons that are exclusionary and Eurocentric. The new canons that are being built on principles of inclusivity are no less "timeless" or "universal" than the traditional canon, because the traditional canon itself is neither timeless nor universal—it is merely a structure upon which many temporally and culturally specific meanings have been hung. It is time to let go of "the myth of still relevant" and embrace the notion that relevance is a product of our own artistry here and now.

The fundamental problem, as I see it, is that our (Western) culture has taught us to think through things in terms of binary opposition: similarity *or* difference, continuity *or* rupture, relevance *or* irrelevance, as though any one of these things precluded the other. In reality, though, both exist simultaneously within the same work/canon/phenomenon, and to ignore that is to deny ourselves half the picture. Take the phenomenon of adaptation itself: adaptation can only be defined by the simultaneous coexistence of similarity and difference, because a work without similarity to a predecessor is simply a new work, while one without differences from its predecessor is merely a copy. Given this notion, you would think that adaptation scholars would be particularly practiced at holding the seemingly oppositional categories of similarity and difference in view simultaneously; and yet when we argue that adaptation is a driver of canonization, that the more adaptations a story spawns the more canonical it is—as though adaptations were copies spreading the source texts to new audiences—we ignore the fact of difference in adaptation and privilege similarity, to the point that we stabilize and reinscribe the (traditional) canon through entirely fanciful means. "The myth of still relevant" is a myth, and one that requires ignoring the fact that, like our human bodies, the reproduction of our cultural touchstones is enacted through recombination more akin to sexual reproduction than the exponential copying of cell division which most discussions of adaptation seem to imply.

When we take the time to deconstruct this myth, and look specifically at difference within adaptation, we see that even the most canonical of the canonical—the plays at the heart of the traditional Western canon—are not stable, unitary, monolithic, nor timeless. Adaptation, the mechanism that has "kept" these stories in the canon, has not so much accorded power to singular narratives as it has installed ruling families. No *Antigone* that you have ever read or seen, even if you are a classical specialist who reads ancient Greek, has been the *Antigone* of Sophocles. That *Antigone* has been dead for a long time, and while her cultural/adaptational descendants are numerous and varied, all they can preserve of her are individual characteristics, parceled out and recombined with new cultural narratives. To live on through descendants is not to continue unchanged, but to continue *changed*, in infinite combinations without copies. The idealized, stable, frozen-in-time ancient *Antigone* that we all think of as one of the most canonical plays of all time does not exist, and even at its center, the canon is not stable. *Antigone* is dead, long live *Antigone*s!

Notes

1 In my classes on world drama and theatre history, I identify four different locations where theatre may have been independently invented: Egypt, Greece, India, and Mesoamerica. We examine the earliest evidence from each of these societies, enter into scholarly debate over whether Egyptian drama might have influenced Greece (see Teeter 2011 on the dramatic qualities of the Abydos passion plays and Moyer 2011 on interactions between the two cultures) and whether Greek drama influenced India (see Kuiper 1979), and discuss how the way in which one defines words like "theatre" or "drama" allow people

to either include or exclude these various cases as examples of "theatre" in the first place. While it is difficult to reach definitive conclusions with any of this, the one thing about which we can be relatively certain is that the Afro-Eurasian lines of influence that may be drawn among ancient theatres do not apply to Mesoamerica (assuming no pre-Columbian contact between the two continent banks), making it clear that theatre was independently invented by at least two societies and not merely a creation of the Greeks which then travelled the world, as traditional narratives would have it (and, incidentally, these traditional narratives require defining "theatre" in such a way as to exclude the Abydos passion plays of ancient Egypt, which predate the surviving Attic dramas by quite a bit. See McConachie et al 2016).
2 For an excellent succinct history of competing definitions of adaptation within the field, see the introduction in Rodosthenous 2017.
3 On translation as a form of adaptation and the difficulty of drawing clear definitional lines between these concepts, see Raw 2012. There is also a deeper look at translation as an agent of significant change in my discussion of the writings of Lawrence Venuti, below.
4 In fact, I commonly do an exercise with my students in which, when we get to the Greek tragedy segment of a class, I assign each student a different translation to read of the same play. In the class discussions that follow, we invariably find that students have come away with very different impressions of the personal characteristics of the main characters, the quality and style of the writing, and even, on some occasions, what happened in the plot.
5 My reference here is to the concept of effigy as a substitution that simultaneously signals and hides the absence of the original, as developed by Joseph Roach in his excellent study *Cities of the Dead: Circum-Atlantic Performance* (Roach 1996).
6 For an excellent examination of this production and its themes, see Taylor 2007.
7 Even, paradoxically, by Peter Hall himself in the very same interview quoted above, in which he both acknowledges the irretrievability of the original *and also* asserts the timelessness and continuing relevance of the writing. See Hart et al 2003: 134-35.
8 For a look at the development of this term and its entrance into scholarly discussion on translation and adaptation, see Raw 2012.

Works Cited

Auger, Bridgette and Itab Azzam, dir. 2018. *We Are Not Princesses*. Beirut: Open Art. Film.
Bluestone, George. 1957. *Novels into Film*. Baltimore: Johns Hopkins University Press.
Bortolotti, Gary R. and Linda Hutcheon. 2007. "On the Origin of Adaptations: Rethinking Fidelity Discourse and 'Success'—Biologically." *New Literary History* 38, 3: 443–458.
Brice, Anne. 2018. "Podcast: Native American *Antigone* Explores Universal Values of Honoring the Dead." *Berkeley News*, 20 November. Accessed 21May2020: https://news.berkeley.edu/2018/11/20/podcast-antikoni/.
Collins-Hughes, Laura. 2018. "Review: 'Antigone' Asserts Whose Lives Matter, With Modern Relevance." *The New York Times*, 9 July. Accessed 21May2020: https://www.nytimes.com/2018/07/09/theater/antigone-review.html.
Doerries, Bryan. 2015. *The Theater of War: What Ancient Greek Tragedies Can Teach Us Today*. New York: Alfred A Knopf.
Foley, Helene P. 2001. *Female Acts in Greek Tragedy*. Princeton: Princeton University Press.
Gainor, J. Ellen, Stanton B. Garner Jr., and Martin Puchner, eds. 2018. *The Norton Anthology of Drama, Third Edition: Volume One*. New York and London: W. W. Norton & Company.
Grene, David and Richmond Lattimore, eds. 2013. *Sophocles I: Antigone, Oedipus the King, Oedipus at Colonus*. Chicago: University of Chicago Press.

Hart, Mary Louise, Oliver Taplin, Peter Hall, Peter Sellars, Peter Stein, and Lydia Koniordou. 2003. "Ancient Greek Tragedy on the Stage." *Arion: A Journal of Humanities and the Classics* 11, 1: 125–175.
Ho Yi. 2013. "Antigone Goes Asian." *Taipei Times*, 20 September. Accessed 23 May 2020: https://www.taipeitimes.com/News/feat/archives/2013/09/20/2003572557.
Hutcheon, Linda. 2006. *A Theory of Adaptation*. New York: Routledge.
Krebs, Katja. 2014. "Ghosts We Have Seen Before: Trends in Adaptation in Contemporary Performance." *Theatre Journal* 66, 4: 581–590.
Kuiper, Franciscus Bernardus Jacobus. 1979. *Varuna and Vidūṣaka: On the Origin of the Sanskrit Drama*. Amsterdam: North-Holland Publishing Company.
Macintosh, Fiona. 1997. "*Tragedy in Performance: Nineteenth- and Twentieth-Century Productions.*" In *The Cambridge Companion to Greek Tragedy*, edited by P. E. Easterling. Cambridge: Cambridge University Press.
McConachie, Bruce, Tobin Nellhaus, Carol Fisher Sorgenfrei, and Tamara Underiner. 2016. *Theatre Histories: An Introduction*. London and New York: Routledge.
McDonald, Marianne. 1997. "When Despair and History Rhyme: Colonialism and Greek Tragedy." *New Hibernia Review / Iris Éireannach Nua* 1, 2: 57–70.
McDonald, Marianne. 2009. "Black Antigone and Gay Oedipus: Postcolonial Dramatic Legacies in the New South Africa." *Arion: A Journal of Humanities and the Classics* 17, 1: 25–52.
Meinel, Fabian. 2015. *Pollution and Crisis in Greek Tragedy*. Cambridge: Cambridge University Press.
Moyer, Ian S. 2011. *Egypt and the Limits of Hellenism*. Cambridge: Cambridge University Press.
Osofisan, Femi. 2007. *Tegonni: An African Antigone*. Lagos: Concept Publications.
Raw, Laurence, ed. 2012. *Translation, Adaptation and Transformation*. London: Continuum International Publishing Group.
Roach, Joseph. 1996. *Cities of the Dead: Circum-Atlantic Performance*. New York: Columbia University Press.
Rodosthenous, George, ed. 2017. *Contemporary Adaptations of Greek Tragedy: Auteurship and Directorial Visions*. London: Bloomsbury.
Sanders, Julie. 2006. *Adaptation and Appropriation*. London and New York: Routledge.
Sophocles. 1994. *Antigone. The Women of Trachis. Philoctetes. Oedipus at Colonus*, edited and translated by Hugh Lloyd-Jones. Loeb Classical Library 21. Cambridge, MA: Harvard University Press.
Sophocles. 2014. *The Three Theban Plays: Antigone, Oedipus the King, Oedipus at Colonus*, translated by Robert Fagles. Penguin Classics. New York: Penguin Books.
Sport for Jove Theatre Co. 2016. "Antigone Press Release." *Sport for Jove Theatre Co. official website*. Accessed 20 July 2020. http://www.sportforjove.com.au/news/2016/08/antigone-press-release.
Taylor, Diana. 2007. *The Archive and the Repertoire: Performing Cultural Memory in the Americas*. Durham: Duke University Press.
Teeter, Emily. 2011. *Religion and Ritual in Ancient Egypt*. Cambridge: Cambridge University Press.
Tiefenbrun, Susan W. 1999. "On Civil Disobedience, Jurisprudence, Feminism and the Law in the Antigones of Sophocles and Anouilh." *Cardozo Studies in Law and Literature* 11, 1: 35–51.
Venuti, Lawrence. 1986. "The Translator's Invisibility." *Criticism* 28, 2: 179–212.

Venuti, Lawrence. 1998. *The Scandals of Translation: Towards an Ethics of Difference*. London and New York: Routledge.

Voutsa, Theodora. 2016. "Antigone: press release." *International Theatre in English*. 4 January. Accessed 19 May 2020: https://internationaltheatreinenglish.com/2016/01/04/antigone-press-release/.

Walton, J. Michael. 2009. *Euripides Our Contemporary*. London: A & C Black.

Zarifi, Yanna. 2007. "Chorus and Dance in the Ancient World." In *The Cambridge Companion to Greek and Roman Theatre*, edited by Marianne McDonald and J. Michael Walton, 227–246. Cambridge: Cambridge University Press.

Zeitlin, Froma. 1996. *Playing the Other: Gender and Society in Classical Greek Literature*. Chicago: University of Chicago Press.

19 Redirecting Canonicity: PhD Exams and Actor Training

Eero Laine and Peter Zazzali

In order to consider "the canon," we must identify the sites of canon formation. Often understood in literary terms, the canon, that nebulous and haunting thing, is actively formed and reinforced throughout university pedagogy and professional practice. The urge to think of canonicity in literary terms might point us toward the usual sore spots of the content of dramatic literature courses or even the two to three course sequence of theatre history required in many US-based theatre and performance departments. However, these courses are largely symptomatic, recurring outgrowths, of the training programs that they inhabit. As these courses produce and reinscribe various ideas about canonicity, behind them and supporting them are the actor training programs that many undergraduate students are actually there to take part in, and the PhD training programs, exams in particular, that train those who most often teach the more literary, theoretical, and historical courses. These seemingly disparate sites—the PhD exam process and actor training—offer significant inflection points for shifting, redirecting, and maybe even eliminating the canon as it might currently be configured in US theatre and performance. Thus, we argue, in returning to what Alisa Solomon calls "the scene of the crime: the Western theatrical canon," (Solomon 1997: 3) that the scene of "the crime" is less a particular course or even set of courses and more a set of regularized practices that can be found in the everyday work of the actor studio and the assumptions of knowledge creation and retention found in most PhD comprehensive exams.

In considering actor training and PhD study as sites of canon formation and potential disruption, we invite the reader to envision more diverse and inclusive approaches to both pursuits. Unsettling the canon thus goes beyond updating reading lists on a theatre history course or changing up a season of performances. That is, we very consciously eschew arguments about making a better syllabus or planning a canon-reconfiguring season of work, precisely because such actions are retroactively applied and can only be seen as counters to the assumptions built into academic and artistic training programs. We open these considerations through a comparative reading of PhD exam processes in the US and by looking toward other potential models for actor training in the US. Here, we take seriously the invitation of this volume to create dialogue.

DOI: 10.4324/9781003031413-19

We put these two aspects of theatre and performance training in conversation through this article in order to reach across apparently (and frequently) separated wings of many departments. By pushing these two topics side by side, we have come to see the overlaps and possibilities for exchange in PhD exams and actor training. We hope that anyone thinking about "the canon" in the US will ask what PhD exams might learn from actor training and vice versa. We argue the canon and its insidious bias is manifested beyond the literary, in the acts of training that will shape the future of the field and the ways we understand it in relation to canonicity.

We come to this as the director of graduate study (Laine) and director of an acting program (Zazzali) on different sides of the planet and at different kinds of institutions: one a research university in a rust belt city in North America and the other a university of the arts in a major metropolis in Asia. We both have taught acting and doctoral courses and earned our PhDs at the City University of New York, the largest and most diverse urban university system in the world. Through our past and current work, we see a direct connection between PhD and actor training. As many know, PhD students often teach basic and introductory acting courses. It is a routine teaching assignment that Clare Syler calls "ubiquitous" and is facilitated through "Stanislavski's method" (Syler 2012: 115). Indeed, as Syler's research indicates: "thirty-six of the thirty-eight US universities that offer a doctoral degree in theatre, dance, or performance studies also offer an Introduction to Acting course with enrollment open to non-majors and sometimes majors," with these courses often fueling enrollment in the degrees offered in theatre and dance departments (Syler, 2012: 115). We build on Syler's reflective work of identifying the interconnectedness of PhD and actor training in no small part because of influence of such training on the field and the ways that canons are formed and considered.

In pointing to these sites as key aspects of canonicity in US theatre training, we actively look past other understandings of the canon and its mechanisms of formation. Christopher M. Kuipers, for example, suggests that *anthologies* are a central part of canonization (Kuipers 2003). We understand, of course, that questioning such assertions lends an ironic twist to our contribution to this volume. Similarly, Milenna Grass Kleiner, Mariana Hausdorf Andrade, and Nancy Nicholls suggest that "at the local level, theatre history is still strongly influenced by the circulation of the dramatic canon" (Kleiner et al. 2019: 79). That is, the texts that circulate widely have a regional influence. This emphasis on the *dramatic* canon is certainly due in no small part to the perceived permanence of the written word and its ability to influence many and across time.

Borrowing from Diana Taylor, our explication of canonicity recognizes the "repertory" on equal footing with the printed text—or archive. Here we argue for an embodied knowing that goes beyond anthologies and subscriptions. This work is already underway in theatre training programs and we see many possibilities for further change in the future. Meike Wagner notes a number of new programs, for example, in Germany that incorporate practical or artistic work:

Performance practice was considered to provide a basis for political agency, collective creativity, and political awareness in teaching and research […] The combination of theory and practice enables an expansion of the academic canon, an emphasis on participatory research and teaching and the elaboration of new visions for theatre (Wagner 2016: 8)

In sum, we contend the canon is not exclusive to literary works and includes PhD and actor training as highly influential sites, wherein we can shift our understanding of canonicity and how we engage our field.

On PhD Training

In the US, most courses of doctoral study require the successful completion of comprehensive or qualifying exams. These exams are often described in student handbook or degree requirements posted on departmental website and provide clear outlines of what faculty and students can expect in preparing and taking doctoral exams. The documents are largely descriptive but are at times aspirational as they indicate the possibilities and objectives for learning. Importantly for our work here, these explications of process guide the formation of a knowledge base for many PhD students who will move into the professoriate as well as a wide variety of arts and arts-adjacent professions, and we must consider the PhD exam as an important part of disciplinary formation and thus canonization. The material that PhD students are examined on becomes the basis of future syllabi and arts programming, and is the collective knowledge of what is considered specialist and general knowledge in the fields of theatre and performance studies.

The impact of these exams should not be downplayed when considering sites of canonization. While many of the volumes and textbooks that collect plays and narratives of theatre and performance history are often essential to the process of studying for exams, the exams themselves are part of a repertoire of work that grows and shifts organically as the field expands and contracts. Noe Montez has been conducting research into graduate outcomes for theatre and performance studies for a number of years (Montez 2018). These graduates are well placed as educators and leaders in the field and will thus have an outsized impact on the state of theatre and performance studies, and by extension, shape our understanding of the canon.

For instance, Montez's recent job data show that these graduates are spread across a growing number of performing arts occupations as literary managers, artistic directors, and in other roles in arts organizations. Even among these diverse career outcomes, nearly 65% of PhD graduates are teaching at institutions of higher learning (Montez 2020). This is not to conflate tenure track and contingent professors, even as all of these graduates are likely to regularly make curricular decisions for their classrooms and/or degree programs. Considered this way, some contingent professors may have a wider impact on what might be considered canonical in that they are most often called upon to teach a higher load of courses as well as more introductory and survey classes and are often assigned general education or appreciation courses. The material that is taught and, significantly, how it is taught will shape students approach to theatrical and performance material whether they go on to be theatre and performance professionals or they just regularly engage as an audience member. While many of those teaching courses will continue to develop their syllabi in light of new theatre and performance work, doctoral research and especially the exam process will weigh heavily on any professor's understanding of the field and its canon. PhD exams thus act as a sort of crude accumulation of knowledge of the field, a baseline of information that constitutes what is known and expected to be known—that is, what is canonical. That knowledge may be expanded upon or even undercut by future learning, but for better or worse, few who hold a PhD, we think, would dismiss the import and impact of the exam process on their work and thinking.

In a survey of available exam descriptions conducted by searching through handbooks, bulletins, and course descriptions posted on university websites, we were able to discern a number of patterns related to PhD exams; notably, that they function to organize knowledge, have pedagogical goals, and depend on scholarly sociality. While there are differences among PhD programs and even proposed content of the exams, many of the exams are quite similar in the intended outcomes and their methodologies. This is in many ways noteworthy because the exam structures span different types of institutions that offer a doctoral degree in theatre and/or performance studies, from public to private to the Ivy League.

The exams themselves vary in structure and length, but most require students to work from some sort of list of books or authors or ideas that must then be written about or otherwise identified. The people, plays, movements, historical events, and theories of theatre and performance that make up the exam lists are thus deemed important enough to be studied and examined by the PhD students and their advisors. Over half of the programs refer to a "reading list" or "reading lists" in their descriptions of the exam process. And some programs mention other forms of lists. Columbia University, for instance, references "orals lists," which are written lists evaluated through an oral examination process. Exam lists are used for both general or comprehensive exams, often covering a large swath of theatre and performance history and theory, as well as area-specific exams that are intended to form core areas of expertise for the dissertation. The act of list making might resemble some of the canonizing efforts of anthologization, but it is noteworthy that only ten of the programs' exam descriptions use the word "plays" in describing what should be included in preparing for exams. Other programs certainly include dramatic texts in those lists and on exams, even as they are referred to more broadly as "materials" or "sources" or are parts of a bibliography. Even if driven individually by a student, the act of list-making serves a canonizing function and encourages us to think of it as such. Considering their potential impact on the field, another study might actually compare the content of exam lists or questions across institutions and generations of PhD students. (We hope a reader will be in touch if that sounds like a project they might want to undertake together.)

In addition to their impact on a student's research, PhD exams, are foundational moments that will have implications for what a graduate will be qualified and able to teach. A number of programs claim outright that the purpose of the exams is to develop a knowledge base for teaching. Bowling Green State University, for instance, requires "a pedagogical position paper" that "is a personal statement of teaching philosophy" as part of the larger exam portfolio. Ohio University, similarly, requires a professional portfolio of syllabi, a teaching portfolio, and other materials. The University of Georgia requires a portfolio related to teaching that "will demonstrate the student's readiness to teach undergraduate courses." The description of the area exams at the Graduate Center of the City University of New York states that "the presumption is that the student should be prepared to teach an upper-level undergraduate course in any of these fields." Columbia University encourages students to "conceive of each field as a possible teaching field, reflecting areas in which they expect to teach, and representing the range of a student's potential teaching interests." Northwestern University similarly requests that "examination fields be made specifically relevant to the scope of dissertation research and the student's intended teaching fields." Tufts suggests that one of the exams "may be of use in preparing for a class that the student might like to teach in the future." At the University of California, Santa Barbara, a stated goal of the oral exam is "to reassure the committee members that the student is prepared to teach at undergraduate and graduate levels in both general and specific areas." Similarly, at the University of Kansas, one of the stated exam goals is to prove "competence for teaching in particular subject areas." At the University of Oregon, material should be included on the exam that is of use to "future teaching." Such exercises should push students to consider the impact of the exams on the field and future students. How does this work uphold or dismantle the canon?

Highlighting the ways that exam lists will be leveraged makes us consider their canonizing effects and even to question how and if the canon might be undone through such exam processes, especially if we consider PhD exams as examining the future of the field, the future canon. That is, PhD exams examine what will be canonical and thus are essential sites for shaping, guiding, and revising what is or what is not part of accepted and understood as the canon as well as our approach to it. The work of developing lists, studying, and successfully passing examinations is work of field building and field defining, especially as such work is so often oriented toward future classrooms and curricula.

This work does not happen entirely individually, but is enmeshed in a social framework that is itself the effect of previous exams and other acts of canon formation. The ways that exams are conducted will influence the ways that the material is absorbed and disseminated. This occurs formally, through rules and guidelines, but the culture of the PhD program will also shape the ways a PhD exam is administered and assessed, and it matters who is part of this culture of the program. From our own experience in studying for exams in the early part of the 2000s at The Graduate Center of the City University of New York, there are also many informal mechanisms for preparation, from peer-to-peer mentoring, mock exams with fellow students, and piles of study materials from past exam responses to dogeared textbooks along with websites and PowerPoints and PDFs. A number of programs build such recommendations into the official exam descriptions. Arizona State University's Theatre of Youth PhD encourages a number of "study strategies" that include using time between semesters to "read plays, critical theories, and to review area-specific material" while taking notes and arranging "study sessions with peers" and writing "practice essays linking playtexts to cultural and theatrical contexts, and to contemporary critical theories, generally and within area of specialization." New York University, Steinhardt encourages students to develop "A student support group" made up "of no more than three or four trusted critical friends who will provide thorough and regular feedback on the students' work before it is shared with the mentor." The handbook clarifies that the student support group is made up of "friends [who] could be other doctoral students or even outside reviewers who you feel can contribute to the quality of your study," emphasizing that "the sooner you have a student support group the better." Indeed, this is advice we might all do well to follow.

All of these study strategies, both formally proposed and informally enacted, encourage a certain approach to thinking through material. The work of studying for PhD exams is *social*, it is embedded in traditions of practice that pass from one cohort to the next, and guided by faculty who bring their own expectations of exams and what is important enough to be examined. Even as each list might be unique to each student or project, the methods of engaging that material is steeped in tradition and influenced by those who uphold such traditions. Indeed, the sociality of exams should underscore the need for diverse and inclusive faculty and graduate student cohorts. It is clear from many of the exam descriptions that the content will be refined with each iteration of the exam, which means, perhaps obviously, that individually and collectively the examiners and students are in a position to actively shape what is considered canonical.

The content of the exams will very likely be taught to generations of theatre and performance students by those who graduate with a PhD and end up teaching in the academy (both on and off the tenure track). Far beyond canon formation as the development of lists and anthologies and syllabi, PhD exams in theatre and performance demonstrate the sociality of canonicity and the importance of who is involved in exam making and exam taking. That is, much depends on the people that support the exams, from teachers in courses to peer networks, and there is a strong and necessary case to be made not only for the diversification of the canon itself but of those in the field and its expected and shared expertise. It matters who is advising exams, just as it matters who your peers are when you take exams. The PhD exam process is necessarily a vital site for rethinking not only the theatre and performance canon, but also the ways that the canon can be reimagined.

On Actor Training[1]

Similar to PhD programs, studies in acting at US universities also are central points of canon formation and potential disruption. This practice is most evident in the reliance on Stanislavki's system. Rebecca Guy, the venerable acting teacher at the Juilliard School, equates his legacy to actor training with Freud's to psychology in stating: "Stanislavski is to actors what Freud is to psychiatry—you really cannot get away from either" (Guy 2014). There are more than 150 BFA/MFA conservatory-styled programs in the US, nearly all of which are somehow grounded in Stanislavski's system (Zazzali 2016: 9–10). Offshoots ranging from Hagen to Meisner are deployed to create characters in his text-driven process for the purpose of having careers on stage or in film/tv. American actor training has been defaulting to Stanislavki since his arrival stateside in 1923, thereby prompting a canonical understanding of acting as well as theatre and the field itself. If most actors are trained in such a particular system, their understanding of what performance is and can do will necessarily be restricted. There are, after all, numerous traditions and epistemologies across the pantheon of actor training. Why, we ask, has the US been comparably reliant on just one of them?

Some trainers are denying the default to Stanislavski-based learning, however, as demonstrated in Sharrell D. Luckett and Tia M. Shaffer's edited volume, *Black Acting Methods: Critical Approaches*. An anthology of contributions from predominantly US-based teachers and practitioners, it offers insights and interventions that disrupt formulaic—canonical—approaches to training. Justin Emeka and Tawnya Pettifor-Wates's respective essays, for example, challenge decidedly "white" ways to perform Shakespeare. Emeka offers a firsthand account of three case studies of working on plays from the Western canon: *Our Town*; *King Lear*; and *A Midsummer Night's Dream*. In doing so, she appropriately debunks "color blind casting" as reductive and shortsighted and instead argues that each actor's racial and cultural identity must be embraced:

> At some point, most students of the acting craft will confront Shakespeare's canon. Each actor in addition to mastering the text will rely on the wisdom of their own experience and imagination to create these roles. Konstantin Stanislavski considered the "embodiment of the role" an essential part of the actor's process [...] For the artist of color, this can pose a unique challenge if there is not a clear discussion or agreement as to the significance of race and culture in the construction of character within the production (Emeka 2017: 89).

Pettiford-Wates also rethinks classical acting from an "Afrocentric" perspective by which the actor identifies their "own creative potency, content, and power" (107). Like Emeka, she too relies on her professional background by expressing her racial and cultural identity towards fostering her artistic voice (and those of her students), attributes that are overlooked in canonical systems for training actors: The traditions of Stanislavski, Chekhov [Michael], and Grotowski may have prepared my physical instrument in pursuit of a professional acting career, but they did not nurture my spirit nor feed my soul (Pettiford-Wates 2017: 107). Both Pettiford-Wates and Emeka's cases can be put in conversation with the important contributions comprising a special issue of *Theatre, Dance and Performance Training* (Evans et al. 2020) that challenges Western pedagogies while centering marginalized approaches. For instance, writers such as Kristine Landon-Smith and Daron Oram address issues of race and identity in the training space toward decolonizing the curriculum. Their arguments for "pluralistic" and "equitable" models elide with the work that Kyle Haden and his colleagues are currently doing at Carnegie Mellon University's Acting Program (Oram 2020). The oldest such department in the United States, it has responded to student concerns in the aftermath of the George Floyd murder by significantly changing its curriculum to empower students of color. In particular, Haden has reimagined what was once a Period Styles module into an offer that centers Black, Brown and non-western nationalities by exploring and playing roles akin to their identity (Oram 2020).

Entitled "The Culture Class," the course jettisons mainstays like Chekhov and Moliere in favor of Suzan-Lori Parks and Dominique Morisseau. Yet this move transcends the literary to include social and ontological considerations of the actor's craft. How one expresses oneself physically, emotionally, cerebrally and otherwise in "the world" of a Parks play is decidedly different from *The Seagull* or *Tartuffe*. The "period" element of the course remains through a unit on Greek tragedy, wherein mythical themes are realized in present-day settings. Haden has effectively contemporized a class that for 20-plus years had generated learning outcomes consistent with a bygone professional model: the repertory theatre actor. In many ways his reboot of a "classical" approach offers students of all identities greater currency in today's industry, insofar as actors are expected to have a keen sense of their own identity and personal experience, an outcome that has frequently been denied students of color for decades. Thus, jointly reimagining and replacing "traditional" texts and methods invites a more diverse and inclusive training experience that disrupts canonistic praxis.

We are inclined to point out a certain irony in how Stanislavski's model has inadvertently flattened racial and cultural identities. Stanislavski built his system in response to the melodramatic performance tradition of the 19th century in addressing the emergence of dramatic realism—it was a radical (noncanonical) approach for its time. Plays of the likes of Ibsen and Chekhov required a more psychophysical and "truthful" representation of a character to suspend the audience's disbelief and share in the actor's immersion with a role. To be effective in doing so, as the Stanislavskian acting teacher Uta Hagen suggests, one must "first learn who [they] are to 'identify' with their character" (Hagen 1973: 22). In some respects, this approach is similar to what Haden has been developing at Carnegie. He too is guiding actors to locate points of entry to a character by bringing themselves to a role. The distinction comes with making available material that allows students from underrepresented backgrounds the opportunity to play people with whom "they can relate" (Oram 2020), thereby disrupting the canonicity of the acting studio and reimagining it as a site of social justice. Donna B. Aaronson laid this point bare over a decade ago in her chapter "Changing Demographics" for the edited volume *The Politics of American Actor Training* wherein she states: "As student populations become more diverse, the expectation for programs shifts. Theatre departments must address casting and production assignment policies to ensure inclusion" (2012: 95). Stanislavksi himself was a proponent of diversity insofar as he recognized the "subtle, complex, and multifaceted" essence of "human life" and the actor's responsibility therefore to bring "who they are" to the roles they play (Carnicke: 14). Thus, the texts and characters our students explore should represent the diverse range of identities constituting a given cohort. If one is teaching a group of Asian actors, which is exactly Zazzali's experience at present, instead of applying Stanislavski's techniques to *The Cherry Orchard*, a common practice among acting teachers, one might consider an adaption such as *A Winter People*, a reworked version by Chay Yew locating Chekhov's play in China during the final days of the nationalist government in 1935.

Stanisalvski's training has been serving American actors for the past two centuries, given its applicability to different genres and mediums. His system is as applicable to realistic and poetic texts rendered onstage as it is for screenplays and TV dramas. Like other examples of canon formation, time and tradition have lent it symbolic value and corresponding credibility. Yet as is the case with other examples of the canon, whether literary or practiced-based, conventionality justified by history and a revolving door of Eurocentric cognoscenti marginalizes the voices and identities of underrepresented races and cultures.

To borrow from Pierre Bourdieu, the canon can be seen as an act of symbolic violence. Bourdieu describes this practice as symbolic power, describing it as a tacit understanding—"a shared belief"—within a community that forms hegemonic structures resulting in the subjectification of some and objectification of others. Trafficking in "misrecognition" and subterfuge, symbolic violence appears innocuous. Indeed, Bourdieu arrived at this theory when studying the ritual of gift giving on the part of colonialists to the tribal leaders of indigenous groups they sought to coerce. The gift forms an inherent indebtedness on the part of the recipient, thereby emboldening the colonialist's dominance through a veneer of generosity (Bourdieu 1982: 23–25). The canon works in similar ways. To be admitted into a training program—acting or PhD—and have proven professionals offer their expertise is perceived as a gift of sorts. Perhaps this understanding is most evident in the "guru" treatment of "master teachers" over the years. From Stanislavski offshoots like Strasberg and Meisner to voice instructors ranging from Linklater to Fitzmaurice, those amassing symbolic credibility prevail at the expense of newer, more inclusive and diverse schools of teaching and learning. In fact, a number of the aforementioned instructors now have accreditations in their instruction, a "designation" that is obtained only after years of study with said guru (or an acolyte), a privilege that often comes at a significant financial cost, another systemic criterion "legitimizing" the canon. The implication being that if one does not go through the designation program, they are not licensed to include the guru's approach in their teaching. While this may seem reasonable in that the guru aims to protect the integrity of their system and its application, in truth such programs reduce the ways in which we could explore, develop, and expand pedagogies. If learning is to be progressive and inclusive, if it is to address what Paulo Freire terms a "pedagogy of the oppressed," we must challenge extant ways of knowing, resist defaulting to tradition, and decipher the ramifications of canonicity (Freire 2018).

Today's actors and PhD students face a moment in history that requires progressive thinking, diverse training, and forward-looking pedagogies. To the extent they are taught to rely on the canon, they are being shortchanged on both intellectual and experiential planes. While a modicum of tradition and what has worked in the past can be useful, educating those who will in turn educate future generations of theatre practitioners and scholars necessitates rethinking our teaching methods and how we define a successful career in our respective subfields. Conventional perspectives of the job market for actors and PhDs have played a determinative role in how we gauge accomplishments, which is yet another example of the canon's reductive reach. A doctorate in theatre or performance studies, for example, is not exclusively validated by landing a tenure-track professorship. Indeed, as Elizabeth Segrin reports in her article for *The Atlantic*, those with a doctorate in the humanities are flourishing in "media, corporate America, non-profits, and government"; they are "all around us," she claims, "and they are not serving coffee" (Segran 2014: 21). A similar paradigm applies to actors who create careers for themselves outside the industry—film/tv/stage—and rely on skills from their training to transcend the canonical. They are problem-solvers, expressive communicators, critical thinkers, content creators, and team players. This range of aptitudes is developed through a diverse and inclusive pedagogy, such as that which is demonstrated at Carnegie Mellon's Acting Program.

Transcending the Canon in PhD and Actor Training: A Path Forward

This investigation has been directed towards pedagogical practices, which might thereby transcend a strictly text-based understanding of the canon. Both

PhD exams and actor training should be thought of as important inflection points to reconsider the theatrical canon. Together, they represent high stakes sites of training that make clear the possibilities and dangers of canonicity and the ways in which the canon might be redirected and reshaped. Whereas actors develop skills for "success" in the entertainment industry, doctoral students will teach many of the classes at universities where theatre students train. Actor training and PhD study hold the possibility to ingrain canonical ways of thinking or disrupt and transcend them. As Haden and his Carnegie Mellon colleagues demonstrate, rethinking curricula towards greater diversity and inclusion empowers students of all racial and cultural backgrounds. They offer a hopeful example of a progressive and forward-facing approach that locates time-honored practices such as Stanislavski in the context of a daring and affirmative pedagogy. Similarly, PhD training can be reimagined through changing the contents, structure, and format of exams. We might offer our graduate students greater flexibility in how courses are organized and delivered as well as reconsider how we identify learning outcomes and perceptions of a successful career. Theatre and Performance PhDs have shifted from academe to become arts managers, artistic directors, arts practitioners, among other distinct—if related—métiers. It is increasingly easy to make parallels between the precarity of PhD study and that of a professionally trained actor. To think narrowly of the possibilities for each form of training is as canonical as the pedagogy giving rise to it.

As trainers of actors and PhD students, we can only change our approach to the extent we let go of some of that which we have taught and been taught in the past. Here we must take tradition as a source of contextual precedence from which we can inspire growth in ourselves and students alike. Especially in areas with such high stakes for the future of theatre and performance as actor and PhD training, we need to challenge ourselves to meet the current moment with a commitment to diverse and inclusive learning praxis. At the risk of cliché, we have returned to Solomon's "scene of the crime," (1997) the canon, wherein we have the choice to either reinscribe decades of wrongdoing or forge a path forward.

Note

1 Zazzali was educated in a Western tradition and in recognition of the limitations therein chose to accept his current role as the director of an acting program in Asia, where he is part of a multinational faculty delivering cross-cultural techniques to a racially diverse group of students. In doing so, he has redesigned the curriculum to reflect a Singaporean identity through significant programmatic and hiring changes, moves that are dialectically positioned to his identity as a white Westerner.

Works Cited

Aaronson, Donna B. 2010. "Changing Demographics: Where Is Diversity in Theatre Programs in Higher Education and National Associations?" In *The Politics of American*

Actor Training, edited by Ellen Margolis and Lissa Tyler Renaud, 94–102. New York: Routledge.

American Society for Theatre Research, "Doctoral Program Directory." https://www.astr.org/general/custom.asp?page=doctoral_programs. Accessed October 15, 2020.

Arizona State University. 2019. "Theatre for Youth and Community Ph.D. Handbook." https://filmdancetheatre.asu.edu/sites/default/files/phd-handbook-2019.pdf. Accessed October 15, 2020.

Bial, Henry and Scott Magelssen. 2010. *Theatre Historiography: Critical Interventions*. Ann Arbor, MI: University of Michigan Press.

Bowling Green State University. Ph.D. in Theatre. https://www.bgsu.edu/arts-and-sciences/theatre-and-film/graduate-program/phd-theatre.html. Accessed October 15, 2020.

Bourdieu, Pierre. 1982. *Language and Symbolic Power*. Translated by John B. Thompson. Cambridge, MA: Harvard University. Press.

Bourdieu, Pierre. 1993. *The Field of Cultural Production: Essays on Art and Literature*. Translated by Randal Johnson. New York: Columbia University Press.

Brown University. 2019. "Theatre Arts and Performance Studies Doctoral Program Handbook." https://www.brown.edu/academics/theatre-arts-performance-studies/sites/brown.edu.academics.theatre-arts-performance-studies/files/uploads/Doctoral%20Program%20Handbook_8-13-19.pdf. Accessed October 15, 2020.

Carnicke, Sharon Marie. 2000. "Stanislavski's System: Pathways for the Actor." In *Twentieth Century Actor Training*, edited by Alison Hodge, 11–36. London: Routledge.

City University of New York, Graduate Center. "Program Handbook." https://gc.cuny.edu/Page-Elements/Academics-Research-Centers-Initiatives/Doctoral-Programs/Theatre-and-Performance/About-the-Program/Program-Handbook. Accessed October 15, 2020.

Columbia University. "Degrees, Requirements, Funding." https://theatre-phd.columbia.edu/degree-requirements/. Accessed October15, 2020.

Emeka, Justin. 2017. "Seeing Shakespeare through Brown Eyes." In *Black Acting Methods: A Critical Perspective*, edited by Sharrell D. Luckett and Tia M. Shaffer, 89–105. New York: Routledge 2017.

Evans, Mark, Cass Fleming and Sara Reed et al. 2020. *Theatre, Dance and Performance Training* 11, 3: 245–410.

Florida State University. "School of Theatre Graduate Student Handbook." https://theatre.fsu.edu/wp-content/uploads/sites/12/2015/10/School-of-Theatre-Graduate-Handbook-1.pdf. Accessed October 15, 2020.

Freire, Paulo. 2018. *Pedagogy of the Oppressed*. Translated by Myra Bergmann Ramos. New York: Bloomsbury.

Guy, Rebecca. 2014. Interview with Peter Zazzali. New York, 24 April.

Hagen, Uta. 1973. *Respect for Acting*. New York: Macmillan.

Kleiner, Milenna Grass, Mariana Hausdorf Andrade, and Nancy Nicholls. 2019. "Theatre History versus Theatre Canon: The Chilean Case." In *The Methuen Drama Handbook of Theatre History and Theatre Historiography*, edited by Claire Cochrane and Jo Robinson, 79–89. London: Bloomsbury.

Kuipers, Christopher M. 2003. "The Anthology/Corpus Dynamic: A Field Theory of the Canon." In *College Literature* 30, 2: 51–71.

Landon-Smith. 2020. "A Pedagogy for Twenty-first Century Actor Training: Intracultural Theatre Practice which Embraces Pluralistic Identity and Plays with Difference." In *Theatre, Dance and Performance Training* 11, 3: 343–350.

Louisiana State University. PhD in Theatre. https://www.lsu.edu/cmda/theatre/admissions/graduate/phd.php. Accessed October 15, 2020.

Louisiana State University. "Department of Communication Studies, Louisiana State University graduate Student Handbook." https://www.lsu.edu/hss/cmst/graduate/graduate_handbook.pdf. Accessed October 15, 2020.

Montez, Noe. 2018. "Strengthening Job Prospects Within and Beyond the AcademyA State of the Field Address for the Fourth Symposium of Doctoral Programs in Theatre and Performance Studies." *HowlRound*, October 7. Accessed May 15, 2020. https://howlround.com/strengthening-job-prospects-within-and-beyond-academy.

Motez, Noe. 2020. Tweet. @noemontez, May 4. Accessed May 15, 2020. https://twitter.com/noemontez/status/1257427061645488128.

New York University–Tisch School of the Arts. "Doctor of Philosophy in Performance Studies." https://gsas.nyu.edu/content/nyu-as/gsas/academics/bulletin/performance-studies/phd-performance-studies.html. Accessed October 15, 2020.

New York University–Steinhardt School of Culture, Education, and Human Development. 2018. "PhD Candidacy Examination in Educational Theatre and Time to Completion." https://research.steinhardt.nyu.edu/scmsAdmin/media/users/cl1097/Educational_Theatre_PhD_Candidacy_Exam_-_2018_Update.pdf. Accessed October 15, 2020.

Northwestern University. 2019 –20. "Department of Performance Studies, Northwestern University Graduate Student Handbook." https://www.communication.northwestern.edu/sites/default/files/phd_pst/graduate-handbook.pdf. Accessed October 15, 2020.

Northwestern University. 2017. "Interdisciplinary PhD in Theatre & Drama (IPTD) Handbook for Students and Advisors." https://communication.northwestern.edu/sites/default/files/iptd/IPTD-Handbook.pdf. Accessed October 15, 2020.

Ohio State University. 2019. "Department of theatre Graduate Handbook." https://theatre.osu.edu/sites/theatre.osu.edu/files/2019–2020%20Dept%20of%20Theatre%20Graduate%20Handbook.pdf. Accessed October 15, 2020.

Ohio University. 2019–2020. "School of Interdisciplinary Arts Graduate Student Handbook 2019–2020." https://www.ohio.edu/fine-arts/sites/ohio.edu.fine-arts/files/sites/fine-arts/interdisciplinary-arts/files/IART-graduate-handbook-2019–2020.pdf. Accessed October 15, 2020.

Oram, Daron. 2020. "The Heuristic Pedagogue: Navigating Myths and Truths of an Equitable Approach to Voice Training. In *Theatre, Dance and Performance Training* 11, 3: 300–309.

Pettiford-Wates, Tawnya. 2017. "Ritual Poetic Drama within the African Continuum." In *Black Acting Methods: A Critical Perspective*, edited by Sharrell D. Luckett and Tia M. Shaffer. New York: Routledge.

Rutgers University. "Graduate Program Ph.D. Qualifying Examination." https://english.rutgers.edu/academics/graduate-92/programstructure/qualifyingexam.html. Accessed October 15, 2020.

Segran, Elizabeth. 2014. "What Can You Do With a Humanities PhD Anyway?" *The Atlantic*, 21 March. Accessed 11May2020. https://www.theatlantic.com/business/archive/2014/03/what-can-you-do-with-a-humanities-phd-anyway/359927

Solomon, Alisa. 1997. *Re-Dressing the Canon: Essays on Theatre and Gender*. London: Routledge.

Stanford University. Doctor of Philosophy in Drama. https://web.stanford.edu/dept/registrar/bulletin1112/7141.htm. Accessed October 15, 2020.

Stanislavski, Konstantin. 2008. *An Actor's Work*. Translated by Jean Benedetti. London: Routledge.

Syler, Claire. 2012. "Personal Narratives: A Course Design for Introduction to Theatre." In *Theatre Topics* 22, 2: 171–181.

Taylor, Diana. 2003. *The Archive and the Repertoire: Performing Cultural Memory in the Americas*. Durham, NC: Duke University Press.

Tufts University. "MA/PhD in Theatre and Performance Studies Graduate Student Handbook." https://dramadance.tufts.edu/documents/gradHandbook.pdf. Accessed October 15, 2020.

University at Buffalo, State University of New York. PhD/MA Theatre Performance Handbook.

University of California, Berkeley. "PhD Program of Study." https://tdps.berkeley.edu/grad/program#qualifying-exam. Accessed October 15, 2020.

University of California, Davis. "University of California, Davis, Graduate Group in Performance Studies Student Handbook." https://arts.ucdavis.edu/sites/main/files/file-attachments/pfsstudenthandbook.pdf?1593015502. Accessed October 15, 2020.

University of California, Irvine. "Comprehensive Examinations." https://drama.arts.uci.edu/graduate-programs/phd/comprehensive-examinations. Accessed October 15, 2020

University of California, Los Angeles. "Graduate Program: Theater and Performance Studies." https://grad.ucla.edu/programs/school-of-theater-film-and-television/theater-department/theater-and-performance-studies/. Accessed October 15, 2020

University of California, San Diego. "Theatre and Dance." https://ucsd.edu/catalog/curric/THEA-gr.html. Accessed October 15, 2020

University of California, Santa Barbara. "Program and Degree Requirements." https://www.theaterdance.ucsb.edu/academics/graduate/degrees. Accessed October 15, 2020.

University of Chicago. "PhD Degree Requirements." https://arts.uchicago.edu/theater-and-performance-studies/graduate-program/phd-program/phd-degree-requirements. Accessed October 15, 2020

University of Colorado Boulder. 2019–2020. "PhD in Theatre Student Handbook." https://www.colorado.edu/theatredance/sites/default/files/attached-files/thtr_phd_handbook_19-20.pdf. Accessed October 15, 2020

University of Georgia. 2019. Department of Theatre and Film Studies Handbook" 39th Edition. https://drama.uga.edu/sites/default/files/inline-files/TheatreFilmStudiesHandbook%20Spring%202019%20Edition.pdf. Accessed October 15, 2020

University of Hawaiʻi at Mānoa. "Doctoral Comp Exams Western Area Description." http://manoa.hawaii.edu/liveonstage/theatre/graduate-admissions/graduate-resources/phd-theatre/. Accessed October 15, 2020

University of Illinois at Urban Champagne. "PhD Theatre Studies." https://theatre.illinois.edu/phd-theatre-studies/. Accessed October 15, 2020.

University of Kansas. "PhD Degree Requirements." http://catalog.dept.ku.edu/201112/6724.html. Accessed October15, 2020.

University of Maryland. "Handbook PhD in Theatre and Performance Studies." https://arhuserv.umd.edu/sites/default/files/2019-11/PHD%20Handbook-UPDATED%2009-27-2019.pdf. Accessed October 15, 2020

University of Minnesota. PhD Requirements. Accessed May 10, 2019.

University of Missouri. "PhD Requirements." http://catalog.missouri.edu/undergraduategraduate/collegeofartsandscience/theatre/phd-theatre/. Accessed October 15, 2020.

University of Oregon. 2018. "Graduate Student Handbook, Department of Theatre Arts." https://cpb-us-e1.wpmucdn.com/blogs.uoregon.edu/dist/7/9559/files/2010/04/GradHandbook-1k2vsd7.pdf. Accessed October 15, 2020.

University of Pittsburgh. 2016–2017. 'Department of Theatre Arts Graduate Student Handbook." https://www.play.pitt.edu/sites/default/files/2016–2017_Grad_Handbook_3.pdf. Accessed October 15, 2020.

University of Texas at Austin. 2017. "Ph.D. in Performance as Public Practice Curriculum Guide." https://theatredance.utexas.edu/sites/files/tad/program_guide_for_phd_ppp.pdf. Accessed October 15, 2020.

University of Washington. 2018. "Academic Policy Memo 6." https://drama.washington.edu/academic-policy-memo-6. Accessed October15, 2020.

University of Wisconsin, Madison. Interdisciplinary Theatre Studies. "About." https://dept.english.wisc.edu/intertheatrestudies/programs/phdstudy/. Accessed October 15, 2020.

Wagner, Meike. 2016. "Expanding the Canon, Creating Alternative Knowledge, Marketing the Field?: Performance Practices in Theatre Studies." *Nordic Theatre Studies* 28, 1: 4–14.

Zazzali, Peter. 2016. *Acting in the Academy: The History of Professional Actor Training in US Higher Education*. New York: Routledge.

20 We Aren't Here to Teach What We Already Know

Jessica Brater and Michelle Liu Carriger

Mechanical Canon

In the long after- (or current-) math of the "Culture Wars" and "identity politics" we have become accustomed to thinking of "The Canon" (when capitalized in this essay, we refer to "The Western Canon" or "The Theatrical Canon" as an idea that has historically contained specific European works) as a moral or political problem. The very notion of a curated, gate-kept collection vetted as The Good Stuff, The Stuff Worth Knowing, activates two strongly binarized tracks of thought that may not be reconcilable. On the one hand, a shared Canon might be considered a prerequisite foundation to a unified society (arguably A Good Thing), on the other hand the process of selection and the scope of the works that have been honored by inclusion has been amply and indisputably revealed to be necessarily in collusion with historical oppressions and privileges. Most arguments about the value of the Canon, however, depend ultimately on groups' and individuals' fairly intractable political and moral persuasions, even if a vast grey area opens up between the poles of "Western Civilization" and its radical critique. In this central morass is where we might locate the ameliorative measures that have been attempted over the years for bringing the poles of Western tradition and progressive change together, such as an "additive" canon which would admit additional texts from beyond the centers of western culture to fill out the picture, or alternative or additional canons to supplement the "original" Canon.

While the Canon indubitably comprises a rich topic for political and ethical discussion, in this essay we would like to consider how our inherited Canon works as a *mechanical problem* instead. The very notion of a canon contains the seeds of its own self-replication and preservation: the works of the canon are central to our shared culture and therefore important to know, but knowing and teaching them causes them to be endlessly recentered as What-Is-Worth-Knowing: that is, canons work like machines for knowledge conservation and dissemination. Generations of scholars, teachers, and students learn canonical works as the standards for "good" art and literature, thus imbuing the standards of those that have gone on before as the benchmark for new works that appear. However, we cannot solve this problem by simply abolishing standards:

DOI: 10.4324/9781003031413-20

the solution to the exclusivity of canon aesthetics is certainly not to say that bad works are just as good as good ones, but to recognize the mechanism of canonicity that endlessly recenters what already is (i.e., that *conserves* its aesthetics, contents, and art forms) at the potential expense, and only incremental acceptance, of the works and artists who function outside that dynamic. Arguably, such a dynamic poses an obstacle to artistic and political innovation and difference of all kinds, but in the US's and larger Anglophone world's contemporary climate of race, ethnicity, gender, and sexuality-based collective activism, the specific ways in which the white, male, straight majoritarian Canon has failed to recognize authors and artworks from minoritarian backgrounds are particularly charged concerns. Another way to say this might be that the mechanics of canonicity may not themselves be politically inflected, but the effect of the mechanical Canon of US and Anglophone theater and drama *is* politically significant.

So how might we be able to establish a more equitable approach to canonicity if we consider the Canon as an expression of the physical limitations of knowledge and academic curriculum: the number of weeks available for a course, the amount of knowledge students can absorb, the limits on the expertise an individual instructor has or can acquire in advance of teaching? Could reexamining the Canon as a mechanical issue allow us to envision new relations within the necessary work of judging and collecting the great artworks of a society by putting aside the activity of parsing moral attitudes and personal convictions and looking at canon formation as a problem of space, time, and expertise?

A (the) canon is less an actual thing—a discrete body of approved texts—and more a mode of thinking, a widespread, agreed-upon, repeated, performative action of designating value. Perhaps this is why at some point the notion of "expanding" the Canon to include more people became more suspect than destroying canons: the mechanics of "expanding" center whiteness as the standard authority in selectively accessioning all cultural outputs into a collective culture, on an unspoken basis of palatability to the dominant norm. The additive "expanded" Canon is a seductive idea: we don't have to give anything up, we don't have to change our overall notion of what is good, of what a true contribution to society or art consists of, and we don't have to displace or demote anything that already exists at the center of this designation. The center never moves but instead is perhaps even buoyed up by everything new appearing ancillary as a sidebar, a one-day unit, an offhand anecdote.

For example, Suzan-Lori Parks points out in her short essay "Elements of Style" how classical Aristotelian dramatic structures have dictated that a "good" play must have forward momentum through a beginning, middle, and end, while Parks' own dramaturgy, fostered by her minoritarian cultural experience, tends toward cyclical "repetition and revision," instead of the straight bolt of Aristotelian tragedy. That is, subjective aesthetic standards are themselves culturally bounded and have invisibly helped to define which works conform sufficiently to majoritarian forms to be recognized as worthy of canonical status. Parks herself has become part of the American dramatic canon anyway, as a Pulitzer Prize winner, and yet there are canons and canons: while Parks most definitely has a place in one, the works of Suzan-Lori Parks remain marginal to the *Oedipus Rexes* and Shakespeare plays of the average college theatre class.

While one way of thinking about canons is to note their exclusivity and gatekeeping tendencies, which have been oppressively applied over generations, we must also recognize that a canon is a document of a society and culture, and it's pragmatic to know and understand a society, even (or especially) if it's as a prerequisite to changing it. Cultures have been exclusionary, yes, but the alternative to the exclusivity of community is [arguably] not to do away with community and culture altogether, just as the "solution" to the politically inflected exclusions wrought by canonical mechanisms cannot be to just include everything (as we have pointed out, no college class, or indeed human, is capable of encompassing *everything*). In what ways, then, can we (must we) deal with canonicity not as an unfortunate, exclusionary imposition, but as fundamental to how cultures and communities are formed and maintained? That is to say, in what ways might we look at the Canon as an expression not only of the historically contingent dominant culture we have inherited, but also as an expression of the material limits of time, brain-space, and curricula, and one that is actually open to revision, adaptation, and change? And *if* we pivot to think of the Canon thus as a material limit, does it change our relationship to what it encompasses and how we imagine ourselves reflected in it? Would removing the ethical or moral valences from our examination of canon formation and thinking more specifically of the finitude of our capacity enable us to approach the project from a new and potentially more energizing angle?

To be clear then, the challenge before us is not to disregard the political and activist aspects of how we work with the Canon, but to recognize that canonicity is inherent in pedagogy and epistemology. By making the limits and mechanics of canons (which are perhaps also the limits and barriers of teaching and knowledge) visible and palpable, making the "container" part of the lesson along with the "contents," we hope to open new avenues of navigating canonicity and our inherited canons. In the remainder of this essay, we describe one pragmatic way in which we attempt to approach the mechanics of canonicity with a mechanical intervention of our own while addressing some of the individual constituent challenges of canonicity along the way, through the design of a syllabus and lesson plan database which has grown out of a three-year working group engagement around issues of pedagogy and theatre history curricula.

Concrete Work on Mechanical Problems

We entered into our own engagement with (maybe) canon formation in the course of organizing a theatre pedagogy working group for the 2017 ASTR

(American Society for Theatre Research) conference, which continued for three years, and which we are now transitioning to an online database. Seeking to provide meaningful support for instructors, rather than merely a repository for play titles, the database will provide teaching tools and content to help enable more faculty at every level of academia to teach more topics effectively—to rewrite, decenter, or disassemble their canons via material or mechanical intervention. Our idea here is to meet the individual mechanical challenges of finite time, training, and expertise with collective knowledge, experience, and practical approaches. The working group and database may thus offer tools with philosophical and political ramifications to instructors, but do not themselves impose new approaches or ideas about canons on individuals.

In the spring of 2017 we generated a call for papers for the first iteration of our Pedagogy of Extraordinary Bodies working group. Still reeling from the 2016 presidential election, we noted that

> at a moment when democratic and diverse bodies are exposed to extraordinary danger, who and what we put on our syllabi, our ability to create safe and brave spaces in which to carry on open conversations, and our commitment to training teachers prepared to organize and lead these classes take on a new importance.

Our goals were to (re)interrogate and (re)assemble our syllabi and our theatre history classrooms, exploring new modes in which to create productive "spaces of discomfort" to speak and learn about difference and otherness with each other and with our students. Though we had not yet considered canon trouble as mechanical rather than philosophical, the challenges we enumerated were largely technical rather than political. These included lingering Euro- and Anglo-centrism in textbooks and curricula (with concomitant tokenization of non-Western topics as colorful addenda), the burden of exposing students to traditionally canonical texts while making space for women and other canonically marginalized artists, the impossibility of any one instructor developing expertise in the wide swath of world performance history given constraints on time and effort such as adjunct remuneration and balancing research and other teaching responsibilities. The problems we identified in our call for participants were borne out in discussion with our working group.

As we engaged in conversation during our working group session, we identified a number of challenges—some technical and others ideological—that make it difficult for us to teach theatre and performance history with the breadth and depth we desire. Nearly every member of our working group teaches theatre and performance history as a survey course and every one of us has experimented with ways to alter our syllabi to include plays, performances, and artists beyond the conventional canon. One challenge our group articulated is including a wider scope of material in a meaningful rather than a cursory way. This concern unlocked a further range of issues, including the knowledge, expectations, preconceptions, and familiarities that both instructors and students brought with them to the classroom. Indeed, we may speculate whether survey courses are primarily vehicles of canonical thinking, and whether or how they could function against or in excess of traditional canons.

One aspect of the mechanical canon problem that emerged particularly strongly for us is how in some sense, the canon resides *inside* us. We as theatre education professionals are finite vessels who only know what we know, and we know those things largely because of who taught us and what they knew. That is, though the concept and contents of a canon are collectively created, so far (for the most part) teaching theatre history is an individual rather than a collective enterprise. So we began to imagine ways that we could harness collectivity and share responsibilities by gathering our time, effort, and training into a communal project so that even if we are still teaching as individuals, we benefit from the experience and expertise of our larger theatre and performance academic community.

Another trouble is the continuing centrality and importance of the conventional canon. While it might be tempting to throw the baby out with the bathwater, many of us feel a responsibility to our students to familiarize them with traditional canonical plays and histories they may encounter in the industry or in graduate school. We are seeking a methodology agile enough to engage with works of the traditional canon without glorifying them or excluding worthy "noncanonical" content. Because our working group included cross-generational participants ranging from graduate students to full professors, we had the opportunity to consider cyclical approaches to this conundrum. Professor Rhonda Blair says

> My experience has basically been that there have been revisitings over the decades to see who's being included and who excluded in terms of what work is valued and how it's supported: what work is being produced, by which theatres, what work is included in curricula, what are the opportunities provided for actors and other theatre artists by these works, what are the values, privileging, and circumstances of history that foreground some works and ignore or render invisible others? (Blair 2020)

Despite previous efforts, we remain in need of pedagogies that embrace the vastness of global performance traditions without othering them by using European traditions as a kind of North Star.

"We aren't here to learn what we already know," Kyla Wazana Tompkins reminds students in an eponymous 2016 article on the Avidly blog of the *LA Review of Books*. Tompkins' declaration is apropos of teaching theory and comes in conjunction with summarizing Judith Butler's famous essay defending the difficult language of theory as necessary to deconstructing the ideology secreted inside "common sense" knowledge. In an analogue manner, students sometimes respond more positively to the "canonical" subjects they already recognize as important. In some sense, it is their (and instructors') prior immersion in dominant Canon culture which subtly frames some topics as 'meaningful' and others, less familiar, as ancillary. Of course, an increasing proportion of students enter college classrooms with a strong sense of historical injustice and a desire to see themselves reflected in diverse subjects, although this doesn't always translate into a clear sense of how or what that might entail, or a sophisticated understanding of the historical structures that maintain the status quo and notions of shared culture.

Not only do students and instructors sometimes betray preferences for topics they already know something about, instructors largely teach how and what our teachers taught us, not only from personal preference but also from lack of tools or time to change. Even those of us in programs with the most diverse faculty and areas of expertise are limited by our training based on the curricula of our alma maters. This problem is not a new one. Blair recalls earlier decades' battles over

> the failure of works by women and people of color (apart from Raisin in the Sun, if memory serves) to be included in the 'canon' when I was in grad school in the 1970s, and the 'wars' in the 1980s and 1990s to get plays by women included [...] And, of course, these decades were fraught by white women's failure to acknowledge and deal adequately with the inclusion of women of color (Blair 2020)

Despite the hard-earned advances Blair describes, the reality remains that for most of us, although we hear and promulgate robust diversity, there was rarely enough training that expanded significantly beyond the conventional Canon.

Furthermore, few of us were taught formally how to teach. And once we have entered the profession, there is rarely time or resources assigned to changing or expanding our teaching abilities. Many of us are trained in graduate school to do depth, not breadth. We were not encouraged or rewarded for attaining broad "survey" type knowledge of the sort that is required for teaching undergraduate theatre history classes. This problem, which began for many of us in graduate school, is exacerbated when we enter the profession. Just as canon formation is hierarchical, so too is the luxury of time to expand our own areas of expertise. Many (though not all) of us who teach theatre history are in the beginning or early stages of our careers and lack the time or institutional support to broaden and deepen our knowledge of global performance traditions. We might thus extend Tompkins' reminder to teachers, for whom there may not be the time, inclination, or support for continually expanding, questioning, and updating what and how we teach: *We aren't here to teach what we already know.* Of course such a statement is paradoxical—you can't teach what you don't know—although conversely the typical adage about the act of teaching being catalytic of deeper learning might also be salient.

What would it mean to take to heart a new adage like "we aren't here to teach what we already know"? It would, for one thing, probably entail thinking anew about the canon of works we take for granted as necessary or central to our traditions. This does not simply mean excising those works, as part of our remit as educators is inducting students into a culture, history, and tradition which pre-exists us, and which will not disappear or cease being the typical frame of operations into which our students will graduate as scholars, artists, and practitioners. But we need to do this while balancing a simultaneous and juxtaposed responsibility to create syllabi that reflect the racial and cultural diversity of our student populations, not to mention the diversity of their fields of study. The authors of this chapter teach at public universities to populations of both BA and BFA students in various combinations who arrive with varying levels of academic training, preparation, and interest. Setting aside the challenge of running a course that accommodates these differing populations, we are left with another lingering problem: there is simply far too much out there to include. The "additive" canon doesn't often leave enough space to substantially decenter classical (canonical) works.

But what if we were to work as a community? The working group aggregated syllabi, lesson plans, position papers, and copious personal experience in our in-person meeting and a shared online folder, which in total began to gesture toward one material response to the problems of canonicity and physical limitations: assembling more than one person or course could ever possibly teach in one place, to be pieced together in different combinations with each course, or by each instructor. A primary idea forged amongst meeting participants was to create a database of lesson plans and syllabuses, peer-reviewed to ensure general quality, which would provide a material resource for rethinking instructors' individual teaching canons. It would provide one mode of supporting us in teaching what we don't already know.

A database of peer-reviewed teaching tools would allow instructors to reinvent approaches to teaching theatre history with the confidence that the resources have been provided by those with specializations in particular areas of global performance traditions. An instructor might, for example, wish to include indigenous performance of the Americas. The database will ideally provide several lesson plans, Powerpoint presentations or lecture notes, and accompanying student assignments from culturally and geographically diverse indigenous American traditions. The instructor can then select one or combine several to create a unit spanning several days. Access to the database will be free, but in an effort to build and sustain a sense of this effort a community-driven project, those who wish to access material will also be asked to submit teaching resources of their own or to serve as peer reviewers. Thus, we hope, our community could pool our time and expertise to surmount two particular mechanical problems identified by our working group.

The difficulty of addressing an "additive" canon that endlessly recenters a central core of hegemonic white Anglophone works is potentially tougher to address. One tactic is to make the mechanics of canonicity the focus of a class. Another is to choose other centers through which to re-constellate course materials, such as the geographical location of the class in question, or theoretical concerns, like formations of group or societal identities—both of these approaches might open up specific opportunities to discuss the mechanics of canonicity and the white Anglophone hegemony of the "Western Canon" most often taught in US colleges. One possibility might be to provide students access to the database with an assignment to develop their own syllabuses for a theatre history course, or to compare and contrast the assembled resources on the database with one or more theatre history textbooks.

Thinking concretely about the typical "delivery systems" of students' basic theatre and performance history education also potentially articulates a common elision we face in our scholarship and teaching practices: that the phenotypic appearance of an instructor should match the course content being discussed. This desire conflates two separate, pressing issues in the academy: diversifying the professoriate and all levels of education professionals and diversifying and decolonizing curricula. While both are important goals, it is deeply important to keep them clearly separate from each other for several reasons. Firstly, academic and pedagogical knowledge is not an essential trait, it is learned and nurtured. Anyone, no matter their ethnic or racial background, has to take the time and energy to be exposed to different forms and while a person of a specific cultural heritage may have been more often exposed to forms and texts from their family's background, such a correspondence does not go without saying, especially in a multi-racial settler colonial society with a clear hegemonic bent toward specific forms like the United States (the location from which we are writing and teaching).

Secondly, the implicit corollary to essentialist attributions of expertise would be that white people are only responsible for knowing "white people culture." This is of course the fallacy that our entire critique of the Theatrical Canon and canonicity rejects. Any curriculum that presents course material as a survey (and potentially any person who believes in a pluralist civic community) is thus responsible for learning far beyond the materials that would seem to match their cultural background. In trying to help build a peer-reviewed, rigorous collection of resources for individual instructors to grow beyond their specializations and the other limitations inherited from those who taught us, and prolonged by neoliberal pressures on our time and energy, we are attempting to remove some of the material barriers that hold people back from putting their philosophical and political convictions about canon reformation into practice. Perhaps then, in some sense, the very format of the survey course could, rather than reiterate its likely origin in the old hegemonic Canon, instead serve as a stage for anti-essentialist, cosmopolitan engagement. Ideally, changes in our current instructors' approaches will foster a more equitable supply line, nurturing more ethnically, racially, sexually, gender-, and ability-diverse people into the professoriate over time, thus helping to address the other half of this complex equation.

It is our hope that the simple solution of collating mass contributions in a relatively uncurated way (i.e., without the singular ideological viewpoint of a textbook, or separated out into central and marginal issues) and directly referring to the individual limitations each instructor and class faces may offer one way to recalibrate our relationships to the "Canon." The database collectivizes knowledge while leaving individual responsibility and choice open in creating classes and charting paths through the excess of knowledge. Agreeing to share lesson plans and teaching styles did not raise significant concerns amongst our working group participants, although we are certainly still enmeshed in a society and academic institutions which subscribe fiercely to mythologies of individual authorship and intellectual property—values which may also infuse traditional understandings of the Canon, with its singular Great Men penning their Immortal Great Works. This collective, non-hierarchical approach may help to further subvert the supremacist fantasy of the isolated artistic genius.

The Too-Big Canon

If we are correct about the mechanical functions of the Canon and canonicity, then canons will never really go away, but perhaps are mutating, developing in the contemporary moment and the near future. As we write this essay in the first half of 2020, the present moment is extraordinarily uncertain, with new diseases and old epidemics of structural racism both in full blown crisis. As we have argued, canons in and of themselves may never disappear, due to the ways in which they are material derivations of the limits of time and knowledge. Perhaps the Canon's next best act will be to grow much bigger, enough for students and instructors to recognize it as a structure of power that is inevitable but not neutral, one that reminds us of the limits and limiters of knowledge formation. Perhaps we need to knock the endlessly centered hegemonic greats not out of the classroom, but to the side, asking how and why they got to the center and have stayed there. By providing our students with the tools to recognize the canon as a mechanical problem with massive social and political ramifications, we prepare them to recognize structures of power in institutions beyond the campus gates. If we do our jobs as educators, theatre students should be uniquely prepared to critique and influence the confluence between "representation" and its enactment, "knowledge" and its containers and trappings of truth. What is the dissonance between election law and election practice? Are police departments and elected officials who march with Black Lives Matter legislating and practicing meaningful change or merely gesturing toward it in the performance of protest? It is not insignificant that in the midst of the moment of crisis in which we write this chapter theatre artists have called for the abolishment of white supremacy on stage and behind the scenes in the American theatre (https://www.weseeyouwat.com). If we can prepare our students for revolution in our theatre history classrooms, perhaps they can move us closer to a community modeled on the kind of collective sharing of knowledge and power we hope to achieve in our approach to instruction.

Works Cited

Blair, Rhonda. 2020. Personal Email with Authors.

Butler, Judith. 1999. "A 'Bad Writer' Bites Back." *New York Times*. 20 March. Accessed 10 June 2020. https://archive.nytimes.com/query.nytimes.com/gst/fullpage-950CE5D61531F933A15750C0A96F958260.html.

Parks, Suzan-Lori. 1995. "From 'Elements of Style.'" In *The America Play and Other Works*, 6–18. New York: Theatre Communications Group.

Tompkins, Kyla Wazana. 2020. "We Aren't Here to Learn What We Already Know." *Avidly,* blog of *Los Angeles Review of Books*. Accessed 13 September 2016. http://avidly.lareviewofbooks.org/2016/09/13/we-arent-here-to-learn-what-we-know-we-already-know/.

21 How Do We Do the Queer Canon?

Zachary A. Dorsey, with Paul Bonin-Rodriguez, Michelle Dvoskin, Lindsey Mantoan, Eleanor Owicki, Jaclyn I. Pryor, and Ramón H. Rivera-Servera

Introduction

Zachary A. Dorsey:
The origins of this chapter can be traced to Jill Dolan's Queer Theory and Performance class, which many of this chapter's authors took together as graduate students once upon a time (the 2000's) in the Performance as Public Practice (PPP) program at the University of Texas at Austin (UT). Jill's "Intellectual Genealogy" assignment - while not explicitly framed as about the canon - pushed us toward research on queer theorists and artists. Her stated aim on the syllabus was to "build a sense of historicity around the work we're reading, and to understand the complexities of writing queer theory/practice even now. I also want us to see these authors as people with whom we're in conversation, rather than simply people with last names whom we quote" (9). Rather than producing dry biographies, these genealogies had us gleefully mapping the field, charting relationships, making connections, and exploring gossip about these authors. Jill's responses to our work generously filled in the gaps of our preparations and our knowledge, but also gave us license to question what knowledge even matters to the field to begin with. During our time in graduate school, Jill and the other PPP faculty brought many of these scholars and artists to campus, moving us from only figuratively being in conversation with these people to literally being in conversation with them. This helped us begin to understand canonicity as relational and curatorial, a complex operation that even as fledgling graduate students we were already a part of. Much later, we came to see Jill's assignment as encompassing past, present, and future, a realization that informs our theorization of the queer canon in this chapter.

My experience of the canon was hugely informed by my fellow graduate students who began their study at UT at or around the same time as I did. This "cohort" of students (give or take a few years) are now in a mid-career moment where we find ourselves exploring the idea of the queer canon with our own students, alternately shoring it up and tearing it down. In our initial discussion about this chapter, we surveyed plays, performances, and theories that one might assign to the queer canon, yet we found something almost antithetical in trying to delineate the canon this way. Queer's ethos of resistance and counternormativity flies in the face of articulating (or preserving,

DOI: 10.4324/9781003031413-21

or enshrining) a list of sacred texts, artists, and theories that constitute and define a field. In *Cruising Utopia: The Then and There of Queer Futurity*, José Esteban Muñoz describes queerness as "not simply a being but a doing for and toward the future" (1). What surfaces in our individual essays is the shared belief that any productive conception of a queer canon must reject simple lists of artists and artworks. Noe Montez and Kareem Kubchamoni, the editors of the 2020 special issue of *Theatre Topics* on "Queer Pedagogy in Theatre and Performance," note that "we must remember that the academy is not the only place to do queer thinking" (xi). Just as Muñoz primes us to examine the "when" of the canon, Montez and Kubchamoni challenge us to rethink the "where" that the queer canon is constituted and contested.

The solo-authored micro-essays that follow are inspired by a shared investment in reframing the queer canon as a doing rather than a being; in reorienting notions of the queer canon as about the future rather than the past; and in recognizing the operations of canon-making in communal, inclusive, and everyday places beyond just university classrooms and libraries. The queer canon is always in motion, is always incomplete, is always in a state of anticipation, and is always just out of reach. It is best understood and experienced as a series of encounters, not just the textual or performed output of a group of authors, but the collective energies and efforts and exchanges between individuals, communities, and institutions, in diverse spaces and places, and across time. Queer canonicity eschews gatekeeping and abhors permanence. If a conventional canon consists of the great texts and authors of the past, the queer canon considers such works and such moments only insofar as they enable thinking with, through, and between, and point toward what might yet be. This vision of the queer canon is the biproduct of our discussions and the aggregate of the individual essays we wrote, each of which grapples with the question: **"How do we *do* the queer canon sales?"**

We Transgress Disciplinary Boundaries

Eleanor Owicki:
For me, one of the most important things about queerness is that it rejects tidy categorizations. It is inherently chimerical, and attempts to rigidly define it are always unsatisfying. So perhaps I shouldn't have been surprised at how difficult it was to identify a (let alone *the*) queer canon. Similarly, I felt much more at ease when we switched to thinking about the queer canon as something we were creating through our own actions and teaching. At UT, we were encouraged to consider ourselves artist/scholars, with the two practices not only informing each other but merging into one. This rejection of boundaries felt inherently queer to me, regardless of whether the topic under exploration was explicitly related to gender or sexuality.

I particularly saw this blending in the prevalence of solo performance in my time at UT. We frequently read or watched these for class, took courses that involved creating them, and brought in guest artists to stage them. Seeing E.

Patrick Johnson perform *Sweet Tea*, Robbie McCauley perform *Sugar*, and Tim Miller perform *Lay of the Land* in the Winship theatre building were highlights of my graduate career. The solo pieces we studied and made were generally autobiographical or autoethnographic meditations on larger social or cultural topics; the writer/performer would use their own thoughts, experiences, and feelings to reflect on a broader issue. The end result was often a type of very personal public scholarship.

While many of my colleagues created brilliant works in this vein, I had little desire to perform publicly. This did not mean, however, that I was unable to explore these hybrid methodologies. Through smaller in-class work, I learned the value of using artistic methods to clarify and deepen my own thinking and analysis. I particularly remember this in Deborah Paradez's "Black and Latino Performance and Popular Culture" course. Each week, one student would offer a "creative response" to the readings; we could basically take that prompt in whatever direction we wanted. Since the goal of this assignment was to thoughtfully engage with the course material, not to create "good art," I felt an increased freedom to play and experiment. I also felt confident that my professor and classmates would respond to my offering with support and generosity (which they indeed did).

In my current position at Indiana University, I continue to encourage this cross-pollination between scholarship and creative practice. I find that students can readily understand that research and critical analysis might enhance their art, but the idea that art might enhance their research and critical analysis is less evident. I particularly try to teach these skills in the graduate classes I teach for our MFA students (who are required to take two courses in the History, Theory, and Literature area). I have adopted the creative response project for these classes, and I give my students instructions similar to the ones I received: explore, take risks, and don't worry about approaching the project in the "correct" way or about creating "good art." My students have taken up this invitation with enthusiasm, creating installations, songs, sculptures, and of course solo performances in a range of styles. These pieces inevitably spark interesting discussions and often help us get to the heart of a piece more quickly than we would have if we had started with traditional analysis. Each student must also write a short paper to accompany their creative response; in most cases, it is clear that the process of creation brought the student to a deeper understanding not only of the specific piece to which they were responding, but to the larger questions of the course.

I doubt my students see these assignments as part of a queer practice. I certainly don't frame them that way. I know, however, that they are rooted in the understanding of queerness that I began to develop at UT, one which embraces messiness, boundary crossing, and experimenting to find new practices and processes. They also help to foster the supportive communities and critical generosity that other contributors discuss in their micro-essays, elements that I agree are essential to how we do the queer canon.

We Practice Critical Generosity

Ramón H. Rivera-Servera:
David Román's notion of "critical generosity" is one of the most cherished gifts from my early education in performance studies (Román 1998). Critical generosity is both a standpoint and a methodology that asks the critic/scholar to advance rigorous analysis of aesthetics and content while considering the contextual world and intention of the work at hand in ways that balance ethically the role of the critic and the advocate. It offered me a model of research deeply invested in the social world of performance and the critic's relationship and responsibility to that world. It moved me away from canons and into communities. It modeled queer methodologies of care where advocacy for art and artists is not about the production of canonical achievement but about the queer relatonality and sustenance of worlds. As Jill Dolan explains, for Román "performance should be taken on in its own terms, and read through the exigencies of a social moment, offering cultural critique equally important as more straightforward aesthetic ones" (Dolan 33).

Critical generosity invites us to move beyond universalist frameworks for selecting which works to deem worthwhile in our engagements with theatre and performance. It also moves beyond the traditional Department of Theatre or Dance and the Euro-American traditions that have so anchored the conceptualization of the field in the United States and into a broader range of contexts and platforms where theatre and performance thrive in community settings; professional, amateur, or otherwise. For me, this move beyond meant focusing on traditions of performance scholarship and practice emergent from Mexican American and Latinx perspectives. These performance forms in their particular contexts shaped my own queer of color approach to performance research, curation, and practice.

The University of Texas at Austin, where I pursued my graduate training, has been home to what I have claimed as a Mexican American/Latinx branch of the performance studies tree. While little known in performance studies circles, this tradition started with the groundbreaking work of Américo Paredes and Jovita González into *corrido* and *vaquero* aesthetics and practices in the early part of the 20th century. It includes the ethnographically driven work of José Limón on subaltern aesthetics, Richard Flores on gift economies, and Amelia Malagamba-Ansótegui on transborder visualities and embodiments. It also includes the influential works of Deborah Parédez and Laura Gutierrez, both former core members of the faculty. They all prioritized ethnography as a relational methodology of "being with" aimed at allowing context, community traditions, and current urgency to determine the canonical, or valued—practices the research goes on to pursue, analyze, theorize.

Tending to the Latinx queer communities that are the central focus of my research and life meant moving beyond a theatrical canon where Latinx work is positioned as a minor note. It required riding the minor frequencies of queer latinidad through the nightlife waterholes, community centers, activist circles, and art collectives my work turns to. Critical generosity advances an understanding of how these minor frequencies animate vast worlds that both diagnose the enduring inadequacies of the past and enacts, affectively and effectively, the experience of a present and future performed within the urgencies and pleasures of Latinx queer life. In inviting "critical generosity" as the queer standpoint, method, and ethic of our performance scholarship, we are invited to see canonical frameworks in theatre scholarship and production as historically authorized platforms to intervene and to move queerly beyond.

We Turn to the Audience

Zachary A. Dorsey:
I will never forget seeing Tim Miller's *Glory Box* at The Vortex Theatre in 2000 during my first semester as a graduate student. Dr. Oscar Brockett – then widely recognized throughout the Austin Theatre community as among the city's most sage and stalwart of theatre-goers – happened to be there that night, and he happened to choose to sit next to me. At one moment in the performance, Brockett leaned over and whispered in my ear, "I wonder if Tim is going to take off his clothes again... Oh! There he goes!" Polite laughter rippled through the audience as Brockett's old-man voice carried throughout the small theatre and onto the stage. Miller's performance was made all the more memorable for all who were sharing it because of Brockett's interjection, which brought with it a joyful reminder of our imperative as theatre-going audiences: we should gather again and again (as Brockett did) to bear witness to the stories shared and the lives enacted onstage, and we should remain ever conscious and elated that we get to do so as a community, together.

Here, I want to stake out as worthy of inclusion in any discussion of a queer canon the methodology of giving significant consideration to "who" we attend the theatre with, and how they contribute substantially to one's meaning making experience. Whenever I can, I assign my students David Román's "November 1, 1992: AIDS/*Angels in America*," an achingly beautiful essay where he anchors a discussion of Tony Kushner's plays with poignant and sustained descriptions of the lives of his friends who attend the theatre with him. Similarly, the acknowledgements section of Stacy Wolf's *A Problem Like Maria: Gender and Sexuality in the American Musical* is seared into my memory, in which she describes the moment where her book project began on a cross-country car trip when she found herself belting out "My Man" from *Funny Girl*. Even re-reading it nearly two decades later, I'm still moved by how Wolf describes Jill Dolan's presence on that road trip as vital to the book, and how their experience listening to cast albums, watching films, and attending productions is central to a joyful life together.

During my MA and PhD work at UT Austin, perhaps the largest part of my education as a Theatre Scholar and Artist came from attending (or being sent to) the theatre multiple nights a week. As vibrant and mediocre and luminous and vexing as those performances were, it was the ritual of going to the theatre with others that lingers for me: my then-boyfriend-now-husband feeling no shame for dozing off during a production of Terrence McNallys' *Love! Valour! Compassion!*, for example, or my Thursday night theatre-going group using theatre (and margaritas) as an excuse to remain a constant presence in one another's lives. By arguing that audience, communitas, and kinship are deeply worthy of attention here as much as the productions themselves, I don't suggest that this mode of criticism is appropriate only to queer theatre or queer artists. Rather, I'm flagging my nascent belief that in all future conversations about a queer canon, the "with whom?" is as essential as the "what, where, and when?"

I was thrilled to have taught the brilliant Azure D. Osborne-Lee in my very first semester as the instructor of the 300 student Introduction to Theatre for Non-Majors class at UT Austin. Now he is writing insanely ambitious plays like *Glass*, which the students in my Dramaturgy class at James Madison University eagerly devour. Osborne-Lee undoubtedly would have found his way to the theatre without me, but I'm grateful to have had the opportunity to offer him support in that direction near the beginning of his journey. I teach Introduction to Theatre far more than I get to teach Queer Theory and Performance these days, which means that my opportunities to engage with students in prolonged conversations about the/a queer canon are limited. But with Introduction to Theatre, I do get to send large numbers of people to the theatre, where I challenge them to commune not just with the play and the production, but with those all around them. Una Chaudhuri uses the phrase "an experiment with the politics of possibility" to describe Kushner's *Perestroika*, but I feel it aptly describes every time an audience comes together in good faith to experience a work of theatre *en masse*.

We Look to Queer Spaces

Paul Bonin-Rodriguez:
In the video of dancer/choreographer Jennifer Harge's *mourn and never tire* (2018) at the National Cathedral, the camera captures both the audience and the performer. From the altar, Harge runs in place for eleven minutes while reciting into a microphone the names of fellow African Americans who have been killed by police violence. As the list grows longer, Harge becomes increasingly fatigued. The dancer's shoulders hunch, her breathing labors. The choir members and featured speakers sitting behind her grow visibly weary. Some fidget, others freeze; and one man wipes his watering eyes repeatedly. The visible discomforts captured on camera invite the question, "On what registers do folks experience this scenario of trauma and ongoing oppression at an event meant to celebrate the anniversary of a speech by Dr. Martin-Luther King, Jr. some fifty years before?" Here the queer meaning-making paradigm exposes the gap between the ideals and outcomes of civil rights struggle and recasts the celebration as an elegiac call to continue the fight.

Figure 21.1 Jesús I. Valles *(Un)Documents*, 2019. Credit: Errich Petersen Photography

In contrast, the video documenting the premiere of trans performer Becca Blackwell's newest show, *Schmermie's Choice* (2020) at Joe's Pub offers up the performance space as a site of shared frolic and laughter about sexual intimacy, as well as the mutability of desire, for the many trans folx in attendance. In nearly an hour of comedy coupled with a massage that Blackwell gives to one audience member, the show demonstrates how trans desire "achieves meta-cultural intelligibility through the ideologies and institutions of intimacy" (Warner and Berlant 553). The spaces, relational configurations, and acts of intimacy invoked and acknowledged between comic testimony and audience response are world-naming, if not world-making.

Jesús I. Valles's poetic and powerful *(Un)Documents* offers the story of a family's crossing into the U.S. and separation by U.S. forces, to draw the subject increasingly back into a queer-affirmative site familial and cultural belonging against a background of xenophobia and oppression. When I see it in February, 2020 at Austin's Mexican American Cultural Center, I sit among other first, second, and third generation Latinx folx, who testify to the show's relevance to our lives in the talkback (Figure 21.1).

While I might teach each of these works and artists as part of a contemporary queer performance canon, I am more likely to point to the spaces they occupy and activate by the queer "movements deployed within" (DeCerteau, qtd. in Rivera-Servera 2012: 30). In each of their works, the artists ask what LGBTQ+ knowledge, experience, and testimony has to offer the world. In so doing, they participate in what David Román has called "a queer worldmaking enterprise" that "open[s] a space in the national culture for a set of alternative sentiments and practices" (2012: 179). Ramón Rivera-Servera expands on the idea asserting that queer performance spaces "build social, cultural, and political" bonds across different experiences and backgrounds (2012: 6). To understand queer space as it is created and elaborated is to recognize a queer canon being composed in real time as LGBTQ + folks come together to memorialize and celebrate our existence, mark our endurance, and share our insights on how to imagine a more inclusive world into existence one gathering at a time.

We Say Why It Matters

Jaclyn I. Pryor:
In her now infamous essay, "Performative Acts and Gender Constitution: An Essay in Phenomenology and Feminist Theory" (1988), feminist philosopher Judith Butler employs the term "performative" to describe how gender "works": gender, she asserts, is not biologically determined but socially constructed and, as such, it *produces a series of effects*. Here, she is building upon the work of philosopher J.L. Austin, whose *How To Do Things With Words* (1962) similarly argues that speech-acts are (or at least have the potential to be) performative: *they do things*.

In our field, we turn this dictum onto itself: we insist that *performance* is performative. To claim that performance (broadly defined) is performative is to insist on the value of liveness in the meaning-making paradigm; it is to insist, that is, upon the crucial role that *the spectator* plays in the act of reception and analysis. As performance theorist Jill Dolan compelling argues in *Utopia in Performance* (2005), performance has the capacity to move us, bind us, and allow us to imagine what a more socially just and affectively connected world might feel like. In this regard, performance is a worldmaking project—and one with great capacity for reimagining social relations past, present, and future.

Here, I would like to suggest that the queer canon is not (only) those groundbreaking works of live art *per se* that sit at the interstices of queer and performance studies but instead what it is that *they do for us* and what, in turn, *we do with them*. When scholars in the field engage live events, whether this be a Pulitzer Prize-winning play like Tony Kushner's *Angels in America* (Román) or Paula Vogel's *How I Learned To Drive* (Pellegrini); a Broadway musical hit like Joe Mantello's *Wicked* (Wolf) or Jerome Robbins' *West Side Story* (Paredez); downtown work like Split Britches' *Belle Reprieve* (Dolan) or Carmelita Tropicana's *Chicas 2000* (Muñoz); experimental documentaries like Marlon Riggs' *Tongues Untied* (Johnson) or Tom Joslin and Peter Friedman's *Silverlake Life* (Phelan); Latinx social dance (Rivera-Servera) or South Asian public culture (Khubchandani); the racialized politics of a moan (Moten) or a scream (Chambers-Letson), queer performance studies insists that performance exists outside the frame of its elocution and resides instead—or at least as well—in its effects (and affects). This methodology, I contend, *is* the canon (at its queer best). It asks us to look not only at what performance *is* but what it *does* (to/for us)—producing a body of (spectators to the) work as varied as the number of people who bear it witness.

Grounded in affect and multiplicity, this methodology is especially crucial at this historical moment in cultural politics in which binarisms such as "good" and "bad" (art, people, politics) reign supreme. As queer-of-color and crip critiques frequently remind us, such carceral logic is animated by the very white supremacies that we seek to dismantle and, as such, "will never dismantle the master's house" (Lorde 2017: 89). *But what will?*

It is my contention that queer methods in performance studies can certainly do their part. To give one concrete example: when performance studies scholar Joshua Chambers-Letson begins his essay about the necessity of Black insurgency, "How to Listen to a Scream: Black Performance and the Anarrangement of Law," by describing two-year old K'Sisay Sadiki's scream—a scream prompted by the 1971 beating by court marshals of her father, civil rights activist and Black Panther leader Kamau Sadiki—his point is not to argue that the arrest, trial, beating, and incarceration of Sadiki (and his colleague Assata Shakur) was unjust. Of course it was. Rather, his aim is to demonstrate, with the kind of breathtaking thick description, intricate performance analysis, and complex historicization that is emblematic of the field, how Blackness, voice, and state violence coalesce, and why and how, in turn, Black performance *matters*. Put differently, it is the politics of "mattering" that performance studies lay bare, and this, I believe, is its canonicity, as well as its vitality, in a culture of violence and harm.

We Acknowledge the Past While We Teach the Present

Michelle Dvoskin:
When I was asked to contribute to this chapter, I was in the final stages of preparing my fall courses. It so happened that this was the first year my annual "Topics in Drama" course focused on, and was officially subtitled, "Queer Theatre." When I had begun brainstorming what the course might look like, I instinctively thought back to my time in the Performance as Public Practice (PPP) Program at UT Austin. I had arrived with an understanding of my own sexuality, an interest in LGBT/Q theatre, and a distinctly limited idea of what that included: *Angels in America,* Terrence McNally's plays, the musical *Falsettos* that captured my high-school heart, etc. Overall very white, very male, and very mainstream.

After starting at UT, experimental artists, particularly the women of the WOW Café, became what I thought queer performance was supposed to be. I saw how essential their work was to my professors and colleagues and was lucky enough to watch performances by, and interact with, Peggy Shaw, Lois Weaver, Carmelita Tropicana, Marga Gomez, and Tim Miller. Their work excited and engaged me... but part of my heart stubbornly clung to earnest, relatively straightforward (forgive the pun) explorations of LGBT lives and loves. I felt guilty for my attachment to conventional, realistic work—a lesbian instead of queer, when queer was the better thing to be. Until I realized that I was the one enforcing that binary. One of the things I loved most about PPP was its assumption that all of our scholarly and artistic work counted as "public practice [s]" that could help create social change. This lack of hierarchy still feels like one of the most productively, joyfully queer aspects of our work together.

With that encompassing spirit in mind, I started planning. Obviously, a unit on WOW with at least one piece each from Split Britches, Carmelita Tropicana, and Holly Hughes, and maybe Five Lesbian Brothers. And Tim Miller, of course. Then more mainstream, realistic work—*Boys in the Band* and *Last Summer at Bluefish Cove*, to start. Definitely a unit looking at AIDS, so *The Normal Heart*, *As Is*, and definitely *Falsettos*. I teach *Angels in America* in my introductory course for majors, so I could skip that. Terrence McNally had to be included, and Richard Greenberg, and Paula Vogel, and... My "must" list just kept growing, a sort of greatest hits album of LGBT/Q theatre and performance I have known. Suddenly I looked down at my notes and realized that I may have stopped imagining there was a "right" kind of queer theatre, but hierarchy remained—not to mention the whiteness that came with it. My class was getting mired down in that most normative of things, a canon. Unacceptable.

I quickly shifted gears. The course—re-subtitled "Contemporary Queer Theatre in the US"—will start with a unit on "canons." Each student will share research on an arguably "canonical" LGBT/Q play. Then, we'll think about how shows like *Belle Reprieve* and *The Normal Heart* both are and are not part of the same "queer canon." We'll consider the limitations and dangers of reifying work as "canonical." We'll discuss ways cultural power and access impact what works are seen as important, and particularly about how whiteness is privileged. We'll also talk about how claiming a queer canon can recognize and honor often-groundbreaking work today's queer theatre builds upon. Finally, we'll read the revised versions of my still-beloved *Falsettos* and *M. Butterfly* produced on Broadway in 2016 and 2017, respectively, and discuss what it means not only to revive but revise a play from "our" canon.

Then we'll move on, spending the vast majority of our semester reading queer plays from this decade. The plays I've chosen are diverse in their creators, characters, styles, and themes; they offer lots of ways to understand what it can mean to be queer or live queerly. I don't really care whether any of them will "deserve" to end up in the canon unit of some mythical future course. And letting go of the assumption that I should has brought me an enormous amount of queer joy that I can't wait to share with my students.

We Value Queer Mentorship

Lindsey Mantoan:
In their article for *Theatre Topics*' 2020 special issue on Queer Pedagogy, "Against Chronology: Intergenerational Pedagogical Approaches to Queer Theatre and Performance Histories," Benjamin Gillespie and Bess Rowen

argue against linear ordering of materials on syllabi for queer theatre courses. They persuasively "demonstrate that chronology is not the most effective approach for teaching queer theatre and performance histories. While it is a common practice to map out significant theatrical events through presenting a linear progression of history, especially in larger survey courses, the essay proposes an alternative model that seeks to uncover the intergenerational connections and queer temporalities embedded within queerhistory" (2020: 69). In other words, given that queer temporality remains one of the primary lenses through which to analyze performances, queer pedagogy ought to avoid enforcing heternormative time.

Shortly after the death of José Esteban Muñoz (1967–2013), the Association for Theatre in Higher Education (ATHE) featured a panel on LGBTQ Historical Scholarship. Kareem Khubchandani's subsequent article "Introduction: Queer Genealogies—Remembering the Future" maps how queer mentorship circulated during the ATHE panel. In a beautiful ode to the ways in which mentorship shapes critical analysis, careers, and even the understanding of self, Khubchandani celebrates the interconnections and journeys of some of the most well-known scholars in our field across multiple generations, writing: "The mentorships named in the room spoke to the ongoing legacy of queer studies. They rendered citation a political practice, and made evident the systems of care that LGBTQ people, women, and people of color know to be necessary in surviving the academy" (2016: 45).

Pairing these two intellectual projects—one which resists straight time and one which prizes mentorship as fundamental to intellectual and creative growth—I seek here to amplify recent calls for multi-directional mentorship. Memes declaring "if you don't have a mentor twenty years younger than you, you're doing it wrong" and articles such as *Entrepreneur*'s "4 Reasons You Need a Mentor Who Is Younger Than You" (2017) and the *New York Times*'s "What Could I Possibly Learn From a Mentor Half My Age? Plenty" (2016) argue for the value of an older person in a mentorship pairing being the learner rather than exclusively the teacher. While a number of people cited in this chapter (and even some people writing microessays here) have mentored me, and while I in turn serve as a mentor for queer students at my institution and elsewhere, I also benefit from the perspectives and knowledge of queer artists younger than me.

Queerness opposes hierarchies and linearity, so multidirectional queer mentorship seems a natural dynamic. Sure, I've taught queer students about the Wow Café and Terrel Alvin McCraney's Brother/Sister plays and that the musical *Wicked* is inherently queer (see Stacy Wolf 2008), but queer students have taught me that Hayley Kiyoko is the Lesbian Jesus. I now regularly teach Hayley Kiyoko's music videos in my classes. My love of Netflix's reboot of *She-Ra* (2018–2020) started when one of my younger queer mentors encouraged me to watch it. After binging, I examined with her the way the show works to repair some of the queer trauma inflicted by "bury your gays" representation and queer baiting in television shows. Now, not only do I talk in my classes about the evolution of queer representation on television, but I've also written a piece on the show's impact on queer families for CNN—a piece which I shared with the same younger queer mentor to hear her notes and advice before submitting.

In this way, younger queer mentors shape pedagogy, scholarship, and queer joy by not only introducing older queer professors to new content but also sharing their experiences coming out/coming to terms with their identity, which in some ways is a very different experience across generations and in some ways is very much the same. There's no canonical queer experience or list of queer texts. But there's a complex web of mentorship that shapes us all, and embracing the ephemeral and profound nature of this kind of sharing over static lists of texts is part of what we might call queer canonicity.

Works Cited

Austin, J.L. 1962. *How to do Things with Words*. Oxford: Clarendon Press.
Berlant, Lauren, and Michael Warner. 1998. "Sex in Public." *Critical Inquiry* 24, 2: 547–566.
Blackwell, Becca. 2020. *Schmermie's Choice*. Viewed courtesy of Author. 22 March.
Bloomgarden, Kathy. 2017. "4 Reasons You Need a Mentor Younger Than You." *Entrepreneur* 27 June. Accessed 14 October 2020. https://www.entrepreneur.com/article/296194.
Butler, Judith. 1988. "Performative Acts and Gender Constitution: An Essay in Phenomenology and Feminist Theory." *Theatre Journal* 40, 4: 270–282.
Chambers-Letson, Joshua. "How to Listen to a Scream: Black Performance and the Anarrangement of Law." Unpublished.
Chaudhuri, Una. 1997. *Staging Place: The Geography of Modern Drama*. Ann Arbor: The University of Michigan Press.
Dolan, Jill. 1993. *Presence and Desire: Essays on Gender, Sexuality, Performance*. Ann Arbor: University of Michigan Press.
Dolan, Jill. 2005. "Queer Performance and Theory." In *Syllabus*. Austin, TX: The University of Texas at Austin.
Dolan, Jill. 2005. *Utopia in Performance: Finding Hope at the Theater*. Ann Arbor: University of Michigan Press.
Harge, Jennifer. 2018. *Mourn and Never Tire*. https://vimeo.com/279055723. 9 July. Accessed 16 September 2020.
Johnson, E. Patrick. 2003. *Appropriating Blackness: Performance and the Politics of Authenticity*. Durham, N.C.: Duke University Press.
Khubchandani, Kareem. 2020. *Ishtyle: Accenting Gay Indian Nightlife*. Ann Arbor: University of Michigan Press.
Khubchandani, Kareem. 2016. "Queer Futures: The Then and There of LGBTQ Theatre Scholarship." *Theatre Topics* 26, 1: 45–46.
Korkki, Phyllis. 2016. "What Could I Possibly Learn From a Mentor Half My Age? Plenty." *New York Times* 10 September. Accessed 14 October 2020. https://www.nytimes.com/2016/09/11/business/what-could-i-possibly-learn-from-a-mentor-half-my-age.html.
Lorde, Audre. 2017. *Your Silence Will Not Protect You*. London: Silver Press.

Montez, Noe and Kareem Khubchandini. 2020. "A Note from the Editors: Queer Pedagogy in Theatre and Performance." *Theatre Topics* 30, 2: ix–xvii.

Muñoz, José Esteban. 2009. *Cruising Utopia: The Then and There of Queer Futurity*. New York: New York University Press.

Muñoz, José Esteban. 1999. *Disidentifications: Queers of Color and the Performance of Politics*. Minneapolis: University of Minnesota Press.

Paredez, Deborah. 2014. "'Queer for Uncle Sam': Anita's Latina diva citizenship" In *West Side Story*. *Latino Studies* 12, 3: 332–352.

Pellegrini, Ann. 2007. "Staging Sexual Injury: How I Learned to Drive." In *Critical Theory and Performance*, edited by Janelle Reinelt and Joseph R. Roach, 2nd Edition, 413–431. Ann Arbor: University of Michigan Press.

Phelan, Peggy. 1997. *Mourning Sex: Performing Public Memories*. London: Routledge.

Rivera-Servera, Ramón H. 2012. *Performing Queer Latinidad: Dance, Sexuality, Politics*. Ann Arbor: University of Michigan Press.

Román, David. 1998. *Acts of Interventions: Performance, Gay Culture, and AIDS*. Bloomington: Indiana University Press.

Stevenson, Noelle. 2018 *She-Ra: Princesses of Power*. Voices by Aimee Carrero, AJ Michalka, and Karen Fukuhara. Los Gatos, CA: Netflix.

Wolf, Stacy. 2003. *A Problem Like Maria: Gender and Sexuality in the American Musical*. Ann Arbor: The University of Michigan Press.

Wolf, Stacy. 2008. "Defying Gravity: Queer Conventions in the Musical Wicked." *Theatre Journal* 60, 1: 1–21.

Wolf, Stacy. 2011. *Changed for Good: A Feminist History of the Broadway Musical*. Oxford: Oxford University Press.

Index

A Raisin in the Sun 25–26, 81, 84, 85, 253
A Tempest 53
A Theory of Adaptation 260
Actor training 44, 150, 252, 273–275, 279–283
Adaptation, adaptions 17, 45, 70, 107–108, 161, 168, 205, 231, 257–270, 290
Ahmed, Sara 79, 91
Althusser, Louis 66
American Revolutions: The United States History Cycle 117–118
American Sign Language 148, 155
American Society for Theatre History (ASTR) 290–291
American Theatre 10, 233
Angels in America 177, 253, 302, 305–307
Anthology, anthologies, anthologize 3, 49, 50, 53, 58, 126–129, 132, 147, 149, 152, 176, 177, 180–182, 184, 185, 195, 219, 224, 226, 245, 246, 248, 250, 251, 254, 264, 274, 276, 278, 279
Antiblack, antiblackness 79, 80, 83–85, 89, 90
Antigone 168, 258, 259, 261–265, 267, 269
Apartheid 59
Aristotle 72, 139, 180, 253
Asian Shakespeare Intercultural Archive (A|S|I|A) 251
Association for Theatre in Higher Education (ATHE) 147, 308
Austin, J. L. 59, 305

Barfield, Tanya 82
Bechdel, Alison 83, 208
Beckett, Samuel 150, 166, 233, 235, 253
Bhagavad Gita 42

Bible 3, 38, 42, 70
BIPOC 17, 50, 72, 119, 138, 158, 205, 241
Black Acting Methods: Critical Approaches 14, 279
Black Boy 70
Black Lives Matter (BLM) 33, 225, 238, 261, 267, 296
Bloom, Harold 23, 25, 27, 28, 30, 33, 39, 134, 137–139
Bourdieu, Pierre 54, 55, 281, 282
Brecht, Bertolt 103, 107, 218, 225, 231, 233, 235
Broadway 12, 81, 84, 97, 118, 156, 179, 201–210, 247, 305, 307
Brustein, Robert 18, 25, 85
Bunraku 163, 221
Butler, Judith 181, 292, 305
Butoh 219–221

Canon Wars, The 12, 245, 247
Capitalism 15, 64, 65, 68, 69, 73, 77, 196, 238, 241
Casting 18, 32, 33, 43, 104, 107, 110–112, 130, 154, 205, 212, 279, 281
Catholic 2, 24, 137, 196, 203
Césaire, Aimé 53
Chekhov, Anton 40, 66, 103, 107, 136, 166, 234, 235, 280, 281
Choreography, choreographer 13, 14, 89, 114, 151, 184, 189, 195, 196, 224, 226, 303
Christian 2, 3, 24, 33, 50, 52, 54, 59, 123, 141, 168, 179, 196
Chromosomes 259
Church 2, 3, 50, 51, 94, 106, 137, 165, 166, 233
Chūshingura 223
Cinderella 103, 112, 114–117

Clybourne Park 25, 26
Cornerstone Theater Company 103, 104–109, 115, 118–120
Covid-19, Coronavirus 1, 32, 63, 64, 77, 157
Cuban Theatre Digital Archive 252
Curriculum, curricula 31, 44, 50, 59, 60, 65, 80, 93, 132, 135, 162, 167, 191, 197, 213, 217, 231, 232, 250, 254, 276, 280, 283, 289, 293, 295

Dante Alighieri 137, 161
Database 13
de Vega, Lope 41
Deaf West 155
Decolonize, Decolonizing, Decolonization 26, 27, 28, 34, 43, 45, 50, 134, 136, 280, 295
Dolan, Jill 12, 155, 156, 175, 182, 245, 298, 301, 302, 305
Doll's House, A 153, 154, 250, 254
Drag 112, 183–185
Drama Corpora Project 250, 256
Dramaturgy, dramaturg 14, 17, 36–37, 46, 81–82, 84, 89–90, 116, 154, 177, 180, 182, 207, 209, 220, 225, 230–232, 234, 240–241, 248, 289, 303
Du Bois, W.E.B 18, 84, 176

Eighteenth-Century Collections Online 251
El Guindi, Yussef 126

Floyd, George 1, 64, 280
Fornés, Maria Irene 181
Friere, Paulo 45, 282

Gardley, Marcus 41
Geiogamah, Hanay 134, 138, 143
Gibran, Kahlil 122, 124
Global South 26, 138, 194
Greece, Greek, Greeks, Grecian 3, 6, 26, 46, 55, 104, 115–116, 156, 161, 163–165, 167, 167–170
Guerrilla Girls, The 248
Guillory, John 104

Hamlet 103–106, 110, 114, 223, 227, 253
Hansberry, Lorraine 25, 81, 84–85, 253
Hartman, Saidiya 26
Hemispheric Institute 129
Hemispheric Institute Digital Video Library 252
hooks, bell 4–5, 26, 206–207

Hudes, Quiara Alegría 64, 71
Hurston, Zora Neale 81, 89
Hutcheon, Linda 257–260

JUBILEE, The 238

Kabuki 219–222, 224–226
Kilroys List, The 13, 183
Kinesthesia 188
King, Martin Luther, Jr 86, 303
King, Rodney 86
Kwan, SanSan 194, 226

Laban (also Labanotation, Laban Movement Analysis) 188–190, 192
League of Resident Theatres (LORT) 18, 230–232, 237
Lew, Mike 156, 158
Lorde, Audre 5, 11, 28, 41, 127, 212–213, 236, 306
Love, Heather 177–178
Lovecraft Country 33
Lovecraft, H.P 33–34

M. Butterfly 59, 177, 180, 307
Mac, Taylor 176
Macbeth, *Macbeth* 40, 103, 112, 114–116, 119
Mamet, David 42, 142
McCraney, Tarell Alvin 41, 308
Medea, *Medea* 103, 112, 114–116
Mee, Charles 152
Molière 80, 107, 179, 253, 280
Montez, Noe 248–249, 275–276, 299
Moraga, Cherríe 8, 150, 153
Morriseau, Dominique 41
Morrison, Toni 25, 88–91
Muñoz, Jose 175, 299, 305, 308, 310
Museum, museums 85–87, 89, 146, 167

NAFTA 65, 68–69
Naimy, Mikhail 122, 124
National Endowment for the Humanities (NEH) 147
Noh 163, 221–222, 224–225, 227
Norman, Marsha 12, 150, 154
Norris, Bruce 25–35
Nottage, Lynn 118, 151

O'Hara, Robert 89
Obama, Barack 91
Oedipus 56, 168–169, 253, 290
Off-Broadway 81, 179

Oklahoma! 103–119, 201–214, 247
Okorafor, Nnedi 34
Opera 114, 161–170, 204, 225
Oregon Shakespeare Festival 36, 103–118
Othello 87

Pandemic 7, 34, 66, 75–77, 205, 232
Parks, Suzan-Lori 41, 280, 289–290
Pedagogy 8, 14–15, 44–45, 79–89, 192, 211, 228, 273–283, 290–291, 299, 307–309
Pedagogy of the Oppressed 45
Pen Group, The 124
Performance Studies 14–16, 23–27, 49–56, 67, 81, 93–95, 132, 217–227, 231, 274–282, 301–306
PhD training, PhD exam 17, 95, 273–283
Physical Actor Training: An Online A-Z 252–255
Play On! Shakespeare Festival 110
Plotting Yiddish Drama 251
Project Gutenberg 250

Quantative analysis 245–254

Raffo, Heather 126
Reading list, reading lists 6, 24, 0276
Religion, religious 141, 262
Revisionist 4, 50, 147, 190–197
Richards, Lloyd G. 81
Rihani, Ameen 122–124
Romeo and Juliet 43, 107, 184, 231
Routledge Performance Archive 252–256

Said, Edward 121
Schechner, Richard 93

Shakespeare 8–15, 31, 36–47, 49–56, 87, 99, 103–118, 127, 136–138, 161–168, 176, 214, 219–221, 231–236, 245–253, 279, 290
Shamieh, Betty 126
Singapore Theatre Festival 40
Smith, Anna Deavere 8, 18, 0150
Sophocles 8, 168, 214, 253, 258–269
Spiderwoman Theater 139
Stanislavski, Konstantin 279
Survey 49–60, 213, 276, 291–295, 298–308
Syllabus, Syllabi 7–11, 29, 176–177, 193, 245–255

Taylor, Diana 26, 94, 129, 209, 239, 274
Teenage Dick 156–159
Textbook, textbooks 259
The Hungry Woman 8, 59
The Internet Archive 250
The Little Clay Cart 104–108
The Orphan of Zhao 225

Uncanny Valley 222

We See You White American Theater; We See You, WAT; WSYWAT 1–18, 64, 72, 241
Weisel, Elie 42
White Savior 23, 33, 59, 142
White Supremacy 1–18, 27, 59, 84–90, 107–117, 132, 157, 192, 207–211, 246, 296
Wikipedia 30, 223, 248–249
Williams, Tennessee 148–159, 253
Wilson, August 17, 25, 41, 83, 110
Wolf, Stacy 12–15, 112, 201–212
Wolfe, George C. 83–90, 204
Wright, Richard 70

For Product Safety Concerns and Information please contact our EU representative GPSR@taylorandfrancis.com
Taylor & Francis Verlag GmbH, Kaufingerstraße 24, 80331 München, Germany

www.ingramcontent.com/pod-product-compliance
Lightning Source LLC
Chambersburg PA
CBHW070746020526
44116CB00032B/1987